ATHENE
SERIES

GENERAL EDITORS
Gloria Bowles
Renate Klein
Janice Raymond

CONSULTING EDITOR
Dale Spender

The **Athene Series** assumes that those who formulate explanations of the way the world works need to know and appreciate the significance of basic feminist principles.

The growth of feminist research internationally has called into question almost all aspects of social organization in our culture. The **Athene Series** focuses on the construction of knowledge and the exclusion of women from the process—both as theorists and subjects of study—and offers innovative studies that challenge established theories and research.

ATHENE, the Olympian goddess of wisdom, was honored by the ancient Greeks as the patron of arts and sciences and guardian of cities. She represented both peace and war, the latter in its cognitive aspect. Her mother, Metis, was a Titan and presided over all knowledge. While pregnant with Athene, Metis was swallowed whole by Zeus. Some say this was his attempt to embody her supreme wisdom. The original Athene is thus twice born: once of her strong mother, Metis, and once more out of the head of Zeus. According to feminist myth, there is a "third birth" of Athene when she stops being an agent and mouthpiece of Zeus and male dominance, and returns to her original source: the wisdom of womankind.

Creating an Inclusive College Curriculum

A Teaching Sourcebook from
the New Jersey Project

Edited by

Ellen G. Friedman, Wendy K. Kolmar,
Charley B. Flint, and Paula Rothenberg
with the assistance of Jill E. Edwards

ATHENE
SERIES

TEACHERS COLLEGE PRESS
Teachers College, Columbia University
New York and London

Published by Teachers College Press, 1234 Amsterdam Avenue, New York, NY 10027

Library of Congress Cataloging-in-Publication Data

Creating an inclusive college curriculum : a teaching sourcebook from
   the New Jersey Project / edited by Ellen G. Friedman . . . [et al.].
        p.   cm.—(Athene series ; 45)
   Includes bibliographical references and index.
   ISBN 0-8077-6283-0 (cloth : alk. paper). — ISBN 0-8077-6282-2
(pbk. : alk. paper)
    1. Education, Higher—New Jersey—Curricula.   2. Multicultural
education—New Jersey.   3. Educational equalization—New Jersey.
4. Women's studies—New Jersey.   I. Friedman, Ellen G., 1944–   .
II. New Jersey Project.   III. Series.
LB2361.6.N5C74   1996
378.1'99'09749—dc20   95-35059

ISBN 0-8077-6282-2 (paper)
ISBN 0-8077-6283-0 (cloth)

Printed on acid-free paper
Manufactured in the United States of America
03 02 01 00 99 98 97 96   8 7 6 5 4 3 2 1

Contents

From 20th-Century to Modern Art
For Openers
Revisiting Inclusion
Difference: Comparing Visual Comparisons
Breaking Ranks with the Timeline

The Place of History in a Theory Course
The Risks of Personal Experience

Sally
Toni
Belle
Ellen

The Journal as Central
Evaluating Journals
Some Words of Caution

**PART III
SYLLABI AND NARRATIVES**

About the Course
Student Composition and Level
Incorporation of Gender, Race, and Class into the Course
Student's Reactions to the Course
Modification of Course Content
Syllabus for Change in Societies
Schedule of Classes and Readings

Foreword

This book includes a selection of essays and syllabi from the New Jersey Project, Integrating the Scholarship on Gender. That unique statewide project spans many disciplines, types of schools, strategies for change, and stages of curriculum development, and this collection of its best to date brings to light a critical mass of challenging information that will be useful to many audiences: faculty, administrators, and students.

There is a heightened public interest concerning educational equity, multicultural education, diversity in the classroom, and interdisciplinary studies programs that focus on gender, race, class, and sexuality. This book can serve as a thoughtful and rich guide to educational equity in the curricula of our colleges and universities. Educators in all fields will find this text an invaluable resource for inclusive curricula that engage all students. We need to bring our college offerings up to date on issues of gender, race, class, and sexuality, and this volume should become a staple in faculty development workshops around the country and a requirement for students in the fields of education and institutional change.

I consider this book a cornucopia of experience and information that can serve to nourish higher education. If we accept this gift, we will learn from one of our nation's best efforts how to enrich and transform college curricula. I join the editors and contributors in inviting you to seek and find what is useful for you, your colleagues, and your students. I trust that when you engage with this collection, you will bring to it your sense of adventure—or a wish to enhance it—and will be open to the unknown possibilities and potential that diverse perspectives and new knowledge can bring to teaching and learning in our college classrooms.

Pedagogy is inseparable from content; practical classroom experience is interwoven with theory, analyses of assumptions, and assignments. The whole is much greater than the sum of its parts. Under the exceptional leadership of Paula Rothenberg, the New Jersey Project has drawn from (and, in turn, augmented) the vast resources generated by decades of scholarship on gender, race, ethnicity, class, and sexuality. The result is a project at the forefront of innovative educational change. This statewide process has both recognized and encouraged many outstanding teachers, scholars, and agents of institutional change, whose contributions are documented in the project's publications, including this book, and from whom we have the great opportunity to learn. Even more broadly, the New Jersey Project serves as a model for statewide and national initiatives on educational reform.

By challenging passive learning, assumptions about scientific objectivity, and unquestioned judgments about universal values concerning truth and beauty, this exemplar of scholarship from the margins recognizes the significance of relations of power in defining what is legitimate knowledge, who is the appropriate knower, and what ends are served by systems of knowledge. Needless to say, this requisite reconceptualizing disrupts our feelings of comfort in what we know, why and how we know it, and what our students should know.

A few words about the necessity and benefits of discomfort are in order. As a scientist steeped in the powerful traditions of Western scientific acculturation, I was knocked off my feet when I became aware of the scholarship on gender—by the conceptual impact of what had been left out of my privileged education and what had constrained my understanding of nature and the world around me. With helping hands, hearts, and minds, colleagues supported and encouraged my reeducation, my reconceptualization not only of the content of knowledge but also of the very process by which knowledge is created and then used. The experience began to transform the meaning of education—and the politics of education—for me as a teacher and learner.

As a veteran of the discomfort generated by shaking foundations, I have seen how the unease becomes transformed into a more fruitful and constructive perspective on the nature of those earthshaking motions. Like the social movements from which educational reform and revolution have sprung, disruption of the curricular status quo can be appreciated as the necessary tilling of the earth that turns the soil over, aerating and redistributing it; this regenerative action provides opportunities for new ingredients that lead to improved and more diversified growth.

Like any endeavor worth doing, curriculum transformation can seem overwhelming, but it has proved ultimately energizing for teachers, students, and administrators alike. This valuable book will move newcomers and veterans of curriculum development toward education for the 21st century.

Bonnie B. Spanier, Associate Professor
Women's Studies Department
State University of New York at Albany

Acknowledgments

This book would not have been possible were it not for the persistent, thoughtful, and rigorous work on inclusive curriculum and scholarship being carried out by faculty and administrators at New Jersey colleges and universities. Graduate assistant Jill E. Edwards and former secretary Joanne Gordon of the Women's Studies Program at Trenton State College helped bring the volume to fruition with dispatch, efficiency, and a sense of purpose. Judy Baker, administrative assistant for the New Jersey Project, contributed her talents to this volume in numerous ways, as did Mia Anderson and Naomi Miller, both assistant directors of the New Jersey Project. The editors gratefully acknowledge their contributions. Also, we wish to thank Pat Beaber and Carol Miklovis, librarians at Trenton State College, who helped us answer bibliographic questions, track references, and find copies of necessary books and articles.

Ellen G. Friedman
Wendy K. Kolmar
Charley B. Flint
Paula Rothenberg

From the start, the New Jersey Project has been a collaborative effort. It owes its beginnings to the vision of Catharine Stimpson, the dean of the graduate school of Rutgers University; Mary Hartman, then dean of Douglass College, Rutgers University; T. Edward Hollander, former chancellor of the New Jersey Department of Higher Education; Edward Goldberg, former assistant chancellor and later chancellor of the New Jersey Department of Higher Education; and Thomas Kean, former governor of the State of New Jersey; and to the 36-member Advisory Board that helped to oversee its design and execution.

Since its creation in 1986, the work of the New Jersey Project has been carried out by hundreds of faculty and staff at New Jersey colleges and universities. In addition to the 45 participants whose work is included in this volume, hundreds of faculty, staff, and students on campuses throughout the state have helped create the scholarship, the pedagogy, and the institutional climate that make curriculum transformation possible. Their efforts have been supported by incalculable hours of paid and unpaid work by staff at the Project office, supplemented by the enthusiasm of a series of energetic student assistants.

The list that concludes this volume includes the names of many, but certainly not all, of the faculty and staff who have played an active role in the New Jersey Project over the past nine years. Because of their efforts and the contributions of their unnamed colleagues and students, and because of an unprecedented statewide collaboration among two- and four-year institutions throughout the state, New Jersey higher education will never be the same.

Paula Rothenberg
Wayne, New Jersey
June 1995

INTRODUCTION

Received Ideas and Curriculum Transformation

Ellen G. Friedman

Satirizing the academic debate on the literary canon and curriculum transformation, Christine Brooke-Rose (1988) populates her novel *Textermination* with characters from hundreds of canonical and noncanonical books. She presents the debate about which books will stay in the curriculum from the point of view of these characters, whose very existence depends on its outcome. They convene at the San Francisco Hilton (the site of the 1988 Modern Language Association Convention, where thousands of English professors meet annually) to determine which of them will continue to be read, for it is by virtue of their being read that they have life. They engage in prayer sessions during which they appeal to the "Implied Reader" to keep them alive. They attend panel discussions with the hope that they will be discussed, because then their existence will continue. The book is replete with literary terrorists and upstarts from television and the movies. From the first page of the book, where Jane Austen's Emma Woodhouse finds herself in a carriage with Goethe conversing in German, it is clear that Brooke-Rose intends to capture the sense of uproar and delirious possibility that curriculum transformation projects have inspired.

In fact, transforming the curriculum—the course of study undertaken by students—involves much more than subtracting some books and adding others. Transformation requires a radical change in the position from which one regards knowledge and the world. It means, for instance, not only putting slave narratives or sentimental novels into U.S. literature courses but also understanding that such narratives and novels interrogate the received ideas that U.S. literature is supposed to convey about our culture. Including these works means that the professor can no longer present the American imagination as unitary, as defined by, for instance, heroic individualism or a dream of a new Eden. Even the universalizing term "American imagination" crumbles with questions that arise from these inclusions, such as, Whose America? Such inclusions also trouble old formulas that have been delivered by U.S. literature professors generation after generation—for example, "heroic individualism." Now they suggest questions such as, Heroism from what point of view and for whose benefit?

Curriculum transformation is serious business. It attacks received wisdom, wrenches internalized values, and contests assumptions held so deeply that to challenge them feels as if one is fighting nature. For instance, Joan Kelly's now classic question "Did Women Have a Renaissance?" in her book *Women, History, and Theory* has forever changed our approach to history (1984, p. 19). Her answer is that women were much better off in the Middle Ages, habitually called the "Dark Ages" when I was in school because, the reasoning went, it was a time marked by "no progress." However, during the "Dark Ages," Kelly points out, women owned and managed vast estates, the maternal name was commonly used for children, the "legitimacy" of offspring was not a great issue, and women participated in creating courtly literature. As smaller political units such as fiefdoms coalesced into nation-states during the "Renaissance," women lost all these rights. Armed with such knowledge, we are able to understand that "progress" is a term historically applied to male achievement. Looking at a historical period through the female gaze may transform how one interprets it. Indeed, not only has the smile been wiped off the Renaissance, but some historians have abandoned it as a meaningful category.

What many people find hard to understand is why, in a country where free speech is thought to be an absolute right, there is such an intense struggle about books. For one thing, this received wisdom entails many complexities and has been contested throughout our history. Thomas Jefferson thought of freedom of speech as a "natural" right guaranteed by a government based on "reason." In a letter to a friend in 1802, he defended even the Federalists, who were his opponents, in their right to lie:

> I shall protect [the Federalists] in the right of lying and calumniating, and still go on to merit the continuance of it by pursuing steadily my object of proving that a people easy in their circumstances as ours are, are capable of conducting themselves under a government founded not in the fears and follies of man,

but on his reason, on the predominance of his social over his dissocial passions, so free as to restrain him in no moral right, and so firm as to protect him from every moral wrong, which shall leave him, in short, in possession of all his natural rights. (Jefferson, 1802/1939, p. 95)

For Jefferson, "reason" would arbitrate the contesting positions that free speech allowed. But who owns reason? By what standards would the most reasonable stance be identified? The authors of *Women's Ways of Knowing* (Belenky et al., 1986) point out that the claim to rationality has historically not been gender neutral but has been used for millennia to describe women as inferior. Even the New York State Regents in their 1989 report recognized that when the framers of the Constitution, like Jefferson, spoke of "reason" and "natural rights," they had in mind a white male with property (Ignatieff, 1991, p. 19). Such questions and insights inform curriculum transformation.

Curriculum transformation is as difficult as it is necessary, because male hegemony informs our habits of thought, our language, our very metaphors. With unintentional humor, a geologist described the volcanic eruption of Mount St. Helens in this way: "Her flanks are shuddering. We don't know her intentions. Scientists haven't been able to probe her deeply enough with their instruments" (Marvin Beeson as quoted in Merchant, 1982, p. 405). This geologist was continuing the tradition of Francis Bacon, for whom nature was a secretive woman: "Neither ought a man to make scruple of entering and penetrating into these holes and corners, when the inquisition of truth is his sole object" (Bacon, reprinted 1968, p. 296). Metaphors of phallic conquest infect language across discourses. For Ezra Pound, "Poetry speaks phallic direction." He gives himself as an example of one who drives new ideas into the "great passive vulva of London" (Gilbert & Gubar, 1987, p. 155). Such metaphors, of course, are the powerful legacy of ancient cultural habits: After all, Aristotle described woman as a mutilated male (Agonito, 1977, p. 46).

All cultural canons—whether ancient, religious, or literary—are "strategic constructs" by which the dominant order both confirms its own values and passes them on to the subsequent generation, thus ensuring that power will remain in similar hands (Altieri, 1984, p. 42). In the United States, the defense of these canons finds columnists, politicians, and intellectuals of opposite stripes in agreement with one another. For conservative columnist George Will as well as 1960s liberal Arthur Schlesinger, curricular diversity means the contamination of universal humanistic values by politics, thereby risking the moral fabric of society for partisan goals (Brodkey & Fowler, 1991, p. 4). Claiming the position of objectivity and universality, they do not concede that their position is political. They do not understand that they are performing as white males and not as objective observers. Intellectuals who are more in tune with the goals of curricular transformation, such as Cornell West (1989) and Arnold Rampersad (1991), try to strike a conciliatory note by pointing out that dissent and discontinuity are emblematic of U.S. intellectual history. They present a more elastic portrait of the culture than the stable, grand social narrative evoked by Will and Schlesinger. Rampersad, for instance, quotes Ralph Waldo Emerson: "We have listened too long to the courtly muses of Europe." Emerson wanted to explode the standard reading list. He wrote, "[T]he only objection to *Hamlet* is that it exists" (Rampersad, 1991, p. 14). Yet some of the very professors who convey the antiestablishment positions of writers such as Emerson and Walt Whitman (who urged the young to escape the libraries and destroy their teachers) to their students have been known to resist both new books and new positions in the curriculum.

In the past, the natural right to free speech, the rule of reason, and the power to overturn the father's books were circulated among the very few. Although Jefferson, Will, Schlesinger, and the phantom professor may speak in universals about freedom and revolution, they mean mostly themselves and those who are not too different from themselves. Women, as well as racial, ethnic, and sexual others, may simply not be within their frame of reference. *House of Mirth* (Wharton, 1905/1987) is about Lily Bart, a woman who must marry well if she is to remain in her own social class. Although she succeeds in attracting rich men, she sabotages each opportunity until she exhausts her options. Left poor and alone, she commits suicide. Contributing to her downward slide is her attempt to live up to the moral standards of Selden, the man she really loves. In the crucial exchange between them, Selden says, "My idea of success . . . is personal freedom." The idea stuns Lily, who must allow herself to be molded by the members of New York's aristocracy who hold her future in their hands. "Freedom?" she asks. He explains, "To keep a republic of the spirit." When Lily says that she hopes he will help her find this country, this republic of the spirit, Selden responds, "It's a country one has to find the way to one's self" (p. 89). The fact is that Lily does try to find the way herself, but her path is repeatedly blocked by others who wish to impose their own ideas about Lily on her, who wish to create her in their image. For Lily, death is the only path to freedom. In the most profound moment of the novel, Lily exclaims to Selden, "Ah, you are as bad as the other sectarians . . . ; why do you call your republic a republic? It is a close corporation, and you create arbitrary objections in order to keep people out" (p. 93). What Lily understands at this bright moment of perception, when she calls Selden's republic a "close corporation," is that Selden's republic, reflective of larger republics, is really a rich men's club from which she is absolutely barred. She complains, "You think I can never even get my foot in the door" (p. 93).

It has taken a revolution to get Lily's foot in the door, but it is in the door now. One of the names for that revolution is curriculum transformation, which attempts to shut down the "close corporation" of patriarchy in the academy and replace it with a republic that has substituted a welcome mat for the closed door.

Curriculum transformation, with a history of over 20 years, is the attempt to mainstream the new scholarship on gender, race, ethnicity, class, and sexuality—to suffuse the academic curriculum with this scholarship and with the points of view out of which it arises. In Susan Van Dyne's words, those engaged in transformation projects aim to right the "power imbalances that structure the culture that surrounds our curriculum and classrooms and that inevitably permeates them" (1990, p. 247).

Fed by the swelling river of feminist and multicultural scholarship, books and articles flowed out of publishing houses and journals; they covered the organizational patterns that these projects follow; what they mean to administrators, students, faculty, academia, and the community; resources for pursuing them, including syllabi and bibliographies; and their theoretical underpinnings. Dale Spender's *Men's Studies Modified: The Impact of Feminism on the Academic Disciplines* (New York: Pergamon, 1981), for instance, spelled out the politics of knowledge at work in academic institutions, interrogated the traditional knowledge that fell under the rubric of "objectivity," and questioned the use of "man" to signify men and women. In the same year, Johnnella E. Butler published *Black Studies: Pedagogy and Revolution* (Washington, DC: University Press of America). Her book, which helped establish black studies as a pedagogy and define its relation to the dominant culture, clearly articulated the implications for general education. These books assisted in the transition from theory to pedagogy, pointing the way to curricular reform. Early publications reporting attempts at curricular change were, for the most part, exclusively focused on women. The experiential book *Learning Our Way,* edited by Charlotte Bunch and Sandra Pollack (Trumansburg, NY: Crossing Press, 1983), detailed alternative classrooms with a women's studies emphasis. It shared attention with more formal guides that grew out of particular transformation projects and conferences, such as Marilyn R. Schuster and Susan R. Van Dyne's *Women's Place in the Academy: Transforming the Liberal Arts Curriculum* (Totowa, NJ: Rowan & Allanheld, 1985), Betty Schmitz's *Integrating Women's Studies into the Curriculum* (Old Westbury, NY: Feminist Press, 1985), and Bonnie Spanier, Alexander Bloom, and Darlene Boroviak's *Toward a Balanced Curriculum* (Cambridge: Schenkman, 1984). The criticism that women's studies and curricular reform pertained mainly to white women was answered early with an important book on African American feminism, *All the Women Are White, All the Blacks Are Men, But Some of Us Are Brave: Black Women's Studies* (Old Westbury, NY: Feminist Press, 1982), edited by Gloria T. Hull, Patricia Bell Scott, and Barbara Smith; it concludes with bibliographic essays and selected course syllabi. In the 1990s, the arena for curriculum transformation has greatly expanded and reflects the scholarship on identity politics and multiculturalism. *Transforming the Curriculum: Ethnic Studies and Women's Studies* (Albany: State University of New York Press, 1991), edited by Johnnella E. Butler and John C. Walter, promotes a curriculum that mirrors national diversity and includes essays not only on women's studies but also on African American, American Indian, Asian American, and Latino American studies. Worth particular mention are two textbooks edited by Paula Rothenberg, both now in third editions, that bring the insights of transformation into class texts: *Race, Class and Gender in the United States: An Integrated Study* (New York: St. Martin's Press, 1995) and, with Alison M. Jaggar as coeditor, *Feminist Frameworks: Alternative Theoretical Accounts of the Relations between Women and Men* (New York: McGraw-Hill, 1993). The current resources for those interested in curriculum transformation are rich and accessible. Books, conferences, consortia, Internet databases, and electronic-mail networks such as WMSTL provide abundant opportunities and materials for administrators and faculty.

In "Changing the Institution," Marilyn R. Schuster and Susan R. Van Dyne (1985) describe three models of curriculum transformation: the top-down model in which a college administrator or state education official mandates change; a piggyback model in which transformation rides the wave of other revisions in general education; and the bottom-up model, originating with faculty and student reform initiatives. The New Jersey Project goes beyond even a synthesis of all three models. It comes closest to what is often called a "greenhouse model," in which every aspect of the climate is made friendly to transformation. It is the only statewide project that, over the course of the last decade, has reached virtually every institution of higher learning in the state. As Paula Rothenberg details in Chaper 1, the New Jersey Board of Higher Education's invitation for grant proposals to initiate statewide curriculum transformation in the mid-1980s gave birth to the project. This top-down initiative quickly engendered a palimpsest of curriculum projects following various models, growing out of faculty efforts and general education reform as well as additional statewide transformation grants. Although it began as a gender integration project, the second phase—the first lasted from 1987 to 1989[1]—under the directorship of Paula Rothenberg, promotes the integration of scholarship on race and ethnicity, class, and sexuality as well as gender. It sponsors international and regional conferences, art exhibits, speakers, an annual summer institute for curriculum reform, regional and statewide faculty networks, a newsletter, student awards, the international journal *Transformations,* and even a curriculum transformation events hotline. The conferences, networks, and summer institutes have put scholars with cutting-edge perspectives face to face with instructors from all over the state who can present their own specific institutional or discipline-related situations and problems, thus smoothing the path from theory to practice. In 1994, the project was the corecipient of the Progress in Equity Award from the American Association of University Women's Legal Advocacy Fund. Participants in the project have gone on to receive Ford Foundation grants for integration plans at their own institutions and are also consultants in national curriculum transformation initiatives such as American Commitments: Diversity, Democracy, and Liberal Learning, sponsored by the Association of American Colleges and Universities.

Trenton State College, where I teach English and direct the women's studies program, exemplifies the truly transformative effects of the project on faculty, students, curricula across the disciplines, and general education within a single institution. In 1990, two faculty members from the Psychology Department and I received a grant from the New Jersey Department of Higher Education for curriculum transformation. As a result, two of us attended the New Jersey Project summer institute and held project network meetings at Trenton State. The expertise we gained translated into a multitude of changes in curriculum and faculty development, as well as new books and periodicals for the library. With the support of women's studies librarian Pat Beaber, faculty in a variety of disciplines, including psychology, English, modern languages, the Honors Program, nursing, and business, rewrote basic courses and introduced new courses. The new dean of arts and sciences, Richard Kamber, impressed with both the need for curricular change and the quality of scholarship and faculty dialogue inspired by transformation activities, sponsored separate requirements in both gender and multicultural studies for all students in the general education program; these requirements became effective in 1993. This philosophy of an inclusive curriculum is also incorporated into the statement of goals and outcomes that all courses approved for general education must reflect. In addition, two of the three interdisciplinary studies core courses, required of all students in their first two years, incorporate perspectives on gender and multiculturalism. The second course in the three-course sequence, Change in Societies, is described in Chapter 16 of this volume by its coordinator, Lois Fichner-Rathus.

Creating an Inclusive College Curriculum: A Teaching Sourcebook from the New Jersey Project has three parts designed to provide models of statewide, institutional, and course reform. Part I, Creating a Statewide Curriculum Project, describes the genesis and development of the New Jersey Project, the institutionalization of reform from the points of view of administrators and faculty at two- and four-year colleges, and techniques to overcome faculty and institutional resistance. Part II, Rethinking Course Content, Perspective, and Pedagogy, contains theoretical and practical essays that focus on issues of pedagogy. These essays range from Rothenberg's chapter on interrogating the posture of objectivity in academia to others on transformation in specific disciplines and fields, including general education. Part III, Syllabi and Narratives, contains syllabi and instructors' accompanying experiential narratives for 32 courses. Although hundreds of courses have been transformed as a result of New Jersey Project efforts, these 32 represent disciplines or approaches not usually covered in readily available resources, including English composition, teaching lesbian and gay perspectives, math anxiety and calculus, technology and science, business, law, education, and nursing.

NOTE

1. See Smith (1990), documenting the first phase of the New Jersey Project under the direction of Carol H. Smith and Ferris Olin.

REFERENCES

Agonito, R. (1977). *History of ideas on woman: A source book.* New York: Putnam.

Altieri, C. (1984). An idea and ideal of a literary canon. In R. von Halberg (Ed.), *Canons* (pp. 41–64). Chicago: University of Chicago Press.

Bacon, F. (reprinted 1968). *The works of Francis Bacon* (J. Spedding, R. Ellis, & D. Heath, Eds.). Vol. 4. New York: Garrett Press.

Belenky, M. F., et al. (1986). *Women's ways of knowing: The development of self, voice and mind.* New York: Basic Books.

Brodkey, L., & Fowler, S. (1991, April 23). Political suspects. *Village Voice,* pp. 3–4.

Brooke-Rose, C. (1988). *Textermination.* London: Carcanet.

Gilbert, S. M., & Gubar, S. (1987). *No man's land: The place of the woman writer in the twentieth century: Vol. 1. The war of the words.* New Haven, CT: Yale University Press.

Ignatieff, M. (1991, September 8). Crazy ideas that make good sense. *Observer,* p. 19.

Jefferson, T. (1802/1939). *Thomas Jefferson on democracy* (S. K. Padover, Ed.). New York: New York Public Library.

Kelly, J. (1984). *Women, history, and theory.* Chicago: University of Chicago Press.

Merchant, C. (1982). Isis' consciousness raised. *Isis, 73,* 398–409.

Rampersad, A. (1991). Values old and new. *Profession, 91,* 10–14.

Smith, C. H. (1990). Creating a state-wide network. In C. H. Smith, F. Olin, & B. W. Kolmar (Eds.), *The New Jersey Project: Integrating the Scholarship on Gender, 1986–1989* (pp. 1–7). New Brunswick, NJ: Institute for Research on Women, Rutgers University.

Van Dyne, S. (1990). Notes on a decade of change. *NWSA Journal, 2,* 245–253.

West, C. (1989). *The American evasion of philosophy: A genealogy of pragmatism.* New York: Macmillan.

Wharton, E. (1987). *House of mirth.* New York: Macmillan. (Original work published 1905)

PART I

Creating a Statewide Curriculum Project

1

Transforming the Curriculum:
The New Jersey Project Experience

Paula Rothenberg

At the heart of curriculum transformation is a long-term commitment to rethinking or re-visioning the content and form of what we teach. As such, curriculum transformation is not particularly noteworthy; it is simply the way good teachers and active scholars go about the business of teaching and learning. Insofar as everything we experience shapes how we think, we inevitably bring new insights, knowledge, or perspectives to our work even as we teach the same book or reading for perhaps the third or fourth time or do no more than replace a single much-used text with a new and fresher alternative.

But there is another sense in which we talk about curriculum transformation, a sense that goes beyond the personal and ongoing growth of individual teacher-scholars. Curriculum transformation on a large scale, the kind that gets talked about beyond the halls of the academy, occurs periodically and in response to dramatic changes in our society, changes that prompt us not merely to reappraise the utility of a particular text but to question the very worldview that informs the perspective from which we teach and write.

Those of us teaching and learning at the close of the twentieth century find ourselves caught up in one of those moments when the foundations of knowledge have been called into question. As a result of the scholarship that has been produced by women's studies, black and other ethnic studies, and lesbian and gay studies, profoundly disturbing questions have been raised about what we have always considered to be knowledge in any field. By focusing on the ways in which this knowledge has been socially constructed, such scholarship has raised revolutionary questions about the way we have defined objectivity, truth—even reality. These questions shape this historical moment in education and frame the intellectual and social context in which we function as educators.

Over the past two decades, various institutions, consortia, and university systems have responded to the imperatives emanating from the new scholarship, the actual and projected changes in the demographics of our society, and the mandates generated by recent movements for social and economic justice to transform not merely their curricula but their institutional climate and character as well. In some cases, these efforts have been funded by grants from public or private agencies or both; in other cases, they have been supported largely through the commitment of institutional resources, often modest at best, which have been used to provide release time and faculty development opportunities to faculty and staff.

NEW JERSEY'S STATEWIDE INITIATIVE

Since 1986, New Jersey college faculty have been able to call upon the support, resources, and expertise of a statewide curriculum project funded by the New Jersey Department of Higher Education. After three years at the Institute for Research on Women, Douglass College–Rutgers University, the project moved to its current home at William Paterson College in Wayne, New Jersey. Established as a project that would focus on the integration of women and issues of gender into the higher education curriculum, the New Jersey Project rapidly adopted a more inclusive orientation, recognizing that it is neither possible nor desirable to separate gender from race and ethnicity, class, sexuality, or culture.

During the mid-1980s, the New Jersey Department of Higher Education saw one of its roles as stimulating and supporting innovative initiatives. By functioning as if it were a state-based FIPSE (Fund for the Improvement of Post-Secondary Education, a federal grant program) or Ford Foundation, the department could encourage curriculum innovation in the colleges and at the same time give New Jersey faculty and administrators experience writing grant proposals, which would then prepare them to seek additional outside funding for such projects. By the mid-1980s, FIPSE, Rockefeller, Ford, and other funding agencies had already funded numerous curriculum transformation projects at institutions around the country; it was in this context that the Department of Higher Education sought a proposal for such a state-wide project in New Jersey.

The grant proposal that provided initial funding for the New Jersey Project was prepared for the New Jersey Department of Higher Education at the invitation of Edward Goldberg, then assistant chancellor. It was developed by a group of faculty from around the state, who later became the core of the project's advisory board. The group worked with the Institute for Research on Women to conceptualize what such a statewide project might look like. The proposal was modeled, in part, on two gender-focused curriculum transformation projects that were already being funded by the Department of Higher Education's Humanities Grants Program—one directed by Wendy Kolmar at Drew University, and the other directed by me at William Paterson College. Multiple factors came together to make the creation of a statewide curriculum transformation project in New Jersey possible—namely, that New Jersey had an institute with a considerable reputation in gender scholarship; that the state had a number of energetic, well-respected feminist scholars, in particular, Catharine Stimpson and Mary Hartman; that the two previously mentioned institution-based gender projects had attracted the attention of staff at the Department of Higher Education; that we had the vision and leadership of Edward Goldberg; and that there was national interest in (and funding of) feminist scholarship, pedagogy, and curriculum reform.

The project was introduced by convening a large Administrators' Day Program in February 1987. Invitations were extended to administrators at all the colleges in the state as well as to a small number of faculty recognized for their feminist scholarship, educational leadership, or both. Chancellor T. Edward Hollander spoke to the almost 400 in attendance about the value of gender integration; Governor Thomas Kean issued a proclamation in support of the project and its goals; and nationally recognized scholars Peggy McIntosh, Johnnella Butler, and Beverly Guy-Sheftall, along with Middlesex County College President Flora Mancuso Edwards, gave presentations on the need to transform the traditional curriculum and extolled the new scholarship. Presentations about the two curriculum transformation projects already under way in New Jersey provided concrete accounts of what could be accomplished and how such work might be carried out. Wendy Kolmar and I were introduced by our dean and college president, respectively, and each administrator talked enthusiastically about the campus-wide benefits of such curriculum efforts. This event made it clear to all concerned that the project had the blessing and support of those at the highest levels and situated the project firmly in the midst of a rigorous and extensive national effort to integrate gender and other perspectives into the curriculum.

Like most states, New Jersey has a fairly broad array of public and private 2- and 4-year colleges and universities that make up its system of higher education. The great challenge to a statewide curriculum project is to find a way to meet the diverse needs of diverse institutions and faculty and to make its presence felt even at campuses located at opposite ends of the state. The New Jersey Project has responded to this challenge by creating a wide variety of projects and activities. In addition to holding statewide conferences and workshops each year, the project holds regional network meetings each month at multiple locations selected to facilitate participation by faculty regardless of where in the state they live or work. Special readings, roundtables, and workshops are held at individual institutions throughout the year, and between January 1992 and December 1993, a traveling art exhibit featuring the work of women artists at New Jersey colleges visited 14 college campuses. A statewide student awards competition designed to recognize excellence in feminist scholarship is held each year and receives submissions from the majority of institutions in the state. *Transformations,* the New Jersey Project journal, has an editorial board and a set of manuscript readers drawn exclusively from New Jersey college faculty, ensuring that state faculty are engaged in producing, reviewing, and disseminating new scholarship and teaching resources on a regular basis.

Because of the extent and nature of such activities, large numbers of faculty, staff, and administrators at virtually all institutions are caught up in an ongoing series of professional development experiences. They receive mailings and materials on a regular basis, and gender-focused inclusive scholarship is made an important part of the intellectual life at New Jersey institutions.

RESIDENTIAL SUMMER INSTITUTES

The heart of the project's activities has always been its residential summer institute, which brings together some of the best teachers and scholars in the state and the nation. Designed to provide New Jersey college faculty and staff with an intensive immersion in the scholarship and pedagogy of an inclusive curriculum, the institute includes lectures and workshops, cultural events, access to an on-site resource room, the opportunity to screen videos, and time for informal discussion between and among speakers and participants. Interested New Jersey college faculty and staff apply individually or in teams. As part of the application process they are asked to formulate their goals for personal course revision and for institutional transformation. Once accepted, they receive a packet of preliminary background readings, and when they return home, they take with them a second set of readings selected to reinforce and supplement the presentations they have heard.

Although the first two project-sponsored institutes were quite long, during the second phase of the project, the institutes have been scheduled over long weekends and have generally lasted no more than 5 days and 4 nights. Longer institutes were more likely to attract faculty who already had a strong commitment to this work and placed a special burden on people with family responsibilities, since they required being away from home from Monday to Friday for 2 consecutive weeks. By shortening the institutes, we were able to attract a more diverse group of participants.

The program at each institute includes speakers who are asked to provide an overview of major discipline areas (English and humanities, history and humanities, social sciences, math and science) and to suggest how placing women and issues of gender, race and ethnicity, class, and sexuality at the center of the disciplines transforms the questions we ask, the paradigms we employ, the language we use, and the conclusions we generate. In addition to these broad overview talks designed for a general academic audience (which often includes counselors, librarians, and other nonteaching professionals), each speaker conducts several nuts-and-bolts workshops on curriculum transformation in her or his discipline. In most cases, speakers spend at least several days in residence, allowing for individual conversations and follow-up questions. Many institute participants are especially pleased with this aspect of the program and comment that it is a welcome change from the usual format, where experts seem to drop out of the sky and then leave as soon as they have imparted their wisdom. Happily, many of our speakers model the project's commitment to seeing us all as teacher-learners throughout our lives, and they become part of the learning community for the duration of the institute. Speakers providing overviews of major discipline areas have included Carole Boyce Davies, Susan Van Dyne, Cheryl Wall, and Paul Lauter in English; Deborah Gray White, Kenneth Goings, and Vivien Ng in history; Sandra Lynn Morgen, Leslie Hill, and James Anderson in social science; and Sue Rosser, Bonnie Spanier, and Sandra Harding in science and math.

In addition to the discipline presentations and workshops, each institute includes a lecture, a workshop, or both that focuses more specifically on issues of sexuality and pedagogy. Although all speakers are asked to talk about pedagogy as well as issues of heterosexism and homophobia, we schedule additional workshops in these areas because they often receive less attention than necessary and because faculty often cite attention to these concerns as the most valuable part of their institute experience. Finally, each institute includes both large group sessions and smaller team meetings, during which the practical aspects of institutionalizing curriculum change are discussed and specific strategies for individual campuses are developed. The core of the program is rounded out with films, talks, and workshops on a variety of topics. For example, the 1993 institute included a screening of *Raise the Red Lantern,* a 1991 film by Zhand Yimou (in Mandarin with English subtitles); a

talk on Latina perspectives on scholarship and the curriculum; an interactive
workshop on dealing with racism, sexism, and homophobia in the classroom;
and a performance by a feminist storyteller that raised issues related to eating
disorders, adolescent romance, and family relationships. Other summer
institutes have included slide presentations on women in art; a slide show,
lecture, and performance on 17th- and 18th-century women composers; readings from the Feminist Press Cross-Cultural Memoir Series; and overview-
lectures on the evolution of women's studies and curriculum transformation
by Florence Howe, Alison Bernstein, and Elizabeth Minnich. Additional lectures and workshops have been offered by Marilyn Schuster, Lynn Weber,
Ada Maria Isasi-Diaz, Ruth Sidel, Marilyn Frye, Elizabeth Higginbotham,
and many others. Because recent institutes have had an increasingly large
male presence, we usually try to include at least one man among the major
speaker-facilitators and now routinely offer a small group workshop on exploring male issues in feminism.

Not surprisingly, the composition of each institute has a significant
effect on its character. One year we had five participants from business and
management, so we brought in an expert on transforming the business curriculum who conducted a special 3-hour workshop for that group. Another
year, the number of faculty from schools of education prompted us to schedule a special small group session on transforming teacher training curricula.

It goes without saying that we aim for diversity among the speakers
and make sure that our selection of experts does not marginalize any group.
Although it would be impossible to construct an institute program that included all the voices that should be in the curriculum, we try to create a
program that makes it clear that there *are* many voices and that this multiplicity adds to both the richness and the rigor of our work.

Each summer's institute produces a new generation of people dedicated
to curriculum transformation who feel closely connected to one another and
to the project. The enthusiasm and expertise these individuals bring back to
their campuses often spark departmental or campus-wide interest in transformation and often result in new teams from those schools attending the
institute the following summer. Equipped with new perspectives on scholarship and with access to a variety of curriculum transformation resources,
institute "graduates" work with others to create a curriculum initiative
uniquely tailored to the needs and strengths of their particular institutions.

REGIONAL NETWORK MEETINGS

Although many curriculum projects, including the New Jersey Project during
its first 3 years, focus on changing (or creating) syllabi, more recently, the

project's emphasis has been on changing people. The emphasis on syllabi is understandable. It's useful, often essential, to be able to go to funding sources with "hard data" about how many courses were or will be revised, and funding agencies often need such a syllabus count in order to justify their funding. Our experience has taught us that teachers with an inclusive perspective who use the categories of race, class, gender, and sexuality as lenses for seeing and analyzing experience do so regardless of the syllabus they employ, whereas syllabi revised by faculty with an inclusive perspective may be taught infrequently or may be used by faculty with little understanding of these broader curricular and scholarship issues and perspectives. In the end, there's no reason to choose. Successful curriculum projects do well to work toward both ends.

Monthly regional network meetings sponsored by the project provide an opportunity for summer institute participants to continue to meet on a regular basis and give the project a highly visible presence around the state. Generally scheduled on the last Tuesday, Wednesday, and Thursday of the month, networks are hosted by three institutions each year, and locations are selected to facilitate participation in a state where hundreds of miles separate the northernmost and southernmost schools. Network sessions are attended both by faculty and staff who are already familiar with curriculum transformation and race and gender scholarship and by those seeking an introduction to such issues. The sessions provide an opportunity to discuss new scholarship, continue to shape a transformed and transformative curriculum, share resources, and explore issues of pedagogy. Faculty engaged in curriculum efforts at their schools often invite colleagues who are less involved to attend special sessions that they know will be of interest to them. Locating a network at a particular site is a good way to spark or rekindle an institution-wide commitment to curriculum work or to recognize the strong efforts of particular schools in this respect. Over the years, network topics have spanned the disciplines and examined diverse aspects of campus life, as the following sampling of topics indicates: The Role of Feminist Scholarship in the Classroom; Revolution in Thought: Science and Gender; Transcending Boundaries in the Campus Culture; Revisioning Business Law: A New Pedagogical Perspective; Teaching and Mentoring New Jersey's Latina Women College Students; The Social Construction of Masculinity; and Through the New Looking Glass: Women in Europe and Japan, 11th–14th Centuries.

Networks also provide an efficient and effective structure for obtaining and distributing information and resources within the state. They begin with light refreshments and informal conversation; in some cases, discussions continue over dinner at local restaurants.

In addition to the summer institute and monthly regional network seminars, the project sponsors at least two statewide conferences each year. Some of these large conference-workshops have focused on specific areas of the curriculum, such as math and science or the introductory Western civilization requirement, or on developing new pedagogy. Several years ago, the project brought Suzanne Pharr, author of *Homophobia as a Weapon of Sexism,* into the state to conduct workshops at a number of schools on the relation between and among sexism, racism, class privilege, homophobia, and heterosexism. More recently, the project held a large statewide conference to showcase the curriculum work of New Jersey college faculty and administrators. In April 1993, the project sponsored a national conference on inclusive curriculum that brought together more than 800 scholars and teachers involved in K–12 and higher education from all across the nation.

MAINTAINING A SUPPORTIVE ENVIRONMENT

In addition to encouraging faculty and staff to transform curriculum, pedagogy, and climate, one of the project's goals is to help create an environment at New Jersey colleges that will help attract, retain, and promote a diverse faculty and staff. In addition to the regional and statewide meetings, the project has worked toward this goal by establishing ALANA (African, Latina, Asian, and Native American), a network by and for women of color in higher education in New Jersey, and by helping to facilitate a network for lesbian and bisexual women at New Jersey colleges. Each of these networks grew out of requests from New Jersey college faculty and staff and reflects a recognition of the unique needs and strengths of these constituencies and the importance of creating opportunities for their members to network and self-define. The most successful ALANA conferences and workshops have focused on "getting ahead in the academy," providing practical, inspirational, and realistic advice about tenure and promotion, career paths for nonteaching professionals, writing and publishing, juggling family and career, pursuing grants, and coping with burnout.

The project also publishes *Transformations,* a journal that focuses on curriculum transformation scholarship and resources. Distributed free of charge to interested New Jersey educators, *Transformations* is available on a subscription basis to faculty in other states. In addition to providing a place where faculty can publish their work and receive appropriate credit toward retention and promotion, the journal puts curriculum transformation materials into the hands of teachers in an efficient and timely fashion on a regular basis. Guest lecturers from project events are often asked to make their presentations available for publication, and faculty creating new courses and updating bibliographies are encouraged to use the journal to make their work available to others.

The project's student awards competition, begun in 1989, is designed both to recognize and encourage faculty and students engaged in creating the new scholarship and to ensure that the new scholarship is integrated into course assignments, since, as everyone knows, if it's not on the exam, it doesn't really count. This statewide competition recognizes essays written by 10 undergraduate students at New Jersey's colleges who employ multiple feminist perspectives in their work. The project is committed to showcasing student work at both introductory and advanced levels and at both 2- and 4-year colleges. Winning essays are selected by a committee of New Jersey college faculty, and the essays are published. The student essay volume lists the author, title, and faculty sponsor of each submission in the hope that showcasing the breadth and scope of this work will encourage other students and faculty to transform their scholarship as well. The volume of student essays is often used in college and precollege writing workshops to motivate, instruct, and empower students.

Awards, which are funded through individual and corporate donations, are presented at a dinner each May that features a speaker specially chosen for the occasion. The dinner also provides a year-end opportunity to celebrate the project's work. Student awards dinners have featured talks by Blanche Cook on Eleanor Roosevelt, Shirley Hune on growing up Asian and female, Peggy McIntosh on the multicultural self, and talks and readings by writer–social activist Grace Paley and poet Abena P. A. Busia.

Since its inauguration in February 1987, the New Jersey Project has gone from an initiative regarded by some with a degree of skepticism to one whose work is widely respected throughout the state. It receives generous support from many New Jersey colleges that provide space for project events, release faculty to serve as project staff, and serve as host sites for regional networks. Many routinely contribute to the fund that provides monetary awards to student essay winners.

The project has gained credibility and respect by holding to task and getting on with its work regardless of the political climate in the state or the nation. We are firmly committed to academic freedom and believe that faculty must retain the right to shape their own courses, but we also believe that the very intellectual curiosity that made most of us teachers in the first place will sooner or later prompt interest in the new scholarship. Our job is to create a climate that stimulates that interest and then provide the expertise and resources to support transformation efforts by those who choose to undertake them.

We have received enormous support from the Department of Higher Education and were very fortunate that Ed Goldberg, who helped create the project while serving as assistant chancellor, became chancellor of higher education on March 1, 1991. In remarks at his swearing-in ceremony, Chancellor Goldberg made a point of reiterating his strong commitment to curriculum development and lauded the two statewide curriculum projects for their groundbreaking work. Clearly this expression of support from the new chancellor was helpful in further legitimating our work.

GETTING STARTED IN YOUR STATE

Although the value of having a statewide project on transforming the curriculum cannot be overestimated, it is also true that a great deal can be accomplished even without such broad support. People often mistakenly believe that change can come about only if large numbers of people are committed to it, but our experience has not borne this out. In fact, extensive and long-lasting curriculum transformation is usually initiated by no more than a handful of people, and sometimes by no more than two or three, who decide that something needs to be done and set about doing it. By circulating a few interesting articles or screening a video and gathering to talk on a regular basis, a small group of faculty can begin an initiative. Once begun, other colleagues will join these groups out of interest, curiosity, or both and can be encouraged to do so by personal invitations (not impersonal flyers). Specific individuals can be courted by selecting an article or topic that is likely to be of particular interest to them. Holding roundtable discussions among faculty who are teaching the same course can help create a community of teacher-scholars who come together regularly because doing so enhances both their teaching and their intellectual lives and will inevitably lead to an exchange of teaching resources and a reexamination of syllabi. Asking the institution to provide anything from money for refreshments and speakers to release time can create a campus faculty development project with fairly limited funding and usually produces a disproportionately large return on a minimal investment. Bringing in one or two outside speakers can often electrify an entire campus community and engage faculty in an exciting reexamination of the curriculum they teach. Even in times of fiscal austerity, there is always some money available, and one or two vocal and imaginative faculty can usually persuade a dean, academic vice president, or student funding agency that money spent on a few exciting speakers will benefit every aspect of the institution. Following up these guest lectures with workshops and roundtables on a regular basis is how many curriculum transformation projects have begun.

Faculty at institutions that are particularly inhospitable to this work should consider creating faculty development seminars with participants from other schools in the region. In addition to being good candidates for outside funding, such arrangements can stimulate interest in curriculum transformation among administrators at previously recalcitrant institutions.

Students too can play an important role in stimulating transformation by taking questions that they have learned to ask in one course and adapting them to another. Many teachers of introductory Western civilization classes came to read Martin Bernall's *Black Athena* because students who had read that work in African American studies began to use it to question the narrow framing of this reputedly "inclusive" history requirement. Faculty in the natural sciences have often been moved to consider feminist perspectives on science because of questions brought by students who learned to ask them while taking women's studies courses. By raising epistemological issues that apply across disciplines, regardless of the particular courses we teach, each of us can empower our students to act as agents of curricular change.

When people first learn about the New Jersey Project, they often say that it would be wonderful to have such a project to draw upon but assure me that their state is the last place in the world where such a project could come into being. In fact, had anyone talked to me even a few months before the proposal for the New Jersey Project was solicited by the Department of Higher Education, I would have said the same thing. The New Jersey Project was sparked by the work of a few committed faculty who began small-scale curriculum projects at their own institutions out of their own need to rethink scholarship, curriculum, and pedagogy, and the bottom line is that it continues for that very same reason.

2
Sustaining the Curriculum Transformation Process: After the First Year

Wendy K. Kolmar

Transforming the curriculum to incorporate the theory, methodology, and content generated by the new scholarship on gender, race, class, and sexuality is a long-term process for both individual faculty members and an institution as a whole. Yet long-term external funding is often difficult to obtain, especially in the tight budget years of the early 1990s. Therefore, when faculty and administrators first undertake these efforts, they must also consider how best to sustain them over time.

Curriculum transformation in an institution can be initiated by administrators, faculty, students, or librarians. It can begin in a women's studies program or in an academic department. In some of the institutions that have participated in the New Jersey Project, curriculum transformation work has been initiated by academic administrators; in others it has been initiated by senior faculty; in others by adjunct or basic skills faculty.[1] On many campuses in New Jersey and elsewhere, faculty or academic administrators have found it possible to get special internal funding or outside grant funding to begin the process of integrating gender, race, class, and sexuality into the curriculum.[2] With that initial funding, usually covering only 1 or 2 years, release time or stipends may be made available to faculty to create and teach transformed courses, outside consultants may be invited to present workshops for faculty, and syllabus revision may be begun. However, when that year ends and special funding is no longer available, projects often founder or dwindle. To help prevent the early demise of projects, the New Jersey Project has created statewide structures that support and enhance faculty efforts by providing speakers and consultants to campuses and organizing semiannual conferences, monthly network meetings, and summer institutes.[3]

Broad and thorough integration of the perspectives of gender, race, class, and sexuality throughout the curriculum requires that faculty have time to read, assimilate, and disseminate throughout their courses the new scholarship in their fields. Given the breadth, complexity, and continual development of this scholarship, as well as the many demands on the time of most faculty members, this is a long process. Even when an institution has funding to give a faculty member release time to develop a substantially revised syllabus, questions remain: Will this course be offered regularly? If this is one section of a larger course, will this faculty member continue to teach it and will his or her colleagues consider adopting the revised syllabus or doing their own revision? After the faculty member has taught the course once, will there be time and support for her or him to revise the course again? Will it be possible for the faculty member to revise the other courses she/he teaches in the near future? What institutional support and rewards are there for faculty who make ongoing course revision a priority? The challenge for those of us who are working for curriculum transformation over the long term is to find ways to address these questions within our institutions.

LAYING THE GROUNDWORK IN THE FIRST YEAR

Any proposal for a 1- or 2-year grant or institution-funded project should be carefully designed to lay the groundwork for sustaining curriculum transformation efforts beyond the initial term of the project. Proposals should set specific and limited goals for the initial years of the project, making it as clear what will *not* be accomplished as what will be. For example, the first year's work might focus on integrating gender, race, class, and sexuality into introductory courses or into courses in a core curriculum. Such a project objective makes it clear that a large portion of the curriculum will remain untouched at the end of those initial efforts. Setting such goals also makes it clear that the kind of curriculum change we are initiating cannot, as some administrators and faculty colleagues wish, be done in a year so we can move on to some other agenda.

If projects are to survive beyond the first few years, it is crucial to cultivate both administrative and faculty support: Administrative support is crucial for resources and for incorporating curriculum change into broader institutional agendas. Faculty support is obviously critical because they are the ones who shape the curriculum and define the content of courses.

The support and involvement of deans and senior faculty are also essential because of their centrality to both the hiring process and the promotion and tenure process. For the work of curriculum transformation to continue in an institution, the faculty involved in this activity must receive tenure and be promoted, and the hiring of new faculty must be done with attention to their expertise in the new scholarship in their fields. For revised courses to stay in the curriculum and for the revision process to be extended to other courses, department chairs must support or be engaged in the process of course revision, because they often make important choices about scheduling and staffing specific courses.

The involvement of a diverse group of faculty—faculty who are both junior and senior in rank, male and female, ethnically diverse, and who come from as broad a range of disciplines as possible—is also crucial to promoting curriculum efforts in a range of departments and by a range of faculty. A project should not depend exclusively on the efforts of a few junior women who are already closely identified with women's studies, although they are often the people who initiate such work.

To support all faculty who engage in the process of revising the curriculum, institutional evaluation systems should be revised to value the work of inclusion. Student course evaluation forms should be reviewed and questions modified or added that ask about the inclusion of new content and approaches. Equally important, deans and promotion and tenure committees should be urged to include curriculum transformation among the work they assess when evaluating teaching excellence.

USING EXISTING STRUCTURES AND RESOURCES

A commitment to curriculum transformation is most likely to be sustained in an institution if it is not seen as a "special project" but can instead be clearly defined as part of the academic mission of the institution, as it is articulated in the mission statement and in other goal and policy statements. In the absence of special internal or external funding, curriculum transformation work can be supported by existing institutional funding sources. Regularly available funds for faculty development can be requested. Departmental or institutional funds for lectures can be used to bring feminist scholars to campus. Library materials for curriculum transformation can be acquired among materials purchased with regular departmental and program library budgets.

Curriculum reform initiatives in an institution also create opportunities for the inclusion of gender, race, class, and sexuality, among them: revision or development of a core curriculum, revision of general education requirements, development or revision of a first-year seminar program, development of an honors program, revision of departmental curriculum. Creating linkages with these other curriculum reform efforts can effectively institutionalize curriculum transformation as one of the goals of that college's or university's curriculum. For example, at many New Jersey institutions, among them Upsala, Fairleigh Dickinson, Kean, and Seton Hall, faculty who are interested in curriculum transformation have made themselves an essential part of the faculty committees charged with revising and ultimately with teaching the liberal arts core courses. Often this work on core committees not only produces an integrated undergraduate core curriculum for students but also creates another locus for faculty development.

By joining institutional initiatives focused on improving teaching, faculty committed to curriculum transformation have also been able to broaden their work with colleagues. Many campuses have recently set up centers for teaching or have developed programs to enhance teaching, such as the New Jersey master faculty program.[4] For example, at County College of Morris, faculty and the dean persuaded their Center for Teaching Excellence to make the steering committee a part of its structure. At Brookdale Community College, the curriculum transformation group worked not only with the Center for Educational Research but also with the Holocaust Center and with the international studies program to interrelate the objectives of these programs.

At many institutions, the number of faculty introduced to curriculum transformation strategies has been substantially increased by using faculty development mechanisms already in place on campus. At Sussex County Community College, a faculty panel made a presentation at the fall faculty orientation. At Upsala College, several faculty forums were scheduled that focused on women's studies and race relations. At County College of Morris, members of the Curriculum Transformation Steering Committee presented their work at an end-of-the-year professional development day. At Camden County College, faculty who had attended the New Jersey Project summer institute made a presentation on one of the regularly scheduled faculty professional development days. At Hudson County Community College, speakers on transforming the curriculum were invited to keynote two of the faculty development days held before the semester began; these days are particularly important because they include many adjunct faculty who are sometimes difficult to reach through other mechanisms. At Drew University, faculty who participated in gender integration seminars presented their work at the regular May workshops for instructors in the first-year seminar program.

Campus-wide or departmental lecture series can also be a tool for introducing the new scholarship. Departments or programs that have funds for lectures can be encouraged to invite speakers whose work focuses on the new scholarship on gender, race, class, or sexuality. Speakers should be asked to provide bibliographies or supplementary reading lists for faculty and students to expand the topic of the lecture. Often, if such lectures are linked to specific courses that need revision or are in the process of being revised, hearing the speaker can provide the course instructor with additional material to integrate or can provide a new approach to the field or perhaps a starting place for course revision. At Ramapo College, faculty created a lecture-workshop series that focused on the transformation of specific disciplines and involved faculty from those disciplines as respondents and discussants. At Drew University, at least one of the speakers sponsored each year during women's history month is asked to come to campus for the day to do a faculty development workshop and to meet individually with faculty in her area.

For faculty who are trying to continue transforming courses, resources are as important as other forms of support. For this reason, it is essential to make librarians a part of curriculum transformation efforts from the beginning, as so many New Jersey projects have done. Librarians need to know in what areas curriculum transformation is under way and what resources are required to support those courses. Only when this kind of information is exchanged can librarians work with faculty to see that library collection development keeps pace with curriculum transformation. Some New Jersey institutions have also developed resource rooms for faculty where they collect course syllabi, bibliographies, and working papers and reports from other curriculum transformation projects and research centers that focus extensively on curriculum (e.g., Wellesley Center for Research on Women, Memphis State Center for Research on Women, Southwest Institute for Research on Women). When librarians are included in curriculum transformation projects, they can be very effective in encouraging faculty work on course revision by notifying them of new materials relevant to their courses as they arrive in the library.

Finally, perhaps the most important resources for sustaining the process of change are the faculty and students who support this work. Individual faculty who are involved in curriculum transformation and course revision should share their work with colleagues in department meetings or over the lunch table. Sending a colleague just the right article or offering one strategy to try in class tomorrow may be the impetus she or he needs to start revising a course. Students who have taken women's studies courses or revised courses elsewhere in the curriculum can push faculty to think about revision by raising questions about gender, race, class, and sexuality during classroom discussions or by choosing paper topics that approach course material from these perspectives. Seeking out material to respond to a student's question or to help a student with research can be the beginning of course revision for many faculty members.

Every college and university is unique and will pose particular problems and have particular advantages for work on transforming the curriculum. Faculty committed to this work have to assess their own institutional situations and climates. Some strategies will work in some institutions, and others will not. What is appropriate depends on the availability of resources, the nature of support for curriculum work at the various levels of the institution, and the nature and fervor of the resistance to curriculum transformation efforts. But whatever the nature of the institution, it seems clear to me that creation of transformed curricula depends on our ability to make the inclusion of the diverse theories, methodologies, and content of the new scholarship on gender, race, class, and sexuality an inseparable part of what we define as good teaching and good research.

ACKNOWLEDGMENTS

The strategies presented in this chapter are not exclusively mine but represent the collective understanding of faculty working on curriculum transformation in New Jersey and reflect the wisdom of the many feminist scholars nationwide who have shared their expertise with us over the life of the project during conferences, workshops, summer institutes, campus visits, and long dinner conversations. They include, among many others, Margaret Anderson, Dorothy Helly, Elizabeth Higginbotham, Sandy Morgen, Sue Rosser, Betty Schmitz, Marilyn Schuster, Bonnie Spanier, Susan Van Dyne, and Lynn Weber. For this chapter's shortcomings, none of them, of course, bears any responsibility.

NOTES

1. Because the initiators of this work are so varied, I have found myself describing many of these activities in the passive voice. I have done this not because these actions have no agents but because I hope that many people will be able to see themselves as the initiators of some of these actions. The people to whom this chapter is addressed are not all faculty members or administrators, not all women's studies faculty or department chairs, but rather, I hope, some people in all those positions who see the strategies I describe as effective ways for them to work for curriculum change in their own institutions.

2. On many New Jersey campuses, the initial year of this process is the year after a faculty team returns from the New Jersey Project summer institute and begins,

with or without administrative support, to try to initiate or expand the work of curriculum transformation.

3. All these efforts of the project are described elsewhere in this volume and will not be discussed in detail here.

4. This program, originally designed and funded by the New Jersey Department of Higher Education, pairs faculty for a year, during which they observe each other's teaching, interview each other's students, and participate in discussions of teaching with each other and with other faculty involved in the program that year. The objective is not to critique colleagues' teaching but to share techniques and strategies so that everyone's teaching is enhanced.

3

Institutionalizing Curriculum Change: College and University Administrators Discuss the Issues

Wendy K. Kolmar, Moderator,
and Wilfredo Nieves, Eleanor Smith,
Cliff Wood, Helen Stewart, and
Catherine Dorsey Gaines

This chapter consists of an edited transcript of a panel discussion at a New Jersey Project conference at Brookdale Community College on November 1, 1991. The moderator was Wendy K. Kolmar, director of women's studies and an associate professor of English at Drew University. The participants were Wilfredo Nieves, dean of liberal arts, Essex County College; Eleanor Smith, vice president for academic affairs and provost, William Paterson College; Cliff Wood, vice president for academic affairs, County College of Morris; Helen Stewart, vice president for academic affairs, Rider College; and Catherine Dorsey Gaines, associate dean, Kean College.

THE ROLE OF ADMINISTRATORS IN CURRICULUM TRANSFORMATION

KOLMAR: What kind of a balance do institutions need between top-down, initiatives for curriculum change and grassroots organizing, organizing that comes from faculty and students?

NIEVES: I think it has to be an integrated approach. For the process to work
   it has to be one in which everyone has ownership. I would like to think
   that I have a little more to do with the implementation of curricular
   transformation than I do. I think my role is as a facilitator—trying
   to make sure that changes are implemented, that there is diversity in
   curriculum development.

SMITH: It is important, when you are trying to stimulate some action, that
   there be a climate and a context for curricular change to take place. So
   it is important for the administration to provide the framework for action. The senior administration has the responsibility for articulating
   values clearly; then it is the faculty that has the responsibility for relating those values to students and coming up with an innovative curricular format. I'm hoping that that will happen with respect to diversity
   on our campus.

   To facilitate new activities, the provost's Faculty Development
   Fund will be utilized to support proposals for curricular development
   in these areas. We are determined to find practical ways to facilitate
   course load and to allow time for developing student interest in a
   new or revised class and to support the course if registration is low
   at first.

WOOD: In 1983, I was fortunate to be one of 9 men along with 300 women
   who spent a couple of weeks at Wheaton College under a FIPSE (Fund
   for the Improvement of Post-Secondary Education) grant for balancing
   the curriculum. I remember Peggy McIntosh saying there how important it was for it [curriculum transformation] not to be an add-on
   but to become part of the institution. So, as I've become an administrator, a dean, and now a vice president, I've kept that idea in mind. Obviously, the curriculum comes from the faculty. But as an administrator,
   I have to be responsible for the curriculum development process—for
   saying to people when they develop new courses, when they look at new
   curriculum, when they revise courses, "Have you given consideration to
   the inclusion of scholarship by and about women?" I think that is the
   most important thing that I can do as an administrator—not only to
   set the climate for inclusion and provide opportunities, but also to make
   people aware that that's what the institution expects.

STEWART: One of the things I'm committed to, no matter where I am and no
   matter what, is the end of dualism. So I'm really a both/and person. As
   an administrator, I try to remember the faculty part of myself that's
   committed to education. If we, as executive administrators, avoid taking an "us/them" view or engaging in a "we/they" struggle with faculty,
   the process will proceed a lot more easily. The faculty are not going to
   force the administration to do anything, and the administration is not

going to force the faculty to do anything. So we have to come up with roles that facilitate the process.

HIRING, PROMOTION, AND TENURE OF FACULTY AND THEIR RELATION TO CURRICULUM TRANSFORMATION

KOLMAR: The next item for discussion is the role of faculty hiring, retention, promotion, and tenure in the curriculum transformation process. These issues become particularly important when institutions are forced to cut their budgets severely.

NIEVES: At Essex, our president has given us a specific directive that our new faculty hires must be representative of our diverse student population. He wants to see an institution that has the faculty diversity for transforming the curriculum. We need individuals who can give leadership in this area and who have the background and experience to take leadership in changing the curriculum.

We look to support those faculty members who have taken the leadership in this area by promoting them. We see faculty who do it [curriculum transformation] on an individual basis in their own classes; we want them to work on making formal changes in the curriculum. That's something we, as administrators, have to encourage more than in the past. That's a contribution we might want to recognize with an award.

SMITH: Institutional commitment is realized when faculty positions are allocated in areas where curriculum change is being encouraged by the college and the faculty. Faculty do the hiring, so if there are going to be changes made in the hiring, it has to begin with the faculty.

Support of curricular change should be apparent in the articulated goals and objectives of the department, the school, and the college. Regarding the issue of retention, promotion, and tenure, the criteria used to determine appointment, retention, promotion, and tenure decisions must be indicators of the value and importance placed on certain types of activities. If the intention of the administration and faculty is to foster curricular change, then those activities must receive recognition in that reward system. If interdisciplinary programs such as women's studies, race and gender, African American studies, Latino studies, Asian studies, and so forth are of value to the institution, then there must be support for those activities.

WOOD: I come from Morris County, a homogeneous community, a fairly affluent community, where fewer than 3 percent of the population are people of color. Yet when I came 5 years ago, one of the goals of the president was to make some changes in the area of student and faculty diversity. At the time I came, of the 210 faculty, fewer than 2 percent were people of color; now it's 14 percent. It's helped that we've had faculty turnover. But you have to make your goals very clear and your expectations very clear. If you're trying to make changes in an institution, to transform the curriculum, you have to bring in people with different values and different perspectives. And so you have to make faculty aware that without a clear commitment to diversity, they will pick someone like themselves, someone who supports their values.

I say we're not hiring "the most qualified person." At the moment, we need to do these things in the institution; we need "these kinds of people" to do "these kinds of things." And therefore, we're looking for people who can bring into the institution the attributes and experience we need at this particular time. The traditional concept of "the most qualified" just doesn't work.

STEWART: I'm going to take a slightly different approach to this topic. The bottom line is that students vote with their feet. If faculty are not teaching courses that our students want to take, the department's going to be in deep trouble. At that point, I think, change will occur whether we plan it, set up goals for it, or do anything else about it. Times have changed, needs have changed, and faculty, by definition—existing faculty and new faculty—are going to be different. I know there's a debate raging right now about whether or not commitment to diversity should be included as part of promotion and tenure criteria. Whether or not we address that directly by making diversity a formal criterion for promotion and tenure, the fact is that some departments are losing students in droves because they are not willing to teach "the new student." And then the big, bad administrators have to go in there and decide whether or not we can afford to continue lines or create new ones in that department or give them other kinds of support.

GAINES: I see faculty hiring, promotion, and tenure as starting from the top down. Seven years ago, our faculty was not as diverse as it is today. The former president made a decision; he told departments: "You will not get faculty lines unless you begin to look at other kinds of faculty coming here. Different kinds of people. A diverse faculty." Once it became apparent that departments were not going to get these lines, departments began to seriously search for "qualified" people to fill these positions. The next step was the retention of these people. The president again made certain stipulations, and we began to work with peer grouping to help the neophyte faculty improve their professional development. As a result, we find that the people who work earnestly with the director of professional development are doing exceptionally well in progressing to tenure. So I think there really must be something from upper administration that says we are not going to accept past practice, but we are going to start looking at other things in order to help get a more diverse staff tenured.

FUNDING FOR CURRICULUM TRANSFORMATION INITIATIVES

KOLMAR: The next issue is funding for projects that transform the curriculum, particularly in a time of budget constraints. What are the possibilities for funding this kind of effort—both institutional and external?

NIEVES: People don't realize that unless something is funded institutionally, it's not really going to last. I think that we've been fortunate to be able to try out things experimentally because creative individuals have sought out other sources, such as grants. But in the end, if something is going to be long lasting institutionally, funding has to come from the institution. Many programs that have been funded through grants originally have proved themselves to be necessary, and money has been found for them.

SMITH: I'm relatively new to New Jersey. One of the things I've found here is that the politics of education disturbs me greatly. I am concerned that the Department of Higher Education and the state legislature often mandate certain things to take place; they give the institution the money to start the program and then nothing happens because at the same time that they're giving with this hand, they're taking away with the other hand. You create a good program, but it can't be the way it's supposed to be because of inadequate funding.

We do need to encourage the faculty or the administration to find other funds external to the institution if we can. We have to be careful when we accept funding that it is for a program that we want to follow through on in a meaningful way, so that we don't have something that is draining resources that we are not honestly committed to institutionally.

The reality is that ultimately the funds are going to have to come from the institution, and I see that happening in only two ways: the reallocation of resources in a creative way and the evaluation of current offerings in the various departments to determine if the present curriculum is appropriate for the present and future needs of our students.

WOOD: I certainly agree with everything Eleanor said, but I also think that if you really believe that change is necessary, then you have to find the resources to support it.

When a project starts with external funds, you have to institutionalize it if it is going to last. I think that any new programs that are begun have to be put in departments. If you set up separate structures outside the faculty structures, it's good while the outside money is there. But then there's no ownership of the programs, and you get resistance when you try to move resources to them. You have to start out in the beginning involving the appropriate faculty and then giving resources—sometimes it's only a small commitment to say that this is important, an hour of release time or whatever. This is what we have to do to get the best use out of our money.

STEWART: I can tell that I'm a provost because funding is the part that really gets me excited. Funding is key, and there are a lot of ways to influence funding. Some of the programs at Rider that have been most effective from both grassroots and administrative perspectives have started with external funding. Most often, you go out and get somebody else interested; you get a little seed money. You hope it works, and 2 or 3 years later, you hope that you've sold it well enough internally that the university will take on the funding. I think those are just the facts of life. We are tuition dependent; we don't have a line in the budget for the great idea you're going to think of next year. Most of our funds are already committed to existing programs. Now we're going to go with that and let it be. I'm going to try to change that process; I'm going to try to help people identify and get the external funds they need to start a program so that we can sell it together.

GAINES: As my colleagues have stated, programs at Kean such as the African American Studies Program, the Cooperative Education Program, the Writing Across the Curriculum Program were all externally funded programs. They have now been incorporated into the curriculum. The most exciting initiatives have been externally funded, but they still have to be incorporated into the curriculum and funding structures of the institution if we want the creative curriculum to continue to benefit the students.

4

Curriculum Transformation at a 2-Year College: Two Views from Brookdale Community College

Irma Lester
Freda Hepner

This chapter, about the creation and development of a gender, class, and cultural diversity program at Brookdale Community College, is written in our two voices. Because the heart of our program is collaboration, we felt that our story could not be told from one viewpoint. Additionally, what we seek and have sought to achieve at Brookdale is the understanding that multiple perspectives are needed if we are to transform our curriculum as well as our vision of the world.

ESTABLISHING A FACULTY GROUP

Irma

In September 1990, I returned to Brookdale Community College after a year's sabbatical leave focusing on women's studies and curriculum transformation, including an inspiring summer institute with the New Jersey Project.

I was eager to bring what I had learned to my own campus, but how could I begin to bring my new plans, my hopes for what I believed was a crucial direction for the college, to reality? I had no grant money or college funds at my disposal.

For me, as always, the answer was to be found in collaboration. Empowered by my relationships with others doing this work throughout the state, I began to set up partnerships at Brookdale. My previous experience overseeing the Writing Across the Curriculum program at Brookdale made me realize the importance of first reaching out to other faculty with interest in this program.

With Mary Lou Wagner, a sociology professor who had attended the New Jersey Project summer institute with me, I began to look for people and resources on our campus to begin a study and discussion group. We realized that we would have to begin with a much more modest plan than that of colleges where funding for release time and materials was available. We decided to cochair a monthly study and discussion group called Multiple Perspectives in the Curriculum and to solicit a volunteer, interdisciplinary core group. The only things we could promise were interesting discussions, new research, and, thanks to the largesse of our college's faculty research institute, a light snack.

We sent flyers advertising the group to all faculty, staff, and administrators, asking for a commitment to attend every meeting listed on the schedule. However, because we wanted our group to reflect diversity in such areas as age, rank, discipline, race, ethnicity, and gender, we reached out individually to people on campus who could contribute to the knowledge and diversity of our group. By the time we were ready for our first meeting, participants included tenured and untenured faculty and learning assistants—men and women of racial, ethnic, and age diversity.

Freda

A full teaching load of five sections and all the other obligations of a community college faculty member leave little time or opportunity for the collegial exchange of ideas across the disciplines. So, when the formation of a group interested in exploring multiple perspectives was announced, I was eager to participate. In my 10 years at Brookdale Community College, I couldn't remember such a campus-wide effort around as publicly controversial a topic as that mouthful "multiculturalism."

Most of the 20 or so faculty members who drifted into the lunchtime meeting with assorted books, papers, and brown bags recognized one another, if not by face, by discipline. We were all from the various social science and humanities departments. We were asked to present ourselves by name and department and to share with the group what our connections, feelings, ideas, and experiences were with issues of cultural diversity.

As people began to speak, I became aware of how much and how little we had in common. Almost all of us spoke with the strong consciousness of the hyphenated American—the outsider who has raised himself or herself through hard work and education. A few others spoke of growing up in stereotypical America—ethnically homogeneous midwestern communities. These were the people who seemed most independent to me. They had consciously had to seek out the "others" in America.

The next month found most of the group returning to discuss an article by Elizabeth Minnich: "From the Circle of the Elite to the World of the Whole." Among the topics of conversation generated by this article was women in the arts. The discussion delineated some of the different perceptions we brought to the issues. Male cultural historians did not think of women's crafts as legitimate art forms. Women in our group raised the question that would be asked again and again in the following months: Who is making the decision about what should be displayed, researched, valued? Passions ran high, but we left this first meeting as we would leave others: minds racing, juices flowing, glad to have been part of it all.

Toward the end of our first year, members of the group began to offer materials, from readings in their own disciplines, for group discussion. We had developed a group dynamic that helped us honestly explore the issues without personal invective. Because each member of the group subscribed to the basic premise that all the diverse American groups had contributed to our nation, the essential question boiled down to what was the most honest scholarship that we could provide for our students. Our goals were alike; our choices differed considerably.

DEVELOPING NEW MATERIALS AND ADDING STUDENT PERSPECTIVES

Irma

As the winter semester drew to a close, Mary Lou and I were anxious to have our group begin to develop materials for course transformation. Although we had attempted to get funding for projects all year without success, we decided to make one more appeal before spring term. To our surprise, after submitting a variety of specific written proposals and speaking to administrators and department chairs, we were granted funds for a seminar that would be open only to those faculty who had participated in our year-long multiple-perspectives group, on which the seminar would build.

Twelve faculty asked to be part of the project. Mary Lou and I worked to plan three sessions for the group as well as independent time to help participants with their projects, which would be due at the start of the fall term. We felt that it was important to have our seminar sessions model the pedagogy that we hoped would be incorporated into their lessons.

We assembled a series of articles and materials for each participant. Included were the following: "Syllabus Redesign Guidelines" by Marilyn Schuster and Susan Van Dyne (1983) and "Classroom Pedagogy and the New Scholarship on Women" by Frances Maher (1985), exercises on sexism and racism for ourselves and our students, bibliographies of materials on gender and multiculturalism, the winter 1991 issue of *Transformations,* and the winning student essays from the New Jersey Project's feminist scholarship contest.

Readings were assigned for each session; group discussion, journal writing, peer response groups, and questioning helped us relate the readings to our own teaching and curriculum. Time was provided each week for sharing our ideas for transforming our courses. We also became resource people for one another, suggesting materials and classroom strategies. Our seminar methods were collaborative, cooperative, and interactive. We incorporated personal experiences along with academic research and had a nonhierarchical approach to learning through shared leadership and participation.

During each session of the seminar, we divided into different kinds of groups to share questions, curriculum ideas, and responses to readings and to serve as resources for one another for our projects. Sometimes collaboration was grouped by discipline so that faculty in sociology, writing, history, or other similar areas worked together; at other times, faculty from diverse ranks and disciplines provided one another with feedback on works in progress. We all found it remarkable how instructive a colleague from another department could be in responding to our materials. In this way, the interaction within the seminar became a pedagogical model for the materials and instruction that would take place in our own classes.

Critical thinking and journal writing helped us focus our ideas, create questions, relate relevant personal experiences, and argue issues. Later, when faculty developed their own course materials, similar techniques were applied in student assignments. Through exploratory writing, students, like the instructors in the seminar, connected their own experiences to societal concerns. Then, through written analysis, they made the connection to the impact of race, class, and gender issues.

Our nonhierarchical approach to leadership was also demonstrated in the way that Mary Lou and I participated in the seminar. Although we were the seminar leaders, we shared that role with everyone in the group. We were also group participants, as each of us worked with a group in planning and developing our own course materials.

At the start of the fall semester, we collected and distributed the new materials and spent time during our meeting discussing the units. Suggestions for revision were made, and we also got reports from one another about how students were responding to the materials. As a group we were able to share all the steps in the development of the new curriculum.

Freda

Each of the participants developed a project that involved a pedagogical change in a particular course. Obviously, this was a discipline-driven transformation. For some, it involved emphasizing aspects of a course that had previously been mentioned only in passing. For others, it meant using text sources and specific student assignments that led to an exploration of gender, race, or class.

For instance, sociology professor Marshall Forman focused more on student experiences and observations in his course Sociology of Marriage and the Family. The course had always included a section entitled The Division of Household Labor: Historical Roots, Contemporary Patterns. What had been only a sidebar in the course became a central theme of the classroom discussion. Students are now asked to include in their papers their own preferences, which, Forman reports, will permit an "analysis of generational differences in gender socialization outcomes"—a valuable achievement for a sociology class.

Professor Richard Sorrell expanded his unit called Industrialization and Immigration, which is part of the history course American Civilization II. His goal is to heighten student awareness of "how multiple cultural perspectives have affected our respective families' lives, both in the past and today." Sorrell starts by describing his own family's background for the students. Students are then sent home to discover their own histories. In class, their demographic data are compiled, categorized, and compared with the national data on immigration. Students reflect on the comparisons and then ask their families a series of attitudinal questions. The students' final papers discuss how their family histories and attitudes are reflected in the historical changes in society.

Students in math professor Terry Healy's course in statistics enjoy the applications nature of the course more than the theoretical components. Healy often uses newspapers and magazines that center around the popular culture—for example, sports and entertainment—to provide statistics for discussion and problem solving in the classroom. She has expanded her pool of articles to include materials that encourage students to raise questions about gender. The data themselves, which the students must analyze statistically, lead to student questions on the reliability of studies that are inferentially biased. For instance, in an article about the relationship between drug testing and gender, students noted that the testing had been conducted almost exclusively on males. They were quick to note that those results could not automatically be extended to include women.

Irma and Freda

In the spring of 1992, the first trial of the Los Angeles policemen who had arrested Rodney King ended in acquittal. Widespread rioting followed. At Brookdale a few days later, the Black Students Union, with the help of some minority staff members, organized a lunchtime meeting for the college community. Students, faculty, and staff members rose to share their sadness and fears about the future. There were calls for change and requests for leadership from the college. Speakers asked that there be a clear acknowledgment of prejudice on the campus and in the community. King's pained message, "Why can't we just get along," was echoed in that lunchroom. The president and the vice president for educational services listened carefully. It was a very somber meeting.

Our group discussed how we might serve the community, as we were the only campus group that had been exploring these issues. We wanted very much to begin to raise the consciousness of faculty and staff, to effect change. After some discussion of ways and means and costs, it was agreed that a small group would be funded to plan a September faculty day on multiple perspectives and a program for the next academic year.

Through our efforts, Paula Rothenberg was invited to be the keynote speaker for our Fall '92 Faculty Day, a convocation attended by the entire faculty of the college. After her informative, rousing speech on the need for a new multicultural curriculum, we divided the audience into small response discussion groups, each led by a member of our planning team. We thought that it was essential for Paula's speech to be more than a 1-day focus on this issue; we wanted it to signal an opening of a new direction for diversity on the campus. From that response we were able to set up two additional multiple-perspectives discussion groups, each led by two members of our original group.

During the fall of 1992, our president, Dr. Burnham, announced the establishment of a Commission on Diversity at Brookdale. Although our proposals and programs were not cited as the reason for this exciting new development, we believe that our work had some impact on his decision.

Now as we look back from the perspective of late winter 1993, we realize that it's never been a matter of a "magic memo" or perfectly worded proposal, but rather a series of ongoing efforts. Our success has been the result of constant interaction with the administration; dedication to a cause no matter how small, unfunded, or hopeless it seemed to be; taking small steps when we could; and, finally, a certain degree of serendipity.

REFERENCES

Maher, F. (1985). Classroom pedagogy and the new scholarship on women. In M. Culley & C. Portuges (Eds.), *Gendered subjects: The dynamics of feminist teaching.* Boston: Routledge & Kegan Paul.

Schuster, M., & Van Dyne, S. (1983). Syllabus redesign guidelines. In *Selected Bibliography for Integrating Research on Women's Experience in the Liberal Arts Curriculum.* Northampton, MA: Smith College.

5

Curriculum Transformation at a 4-Year College: Taking the First Steps

Frances Shapiro-Skrobē
Kathleen Fowler
Rosetta Geller

Our goal at Ramapo College of New Jersey is to transform the curriculum across all disciplines and to adopt an inclusive model, one that examines and explores many selves and reflects the diversity of voices in "our" and other cultures. The challenge set for us by the New Jersey Project (to Integrate the Scholarship on Gender into the Curriculum) and its director, Paula Rothenberg, was to question what would happen when we placed issues of women, race, class, ethnicity, sexual orientation, physical challenges, and so on at the center of our focus rather than in the background and used them as standards against which to measure other issues. What would happen when we foregrounded issues that had been ignored or, at best, treated peripherally—issues that had been added on at the end of a course and easily dropped when time was short?

At the New Jersey Project's 1991 summer institute, Wendy Kolmar, associate professor of literature at Drew University, suggested that to begin this process of curriculum transformation, we needed to ask five fundamental questions: (1) Who defines the content of the course? (2) Whose interests are represented by this choice? (3) What does this course tell students about what is important and what is not? (4) What does the course tell students about race, gender, class, and so forth? (5) What does the structure of the course and its pedagogy tell students about whose perspective is important and about what it means to know something? At Ramapo, we have started asking these questions and have taken the first steps toward curriculum transformation.

BACKGROUND

Ramapo College, a 4-year New Jersey public institution of higher education, was established in 1969 as an innovative college offering traditional academic values in a nontraditional setting. "Experimental," "student-oriented," "informal," "alternative," "interdisciplinary," "international," and "multicultural" are other adjectives that have been applied to Ramapo. We have been lauded as "a small public ivy" and "the college of choice for a global education."

However, despite our history and various efforts to transform our curriculum to be more international, gender issues remained secondary. It was not until the summer of 1988 that we began to see some institutional change. Two Ramapo faculty members—Donna Crawley, associate professor of psychology, and Martha Ecker, associate professor of sociology—attended the New Jersey Project's summer institute. Upon their return, they conducted faculty development seminars to incorporate feminist perspectives into social science methodology courses.

A year later, Ramapo College President Robert A. Scott formed the Task Force on Gender Issues (with Crawley as its chair and Ecker as one of its members) and charged it with reviewing and presenting suggestions on four areas of campus life: personal relationships, including discrimination; curricular issues; campus awareness about sexism and sexual harassment and related topics; and issues of institutional policy and organizational development, including affirmative action goals, as they relate to gender.

The task force recommended that the curriculum committees evaluate courses with respect to appropriate inclusion of material on gender and minority issues. They identified the general education core curriculum as the logical starting point for gender awareness and integration and targeted College English I and II and College Algebra courses, all offered by the Division of Basic Studies (DBS).

However, since these and many other valuable recommendations went only to the administration and to very few faculty, little or nothing ensued. Ecker later expressed her frustration at being too few in number to make a difference. The college lacked the "critical mass" that we know is so essential for effecting any meaningful change. We (Fowler, Geller, and Shapiro-Skrobe), along with Ramon Reyes, coordinator of DBS's developmental writing program, provided part of that "critical mass" when we formed the DBS Curriculum Transformation Team and attended the New Jersey Project's 1991 summer institute. Representing administration, faculty, and professional staff, as well as the fields of composition, English as a second language, mathematics, literature, teacher education, and women's studies, we were eager to learn more about curriculum transformation and to facilitate positive changes within basic studies courses.

We came back to Ramapo excited by the possibilities before us, only to find that the college had decided that the erupting state and campus fiscal crisis had made the Women's Center expendable. Gender was once again a "frill" to be easily discarded. After angry voices reminded the institution of the value of and critical need for services and attention to women and women's issues, continued funding for the Women's Center's space and remaining personnel was assured. In addition, the administration designated $20,000 to be awarded by the Center for Intercultural Education (CIE) to proposals for curricular projects that would integrate global, multicultural, and gender studies across the instructional and student development programs of the college. Projects that addressed gender issues were to receive priority. Our DBS Curriculum Transformation Team received a grant from the CIE to conduct a series of faculty training workshops on transforming the curriculum across many disciplines in the spring of 1992.

THE WORKSHOP SERIES:
DESCRIPTION, OUTCOMES, AND ANALYSIS

As we enacted our grant proposal, several exciting opportunities arose, allowing us to include additional live speakers and facilitators in place of the videotaped presentations we had proposed. We were also able to take advantage of technology in our International Telecommunications Center and hold an audio conference with one of our videotaped presenters. Although our grant ($1,875) was significantly less than our request, it was, nonetheless, the second largest sum awarded that year. Fowler, the project leader, received three credits of release time, and the others volunteered their services. The DBS and Robert Hatala, the vice president for academic affairs, contributed supplemental funds for publicity and refreshments. Rothenberg accepted a reduced honorarium (which she then donated to the New Jersey Project), thus freeing funds for additional speakers.

Best of all, considerable interest from numerous groups on campus enabled us to attract attention from a broad cross section of the college community and to send a message that our efforts were supported from the top down. Our cosponsors were the vice president for academic affairs, the DBS, the Women's Studies Convening Group, the Women's Center, the Ramapo Focus on Teaching (Ramfot) Team, and the All-College General Education Committee. The faculty assembly president agreed to place our workshop schedule on the academic calendar distributed to the college community.

We did extensive research on appropriate books and materials and were able to set up book displays at each workshop. Elaine Risch of Ramapo's library prepared comprehensive bibliographies of relevant materials located on campus, and the New Jersey Project provided us with a variety of bibliographies that it had prepared, especially on science and on pedagogy, which we then duplicated for interested participants.

The workshop series proved very successful. Quite important to this success was the fact that we invited as official discussants faculty whom we knew, suspected, or hoped would be open to these ideas; we left alone those who were openly opposed to such "heretical" changes. Cosponsorship proved to be key, as were the breakfasts we served at each workshop, the publicity we continually generated, the phone calls we made, and the personal letters of invitation we sent to faculty members. We also scheduled our workshops on Wednesday mornings, when the fewest classes were held. Thus, we largely eliminated the problem of conflicting schedules. Most important to the success of the series was the smooth, collaborative effort of the four members of our team, who shared in all facets of planning and mounting the workshops, in encouraging participation, in moderating discussions, and in following through on each session.

We kicked off the series with an inspiring talk by Rothenberg, who discussed the challenges and rewards of curriculum transformation. At our request, our vice president for academic affairs introduced Rothenberg and the workshop series. Rothenberg gave an acute and persuasive philosophical and epistemological analysis of the way in which the categories of white, male, heterosexual, middle class, Christian, and so on are perceived as central and normative in our society and in our teaching. As she noted, marginalizing members of other categories not only devalues them but makes them invisible. Rothenberg analyzed the biases evidenced in such unconscious language choices and common visual images as Little Mermaid Band-Aids and "flesh"-colored crayons. "Whose flesh," she asked us, "are we talking about?" A question and discussion period followed, involving more than 70 faculty, administrators, staff, and students.

For our second workshop on history and American studies, we showed a portion of a videotaped speech that Kenneth Goings, professor of history at Florida Atlantic University, had delivered at the New Jersey Project's 1991 summer institute. In his talk, Goings analyzed the three stages of curriculum transformation: (1) the "add-on" stage, where particular examples of out-standing figures from various groups are pointed to and included; (2) the "trail of tears" stage, which focuses on these groups as victims of oppression and often reflects them as passive in their own history; and (3) recent rethinking, which examines these groups in their full range of activities, experiences, and contributions and allows them to speak to us in their own voices through primary sources.

Goings offered us three histories, African American, women's, and gay and lesbian, as models and showed how they would look in each of the three stages. After our participants—all faculty in history and American studies—reacted to his videotaped remarks, we participated in a prearranged audio conference with Goings, who expanded on his points and responded to questions raised by both the discussants and members of the audience. We were pleased to see several adjunct faculty in history, political science, and American studies among the 30 who attended this session.

Because a number of our social science faculty had already been actively engaged in curriculum transformation for several years, an introductory session for this area seemed inappropriate. Hence, we chose to examine a particular social science discipline, anthropology, which had received little attention. Our third workshop, Inventing Anthropology, was planned around an excerpt of a videotaped presentation by Sandra Morgan of the Center for Research on Women in Oregon. Morgan reinterpreted the hunter-gatherer concept, emphasizing the extensive reliance on grains and plants in the diets of these early people and the recent recognition that it was, indeed, the gathering role that had been essential to the survival of the species. Morgan suggested, among other things, that reviewing anthropology with attention to the female role subtly shifts the entire paradigm of how cultural constructs are perceived. Our discussants, all from the School of Social Science/Human Services, conducted a lively and provocative discussion with our audience of almost 60 faculty and students.

Our fourth workshop, featuring excerpts of a videotape of Sue Rosser, professor of women's studies and physiology at the University of South Carolina Medical School, centered on the inherent biases in the so-called objective world of the biological and hard sciences. Rosser pointed out that scientific theories and the language in which science is discussed are products of historical and social contexts, and that these theories and expectations can and do influence what is actually observed. Rosser warned that such restricted perspectives often lead to outright bad science; one example is that subjects of scientific studies are often only males, even when the goal is to evaluate the use of a particular technique or medication on the female physiology. The 14 people present avidly debated Rosser's concepts.

Our fifth workshop returned to a live format, with Wendy Kolmar facilitating small and large group discussions on literature. Kolmar first presented an overview of the changes that have reshaped the literary canon and the teaching of literature and then gave an example of how in her Victorian literature course she places a canonical text in the context of such underrepresented works as broadsides, ballads, diaries, and prison accounts. The 30 participants included full-time and adjunct writing and literature faculty.

Our sixth workshop on liberating pedagogy was led by Nancy Leech, director of the writing program at Rockland Community College, who addressed the nature of feminist pedagogy, issues of nurturing and empowerment, and collaborative learning techniques. Leech modeled collaborative learning pedagogy by breaking us almost immediately into small groups and asking us to first identify ways to empower students who feel marginalized and then share with one another our own experiences of feeling excluded during our educational lives. She later processed with us the group dynamics that had ensued, and we discussed the subtle and not so subtle ways that students are made to feel "othered." Some 35 faculty and staff from all across the college participated in this session.

Our seventh and final workshop was a wrap-up session led by the team members and several discussants from the previous six workshops. Scheduled after the completion of the spring semester during Faculty Development Week, we merged with the college's Ramfot Team and the college seminar training group to discuss the suggestions and ideas that had been raised throughout the semester. We worked in small groups to define precise ways in which our syllabi and our class plans for the upcoming semester would reflect these concepts. Approximately 40 people came together in this final session.

SUBSEQUENT DEVELOPMENTS

One immediate positive outcome of this series was that it began to identify and bring together faculty who were interested in or already committed to the concept and process of curriculum transformation. For example, one of our DBS colleagues, English professor Peter Scheckner, had been actively involved in New Jersey's International and Global Education Project and had already reshaped his sections of English II to reflect international, multicultural, and class concerns. One result of his interest in our workshops was his decision to infuse gender more prominently into this mixture. He then led a team of five adjunct writing faculty members to the New Jersey Project's 1992 summer institute.

Working together with the earlier DBS team, these faculty members then transformed the English II courses to use texts by multicultural and women writers and to raise issues of gender, race, and class as themes of class discussion and as topics for research and writing. Our commitment to nurturing pedagogies and exploring cultural issues in English I courses was reaffirmed and strengthened.

Other initiatives have followed our original workshop series. As a result of their subsequent participation in the New Jersey Multicultural Project's 1992 summer institute, Crawley, Fowler, Reyes, and Shapiro-Skrobe planned a new 300-level course, Advanced Writing Multiculturally, which would allow students to work simultaneously on enhancing their writing skills while pursuing research, fieldwork, and extensive discussion on issues of personal and social concern. Reyes and Fowler team-taught this course in the spring of 1993 and 1994.

In the fall of 1993, Geller and Fowler integrated the seemingly disparate fields of mathematics and writing by pairing developmental writing and development mathematics courses. The structure of these two courses was profoundly influenced by the move toward an inclusive pedagogy that reflected diversity and gender issues and integrated computer technology, including E-mail communication. In other mathematics courses, writing and research paper assignments were given, and instructors integrated the scholarship on female mathematicians and mathematicians of color.

Our experience with the New Jersey Project has energized and regenerated us in our teaching, our scholarship, and our personal lives. In turn, we believe that we have been a part of giving a new life and a new emphasis to our institution. Long-term results, we suspect, will be so pervasive and so complex that they will be immeasurable.

6

Involving Faculty in Curriculum Transformation: Overcoming Resistance at Richard Stockton College

Nancy L. Ashton

This chapter offers suggestions for motivating people and dealing with faculty resistance to curricular transformation. In our attempts to improve curricula, we must convert others and help them and ourselves in the process of revising courses and designing new courses.

Stockton has had two formal (i.e., externally funded) curriculum transformation projects: One consisted of three half-day faculty workshops, guest speakers for the whole college community, and library acquisitions; the second involved a 2-week intensive summer institute for 15 faculty, plus guest speakers for the entire college during the academic year. Each situation differs, but my ideas can be adapted to help overcome resistance to other programs.

RECOGNIZING FACULTY DIVERSITY

The first difficulty is that college faculty members are a diverse group in terms of both the particulars of their home campuses and their own individual perceptions, styles, and needs. It helps to keep in mind that faculty move gradually in their individual transformation and that any group process usually includes a variety of phases. It is cost effective to forget the die-hard resisters and address only those with some interest. Then, as the numbers grow, some of the previously resistant will become interested. Similarly, I advocate meeting faculty members where they are, helping them to move forward from whatever stage they have achieved.

The heterogeneity among faculty can be a counterproductive force, but we can prevent this by acquainting participants with the idea of phases of development, pointing out that as individuals we move through a series of stages in curriculum transformation and may be at different levels in different courses. A diverse group also has advantages, however, such as stimulating discussions, providing role models for newcomers, and allowing "advanced" members to practice with the neophytes strategies that may be applicable in their work with students. But each program or person must fashion an approach that is appropriate for the particular campus and program goals.

There is also variability in the rewards and incentives that are effective in motivating individual faculty. Some people will be motivated by intellectual stimulation, exchange of ideas, or resources for use in the classroom or in research. Others will need different incentives or are so busy that tangible rewards are needed to win their participation in a project. These can include food at events, bibliographies and resources, small stipends, and book and travel stipends. It helps if administrators formally recognize faculty with letters of appreciation and public commendation.

Having a multifaceted project such as ours—with guest lectures, half-day workshops, a 2-week institute, and library development—enabled us to reach many people on campus and led to informal discussions, such that curriculum integration became a widely discussed topic. Faculty have encouraged college committees to propose policies or projects that are consistent with curricular transformation. These wider ripple effects produce and are evidence of broader support. They also help to get more people involved.

OVERCOMING FACULTY RESISTANCE

There are many sources of faculty resistance, which shift in kind and in subtlety. A major culprit is the complex of "isms"—sexism, racism, and classism, among others. Feminist scholarship challenges masculine self-images, and some men fear being "unmanned" by having women as experts or by having male experience and male-oriented research moved from the center to the periphery. A parallel process can occur with people accustomed to and benefiting from white, middle-class views of the world. Dealing with these is like dealing with the racism and sexism that are rampant in our culture, and one makes a choice about how to react. It helps a great deal to have members of privileged groups as part of the team or as presenters. They appear to have less vested interest and can help draw in reluctant people.

We all have been influenced by exclusive views of the world and of the academy. As academics, many of us feel attacked when we are told that our discipline's canon is distorted or incomplete. Some people resist the implicit conclusion that our own knowledge and views of the world are flawed; others feel guilt at complicity in the process. Teachers and researchers may need to be reminded that at the heart of the academy is the quest for truth—or at least for validity.

Related to this is the phenomenon of reluctance to move out of one's field of expertise. Most academics were trained in and think along a very narrow discipline base. Too many faculty still hold to traditional standards of excellence ("this feminist stuff is not in the prestigious journal in my field") and are wedded to their discipline's canon and favorite paradigms. Given a limited number of weeks in the semester, teachers are often concerned about sacrificing something in order to bring in new perspectives. There are some choices in dealing with this concern: Some people pull no punches and say, "Yes, in order to do the right thing, you will have to delete material from the syllabus, but it will be worth it." Others suggest that material on excluded groups can be incorporated in small ways, for instance, in the examples that are used to illustrate broad concepts and theories, or by assigning student papers on women, people of color, or underclass activists.

OVERCOMING FRUSTRATION AND INERTIA

Some of those who question tradition will realize that changing the curriculum and dismantling the canon will take a lot of work. The breadth and scope of the new scholarship are overwhelming, and laziness or inertia may win out over challenge, stimulation, and professional authenticity. This is especially likely if, as is proper, projects do not focus of just one of the dimensions of exclusion. When participants realize how many groups of people have been excluded, they may throw their hands up. This sense of frustration can occur in even the most well-meaning, committed people; it may be especially evident to them, because they see the need for and the enormity of curriculum revision. A couple of tactics are available here, depending on the faculty members' level of commitment. For those who are less committed, one can point out that "Rome wasn't built in a day" (and neither was our incomplete curriculum) and that they will be doing their part by starting with some small changes. In my experience, when people do one small thing, it leads them to do more, either because they have come to realize that more change is needed or because their efforts have been so well received by students. We need to remind ourselves that this is a developmental process. It will take a long time with many of us doing different things in our own ways in order to gradually build a more valid curriculum. For the more committed, the support of others in facing a formidable task together is helpful; faculty can be buoyed by knowing that others are in the trenches too.

The sometimes unconscious stance of "Why change? My life is okay now" will become evident in those who have different goals of education than we do. For instance, there are those who believe that liberal arts education should acquaint students with the classics and equip them to move into positions of power in capitalist society. Others of us are committed to feminist teaching and other goals for education. A changed pedagogy and a content that is different from our own training and expertise mean that our place in any course is less power wielding, less "in charge," and removed from grandiose notions of being *the authority.* This is asking too much of some faculty, many of whom love the attention an exhibitionist gets or are too insecure to share authority, control, and power. Bringing oneself down from the ivory tower or the pedestal is a big step.

OVERCOMING PERSONAL POLITICS

An insidious syndrome that can do considerable damage to our projects and our curriculum integration efforts is that some who appear to be interested in curriculum revision are just using such projects for their own career advancement or external rewards. They may not really want change but want to look as if they do. Some people like to give the impression that they are doing the "correct" thing. The vehicle that such opportunists hitch their advancement to may be curriculum transformation. Some of these folks are publicizing curriculum transformation and collecting rewards for participating.

Others object to what they term the "politicization" of the curriculum and the academy itself (as if institutions of higher education were not political). We've heard charges of bringing social movements, such as feminism, into the classroom and comments that "my field is not one where we can or should bring political movements in." What they fail to point out or even perhaps recognize is that the traditional curriculum is not value-free but rather came from and still supports vested interests. We must expose the ideology of so-called neutral scholarship.

I hope this discussion of resistance factors, sources, and manifestations has not given the impression that it is only our "opponents" who are potential problems in blocking our success. Some blocks may also come from our allies. For instance, some worry about what curriculum integration efforts will do to women's studies (e.g., the fear that if the curriculum becomes inclusive, administrators will see no need for African American studies, women's studies, and so forth and will withdraw the small support they have given). Others may worry that our projects "won't do it right." These people care about an inclusive curriculum and do not want hasty efforts to backfire and do damage by turning people away from curriculum transformation or by failing to provide participants with the full picture and complexity of the now-incomplete curriculum. We allay these concerns by being modest in what we undertake and by encouraging the assistance of these potential allies.

A final concern is that subgroup who think that they've already changed and want to tell others how to do it. Two groups are most susceptible to this: newcomers to one of the "studies" (or to curriculum integration) and the "white liberal boys," as friends of mine refer to them. (We need to be open to the possibility that we may come across this way to our peers, especially to those in other "studies.") We need to work with these people and may want to encourage their help to keep them from damaging our efforts. They may help by talking to the most resistant faculty on campus or by devising bibliographies or transporting guest speakers. And in subtle ways, by putting relevant articles in their mailboxes or bringing in speakers who appreciate the complexity of curriculum transformation, we can expose them to ideas that challenge their arrogance.

STAYING MOTIVATED

Through all this, keeping the lights and fires on is critical, but this can often be done in very simple, informal ways. For instance, words of support to one another in the cafeteria line, intercampus mail and E-mail as conduits for relevant articles, and public commendation for people who are involved keep the issue alive and provide us with the encouragement we need. There is a large network of people committed to changing our warped curriculum. We call on one another for help and want others to join us and call on us for ideas or assistance.

PART II

Rethinking Course Content, Perspective, and Pedagogy

7

The Politics of Discourse and the End of Argument

Paula Rothenberg

*Too often the attack on diversity is a rhetorical strategy by conserva-
tives and neoconservatives who have their own agenda. Under the
guise of defending objectivity and intellectual rigor, a defense that
can be a lot of mishmash, they are trying to preserve the cultural and
political supremacy of what, in shorthand, we might call white, heterosexual males.*

—*Catharine Stimpson*

The beginning is everything. As any student of philosophy knows, the answer
is already contained in the way we ask the question. Here is where I choose
to begin—on the streets of our cities, battlegrounds, where too many children
are dying. Random gunfire kills a 14-year-old girl in the south Bronx, a 33-
year-old white teacher sitting in her car at a stoplight, hits a 12-year-old boy
playing in front of his house in Brooklyn and penetrates the doors and win-
dows and bathtubs of tenement buildings where women and children of many
colors wait out the violence of the night and leave only because they are
forced to take a chance on the violence of the day. Here is where I begin—
with 11- and 12-year-old black and Hispanic children beaten, cursed, sprayed

with white paint on the way to school, smeared with filthy white creams by white-skinned youths wielding scissors that chop off curly black hair from the heads of screaming children. Here is where I begin—with virile and patriotic boy-men who torture and maim and exterminate those who are gay, or suspected of being gay, or not white or just different but who, being gentlemen, stop short of killing and only beat up or maim or taunt or torture or rape but sometimes stop short of killing their wives, mothers, daughters, children. Exercising their rights of free speech, they scream Nigger, Cunt, Bitch, Spic, Queer—quoting Shakespeare and Milton Friedman and *Moby Dick* in the clear, crisp, clean prose style of some of our best rhetoricians, journalists, and presidents.

BOTH SIDES OF THE STORY

In this chapter I want to talk about the politics of knowledge, the politics of education, and the politics of language and analyze the way in which the Right is attempting to suppress or co-opt the discourse on issues of social justice in our society.

When I began teaching college in the mid-1960s, I entered the classroom with a clear understanding of what constituted a fair and neutral way of teaching and arguing. The paradigm I had been taught, the one I practiced and taught in turn, was that there were two sides to every question and fair-minded people and well-constructed arguments attempted to present both sides as clearly and completely as possible. I was so good at doing what I had been taught that at the end of my first semester, a group of students in my introductory philosophy course came to me and said, with awe and appreciation, "We've been in your class all semester and still don't know what you think about anything." This, mind you, in a course in which we discussed issues such as the existence of God, life after death, and free will. I was flattered and pleased. Like my professors, I was simply presenting both sides and allowing my students to think for themselves.

The year was 1966. Within a year or two, I, along with many others, would reject this liberal paradigm and embark upon a radical critique of the politics of education in general and the politics of the curriculum in particular. My initial disillusionment came when a colleague of mine, a liberal whose antiwar sentiments predated my own, became concerned about the failure of the media to present "the other side" with respect to the war in Vietnam. He responded by collecting money from academics around the country in order to buy an hour of prime time on one of the major networks for a program that would offer an antiwar perspective. Two networks refused outright, privately expressing fears that if such a program were aired, they would have trouble with the Federal Communications Commission when their licenses came up for renewal. The third network was willing to consider such a program only on the condition that half the airtime be devoted to presenting a prowar position. This, the network assured my colleague, was required by its obligation to be fair and unbiased. Since in his eyes the prowar position was already receiving more than enough airtime, he was hardly willing to spend the money collected from antiwar activists to provide yet another forum for that point of view. More importantly, on a personal level, I began to see that, in practice and under certain conditions, an insistence on presenting both sides might undermine the possibility of opening discourse rather than encouraging it.

This suspicion was further reinforced by the furor provoked when it was announced that Angela Davis, a member of the Communist Party USA, would appear as the guest on a late-night TV talk show shortly thereafter. In response to protests, it was agreed that Davis would be permitted to appear only if her appearance was followed immediately by someone presenting the opposing point of view. The implication was clear. This rebuttal would serve as a kind of instantaneous antidote to the poisonous doctrine that Davis could be expected to spread. Davis, a former student of Herbert Marcuse, quite rightly refused to agree to these terms. I learned another lesson about free speech and who enjoyed it, and I began to understand more about the way in which discourse can be limited in the name of being fair, neutral, and objective and presenting both sides.

THE POLITICS OF EDUCATION

It was about this time that many of us turned our attention to the politics of education. Much of the discussion focused on the ways in which both the form and the content of education and educational institutions reproduced hierarchy in general and class divisions in particular. Issues of gender and race were discussed too, but most often they took a backseat to class. Similarly, although certain so-called scholarship and research came under indictment for being politically motivated, more attention was paid to pedagogy and institutional structures than to the curriculum or the canon. Edgar Friedenberg wrote books and essays in which he argued that the real lessons our students learned in school came less from the subject matter they studied than from the ways in which they were treated by the particular schools they attended. And of course Paolo Freire's *Pedagogy of the Oppressed* (1970/ 1984) prompted many of those who were in college or just beginning their teaching careers to experiment with new teaching techniques and new ways of structuring the learning experience.

Not surprisingly, many of those now active in women's studies, Africana studies, and ethnic studies became politicized as part of this movement. Because these groups often found themselves the focus of highly politicized research and scholarship (for example, sociobiology) that was then used to rationalize their subordination, they began to turn their attention increasingly toward the content of the curriculum and scholarship. Beginning by documenting the absence of women, feminists and other thinkers began to uncover gender bias (and sometimes race and class bias as well) in the most basic assumptions, language, and paradigms used throughout the disciplines. Those in Africana and ethnic studies documented similar omissions, and some began to sketch what they called "an Afrocentric perspective" in order to expose the largely white, Eurocentric, and elitist starting point from which much history and culture has been taught and evaluated.

Not coincidentally, at the very moment that these constituencies were offering their indictment of traditional educational curricula, the changing demographics of the U.S. population and workforce and the globalization of U.S. corporations produced a confluence of needs and interests that helped propel the burgeoning movement for curriculum transformation into a significant movement for educational reform. Some are understandably frightened by this turn of events and seek to reaffirm the worldview and accompanying curriculum that confer power, authority, and privilege on themselves or those with whom they have been taught to identify.

CURRICULUM AS POWER

The curriculum is enormously powerful. It defines what is real and what is unreal, what counts and what is unimportant, who or what is normal and natural versus who or what is abnormal and deviant. It determines where the margins or peripheries are and who occupies them. It has the power to teach us what to see and thereby the power to render people, places, things, and even entire cultures invisible.

In spite of attempts by some to treat the traditional curriculum as if it were absolute, exhaustive, and eternal, the curriculum itself has always been in a process of evolution. And, of course, we have never taught "everything." Those who teach have always made difficult choices, and those choices have always had political implications and consequences; they have always privileged some people's lives and cultures and demeaned or obliterated the cultures and histories of others. Those who found themselves in the curriculum have been empowered by it. And those who found themselves, their ancestors, and their cultures absent or peripheral have learned their lesson too.

The debate about curriculum—and about speech, for that matter—

raging at institutions of higher learning around the country as well as on the covers and in the columns of our leading magazines and newspapers is, of course, about power: Who will exercise it, and to what end? In debating the content and orientation of the curriculum, educators, politicians, and those who frame the public debate are really debating who will control the way we are taught to conceptualize our past. As Edie Mayor, curator at the Smithsonian, observed in a talk sponsored by the New Jersey Division on Women in March 1991, they are debating who will control the economics and politics of the present and the future. The stakes are high.

Caught off guard by the initial successes of the movement for curriculum reform, the Right now seeks to reinstate its worldview. It does so by standing reason, logic, and language on their heads, falsely portraying those who seek to open and extend the public debate as the ones seeking to narrow it. Conservatives advocate a curriculum of exclusion in the name of us all and attempt to portray the inclusive curriculum as narrow and self-interested. They do so in part by misrepresenting the current distribution of privilege and opportunity in this society, creating what *New York Times* columnist Anna Quindlen (1992) called "the great white myth." By exaggerating the real but limited gains made by women of all colors and men of color over the past several decades and failing to acknowledge the extent to which what has masqueraded as equal opportunity in the past was just another form of white male privilege, the Right seeks to frame issues of social justice in terms that serve its own interests, portraying itself as the victim rather than the beneficiary of a policy of special privileges.

SUBVERTING FREE SPEECH

Since the Right is in the minority, it is necessary for it to mobilize the support of others. Its task is to persuade the very individuals whose possibilities are diminished by capitalism, patriarchy, and white privilege that their interests somehow lie in continuing to defend the status quo. They do so using a variety of techniques designed to close or misdirect discourse. These include usurping the meaning of words and denying or distorting the historical context in which social issues have taken shape and must be understood. In the words of Herbert Marcuse (1965):

> The meaning of words is rigidly stabilized. Rational persuasion, persuasion to the opposite is all but precluded. The avenues of entrance are closed to the meaning of words and ideas other than the established one—established by the publicity of powers that be, and verified in their practices. Other words can be spoken and heard, other ideas can be expressed, but, at the massive scale of

the conservative majority (outside such enclaves as the intelligensia), they are immediately "evaluated" (i.e. automatically understood) in terms of the public language—a language which determines "a priori" the direction in which the thought process moves. Thus, the process of reflection ends where it started: in the given conditions and relations. Self-validating, the argument of the discussion repels the contradiction because the antithesis is redefined in terms of the thesis. (p. 96)

This is clearly illustrated in the contemporary debate, which finds progressives arguing that racist, sexist, anti-Semitic, homophobic language in itself constitutes a form of violence and should be actively discouraged. The argument continues that tolerating this kind of language perpetuates an educational and social environment where some are silenced, terrorized, brutalized, and denied the freedom to speak or to be, for fear of death or worse. Most of those who make this argument place a high value on free speech and in this way seek to create its possibility, not preclude it. But the neoconservatives seek to draw attention away from these social injustices for which their policies and privileges bear responsibility and seek to redefine the issue as one of free speech. Quick to protect the rights of individuals to hurl vicious racial and other epithets as they choose, these same neoconservatives are usually vocal in their opposition to the distribution of union literature at privately owned workplaces and to informational picketing outside of stores to alert consumers to health risks in the products available for purchase. These, they tell us, infringe on the right of private property and the ability to make a profit. In addition, these same defenders of free speech have no compunction about limiting the speech of doctors and health care practitioners at family planning clinics, literally barring them from even speaking the word "abortion." The issue for the Right is clearly not the absolute value of free speech but the values and interests that speech promotes or frustrates. By refocusing the debate so that the issue is free speech rather than racism or sexism, the Right frames a discourse in its own interests, obscuring the nature of those interests from ordinary citizens who have been taught to adopt those interests as their own and to see the protection of free speech as "democratic" rather than "political."

In these efforts, conservatives receive considerable assistance from the traditional curriculum, which teaches us to define democracy and prioritize "democratic freedoms" in ways that protect the privileges of those who already have them. "Safeguarding free speech" or "protecting the Bill of Rights" or "reaffirming democratic values" are all code phrases for protecting the power and privilege of wealthy white European males and those selected individuals from other groups whom they choose to share that privilege with temporarily. The ultimate victory of this manipulation and inversion of logic is to succeed in portraying demands for the extension of civil rights to women as a group or to particular racial or ethnic groups or to lesbians and gays as a defeat for democracy rather than an extension of it. Not surprisingly, this same curriculum and attendant popular culture form an ironclad association between capitalism and democracy. So closely have these two been linked in the minds of ordinary citizens, and so long have they been treated as interchangeable, that it is almost impossible to frame a discourse that asks whether political democracy is compatible with economic inequality rather than undermined by it. It is not merely that many would dispute this claim. The question simply cannot be asked because the language available precludes it.

RECOMMENDATIONS

What are the implications of this analysis for us as educators? How can we use our classrooms to empower students? What kinds of skills and information do they need for their empowerment? I believe that the most serious failing of education has been its failure to provide students with an adequate context for thinking about important social issues and values. The problem is less with the ways in which we have been taught to argue than with the absence of an accurate and adequate historical and political context in which to situate those arguments. Let me try to outline briefly the kinds of understandings that I believe students (and others) need in order to make sense out of what they see, hear, read, and do.

Students need to learn to identify and reject narrow oppositional thinking that teaches them to see the world in terms of good and bad, right and wrong, black and white, male and female, winners and losers. They need to know that there are always more than two sides to an issue and that alternatives can often be situated on a continuum rather than framed as diametrically opposed. They need to explore the liberating possibility that a number of conflicting and even contradictory things can be true at the same time and to examine models for thought and analysis that are more like spider webs than railroad tracks. Similarly, students need to acquire a respect for diverse styles of writing and arguing, which will in turn affirm the diversity not merely among us but within us—a diversity (richness) that has been suppressed by the imposition of categories of both gender and race as narrowly oppositional and hence mutually exclusive.

I chose to begin this chapter by adopting a literary form that is used infrequently for this kind of presentation. I did so deliberately in response to the journalist who, in an article on "p.c." (political correctness), bemoaned the fact that my racism-sexism anthology was being proposed for use in writing classes at the University of Texas. What disturbed him was that, in his own words, "instead of models of clarity like E. B. White," it contained "essays [sic] such as 'is not so gd to be born a girl,' by Ntozake Shange." His discomfort exposes the paucity of his own education and the narrowness of the definition of "clarity" he has been taught to employ (and which so many of us share), one that has room for White but not for Shange. And of course, he never stopped to ask, Why elevate clarity over passion? Why choose between them in the first place? Students need to understand that clarity comes in many sizes, shapes, and colors and that argument can be framed in poetry as well as prose.

In addition to learning to explore and integrate different styles of writing and literary forms as well as models for thinking and arguing, students need to be taught to use race, class, and gender as categories for making sense out of experience. Many of us unthinkingly assume a naive epistemological framework according to which we believe that all people "see" or experience the same reality and then go on to interpret it differently based on personal variables. In point of fact, what we see already reflects the categories of analysis we bring to experience. A feminist and someone who has never been exposed to feminism can walk down the same street side by side and have totally different experiences in the space of a minute or two. This is because what we notice already reflects what we have been taught to look for. A curriculum constructed by those who have a vested interest in rendering racism and other systems of oppression invisible must be deconstructed so that students can come to terms with the different realities that different groups in our society have lived over the past several centuries.

If the traditional curriculum merely left out certain content, our job would be easy and obvious. We would fill in the missing dates, events, heroes, and heroines and go on about our business. But the problem and hence the remedy are infinitely more complex. Insofar as the traditional curriculum actively teaches students *not* to see gender, race, and class as categories in and of history (and literature, and art, and politics, and the sciences, and so on), our first task is to help students understand the politics of the traditional curriculum, the politics of the way they have been taught to see the world. We must demonstrate how the traditional curriculum creates the erroneous impression that most of knowledge and culture is the creation of a small group of individuals who, by implication, are superior to the rest of us and hence deserving of special powers and privileges. We must help our students and indeed ourselves understand how the equation of "civilization" with "Western civilization" is part of a process that universalizes the needs, interests, and perspective of a small and elite group so that all of us come to see the world through their eyes and in ways that suit their interests. We must help them, and ourselves, recognize that the worldview we have been taught to equate with "objectivity" really creates and perpetuates a world of privilege and power that portrays white male supremacy as natural, desirable, and inevitable.

In addition to learning to employ these categories for organizing experience and analyzing it, students need to learn to see the world through many different sets of eyes. Although it is not possible to include every voice in the syllabus for a single class or even in 4 years of undergraduate education, it is possible to teach our classes and organize the curriculum to make it clear that there are many voices. Students must understand that meanings are in some sense tailored to the individual by virtue of his or her personal history and experience. The logical conclusion of this is not that "everything is relative" but rather that one cannot and should not assume that the way things appear to a particular person is the way they "are" in some absolute sense or that one's values are the only viable values for making aesthetic or moral judgments. Students need to learn that their understanding is enriched by the diversity they explore and that their confidence in the adequacy of their conclusions should be in direct proportion to the number of different perspectives they have temporarily adopted in the course of arriving at them.

All this requires that we teach students history and that we help them develop a sense of history. For too many of them, everything started a moment ago or perhaps yesterday, and too many believe that things have pretty much always been the same. Students who have never studied the slave codes of the early 18th century, which carefully circumscribed the movement and behavior of "Negroes and other slaves," making it a crime for African Americans to be found walking the streets of white towns and cities, will not be able to understand the full meaning of the attacks on black men in Howard Beach and Bensonhurst or the full meaning of the deaths of Phillip Parnell, Edward Perry, and others like them, who die at the hands of white police officers who shoot to kill. Students who have never studied the history of white privilege, male privilege, and class privilege are in no position to tackle the complex moral and social issues that threaten to tear this society apart. They have no context in which to place the competing claims of various ethnic and racial groups. For students who have never seriously studied the history of sexism in this country or the history of the women's rights movement, feminists will remain bra burners and misfits, the appropriate butt of nightclub comics and locker room ridicule.

Closely related to the need for a knowledge of history and a sense of history is the need for a sense of the social dimension. Impatient with never-ending talk about racial justice, some white students seek to deny responsibility for addressing racism by pointing out that their ancestors didn't own slaves or perhaps had not even immigrated to America during the early years of the republic. For these students, all problems and all solutions are individual. If it's not conscious and not intentional, it's not racist or sexist. They need to understand in what sense some problems are part of the social fabric we inherit and from which some of us profit quite apart from our actions or conscious choices. To this end, they need to learn to identify their own race, class, and gender privileges and to analyze them according to a model that helps them see that individuals can be oppressed in some respects and privileged in others, depending on a host of interconnecting variables.

Finally, an education that empowers our students will help them deconstruct the politics of ordinary life and everyday language to reveal the truth that virtually everything is political. The secret of the past is that it always was. Instead of seeking some mythical objective and neutral perspective or voice to learn from or speak with, students (and the rest of us) need to get in the habit of asking Whose view of the world am I getting in this class, book, newspaper, TV show, or political campaign? and its corollary, Whose interests are served when I define the issues and options in this way? Armed with this perspective, they will come to understand that the real challenge is not in trying to attain some kind of false objectivity or neutrality but in learning to evaluate programs and policies with full awareness of whose interests or needs they reflect and promote. It is only then that they and we will be in a position to make conscious and intelligent decisions about which needs should be prioritized. The best protection from the harangues of the demagogue and the manipulation of sophists lies in our ability to identify competing and conflicting interests and enter into a deliberate debate over which ones deserve our attention. It is only with a full awareness of the thoroughly political nature of politics and life that we can undertake a meaningful national debate about issues of social justice and survival. Our responsibility as educators is to prepare our students to engage in that debate as critical thinkers, grounded in multicultural and gender studies, who bring a sense of history to this awesome task.

NOTE

A slightly different version of this chapter was presented at a conference at Bard College in January 1992. Portions of this chapter have appeared previously in "Critics of Attempt . . . ," *Chronicle of Higher Education* (April 1991), and *Transformations* (Spring 1993).

REFERENCES

Friere, P. (1984). *Pedagogy of the oppressed* (M. B. Ramos, Trans.). New York: Continuum. (Original work published 1970)

Marcuse, H. (1965). Repressive tolerance. In R. P. Wolff & B. Moore Jr. (Eds.), *A critique of pure tolerance* (p. 96). Boston: Beacon Press.
Quindlen, A. (1992, January 15). The great white myth. *The New York Times,* p. A21.
Stimpson, C. (1994). Personal correspondence.

8

Teaching About Affirmative Action

Stephen R. Shalom

In some subjects, the teacher's job is relatively straightforward: Present the students with a body of knowledge, provide them with opportunities to use and work with that knowledge, and the students will master the subject matter. The issue of affirmative action, however, has become so emotionally charged for most white students that many of them come to class with psychological barriers preventing them from openly considering the topic. The information can't get through these barriers, and no learning takes place.

If it were simply a matter of students' understanding the various points of view on affirmative action and coming to a conclusion different from my own, I would be disappointed, but there would be no special problem. But when students close their minds to a view that does not conform to their preconceived notions, this *is* a problem, and some teaching techniques beyond simply transmitting information are necessary. In this chapter, I describe an approach for teaching about affirmative action that I have found helpful for penetrating some of the psychological barriers.

My lesson on affirmative action takes two class periods (about 2½ hours). I include it as part of a larger Introduction to Politics course that I teach at a 4-year state college with "nonselective" admissions criteria and a largely white student body. Introduction to Politics is one of the courses that students can take to fulfill their general education requirements. My general approach in the course is to hold students responsible for understanding the arguments on the various sides of an issue but also to encourage them in class discussion and in journals to express their own views. To discourage students from disingenuously parroting my opinions, I rarely state my own views explicitly. For readings, I use a book of debates on political issues that includes pro and con articles on affirmative action.

FAIRNESS

Affirmative action raises the question of fairness: fairness to those who apply for jobs or for admission to schools, and fairness to those who will be using the services of those holding the jobs or graduating from the schools. My own view is that affirmative action is more or less fair in both these senses of fairness: I say *more or less* fair because I believe that no method of allocating social rewards under a capitalist system is truly fair. I believe that people are entitled to an equal share of society's fruits regardless of their innate characteristics or capital, or their parents' innate characteristics or capital. If you are smarter than others, you are fortunate, but I see no reason why that entitles you to a higher standard of living than theirs. Affirmative action represents a fairer way to allocate resources in the context of a system that assumes that the resources will be distributed unequally. So, in my view, those concerned with justice and fairness have to work for affirmative action and an end to capitalism at the same time.

In class, however, all I try to do in my lesson on affirmative action is to get the students to understand the position that argues that affirmative action programs are fair. Contrary to the conventional wisdom, I believe that, properly presented, affirmative action corresponds to the basic sense of fairness of most of my students—if they can get beyond their psychological barriers. To try to tap into that sense of fairness, I begin teaching about affirmative action with an exercise, for which I give no introduction. I just write the headings and lines A and B from the accompanying chart on the board. Then I say to the class, "Imagine that there are two graduates of this college who are applying for the same job. They're both white males; they have the same major; they both have excellent recommendations. In fact, the only difference between them is their transcripts. Applicant *A,* as you can see, had a 3.0 (out of 4) grade point average (GPA) every semester. *B,* who took the same courses, had a 2.6 GPA in his first semester, then 2.7, 2.8, 2.9, up to 3.3 in his last semester, for an overall GPA of 2.95. Now, if you could hire only one of these people, who would it be?"

There is no "right" answer to this question; some students choose *A,* and some choose *B.* I call on a few students and ask them their choices and their reasons for making those choices. I usually get such responses as "*A* is

Semester

Applicant	1	2	3	4	5	6	7	8	Overall
A	3.00	3.00	3.00	3.00	3.00	3.00	3.00	3.00	3.00
B	2.60	2.70	2.80	2.90	3.00	3.10	3.20	3.30	2.95
C	3.40	3.30	3.20	3.10	3.00	2.90	2.80	2.70	3.05
D	1.80	2.10	2.40	2.70	3.00	3.30	3.60	3.90	2.85
E	4.00	3.75	3.50	3.25	3.00	2.75	2.50	2.25	3.13
F	2.00	4.00	2.00	4.00	2.00	4.00	2.00	4.00	3.00
G	3.20	3.20	3.20	0.80	3.20	3.20	3.20	3.20	2.90
H	2.90	2.90	2.90	2.90	2.90	2.90	2.90	2.90	2.90

solid and consistent" or "B has been improving and by now is a better student than A." I ask for a show of hands in favor of each of the two applicants, and usually B wins by a considerable margin. But even if A comes out ahead, I say to those who picked B, "But A has the higher GPA." The B supporters adamantly insist that this doesn't matter, that B is the best choice, that B has shown improvement and is capable of more than A. I say, "Okay, let's add another applicant, C, and see what you think now." I write line C on the board.

"Which of the *three* applicants do you like now? C has the highest GPA of them all, A is in the middle, and B is the lowest." Again there won't be unanimity, but quite a few students, usually a majority, still choose B. I call on a few more students to get their reasons, and to those who select A or B, I say, "But C argues, 'Hey, I had the highest GPA! Doesn't that count for anything?'" And again one of the A or B fans will always point to C's downward trend or lack of consistency. "Okay, here's student D," I continue. "Whom do you like now?" To those who choose D, I remind them that D has the lowest GPA of all the applicants. To those who choose A or B, I repeat that C has a higher GPA. Then I add applicant E. "E has the best GPA of all," I triumphantly declare. "How many like E?" Not too many do. I take a few more class responses and then add applicant F.

Someone in the class is likely to try to explain F's pattern of grades (maybe he plays football in the fall semester, or maybe it takes him a long time to adjust after summer vacation). I acknowledge these possibilities, and then write in the grades for applicant G. "How many like G?" I ask. "Who prefers G to A? After all, except for that one bad semester, G's performance was consistently better than A's." Usually, a student in the class will ask at this point what happened to G in that fourth semester. (If no one raises the question, I ask whether they want to know.)

"Well," I tell them, "let's assume that there are two different G's, call them G1 and G2, and you call each one in for an interview and ask him what happened. G1 says, 'I'm a great believer in hard work, but every so often, you just gotta party!' Okay," I ask, "how many would want to hire *G1?*" A few students may jokingly express their admiration for *G1,* but everyone gets the point, so I go on.

I then give *G2*'s explanation for what happened to him in that fourth semester: His father got laid off from his job and started drinking, and the situation at home got so difficult that *G2* had to move out for a while. But finally his father got another job and got his act together, things settled down at home, and *G2* was able to return his focus to his schoolwork. I then ask, "Who would like to hire *G2?*"

A few students worry about what might happen to *G2* the next time his father gets laid off, but most students eagerly want to hire *G2.* I listen to a few of their arguments without comment and then say, "Okay, here's applicant *H.* Let's assume you're just deciding between *A* and *H.* And let's assume you call each one in for an interview, and this is what you find out about them. *A* comes from a very wealthy family, and *H* grew up amidst great hardship." I then describe their backgrounds in melodramatic detail and ask the class which one they would hire. My experience has been that a large majority of the class chooses *H.* A few students might argue that *A* has the family contacts that will make him a more useful asset to the company, but almost everyone else strongly favors *H.* This is not surprising, given that my students—who typically come from middle- and lower-middle-class families—more readily see themselves as *H.* I play devil's advocate: "But *A* says, 'It's not fair, I've got the higher grade point average!'" The class easily answers me: "With all those advantages, *A* should have done a lot better than just one tenth of a point higher. *H* is a much harder worker. *H,* given his background, accomplished more than *A,* given his."

"So what is our conclusion?" I ask rhetorically. "It seems that the person you think is *most qualified* for the job might not be the person with the highest GPA. At least one of the things you seem to want to take into account is what obstacles the applicant has had to overcome." I then suggest that they keep this conclusion in mind in coming days as we discuss the issue of affirmative action and the question of who is most qualified for a particular job.

Next I give the class a different situation. I tell them to assume that the Math Department at a local college has an opening. Two people apply for the job. For simplicity, I again assume that they are both white males. Candidate 1 is absolutely brilliant: He had a perfect 800 on his math SAT and is considered a real contender for winning a Nobel Prize in mathematics. However, this person has nothing but contempt for students who cannot do advanced calculus and considers it beneath his dignity to teach anything but the most obscure topics in mathematics. Candidate 2 had a 750 on his math SAT. He loves students and has a great deal of experience teaching mathematical concepts to students of different abilities. "Which candidate," I ask the class, "is more qualified for the job?"

The students in the class overwhelmingly rate the second candidate the more qualified. I press them: "I'm not asking you which one you hope the department would hire. I'm asking *who's more qualified.*" The students still maintain that candidate 2 is more qualified. "But candidate 1 had a higher SAT score," I argue. "So why isn't he more qualified?" It's not long before a student says that the job is to be the best possible math teacher, not the best mathematician. Persevering, I ask, "What about the test score?"

"The test doesn't measure whether you are the best teacher, just whether you are a good mathematician," students loudly insist.

"What you're telling me," I conclude, "is that to figure out who's most qualified for a job, we first have to determine what the real purpose of the job is. And we also have to make sure that our job requirements (like test scores) actually measure people's ability to do what the job is really about." The class agrees that if candidate 2 really knew no math at all, he would not be a good math teacher, but that lots of people could score considerably lower on the SAT than candidate 1 and still be excellent teachers.

I next ask the class to consider another job, that of police officer. What are the purposes of that job? With a little prompting from me, we arrive at a job description involving stopping crime and making citizens feel secure. Imagine a city, I then tell them, where half the population is white and half black, and where all the police officers are white. The police officers are all white because the police department used to discriminate against nonwhite applicants. Imagine further that, on a regular basis, some of the white police officers use racial slurs against black citizens and frequently beat them up.

"Do you think the citizens of this hypothetical city *feel secure?*" I ask. Everyone agrees that at least the black half of the population does not. "Now let's say that there's a job opening in the police department. Imagine there are two candidates for the job. Candidate 1, a white male, scores 82 on the department's written examination. Candidate 2, a black male, scores 80 on the examination. On all other tests—physical ability, and so on—they score the same. Who is more qualified for the job? And remember, the purposes of this job are to stop crime and make citizens feel secure. Which of the two candidates would be more qualified in serving those purposes?"

Sometimes the class will judge the black candidate more qualified. I challenge them: "But the white candidate complains that he scored higher on the test. He says that he's a victim of reverse discrimination." And I let the class answer the charge. More typically, however, many students maintain that the white candidate is more qualified. Since these students seem to have difficulty empathizing with the feelings of security and insecurity of the black community, I extend the example in a way that appeals to the insecurities of *whites.* "Let's say that you were a police officer in that same city. You and your partner are sent in to deal with a situation involving a black family, where the man is drunk and acting abusively toward his wife. You find that you have to subdue the husband, but you know that in numerous other incidents like this, there have been accusations that the police engaged in racist behavior and used excessive force, accusations that may or may not have been warranted in any particular incident. Occasionally, such situations, in which white police officers have had to overcome black men, have resulted in altercations that set off chains of events culminating in race riots. Imagine that your partner is the new person hired by the police department. Which of the two candidates do you think would be more likely to be able to help you deal with the situation without causing a crisis: the white candidate who scored 82 or the black candidate who scored 80? Who's more qualified for doing what police have to do in this environment?" I find that most students will agree that this is a situation in which being black *automatically* makes a person more qualified for the job.

RACIAL DISCRIMINATION: DE JURE AND DE FACTO

This discussion usually takes me to the end of the first class session. Starting with the next class period, I turn more directly to the topic of affirmative action. I begin by reviewing some of the ways in which de jure discrimination—discrimination by law—operated in the United States. I remind them of the schools separated by race in the South, the separate water fountains, bus seats, and so on. I explain that, since 1954, governmental racial discrimination has been unconstitutional, so today there is essentially no de jure racial discrimination in the United States. De jure gender discrimination continued much longer, but with some narrow exceptions (such as women in combat), the only governmental gender discrimination that remains is on matters such as separate bathrooms, and most Americans—male and female—believe such gender distinctions to be reasonable and legitimate. This does not mean that de jure discrimination no longer exists in the United States: Laws deny gay men and lesbians equal rights in a wide range of activities. I tell the class that we will take up the issue of civil rights for gays and lesbians later in the course, but that in terms of race and gender, legal discrimination is largely a thing of the past. I further point out that a wide variety of laws make it illegal for an employer or an apartment building owner or a store owner to discriminate on the basis of race or gender. Then I give the class a handout with data on race and gender in the United States. I briefly go through the data, noting, for example, that a household headed by a black high school graduate earns less money than a household headed by a white high school dropout. Then I ask the class, "Given the fact that there is virtually no de jure discrimination against blacks or women, and given the fact that employers and landlords are not allowed to discriminate, why is it that women earn substantially less than men, and blacks earn less, die earlier, and have higher unemployment than whites?"

Students usually don't have much difficulty coming up with one answer to this question, namely, that—despite the laws—employers and landlords *still do* discriminate. I confirm that this is indeed the case, and that there is extensive hard evidence showing this to be so. But then I tell them that *even if everyone obeyed the law,* there would still be problems. And I give them a list of a few of the ways in which the discrimination of the past, even if it never happens again, continues to have harmful effects today:

- Past discrimination made some people poor. Even in the absence of discrimination, the children of poor people have a harder time succeeding than do the children of nonpoor people.
- Most people (including my students) got their jobs by knowing someone. But if blacks were discriminated against in the past, there will be fewer blacks today with the kinds of job connections that can be helpful to friends and relatives.
- Previous discrimination (plus much covert present-day discrimination and violence) has led to massive residential segregation on the basis of race. In states where education is controlled by localities, the schools will be as segregated as the housing. There are no longer signs over the schoolhouse door saying "White Only," but the result is not very different. This is segregation in fact—de facto—if not by law.
- Previous discrimination gives blacks and women lower seniority today and gives them less job experience, which is often a prerequisite for a better job.
- Many union apprenticeship programs give special consideration to the children of members, but membership in the past may have been restricted by race (and gender).
- Many colleges give special admissions consideration to the children of alumni, but not everyone was equally able to attend in the past.
- There is evidence showing that teachers' prejudices, even subconscious ones, can affect the performance of students. Teachers' beliefs that girls can't do math or that blacks have low intelligence influence teachers' interactions with students and become self-fulfilling prophecies.
- Our present-day culture—from language to expected behaviors for different genders or races—was formed in part during times when discrimination was prevalent. Current norms and practices are likely to reflect the discrimination of that earlier time, even if discrimination is no longer permitted. For example, wages and salaries for jobs were set in the past on the basis

of gender; as a result of this established pattern, traditionally female-dominated jobs earn less today than comparably valued male-dominated jobs.

In short, even if there were currently no legal or illegal discrimination in the United States, our past history of discrimination harms blacks and women today.

AFFIRMATIVE STEPS

I explain to the class that those who support affirmative action make the following argument: It would be wonderful if just saying "no more discrimination" could wipe out all the harmful effects caused by previous discrimination. But things don't work that way. It is not enough to stop discriminating; we must take some positive steps—affirmative steps, affirmative action—to remedy the damage that was set in motion in the past but continues into the present.

In the United States, we often think of life as a race, a sort of contest in which the fastest runner gets the good things in life. Imagine if we scheduled a race for 2 weeks from now. One of the runners, however, is kidnapped, chained up into a little ball, and squashed into a 4-foot cube. Two weeks later, just before the race, the police capture the kidnappers and free the runner. They rush the runner to the starting line of the race and say, "Okay, we've taken off your chains; it'll be a fair race now." But the runner can hardly stand up and aches from sore muscles. The chains are gone, but the harm caused by the chains still remains. According to the advocates of affirmative action, racism and sexism are like those chains. Even after they are removed, their harmful effects remain. The race won't be fair. If the race is to be made fair, we first have to massage the runner's muscles, and if we are to make the race of life fair, we need to design affirmative action programs to remedy the harm caused by discrimination.

Opponents of affirmative action argue that although past discrimination was wrong, we must now pay no attention to race or gender; we must be *color-blind* and *gender-blind.* Supporters of affirmative action argue that if there had never been racial or gender discrimination, we wouldn't need to be *color-* or *gender-conscious* today; indeed, their hope is that affirmative action policies will wipe out the vestiges of previous discrimination so that, at some time in the future, we will be able to be color-blind and gender-blind. A person's race and gender will never be irrelevant, but our goal is a society in which these would not be relevant factors in applying for a job or for admission to a school. This is a long-range goal, however, say the advocates of affirmative action. And because the effects of past discrimination are still clearly with us and people were harmed on the basis of their race or gender, we need to take account of race and gender in working to redress that harm.

Some affirmative action programs need to be color-conscious in only minor ways. For example, in a workplace where previous discrimination has not been widespread, the employer might place advertisements for job openings in newspapers that are read largely by minorities, in addition to the mainstream newspapers. Such a policy is color-conscious because the newspapers are chosen on the basis of the race of their readers, but it is not likely to be controversial. In contrast, when an employer has a long and persistent history of discrimination and has rejected and subverted other approaches to integrating the workforce, the courts have sometimes ruled that a certain percentage of new employees must be minorities. This remedy, a quota, has rarely been imposed, and only after less extreme remedies have proved insufficient.

Affirmative action advocates point out that one could use moral grounds to make a reasonable case for even more extreme remedies. For example, many of the white males who hold jobs today obtained their jobs in an unfair contest, one from which minorities and women were excluded. Instead of waiting for job openings to become available and using affirmative action to fill those positions, one could argue that we should declare all jobs obtained unfairly to be vacant and conduct new job searches, allowing the present incumbents to apply but giving them no special preference. After all, why should someone be permitted to retain the fruits of an unfair contest? Compared with this arguable position, most affirmative action policies are moderate indeed.

U.S. SUPREME COURT DECISIONS

In order to help the class explore some of the issues involved in affirmative action, I present one of the key Supreme Court cases on the subject. I first explain, however, that the Supreme Court is a *political* body and its decisions represent not the last word in terms of justice but the political opinions of its justices. When I ask the class how they would have decided a particular case, it is certainly not to see if they are wise enough to agree with the Court; rather, some of the cases before the Court have posed important questions that are worth exploring further.

The case we consider is *Bakke,* in which a white male had been denied admission to the medical school of the University of California at Davis (*Regents v. Bakke,* 438 U.S. 265 [1978]; much of my discussion of the case is based on Joel Dreyfuss and Charles Lawrence III, *The Bakke Case: The Poli-*

tics of Inequality [New York: Harcourt, Brace, Jovanovich, 1979]). I begin by briefly describing the problems of the U.S. health care system. Although the United States spends more money on health care than any other country, both in per capita terms and as a fraction of gross domestic product, the quality of its health care as measured by infant mortality rates or life expectancy is worse than in most industrialized nations. The reason for this is that our health care resources are not equitably distributed. If a medical school were concerned with making the greatest possible contribution to public health in the United States, it would want to train doctors who were going to practice medicine in areas where there were doctor shortages, such as inner cities and Indian reservations. How does a medical school know where a medical student will ultimately choose to practice? One could ask the students before they are admitted, but people change their minds, and people lie. As it turns out (not surprisingly), students who grew up in underserved areas are far more likely to end up practicing there than are other students. (No group of students is *likely* to end up in these places, but those who grew up there are *more likely* to do so than are others.)

UC Davis Medical School had seats for 100 students a year. Of these, 16 were set aside to be filled by a task force seeking applicants from economically and educationally disadvantaged backgrounds. All the students admitted under this program were minorities. These students generally had lower grades and test scores than the students admitted to the 84 regular seats, but the admissions committee believed that there were other indications in their records that they would make excellent doctors. One of the students admitted through the task force was Orel Knight, a poor immigrant from Guyana who 4 years later was voted by his peers to be the best doctor in the graduating class; another was Toni Johnson-Chavis, who grew up in an impoverished black community and while at Davis set up a clinic in a poor neighborhood.

Allan Bakke went through the public schools in Florida at a time when they were segregated (attending the privileged white, not the disadvantaged black, schools). He was an excellent student, and his grades and test scores were higher than most, though not all, of the 16 task force students. His scores were also higher than those of some of the white students admitted to the 84 regular seats. The faculty members who interviewed Bakke were favorably impressed with him but noted that the applicant had "apparently not looked to any extent into the problem of health care delivery." When Bakke was denied admission to the medical school in 1973 and again in 1974, he sued, charging that the fact that minority applicants with lower scores than his had been admitted made him the victim of reverse discrimination.

After providing this outline of the case, I invite comment from the class. Was Bakke treated unfairly? Or was the UC Davis task force a reasonable way to deal with some of the problems of previous discrimination in the medical field? As the discussion gets going, I remind the class of their earlier conclusions that in determining the person most qualified for a position we need to take account of the obstacles overcome, figure out the real purposes served by the position, and be sure that our entrance requirements are actually measuring people's ability to fulfill those real purposes. As a final prod, I mention that it was discovered that the dean of the medical school was entitled to admit up to 5 students a year who may not have met the regular admissions requirements but who came from families with the right connections. Why do you suppose, I ask, that suit was brought over the students admitted through the task force but not over those admitted by the dean?

SOCIAL GAINS

It is useful to end the lesson by telling the class that supporters of affirmative action programs believe that such programs benefit not just minorities and women but the whole society. I ask the class to try to think of some of these social benefits. Although I believe that it is necessary to appeal to students' sense of fairness, it is also important to help them understand that they all stand to gain on some level from promoting equality. I let the class brainstorm for a while and list their answers on the board, occasionally suggesting some answers they may have missed:

- Continued racial inequality promotes anger and rage on the part of those kept down, leading to violence and crime that endangers everyone.
- Employers used to tell their white workers not to get too uppity or they would be replaced by blacks. Racial division still makes it harder for black and white workers to join together to fight for decent wages, or for black and white communities to join together to demand that the country's resources be redirected to serving human needs.
- If the country doesn't tap the potential of its minorities and its women, who together are an increasing majority of the population, our economic well-being will inevitably decline. Every minority and every female blocked from reaching her or his full potential is a loss to the country as a whole.
- People trying to solve society's problems are likely to be more successful if they come from a variety of backgrounds—and bring a variety of different perspectives to bear—than if they all come from similar backgrounds.
- Affirmative action has made us look carefully at job requirements to determine which ones in fact bear no relationship to performing the job (for example, height requirements for police officers). By eliminating these irrelevant factors, jobs have been made fairer for all.

From the class discussions and from the journals the students keep, I find that a good proportion of them take the argument for affirmative action seriously, and many seem to accept it. I wish I could report that they all come to this conclusion, but I think that in many cases there is just too much psychological baggage to overcome in a few class periods. Given the views that students began with, however, I have found this lesson to be quite helpful in transcending their gut hostility to the idea of affirmative action.

NOTE

A slightly different version of this chaper appeared in *Transformations* (Fall 1994).

9
Teaching About Gender, Ethnicity, Race, and Class: Using African Biography and Autobiography

Allen M. Howard

African biographies and autobiographies are valuable for teaching about issues of race, ethnicity, gender, and class in a wide variety of courses. Such works deal with virtually every aspect of individual life and social change: personal identity, kinship, community, marriage, education, aging, religious beliefs, nationalism, and on and on. Moreover, they depict historical and contemporary struggles involving race, ethnicity, gender, and class. Through reading biographies and autobiographies, students comprehend what African peoples have experienced and discover similarities and differences between African societies and their own.[1] They gain a multicultural approach to history that reveals the common experiences of humanity along with the uniqueness of time and place.

COLONIAL AFRICA

This chapter focuses on the Republic of South Africa and on western Africa during the 19th and 20th centuries, an approach that presents general patterns while also defining regional and national differences. The history of South Africa is distinctive because of the large European population, the deep impact of industrial capitalism, and the extreme forms of racism under apartheid. Many of the biographies and autobiographies cited below can be used to teach students how supposedly given racial, ethnic, and gender categories and identities have been constructed and reconstructed.[2]

Precolonial African societies were organized in governments ranging from decentralized forms to highly centralized states, typically kingdoms. Up to the second half of the 19th century, most such governments were independent, but then European imperial expansion brought them under colonial domination. Thereafter, Africans struggled against and accommodated to colonial rule until about 1960, when most countries were independent or on the road to national sovereignty.[3] These political processes are depicted in the biographies and autobiographies of major leaders. Such studies balance Eurocentric material by illustrating a range of African actions in a complex field where opposition to the European presence was only one consideration among many. Some of these works, however, tend toward the "Great Man" and his state or people approach.[4]

For the 19th century, there are several edited collections that concentrate on the confrontation and cooperation between African leaders and Europeans. In addition, numerous full-length and partial biographies deal with state formation, commerce, and religion. Leaders of Islamic reform movements are well examined.[5] The few existing studies of 19th-century female political leaders reveal them as important historical actors who utilized women's and national institutions. Madam Yoko of the Mende area built her own power base—in part through her position as a leader of *Sande,* the women's society—and then collaborated with the British to try to protect her position and the ministates she ruled (Carol Hoffer, "Madam Yoko: Ruler of the Kpa Mende Confederacy," in *Women, Culture, and Society,* ed. M. Z. Rosaldo and L. Lamphere [Stanford, CA: Stanford University Press, 1974], pp. 173–187). Agnes Akosua Aidoo has shown how Asante queen mothers promoted their own and their sons' (future kings') interests within the state and were vigorously involved with foreign relations, particularly defense against the British imperialists ("Asante Queen Mothers in Government and Politics in the Nineteenth Century," in *The Black Woman Cross-Culturally,* ed. F. C. Steady [Cambridge, MA: Schenkman, 1983], pp. 65–77).[6]

Another set of life histories presents the challenge faced by intellectuals and early nationalists such as Edward W. Blyden and Africanus Horton, who lived under European colonial rule in the age of European imperialism and pseudoscientific racism.[7] On the South African side, *Sol Plaatje, South African Nationalist 1876–1932* (Berkeley: University of California Press, 1984) by Brian Willan depicts the ambiguous life of someone who trusted in the possibilities of African advance through education, written protest, and direct appeals to the colonialists but who also confronted them over land seizure, loss of African political rights, and racial affronts. Some of these figures—notably Blyden and Plaatje—were prolific writers whose published volumes on such issues as race, nationality, and land are available for classroom use.

Although biographies from the era of nationalist struggle were often designed to enhance public images, some are valuable for teaching. They usually combine personal narrative, descriptions of major historical events, and ideological statements. Several leading figures who attended college in the United States depict racism there and their relationships with African Americans. In describing the road to independence, they convey the growth of regional, national, and often Pan-African identities. *Ghana: The Autobiography of Kwame Nkrumah* (New York: International Publishers, 1957) remains one of the best of this type, despite self-celebration and other shortcomings.[8]

WOMEN IN AFRICA

Women played an important role in the anticolonial struggles of West Africa, but there are few life histories. LaRay Denzer's study of Constance Cummings-John portrays one of the most prominent women nationalists and Pan-Africanists ("Constance Cummings-John of Sierra Leone: Her Early Political Career," *Tarikh, 25* [1981]: 20–32). Coming from an elite family, she was radicalized through her encounters with racial discrimination and African Americans while studying in the United States. Eventually she turned toward girls' education and the organization of market women and later helped found a nationalist party.[9] Cheryl Johnson-Odim has presented the careers of elite Nigerian women ranging from the conservative to the radical; of particular note is Funmilayo Ransome-Kuti, who, like Cummings-John, was a feminist, Pan-Africanist, and anti-imperialist who engaged in educational and family welfare activities.[10]

POLITICAL LEADERS

Biographies of a few major South African leaders are available, most notably Nelson Mandela in Fatima Meer, *Higher Than Hope: The Authorized Biography of Nelson Mandela* (New York: Harper Perennial, 1990), and Mary Benson, *Nelson Mandela: The Man and the Movement* (New York: W. W. Norton, 1986). The founder of the rival Pan-Africanist Congress, Robert Sobukwe, has also been sympathetically handled (B. Pogrund, *Sobukwe and Apartheid* [New Brunswick, NJ: Rutgers University Press, 1991]). There is a growing list of autobiographies by significant figures, among them Albert Luthuli, *Let My People Go* (London: Fontana Books, 1963); Helen Joseph, *Side by Side: The Autobiography of Helen Joseph* (New York: William Morrow, 1986); and Winnie Mandela, *Part of My Soul Went With Him,* ed. Anne Benjamin (New York: W. W. Norton, 1984).[11] Such autobiographies enable a teacher to trace changes in race relations and attitudes from Nobel Prize–winner Luthuli's description of the multiracial nonviolent defiance campaigns of the 1950s through Winnie Mandela's explanation of how her torture in prison caused her to turn from nonviolence and reject dialogue with the white authorities to the present. Such works also allow students to explore parallels—and differences—with the civil rights movements in the United States.

The lives of middle-level and grassroots leaders and of the ordinary participants in political groups demonstrate the energy, ideas, and organizing skills coming from below. Moreover, these works reveal the complex intertwining of gender, nationality, class, and other shaping factors. Many women's actions were concerned with control of women's space and welfare, not only with nationalism. For instance, a study of Madam Pelewura and the Lagos, Nigeria, market women shows them protecting and advancing their interests through struggle with the British colonial government, eventually teaming up with male trade unionists and nationalist parties (C. Johnson, "Madam Pelewura and the Lagos Market Women," *Tarikh,* 25 [1981]: 1–10). Claire Robertson's *Sharing the Same Bowl: A Socioeconomic History of Women and Class in Accra, Ghana* (Bloomington: Indiana University Press, 1984) contains a number of brief, illuminating life histories. Robertson shows how the world economy and the colonial and, later, national commercial and political structures have governed the opportunities of trading women. Particularly since the 1960s, poverty has been the shared bowl.

ARTISTS

Many South African writers depict the conditions, personal situations, and exposure to Leftist or nationalist ideologies that caused them to become committed activists. In *Call Me Woman* (San Francisco: Spinsters/Aunt Lute, 1985), Ellen Khuzwayo tells how she fell from a relatively comfortable rural life to a proletarian existence and how she organized and led social service groups before being drawn into politics. As in many other South African life histories, Christian beliefs and church membership strongly affected her attitudes and actions. A sampling of the voices of young women influenced by Black Consciousness and the Soweto uprising is found in the collection edited by Beata Lipman, *We Make Freedom* (Boston: Pandora Press, 1984), which also contains the views and experiences of women in squatter communities, rural areas, and various political groups. Another useful collection is D. E. H. Russell, *Lives of Courage: Women for a New South Africa* (New York: Basic Books, 1991). Many men's lives have also been recorded, among them Don Mattera's *Sophiatown* (Boston: Beacon Press, 1985), which portrays his ascent from criminality to become an organizer and creative artist.[12]

The life stories of other internationally known artists contain much of interest for teaching. For instance, because Peter Abrahams (*Tell Freedom: Memories of Africa.* [New York: Collier Books, 1970]), Bloke Modisane (*Blame Me on History* [New York: Simon & Schuster/Touchstone, 1986]), and Mark Mathibane (*Kaffir Boy: The True Story of a Black Youth's Coming of Age in Apartheid South Africa* [New York: Signet, 1986]) belong to three successive generations who rose up out of urban slums and then left South Africa, their lives can be compared and used to chart changes in gender, racial, class, and other dimensions of South African society.[13] For example, Abrahams reveals how within "colored" communities people recognized differences in ancestry, skin tone, religion, and class. Such lives provide a counterpoint to the notion of holistic, static racial and ethnic groups.

WORKERS

A fairly prosperous body of African farmers once existed in South Africa. In *Facing the Storm: Portraits of Black Lives in Rural South Africa* (Athens: Ohio University Press, 1988), Timothy Keegan movingly records their striving for economic gain, ambivalent relations with whites, and tragic dispossession, as well as the decline of patriarchy. A unique collective biography of one generation of South African women is *Women of Phokeng: Consciousness, Life Strategy, and Migrancy in South Africa, 1900–1983* by Belinda Bozzoli with the assistance of Mmantho Nkotsoe (Portsmouth, NH: Heinemann Educational Books, 1991). Educated as Christians in a relatively well-off part of the countryside, they sought personal independence in the cities. After careers as domestic workers and then beer brewers, which accommodated their status as married women and mothers, they ended their days as householders in a much-changed hometown.[14]

Urban workers are well represented. The most prominent early trade unionist, Clements Kadalie, interpreted his movement toward radical unionism and away again, plus the maneuvering among Africans and Europeans in the 1920s, in *My Life and the ICU: The Autobiography of a Black Trade Unionist in South Africa* (London: Frank Cass, 1970). To illustrate changes in work, unions, and race relations, excerpts from Kadalie could be compared with works depicting later periods, such as Naboth Mokgatle's *The Auto-biography of an Unknown South African* (Berkeley: University of California Press, 1971) or Eddie Webster's *Cast in a Racial Mould* (Johannesburg: Ravan Press, 1985).

Questions of gender, race, and class identity emerge powerfully in the histories of women labor organizers. Bettie DuToit's semiautobiographical *Ukubamba Amadolo: Workers' Struggles in the South Africa Textile Industry* (London: Onyx Press, 1978) portrays conditions and organizing efforts in the textile and canning industries, where women and men of all the so-called racial groups, acting as committed union members, faced banning, harassment, and imprisonment. *Strikes Have Followed Me All My Life* (London: Women's Press, 1991) by Emma Mashinini deals mainly with the period of black working-class power and militancy since the early 1970s. It reveals how women's experience as mothers, community builders, and political activists shaped their perspectives as workers and unionists.[15]

RELIGION AND EDUCATION

Recent scholarship has examined gender at different points along the class spectrum and shown the saliency of religion and education. Life histories from the Muslim Hausa-speaking areas and elsewhere demonstrate that age, social status, and religion must be added to class and gender for a rounded analysis. Not uncommonly, African women gain in rank as they marry up socially; give birth to children and have grandchildren; acquire wealth, personal stature, and titles; and exert authority over younger women and men. The classic *Baba of Karo: A Woman of the Moslem Hausa* (London: Faber and Faber, 1954), edited by Mary Smith, remains unmatched for depth and time span and is now supplemented by shorter accounts.[16] The remarkable full-length life stories of Adelaide Smith Casely Hayford (A. M. Cromwell, *An African Victorian Feminist: The Life and Times of Adelaide Smith Casely Hayford 1868–1960* [Totowa, NJ: Frank Cass, 1986]) and Phyllis Ntantala (*A Life's Mosaic: The Autobiography of Phyllis Ntantala* [Berkeley and Los Angeles: University of California Press, 1993]) demonstrate the enduring influence of Western-style education on women and the complex interrelationship of marriage, family, race, social and political commitment, and personal accomplishment.

CURRICULAR AND CLASSROOM STRATEGIES

After this tour of recent literature, what themes emerge as most relevant for curriculum development? The first is obvious: A historical approach must be central. Generalizations about "the African woman," "the Zulu," or any other fixed and homogeneous category are distortions. Second, group identities and boundaries have been and continue to be fluid: In reshaping group identities, people give cultural material new meaning and contest social practices and beliefs. Third, personal identity—manhood, womanhood, humanity—is not gained simply through acculturation but through struggle in a context of gender, racial, class, and other forms of domination. Fourth, nationality, ethnicity, age stratification, and religion are factors that must be considered along with race, gender, and class since they affect identity and action in complex, cross-cutting ways.

Although life stories are attractive for classroom use, teachers must be careful about glorifying individual accomplishment or emphasizing the autonomy and strength of social groups, such as market women. International capital, along with actions by national power holders, have deeply affected the environment in which people attempt to shape their lives. Because such forces—and racism and sexism—have operated globally, comparisons of life histories in Africa, the Americas, and Europe prove enlightening.[17] As teachers and students, we need to keep a humanistic focus on individuals while exploring both the universal and the historically specific dimensions of gender, race, class, ethnicity, nationality, religion, and age.

NOTES

1. Students, of course, need to be able to assess biographies and autobiographies alongside other materials. For most of the works cited here, complementary primary sources are available.

2. This article does not deal critically with autobiography as a genre or type of source. See, for example, T. Hofer and P. Niedermuller, eds., *Life History as Cultural Construction/Performance* (Budapest: Ethnographic Institute of the HAS, 1988).

3. For a general history, see P. D. Curtin et al., *African History* (Boston: Little, Brown, 1977). See also M. J. Hay and S. Stichter, eds., *African Women South of the Sahara* (New York: Longman, 1984).

4. A. J. Temu and B. Swai have pointed out that such works may serve the interests of the ruling groups in independent countries by blurring class distinctions and by stressing formal political independence rather than the continuation of economic dependence. See *Historians and Africanist History* (London: Zed Press, 1981).

5. See R. I. Rotberg and A. Mazrui, eds., *Protest and Power in Black Africa* (New York: Oxford University Press, 1970), and C. Saunders, ed., *Black Leaders in Southern Africa* (London: Heinemann, 1979). Among the best in this genre are D. Robinson, *Chiefs and Clerics: Abdul Bokar Kan and the History of Futa Toro, 1853–91* (Oxford: Oxford University Press, 1975), and L. Thompson, *Survival in Two Worlds:*

Moshoeshoe of Lesotho 1786–1870 (Oxford: Oxford University Press, 1975). For student use, see *Tarikh, 1,* no. 2 (1966); *1,* no. 4 (1967); *4,* no. 3 (1973); and *4,* no. 4 (1974).

6. See also I. Wilks, "She Who Blazed a Trail: Akyaawa Yikwan of Asante," in *Life Histories of African Women,* ed. P. W. Romero (Atlantic Highlands, NJ: Ashfield Press, 1988), pp. 113–139.

7. Full-length studies include E. A. Ayandele, *Holy Johnson: Pioneer of African Nationalism 1836–1917* (London: Frank Cass, 1970); C. Fyfe, *Africanus Horton: West African Scientist and Patriot* (New York: Oxford University Press, 1972); and H. Lynch, *Edward Wilmot Blyden Pan-Negro Patriot, 1832–1912* (London: Oxford University Press, 1967). See also Rina Okonkwo, *Heroes of West African Nationalism* (Enugu, Nigeria: Delta Publications, 1985).

8. Many Nigerians have written their autobiographies. See, for example, O. Awolowo, *Awo: The Autobiography of Chief Obafemi Awolowo* (Cambridge: Cambridge University Press, 1960).

9. Constance Cummings-John's autobiography, coauthored with LaRay Denzer, will soon be published.

10. "On Behalf of Women and the Nation: Funmilayo Ransome-Kuti and the Struggles for Nigerian Independence and Women's Equality," in *Expanding the Boundaries of Women's History: Essays on Women in the Third World,* ed. C. Johnson-Odim and M. Strobel (Bloomington and Indianapolis: Indiana University Press, 1992), pp. 144–157.

11. See also N. Harrison, *Winnie Mandela* (New York: George Braziller, 1986).

12. A fine analytic study of the apartheid era is Tom Lodge, *Black Politics in South Africa Since 1945* (New York: Longman, 1983).

13. Highly popular with students is Miriam Makeba, *Makeba: My Story* (New York: New American Library, 1988). Poems of exile penned by Dennis Brutus, Abena Busia, and others could be read along with such lives. For West African artists, a fine place to begin is Wole Soyinka, *Ake: The Years of Childhood* (New York: Aventura, 1983).

14. See also H. Scheub, "And So I Grew Up: The Autobiography of Nongenile Masithathu Zenani," in *Life Histories,* pp. 7–45.

15. See Iris Berger, *Threads of Solidarity: Women in South African Industry 1900–1980* (Bloomington and Indianapolis: Indiana University Press, 1992).

16. Marked differences in class and education are revealed in the accounts of Hajiya Ma'adaki by B. Mack and Hajiya Husaina by E. Schildkrout in *Life Histories.* See also C. Coles and B. Mack, eds., *Hausa Women in the Twentieth Century* (Madison: University of Wisconsin Press, 1991), and B. Callaway, *Muslim Hausa Women in Nigeria: Tradition and Change* (Syracuse, NY: Syracuse University Press, 1987).

17. See L. Spitzer, *Lives in Between: Assimilation and Marginality in Austria, Brazil, and West Africa 1780–1945* (Cambridge and New York: Cambridge University Press, 1989).

10
Critical Science Scholarship and Curriculum: Beyond Androcentrism

Lynn Hankinson Nelson

The call for papers for a recent conference on critical thinking and science invited consideration of ways in which the undergraduate science curriculum encourages critical thinking and threatens it.[1] The suggestion that the science curriculum might threaten critical thinking is provocative. For many, "scientific method" characterizes the spirit (if not the core) of critical thinking. I agree, to a point (and the source of this qualification will become clear), but my experience in conducting an upper-level seminar in philosophy of science for senior science and mathematics majors and teaching courses in epistemology taken by undergraduates representing a variety of majors has convinced me that many undergraduates do not have an adequate sense of the epistemology of science and that the model many do have does indeed work to undermine critical thinking about science. Moreover, students' views about science also impact, largely negatively, on the value they attribute to the engaged and pluralistic thinking many of us work to encourage in other areas of the curriculum.

Many undergraduates view the sciences and mathematics as fundamentally autonomous, monolithic, and cumulative enterprises engaged in a project to discover the one true theory of nature (pieces of which are to be found in boldface in science and mathematics textbooks). As there is only one true theory, gaining pieces of it is viewed as a rather passive affair: That is, however much work might be involved in constructing and testing hypotheses, designing experiments, collecting data, and so on so that the truth can "emerge," the "acquisition" of knowledge really involves "just looking" (albeit careful and well-prepared looking).

Indeed, insofar as students think of science as an activity at all, many are of the view that it is, as Karl Popper put it, "a process without a subject." [2] The directions of research, the distribution of knowledge and ignorance (the things we come to know about and those we do not), and, ultimately, the *content* of scientific knowledge seem to them determined inexorably by "the world" and a logic of inquiry (unless we make mistakes or tinker with the evidence). Thus, although evidence may be, as Thomas Kuhn (1970) describes it, "collected with difficulty," it is also at some level "self-announcing." From this perspective, neither the social nor cultural identities nor the values of scientists will or could have an impact on the knowledge generated in science communities (at least when things are going as they should). In short, science (at least good science) is insulated from the values and the politics of the social contexts within which it is practiced.

There seem to be several sources for these views. Students rarely recognize connections between a specific theory or research question and a larger research tradition or body of current scientific theory. They are largely unaware of the relationships between scientific theories and research questions on the one hand (e.g., the search for a cause of homosexuality, or for an explanation of alleged cognitive differences in the races or the sexes) and current social and political contexts and concerns on the other, and they have little if any awareness that theories are and will forever be underdetermined by the evidence. These views are often reinforced by the idea that the history of science represents a series of blunders that scientists have now (somehow) overcome. (Indeed, in terms of mathematics and formal logic, many undergraduates seem unaware that these fields even *have* histories.)

In addition to their inadequacy as models of science, these models of knowledge and knowledge-making function to reinforce the view that there is a basic division between the knowledge generated within the so-called hard sciences and that generated in the softer disciplines. More specifically, the models suggest that it is only in terms of the humanities and social sciences that contextual thinking and values do, or should, play a role. Thus, the contextual, pluralistic, and engaged ways of approaching questions and issues that many of us are exploring and advocating can be safely passed up, and insights gained by more inclusive ways of thinking can be safely ignored, if we are of a mind—or when we are being *serious,* such as when we are doing science or mathematics.

MODELS OF CRITICAL THINKING

The strategy sketched here for challenging these views presumes the broad outlines of a model of critical thinking. The model has been developed by Craig Nelson (1989), a molecular biologist who designed his courses in evolutionary biology and genetics to encourage critical thinking about science. Nelson's schema and those on which he draws are richer than my summary will suggest,[3] and I am not concerned here about defending the specifics of his schema of stages of thinking—or the notion that there are discrete stages in ways of thinking. I use his insights and experiences to clarify the kinds of thinking in and about science that I suggest we should encourage.

Nelson outlines four stages or modes of thinking and recommends strategies for enabling students to make the transitions between these. His account of the first stage, which he calls a "Sgt. Friday mode of thinking" in which students demand "the truth and nothing but the truth," is significantly like the views of knowledge and knowing that I earlier attributed to many undergraduates. (It is also close to the stage of "received knowledge" outlined in Belenky et al., 1986, and that of "dualism" outlined in Perry, 1981.) For students to move beyond this stage, Nelson argues, requires that they be encouraged to see that uncertainty is part and parcel of science. Hence, instead of focusing exclusively on imparting the content of current theory, Nelson recommends that attention also be paid to the field's history, particularly its now discarded theories and the reasons they were once viable, and to the current half-life of theories in particularly dynamic areas.

But, Nelson (1989) notes, as important as the recognition of uncertainty is, it does not automatically lead to a sound view of the epistemology of science or to critical ways of thinking. For one thing, the recognition of uncertainty often prompts students to embrace a naive relativism (in Nelson's terms, "Baskin Robbins" thinking): Roughly speaking, "if knowledge isn't objective, then it is personal and intuitive . . . and each person's view is good for him or her" (p. 21). Thus, for some students, Nelson points out, stressing that the evidence *warrants rather than proves* the claim that evolution occurred leads to the conclusion that "since evolution is not certainly true, I can legitimately ignore it" (p. 21). A first step in helping students recognize that whether it is reasonable to believe evolution occurred is not a matter of opinion, Nelson argues, involves helping them understand and appreciate the criteria and evidence used within the field to select preferable claims or theories, a way of thinking he calls "contextual relativism." At this stage, students need to be made aware of the criteria and methods by which choices are made between competing theories and against which claims are offered and evaluated.

But although contextual relativism represents an advance over the first two stages, it also has severe limitations, as Kuhn's notion of incommensurability reminds us (Kuhn, 1970). Contextual relativism, Nelson points out, does not permit comparison between scientific paradigms, or criteria for choosing appropriate applications in complex situations, or understanding of the interrelationships between science and public policy (Nelson, 1989). Each of these situations requires an ability to relate and make choices between different, and in some cases competing, criteria. Such ability—which, following Belenky et al. (1986), Nelson calls "constructed knowing"—requires that one be able to "delineate *the values that underlie* a field's criteria and its applications, demonstrate a field's *limits,* and *relate [both]* to other fields or contexts" (1989, p. 18). Moreover, comparing and evaluating discipline-specific or context-specific criteria requires that students learn to draw on their own values in making comparisons and choices, to be active and engaged participants in the process. Mature, critical thinking, Nelson concludes, "involves the ability and willingness to address tradeoffs, to articulate why [one] advocates a particular approach . . . and to take responsibility for the validity of one's beliefs and for making a difference in the world" (p. 18).

I suggest that issues raised in and by recent critical science scholarship can be used to encourage what Nelson calls constructed knowing in science courses and to encourage more sophisticated views of science. The example I use draws on current research in feminist science scholarship—in particular, that surrounding a debate concerning human evolution—but many cases in the history of science and contemporary science could be used to similar ends.[4]

BEYOND ANDROCENTRIC SCIENCE

Feminist scientists and science critics point out that research into animal and human behavior and social organization often incorporates the basic organizing principle that males are socially oriented—that their activities are skilled and determining of social organization—and females are biologically oriented—that their activities are "natural," unskilled, and largely without consequence for the social dynamics of human and animal groups. In models and theories incorporating this assumption, females are satellites to male actors who determine and dominate social dynamics (Bleier, 1983; Hubbard, 1982).

As feminist critics note, the "man, the hunter" theory incorporates this organizing principle and credits the evolution of *Homo sapiens* to what are assumed to be activities and behaviors that were engaged in and exhibited by our male ancestors. Females appear to have gotten a free "evolutionary ride."

According to the theory, they were menstruating, childbearing, lactating, and child rearing, with none of these activities credited as contributing to the evolution of bipedalist and speaking "man" or to the development of the hierarchical, social arrangements that "man, the hunter" theorists assume characterized early hominid and human groups (see, e.g., the account offered in Washburn and Lancaster, 1976).

Feminists argue that there are fundamental problems with the "man, the hunter" explanation of human evolution and that some of these are directly related to the androcentric organizing principle used by its advocates. For one thing, some have argued, there is no reason to assume that our female ancestors were completely occupied with procreation and child-rearing activities, that they were dependent on male providers, or that male dominance hierarchies characterized the social dynamics of early hominid and human groups (Hubbard, 1982). But in fact, things are not as straightforward as the criticism, so stated, would suggest.

Some "man, the hunter" theorists do appear to have simply assumed that males were dominant and the only hunters. But others have drawn on anthropological accounts of the social dynamics in contemporary hunter-gatherer societies to reconstruct early hominid and human behavior and social organization, accounts that include descriptions of gender roles and behavior in these societies. The theory's advocates have also drawn on models in primatology and animal sociology and used these as evidence for the view of early human social groups incorporated in the theory (Bleier, 1983; Hubbard, 1982; Nelson, 1990).

This is not to say that the charge of androcentrism is unwarranted. Feminists in anthropology, primatology, and biobehavioral science have shown that the organizing principle at issue, which assumes a social male–natural female dichotomy, is also at work in these other fields (Bleier, 1983; Hubbard, 1982; Tanner & Zihlman, 1976). Their research indicates that the principle has shaped (and often distorted) accounts of the social dynamics and behavior of primate and other animal groups, as well as accounts of the social dynamics, including gender arrangements, characterizing contemporary hunter-gatherer societies. In short, feminist science criticism has revealed a substantial feedback system across fields and sciences, functioning to underwrite the organizing principle at the core of the "man, the hunter" explanation of human evolution (Bleier, 1988; Harding, 1986; Nelson, 1990).

The consequences of the organizing principle are beginning to emerge even in the results of cross-cultural and historical studies and research in primatology and animal sociology that are not shaped by it. It now seems clear that the principle precludes recognition and analyses of the interaction between so-called reproductive and productive activities, of variation in procreative and reproductive activities, and of the relationships between such variation and other features of the social and physical environment (Bleier, 1983; Hubbard, 1982; Nelson, 1990). And in terms of the "man, the hunter" theory, it now seems clear that the emphasis on male behavior and activities effectively precluded analysis of the role that procreative and other so-called reproductive activities, as well as gathering, played in human evolution. When such activities are taken into account, alternative accounts of human evolution and of the social dynamics of various human and animal groups gain plausibility (Hubbard, 1982).[5] In one alternative account of human evolution, the "woman, the gatherer" theory, women's activities as gatherers and mothers are central factors, with the greater dependency of the young (the solution to the "obstetrical dilemma"), the environmental pressures for bipedalism, and the importance of women's gathering for themselves and their young placing at least equal selection pressure on females for tool use, language, cooperation, and social organization (Slocum, 1975).

UNDERSTANDING EVIDENCE

I suggest that this debate—and the point holds for other research that reveals relationships between science and sociopolitical context—can be used to encourage a more sophisticated and critical understanding of evidence and thus a sounder view of the epistemology of science and broader critical thinking. For starters, it is important when considering such cases that it be made clear that the connections revealed between methodologies, assumptions, and theories among fields and sciences are not themselves problematic. We would not, for example, expect a theory of human evolution to ignore current research and models in primatology, anthropology, or animal sociology, any more than we would expect it to ignore current theories in population genetics, paleontology, or geology. (Students should be encouraged to recognize, however, that the assumption that primate behavior or contemporary hunter-gatherer societies provide clues into early hominid and human behavior is *itself* dependent on a large body of theory and not self-evident.) So, too, it is important that students recognize that feminist scientists who criticize the "man, the hunter" theory or engage in research to develop the "woman, the gatherer" theory are also not working in a vacuum—scientific or sociopolitical. Like "man, the hunter" theorists, they are synthesizing the results of research in primatology, anthropology, and biology—particularly research that was not informed by the organizing principle they have criticized. Moreover, a decision to explore or adopt an alternative to the "man, the hunter" theory is itself related, at least in part, to results in a number of these fields that suggested that androcentrism leads to partial accounts of social behavior and dynamics at best. Finally, the decision is also related to feminist politics, which includes attention to the so-called commonsense assumptions about gender found to inform this theory and others.

An example may clarify these several points. A matter of debate between the advocates of these two theories of human evolution has been the significance of chipped stones found near fossil remains of *Homo erectus* (Longino & Doell, 1983). Are they evidence that males made tools for the hunting of large animals, as "man, the hunter" theorists assume; evidence that women were making tools to assist them in gathering; or evidence of some other activity that some future theory might posit? One of the things that students should be made aware of is that the evidence we use to try to answer the question of the significance of these stones is *vast,* the explanation of them far from "self-announcing." Current research and knowledge in primatology and anthropology and a host of other fields will constitute part of the evidence for any explanation we construct. Moreover, the very existence of feminist science criticism, no less than its findings, indicates that part of what has been and continues to be brought to bear on the question of their significance is experiences of and views about gender. Again, it is not the connections among scientific theories or the borrowings of methodologies or results that are new or problematic. What is new (and, in some views of science, problematic) is the evidence that "extrascientific" experience and views, and in particular those that are recognized as value-laden and political, play a role in scientific theorizing. That role is evident in both androcentric theories and methodologies and in feminist criticisms of these.

This case study can also be used to explore what Nelson calls "the unavoidability of uncertainty." On the most obvious level, the existence of alternative accounts of human evolution underscores some of the constraints on historical explanation. In reconstructing human evolution, we need to contend with the relative lack of evidence and its unevenness; in terms of the question of female and male contributions, for example, we need to take into account that things such as metal tools associated with hunting will survive, whereas baskets associated with gathering will not.

But these problems are not the most telling. Students also need to recognize that having an abundance of evidence would not provide us with a goddess's view of human evolution. We would still need to make judgments concerning what is to count as evidence for an account of that process, and other theories and current context play a role at every stage. In short, they need to recognize that what we will countenance as evidence emerges concomitantly with the process of constructing theories—it is not laid down prior to that process (Nelson, 1990). Of equal significance in terms of using this example to explore the nature and strength of the evidence for our theories is the point that slippage between the amount of evidence available and our theories, and the use of a larger body of current theory to shape our construing of what constitutes evidence, are factors in *all* theorizing, not just historical explanation.

A further implication of this case that is relevant to critical thinking about science is that the relationship between what we will countenance as evidence and our current theories does not limit us to contextual relativism or condemn us to incommensurabilities. Those advocating the "man, the hunter" and "woman, the gatherer" theories disagree about some things (indeed, as we might suspect, a lot of things), but not everything. They can, for example, meaningfully discuss and disagree about the significance of chipped stones (as, in Kuhn's celebrated example of alleged incommensurability, Galileo and his inquisitors could discuss torture instruments and Aristotelian physics). Neither theory is a closed system, for neither is isolable from a larger body of theory—including commonsense beliefs. And on large parts of that larger body (a heliocentric view, for example, and the view that humans evolved), we can expect "man, the hunter" and "woman, the gatherer" theorists to agree. Nor, without incommensurability, is there reason to think that the current debate will not be resolved.

The issues considered in this case are evidence that the ways of thinking that Nelson calls constructed knowing are, in fact, features of scientific practice. We might be tempted by the view that the moral to be drawn is that, given different or neutral assumptions about gender, race, class, or sexuality, we could just "do science"—or that what is needed is stricter methodological controls to filter out all the sociopolitical, historical, and culturally inflected noise revealed by critical science scholars. But I don't see how we can understand or teach the moral as such, in part because the relationships between approaches to nature and values and sociopolitical context *are neither overcome nor absent in feminist criticism.* To try, for example, to disassociate feminist criticism of "man the hunter" theory, primatology, or anthropology from feminist politics seems as ad hoc as trying to disassociate the androcentrism that feminist criticism reveals in science from the androcentrism and sexism in the societies in which science has been undertaken.

The basis for my earlier qualification—that it is only to a point that science characterizes the spirit of critical thinking—may by now be clear. What we might call "science as usual" is often, and for a variety of reasons, not self-conscious of the ways in which it reflects the social and political contexts in which it is undertaken, or of the ways in which even its constitutive values are discipline specific, as well as historically and culturally specific. But cases such as that explored here, and two decades of critical science scholarship, indicate that attention to these relationships, and to the values underlying and informing scientific knowledge making, is integral to critical thinking *in* and *about* science. Hence, it indicates that encouraging the kind

of thinking that Nelson calls constructed knowing is an appropriate goal of
the science curriculum.

NOTES

1. "Critical Thinking: Focus on Science," Institute for Critical Thinking,
Montclair State College.
2. In fairness to Popper, his view was more sophisticated than those I next
outline.
3. Nelson builds on Perry, 1981, and Belenky et al., 1986.
4. Historical case studies include the theories of race and sex differences developed in nineteenth-century biology and anthropology, and drawn on by Darwin.
Contemporary case studies involve ways in which class, race, gender, and heterosexist
bias inform research programs and theories in primatology, biobehavioral science,
endocrinology, cognitive science, cell biology, and genetics. (Tuana, 1989) provides a
useful bibliography of recent critical science scholarship.
5. I can here do no more than scratch the surface in outlining the consequences
of the organizing principle. The works cited in the text of my discussion should be
consulted.

REFERENCES

Belenky, M. F. et al. (1986). *Women's ways of knowing.* New York: Basic Books.
Bleier, R. (1983). *Science and gender.* New York: Pergamon Press.
Bleier, R. (Ed.). (1988). *Feminist approaches to science.* New York: Pergamon Press.
Harding, S. (1986). *The science question in feminism.* Ithaca: Cornell University Press.
Hubbard, R. (1982). Have only men evolved? In R. Hubbard, M. S. Henifin, & B.
        Fried (Eds.), *Biological Woman* (pp. 17–45). Cambridge, MA: Schenkman.
Kuhn, T. (1970). *The structure of scientific revolutions* (2nd ed.). Chicago: University
        of Chicago Press.
Longino, H., & Doell, R. (1983). Body, bias, and behavior. *Signs: Journal of Women
        in Culture and Society, 9,* 206–227.
Nelson, C. (1989). Skewered on the unicorn's horn. In L. Crow (Ed.), *Enhancing criti-
        cal thinking in the sciences* (pp. 17–31). Washington, DC: Society for College
        Science Teachers.
Nelson, L. H. (1990). *Who knows: From Quine to a feminist empiricism.* Philadelphia:
        Temple University Press.
Perry, W. G., Jr. (1981). Cognitive and ethical growth. In A. W. Chickering (Ed.), *The
        modern American college* (pp. 76–116). San Francisco: American College.
Popper, K. (1959). *The logic of scientific discovery.* New York: Harper & Row.
Slocum, S. (1975). Woman the gatherer. In R. R. Reiter (Ed.), *Toward an anthropology
        of women* (pp. 36–50). New York: Monthly Review.

Tanner, N., & Zihlman, A. (1976). Women in evolution. *Signs: Journal of Women in Culture and Society, 1* (3), 585–608.

Tuana, N. (Ed.). (1989). *Feminism and science.* Bloomington and Indianapolis: Indiana University Press.

Washburn, S., & Lancaster, C. S. (1976). The evolution of hunting. In R. B. Lee & I. Devore (Eds.), *Kalahari hunter gatherers.* Cambridge, MA: Harvard University Press.

11

"Mainlining" Transformation in the General Education Curriculum

Virginia Ramey Mollenkott

At William Paterson College of New Jersey, we are fortunate to have a faculty seminar on race and gender that meets once a month to discuss salient issues. One of the major purposes of that seminar is to update the faculty who are teaching related general education courses, especially Racism & Sexism in the United States. Although I find the seminars stimulating and deeply believe in the course they fuel, I have never wanted to teach Racism & Sexism myself. Why? Because I am committed to "mainlining" the teaching about race, gender, class, sexual orientation, and other issues that have proved divisive in our society. By "mainlining," I mean introducing these topics into traditional courses so that they become a part of everyday garden-variety academic discourse. In these transitional times, we need both. We need specific courses, such as Women's Changing Roles, Racism & Sexism, and Justice & Racism, but for the long haul, we need to mainline a politics of inclusion.

I agree fully with Margo Culley that what I'm referring to as "mainlining" cannot stop with merely adding on a few works by women, gay people, people of color, and a variety of cultures, or even integrating such works into every unit we teach. As Culley puts it, "adding multi-cultural material . . . entirely change[s] the questions we need to ask and the conceptual framework of our enterprise" (1991, pp. 8–9). In addition, as a professor, I find myself being elbowed out of the spotlight and into the role of colearner and facilitator of learning.

This chapter outlines some of the ways I have mainlined in my English courses at William Paterson College. I have done so within three basic categories: First, when I am working with traditional textbooks or literary works, I point out the effects of exclusive language or unconscious stereotyping or insensitivity, even while admiring other aspects of the works in question. Second, when teaching with an excellently inclusive text, I try various experiential ways of overcoming the resistance that can sometimes develop. And finally, in a first-year writing course, where the students themselves provide the major subject matter, I devise ways of raising consciousness about multiculturalism and humane, intelligent responses to it. The purpose of this chapter is to describe some methods of mainlining in each of these three categories.

WHEN THE TEXTS ARE TRADITIONAL

In over 40 years of college teaching, I have had ample opportunity to mainline inclusiveness while working with traditional or even overtly sexist textbooks. In courses in which the Bible is a major issue, such as The Bible & Literature, or Women, the Bible, & Modern Literature, I sometimes utilize an imaginative exercise to illustrate the nature of interpretative communities and the difference it makes when a person's own interests are directly affected by other people's interpretations. Students should be warned to imagine themselves in the situation fully before checking any answers, and to pay attention to their own reasoning process as they choose between the two passages in each category.

> *Imagine:* You are appointed to a futuristic board of planners to set forth the structure of a society into which you will later be born. Your charge now is to make the moral and ethical rules for that future society. Yet as you work on those rules, you are constantly aware that *you* do not know whether you yourself will be born into that society as female or male; black, yellow, red, or white; homosexual, bisexual, or heterosexual; able-bodied or physically handicapped; mentally capable or incapable; poor or wealthy; nor do you know whether your nation will be powerful or underdeveloped. The Bible has been specified as the basic foundation for the moral and ethical rules of the future society, and your planning board is committed to providing biblical justification for each of its rules. Which of the Bible passages below—taken at face value and out of context as they are—would you be more likely to

emphasize, knowing that in your own future life you will be forced to submit to the rules that are going to emerge from each choice?

ON RACE AND CLASS RELATIONS

Let all who are under the yoke of slavery regard their masters as worthy of all honor, so that the name of God and the teaching may not be blasphemed. (1 Timothy 6:1 [NRSV])

Slaves who have escaped to you from their owners shall not be given back to them. They shall reside with you, in your midst, in any place they choose in any one of your towns, wherever they please; you shall not oppress them. (Deuteronomy 23:15–16 [NRSV])

ON MALE-FEMALE RELATIONS

To the woman [God] said, "I will greatly multiply your pangs in childbearing . . . yet your desire shall be for your husband, and he shall rule over you." (Genesis 3:16 [NRSV])

Be subject to one another out of reverence for Christ. . . . Each of you [men] should love his wife as himself, and a wife should respect her husband. (Ephesians 5:21, 22 [NRSV])

ON SEXUAL ORIENTATION AND BEHAVIOR

Neither the sexually immoral nor idolaters nor male prostitutes nor homosexual offenders nor thieves nor the greedy nor drunkards nor slanderers nor swindlers will inherit the kingdom of God. (1 Corinthians 6:9 [NIV])

For I am convinced that neither death nor life, neither angels nor demons, neither the present nor the future, nor any powers, neither height nor depth, nor anything else in all creation, will be able to separate us from the love of God. (Romans 8:38–39 [NIV])

This exercise, which contains several other components, is drawn from Mollenkott (1992, pp. 56–57).

There are bound to be plenty of questions about biblical intentions immediately after doing this exercise, and those are best answered by placing the passages in their historical social and religious contexts. (A Bible dictionary and some commentaries would be helpful here.) But the main purpose of the exercise is to try to elicit from students the realization that since they knew that their own lives would be influenced in unknown ways by the choices they made, they were drawn to the more charitable and humane passages rather than the more rigidly restrictive ones. It should be pointed out that this exercise is *not* meant to suggest that the Bible should actually be used as a basis for future societal laws and structures. Indeed, one of its purposes is to illustrate the danger of enforcing the views of any one interpretive community on everybody else in what would amount to a civil religion.

As a teacher of literature, I work mostly with traditional texts—the classics of English and American literature, most of which were written by white men of ample means. In the course English Literature: Romantic to Modern, I use volume 2 of *The Norton Anthology of English Literature* (1986), assigning most of the women whose works are included: Mary Wollstonecraft, Dorothy Wordsworth, Mary W. Shelley, Elizabeth Barrett Browning, Emily Bronte, Christina Rossetti, Virginia Woolf, and Edna O'Brien and other contemporaries. Obviously, many important issues are suggested by their work, and students are frequently astonished at the awareness of systemic oppression these writers manifest. But a great deal can also be taught from the texts of the male "stars" of the traditional curriculum, especially when white male interpretations are contrasted with interpretations that arise through the vision of non-normative groups. For instance, I was taught that lines 255–278 of Samuel Taylor Coleridge's "Christabel" depict a lesbian love scene. In one of the study questions provided with the reading assignments, I ask students whether that's what they see in the passage. Geraldine, who takes Christabel into her arms in bed, has some horrible disfigurement of "her bosom and half her side," though Coleridge does not tell us what it is. Geraldine holds Christabel in order to take *power over* Christabel: to cast a spell so that Christabel will not be able to reveal what she has seen (*Norton,* pp. 363–364). As a young lesbian student, I was confused and dismayed at being told that this passage describes lesbian love, although at the time I was not politicized enough to do anything other than take into myself the negative implications. My own students also express great confusion over that interpretation. If no one else speaks up, I point out that most lesbian women value equal-partner relationships and that Coleridge says nothing about sex, specifying, in fact, that Geraldine held Christabel "as a mother with her child" (line 300). Thus the traditional interpretation is shown to be inaccurate, heterosexist, and indicative of a genital fixation if not a rape mentality.

During the course of the semester, we notice that certain lines that seem sexist out of context may not seem that way at all in context. Take, for instance, Byron's "Man's love is of man's life a thing apart, / 'Tis woman's whole existence" (*Don Juan,* lines 1545–1546, *Norton,* p. 618). These words occur in a letter written by a young married woman to her even younger lover, Don Juan, who has just been banished from England because his mother found out about the affair. The words are, in fact, a very precise description of the differing fates of Donna Julia, who will be stuck in her unhappy marriage, and Don Juan, who will soon be happily engaged with Haidee and other adventures all over the world. And the words perfectly describe the fate of most 19th-century women. By noticing such cases, students are taught to distinguish between bigoted attitudes on the part of the author and accurate descriptions of the inequitable status quo.

But there are enough bigoted or insensitive attitudes to go around, and pointing them out is an important form of consciousness-raising. During my undergraduate and graduate education, nobody mentioned the racism and religious triumphalism in Tennyson's "I count the gray barbarian lower than the Christian child," or the arrogance of saying "Better fifty years of Europe than a cycle of Cathay" ("Locksley Hall," lines 174, 184, *Norton,* p. 1121). Cathay is China, of course, and a cycle is 1,000 years; so the ranting racism of the character who speaks this dramatic monologue is all too evident. However, in a culture where some people viewed Archie Bunker as a hero and a role model, not a buffoon, it is vital that teachers avoid assuming that everybody automatically sees and rejects such bigotry.

WHEN THE TEXTBOOK IS INCLUSIVE

Teaching with an excellent multicultural and politically correct textbook presents a different set of challenges. So far, I have had just one opportunity to teach Introduction to Literature with the anthology edited by Pamela J. Annas and Robert C. Rosen, *Literature and Society* (1990). During my opening unit on Growing Up and Growing Older, I made the mistake of assigning Whitman's "We Two Boys Together Clinging" as part of the first group of poems. When we began to talk about it, heterosexism and even homophobia squatted in the air like a rancid toad. Nobody said anything overt, but I could feel a resentment that I am not accustomed to.

Things became overt when I later assigned "A Boy's Own Story" by Edmund White. We got to the story late in the period, and just as class was ending, one young man (I'll call him Hal) blurted out that the protagonist of this story was "only a faggot." Hal's tone indicated that, in his opinion, the story wasn't even worth discussing because the central character was not fully human. The silence in the room was palpable, everybody waiting to see what would happen to somebody who had said what many others had not dared to say. I was aware that Hal might be struggling with questions about his own sexual orientation, since it is well known that gay-bashing often springs from sexual self-doubt and self-hatred. In my calmest voice, I warned against using derogatory language and promised to return to the topic the next time we met. Before the next class, I wrote on the board in large letters, *"Nothing human is alien to me."* And in that atmosphere, we managed a more sympathetic discussion of "A Boy's Own Story" and, later in the semester, other works by or about homosexuals.

As the semester wore on, I noticed that many contemporary first-year students will not reveal much about their personal values in front of 39 other first-year students. So I began to use small discussion groups a great deal (6 students maximum), often giving group quizzes in which everybody contributed ideas to the group's elected secretary and for which everyone in the group got the same grade. A sample group question might be, "In Marge Piercy's poem 'Right to Life,' identify at least 12 things a woman is *not* to be confused with." Or I would ask students to write personal response papers, either at home or in class; the most sensitive papers would then be read aloud as a basis for discussion. These could be less fact-oriented than the group-quiz questions, such as "How do you *feel* about Miss Moore's statement that there's something wrong with a society in which 'some people can spend on a toy what it would cost to feed a family of six or seven for a year'? What can be done about these problems?" I noticed that Hal, who had been so brutal about homosexuals, wrote with exquisite sensitivity about the plight of women, poor people, or racially oppressed people, but he refused to read his responses aloud. Once I asked him about the difference between his public and private personae, and he explained in a long note that he could not talk sensitively in front of other students because he feared what they would say about him. At one point in the semester, the class seemed to become polarized between male and female perspectives, with Hal and others expressing the view that you could always count on the women to side with the female characters. So I proposed an experiment. The class was split into seven same-sex groups, each of which was asked to compose a response related to Anne Sexton's poem "For My Lover, Returning to His Wife." I asked both the male and the female groups to respond to the question posed by Annas and Rosen (1990): "How would a poem with a male persona, entitled 'For My Lover, Returning to Her Husband,' have to be different?" (p. 502). I collected the descriptions—and they were vivid! read and classified them at home, and in the next class read them aloud, having the students guess and vote individually on whether each response came from women or from men. I put the tally of each vote on the board. The voting was predictable: If the response depicted the male as egotistically irresponsible, the majority thought that it must have been written by women; only the more male-sympathetic responses were thought to have been composed by men. At the end, we discovered that the majority had been right about the sexual makeup of four of the groups, but wrong about three of them, indicating that people *do* have a sense of justice and will not necessarily make knee-jerk reactions, siding with the gender group to which they belong. What was remarkable was that all the groups, both male and female, to one degree or another said that the average male would be far less selfless and generous in his concern for the future success of the female's marriage than Anne Sexton's speaker was for her lover as he returned to his wife. We were then in a good position to discuss why we all felt that way and what could be changed in our society to facilitate more mutually responsive male-female relationships.

On the day after the semester had ended, I happened to see Hal at the other end of a crowded hallway. I waved, and to my surprise, he not only waved but began to make his way toward me. I put out my hand for a farewell handshake, but instead he gave me a warm hug. With an embarrassed smile, he said, "Hey, it was a pretty good class!"

WHEN STUDENT WRITING IS THE PRIMARY TEXT

In the required first-year writing course, the primary text is the writing generated by the students themselves, and this offers a wonderful opportunity for mainlining democratic principles of inclusiveness. Simply urging students to write about their own backgrounds and the views that grow out of those backgrounds, and having them read aloud their most successful essays, frequently results in important multicultural experiences. For instance, in one section I had a brilliant young man from the former Soviet Union who had been denied a scholarship because he was Jewish; from him, the class learned a lot about Eastern European politics and educational standards. One of the women in the same class had been physically abused by her high school boyfriend and had been forced to get a restraining order to stop him from stalking her; from her, the group learned something about sexual terrorism. Another man was currently working at a New York television station and shared the high-tech pressures of that career. A woman wrote about her parents' poverty and her determination to succeed in school in order to better herself. A baseball player from Cuba described his lifelong passion in colorful prose. We were quite a group. But even such students need to learn that their own experiences are worth writing about, that precisely *in their own particularities* lie their value to an inclusive society.

A second mainlining technique I use in the writing class is an exercise I call "What's Wrong with This Picture?" Ordinarily I present two or three "pictures," asking students to choose the one that stimulates the strongest response in them and to write a paragraph explaining what, in their opinion, is wrong with the "picture" they have chosen. Here is a sample set of choices I plan to use in the upcoming semester:

WHAT'S WRONG WITH THIS PICTURE?

Pick one and write a unified paragraph explaining the problem you see. You have 10 minutes.

Picture 1: A 1990 issue of *Sports Illustrated* reprinted a photograph from *Vogue* magazine showing tennis star Steffi Graf in spike heels and a short, low-cut, very revealing black dress. The caption explained that Graf had received more congratulations for that photograph than she had received for winning the Grand Slam (Mollenkott, 1992, p. 154).

Picture 2: Time magazine reported that ballet star Peter Martins had been arrested for beating his wife, ballerina Darci Kistler, who later dropped the assault charges. *Time* commented: "Martins might do well to remember a line about ballerinas in his book *Far From Denmark:* 'Some are nice, some not so nice. But they are all tough, merciless'" (*Time,* August 3, 1992, p. 77).

The major insights I would be looking for would be these: In the first picture, the outpouring of congratulations for a "cheesecake" photograph—more than for winning the world's four most prestigious tennis tournaments in a single calendar year—indicates widespread relief that Steffi Graf is willing to advertise her heterosexual availability to men. Whereas her chief struggle to achieve number-one tennis status was against a lesbian, Martina Navratilova, Steffi's *Vogue* shot told the world that she was "normal." What's wrong with this picture is that women's individual achievements should be honored at least as much as their physical appearance, and that the heterosexual orientation should not be regarded as the only normal human sexual behavior. In the second picture, one wonders why *Time* would warn Peter Martins about the toughness and mercilessness of ballerinas after he has just beaten one and then been forgiven by her. How misogynistic can society become?

But even if students write responses that are completely different from the ones I am looking for, I will learn a great deal about them, and they will gain valuable thinking and writing experience. And when some of the best responses are read aloud, I will interject my own responses as well. Simply by collecting news items and encouraging students to collect them too, I provide the class with grist for several such impromptu writing exercises a semester.

Finally, brief poems or quotations by diverse authors provide important opportunities for mainlining transformation in the first-year writing course. The most successful set of exercises I have administered to date is described at length in my article "Awareness of Diversity: A Classroom Exercise" in the winter 1991 issue of *Transformations: The New Jersey Project Journal.* The exercises were based on Audre Lorde's "Thanks to Jesse Jackson," a powerful poem that shocks and stimulates students with its global perspective. But any poem or prose excerpt that looks at things from a multicultural point of view may become the basis for imaginative and creative writing exercises.

Apart from providing practice in reasoning and writing, my goal in mainlining is to stimulate awareness of global diversity, the interrelatedness of the world's population, and the fact that together we must develop a sustainable world community. It seems to me that whatever we can do to take responsibility for our own power, and to empower other people, can only add honor to our individual cultural heritages and provide a better future for us all. As Audre Lorde put it, "If we can envision the future we desire, we can work to bring it into being. We need all the different pieces of ourselves to be strong, and we need each other and each other's battles for empowerment as fuel for a livable tomorrow" (1989, p. 12).

REFERENCES

Annas, P. J., & Rosen, R. C. (1990). *Literature and society: An introduction to fiction, poetry, drama, nonfiction.* Englewood Cliffs, NJ: Prentice-Hall.

Culley, M. (1991). "We are here to stay": Curriculum transformation in the 90s. *Transformations* (Winter), pp. 4–14.

Lorde, A. (1989). A question of survival: A commencement speech delivered at Oberlin College, May 29, 1989. *Gay Community News* (August 13–19), pp. 5–12.

Mollenkott, V. (1992). *Sensuous spirituality: Out from fundamentalism.* New York: Crossroad.

Norton anthology of English literature (5th ed., Vol. 2). (1986). (M. H. Abrams, Ed.). New York: W. W. Norton.

12

Teaching Art History: Recognizing Alterity

Neil Printz

The painter Cynthia Carlson once remarked that decoration in art is "the amount of eyeball left after you've finished looking at the main event" (1980–81, p. 5). We might well apply her observation to the representation of art's excluded and marginalized discourses, visualizing it as a recovery of the perimeter, or the background. The foreground and the center become preempted, or, better, they get constantly shifted.

FROM 20TH-CENTURY TO MODERN ART

Twentieth-Century Art, as listed in Caldwell College's catalog, was a one-semester survey of the major movements, artists, and works of the period. During 4 years of teaching it, I became increasingly aware that I was devoting more and more time to the century's historical roots. The background was eroding the foreground. Accordingly, I changed the course's name to Introduction to Modern Art and its content from a sampler of textbook artists and "isms" to an attempt to elucidate the meanings and examine the functions of the concepts of modernism and modernity.

An observation by Edward Said (1989) has become axiomatic to my thinking on this question. According to him, modernity may be tracked in terms of a growing recognition of alterity. Said's insight has informed and reformed my teaching. In class, my students and I examine the textbook cases, but with an altered threshold. We cover well-trodden territory, but we go in search of others. We scrutinize the background and ask how divergent conditions of gender, race, class, and sexuality have been historically represented.

FOR OPENERS

Although most of the students enrolled in Modern Art are art majors, they come with little information beyond the biases and other baggage they carry into class. On the first day of class, to start the discussion and to begin to unpack some of that baggage, I like to ask my students some loaded questions. For openers, I recommend Linda Nochlin's (1989) simple but explosive query, "Why are there no great women artists?" It raises a series of important issues from the outset: Are there really no great women artists? Can the students name any great women artists? Can they name any women artists at all? Can they name any great male artists? What does it mean to be a "great artist"? Who determines "greatness"? Are the standards of "greatness" absolute and universal, or subject to different criteria during different periods of history and in different cultures? Why does "greatness" matter? Whose interests does it serve?

A corollary set of questions follows. One might ask one's students to ponder some of the following: Why are there no great artists of color? Why are there no great gay artists? Might there be great gay artists about whose sexuality we are uninformed? Does one's sexuality affect one's art? Does one's gender affect one's art? Does one's color? One's class? One's ethnicity? Why are there no great Italian American artists? Irish American artists? Jewish American artists? A brief writing assignment or an oral presentation might be developed from these questions: Students would be asked to "find" a work of art by an artist from any, or any combination, of these groups and to consider how the artist's gender, class, color, sexuality, or ethnicity is, or isn't, visible in the work selected.

These questions of identity and affiliation ultimately open onto another question: What is an artist? What words, I ask my students, would they use to describe what artists are like? These are written on the blackboard, edited, regrouped, and used during the class session to cross-examine a series of portraits and self-portraits of artists. I like to begin with Delacroix's "portrait" of Michelangelo brooding in his studio, since it both raises the question of what constitutes a portrait and helps me extract a Romantic notion of genius. This is followed by several gendered comparisons, for example: Fantin-Latour's portrait of Manet as a *flaneur,* a man-about-town, and Romaine Brooks's portrait of herself in the not-so-dissimilar attire of a riding habit; a Gauguin self-portrait and one by Paula Modersohn-Becker; Marcel Duchamp as Rose Selavy and a Cindy Sherman "film still."

REVISITING INCLUSION

Gender difference is so visible that it readily becomes one of the first, most constant, and most effective issues to work with in teaching art history. This is not meant, however, to beg the question of its importance. For over 20 years, feminist revisionism, employing a twofold method of inclusion and critique, has been instrumental in revitalizing art history and, in a very real sense, reinventing it.

In my own work, I have been more involved with the critical functions of a gender-informed history than with the methodology of inclusion. At the introductory level, I am committed to teaching the canon or, better, to teaching *with* the canon, since I use it not as a standard of value but as a stimulus for developing my students' abilities to think critically. I first realized the dangers of adhering too closely to the canon, however, when one of my students wrote in an exam that Mary Cassatt was important because she was the first woman artist. Indeed, to this student and probably to most of the rest of the class, Cassatt was the first woman artist because she was the first and one of the very few women artists that we had studied that semester. Clearly, I needed to reassess how I approached issues of inclusion in the classroom.

Initially, this appears to be an unproblematic task. To assemble a more inclusive curriculum, the teacher simply needs to add more women artists, more artists of color, and so forth. I began to make lists. Let me offer as an example 25 women artists of the modern period:

> *Mary Cassatt, Berthe Morisot, Paula Modersohn-Becker, Gabrielle Munter, Varvara Stepanova, Liubov Popova, Sonia Delaunay, Hannah Hoch, Georgia O'Keeffe, Florine Stettheimer, Meret Oppenheim, Dorothea Tanning, Kay Sage, Frida Kahlo, Lee Krasner, Louise Nevelson, Louise Bourgeois, Helen Frankenthaler, Lee Bontecou, Agnes Martin, Eva Hesse, Elizabeth Murray, Lynda Benglis, Laurie Anderson, Jenny Holzer*

The number 25 may have been arbitrary, but the individuals were not; each had made an uncontestable contribution. Scanning this list, I became aware of two implications: It might constitute an alternative history of modernism, and it suggested other oversights and omissions.

This list generated another list of 25 less canonical women artists of the modern period:

> *Edmonia Lewis, Hilma Af Klint, Sophie Tauber-Arp, Kathe Kollwitz, Isabel Bishop, Elsie Driscoll, Romaine Brooks, Agnes Pelton, Gertrude Greene, Maria Izquierda, Remedios Varo, Augusta Savage, I. Rice Pereira, Joan Mitchell, Barbara Hepworth, Marisol, Niki de Saint-Phalle, Anne Truitt, Jay DeFeo, Bettye Saar, Gladys Nilsson, Nancy Spero, Hanne Darboven, Magdalena Abakanowicz, Ana Mendieta*

This second list included more women of color, more women who tended to work outside the dominant modes of production and the capitals of culture, and more women who operated from the center of that discursive context we call art history but who are constantly overlooked, forgotten, devalued.

I wonder how many of my colleagues in the academy have tried this kind of list making at least once. Curators do this all the time. It's worth trying again and trying periodically. One might even keep one's old lists and date them like a journal. At this point, however, the mind rebels. The practice of history, I remind myself, has long since bypassed the notion that it is simply a matter of lists of events and lists of names. The modern mind envisions history as a battleground of issues and ideas; the postmodern mind represents it as a field of interpretations. Lists? Aren't we well beyond lists? Are we? Should we be? As reductive as a history assembled from lists of names might seem, isn't that how our students first gain access to the history of a period? It seems to me that names, or what those names represent, occupy a position from which they, and we, can begin to work and rework our way into history, into the history of art. Moreover, I believe in the power of names. Think of Maya Lin's *Vietnam War Memorial* and the collective work of art known as the *AIDS Quilt;* each name bears witness against the acts of denial, each testifies to presence in number within that most contested of bodies, the body politic.

One semester, I toyed with the possibility of distributing a syllabus consisting entirely of artists' names, but which names? From which list? How many names? How many women? How many artists of color? Who gets cut? Who gets included? What criteria should I apply? Wasn't one list as bad as another? Wouldn't I be revising the canon by installing another with a variant set of exclusions? Lists might serve a purpose when a census is taken—when numbers and names need to be counted, recovered, and recalled—but they simply wouldn't do as the basis for a historical practice and a transformed curriculum.

I resolved my dilemma by returning to my opening axiom, Edward Said's formulation that modernity might be registered as the growing recognition of alterity. The example he offered was the greater visibility of servants in the 19th-century English novel. I remembered Linda Nochlin's (1989) essay about a painting by Berthe Morisot. It depicts a woman nursing a child in a Paris park, a woman whom Nochlin reveals is not the child's mother but its nurse. How vividly it invited a comparison with Elisabeth Vigee-Lebrun's self-portrait as a mother (or with her portrait of Marie Antoinette and her children) or with a painting of a mother and child by her contemporary Mary Cassatt. It began to seem stunningly obvious to me that Morisot and Cassatt had as much to say, but with very different voices, as Manet and Degas about the collision of public and private spheres in the new urban spaces of Haussmann's Paris. To get beyond merely inserting names, inclusion would require inscribing works into the core question: What is modernity?

Let's revisit my first list: Modersohn-Becker at the artists' colony of Worpswede and Munter in the Bavarian retreat of Murnau vitally contributed to modernism's primitivist discourse of other spaces and other cultures. Delaunay in Paris and Hoch in Berlin envisioned a "new" woman, who moved with and manipulated the rhythms and disjunctions of the modern technological metropolis. Surrealist artists Oppenheim, Tanning, Sage, and Kahlo, all radically reconfigured the representation of the female body and femaleness itself. Here, I delighted in juxtaposing Oppenheim's disturbing fur-lined cup and saucer of 1936 with Cassatt's demure *A Cup of Tea*. With thought, inclusion could fold seamlessly into critique.

DIFFERENCE: COMPARING VISUAL COMPARISONS

If the visual comparison is one of the foundations of art history's pedagogy, it is also one of its most resilient methods. I remember and still use certain comparisons from my first art history classes, such as Courbet's *Burial at Ornans* compared and contrasted with El Greco's *Death of Count Orgaz*. It seems that sometimes we can broach modernity only by setting up the "old" against the "new" so that the threshold of difference can become visible to our students. But as we compare the old with the new, or the traditional with the modern, aren't we also setting up the new as constantly better and improved, more enlightened and livable? Aren't we privileging progress? The visual comparison is a powerful polemical instrument, and it may well be the moment to reappropriate it for other polemical uses—for gender comparisons—and make other thresholds, wrapped in modernity's portmanteau, visible to our students.

Gendered comparisons may move from questions of identity, exempli-

fied by portraiture and self-portraiture, to questions of other kinds of difference, such as differences in subject matter, context, or theme. Comparing
divergent approaches to the same or related subjects has been a staple of the
art history class. I confess to leaning on it often and without shame. Subject
matter is such a good place to begin because it is often the most accessible
point of entry into the work. I don't think that we can ask our students
often enough What is being shown? before we ask them How? or How is
this different?

By gendering comparisons of subject matter, one can work effectively
within the pedagogy to begin its transformation. I like to compare contemporary works, such as Cassatt's *The Bath* and Degas's *The Tub,* and works from
adjacent and not-so-adjacent periods, such as a flower "portrait" by Georgia
O'Keeffe and Andy Warhol's paint-by-number composition *Do It Yourself
(Flowers)*.

In this context, at least two sorts of limitations come to mind. The first
concerns the diminished role of recognizable subjects in much of the work of
the later modern period. It makes this kind of comparison more difficult
but not completely out of the question. For example, consider a comparison
between two wall-mounted sculptures of the late 1960s, Eva Hesse's *Hang
Up* and Bruce Nauman's *From Hand to Mouth*. Here, subject matter is not
absent so much as attenuated, and the comparative problem must shift its
focus from subject matter to metaphor, from what is shown to what is being
suggested.

The other limitation of gendered comparisons based on subject matter
derives from the hermeneutic literalness it tends to affirm. Subject matter
may too easily fuse with meaning, description pass for interpretation. Moreover, certain images or forms may become too readily construed as typically
female or typically male. For this reason, I have always avoided too many
gendered comparisons, as well as the kind of comparisons that seem to court
stereotyping, such as juxtaposing works by Lee Bontecou and John Cham-
berlain. I believe that gendered comparisons work best when they suggest
how rich and complex the question of gender may be, how cross-gendered
we all are.

BREAKING RANKS WITH THE TIMELINE

If inclusion asks that we revisit questions of individual contribution and authorship, the practice of a gender-informed critique presupposes that we
reframe the issues of cultural representation and authority. In this context,
critical theory has complemented feminist studies (see Owens, 1983). The
concept of a "male gaze" is one such vantage point that has gendered the

conditions of authorship (creating), spectatorship (looking), and power (possessing).

How gazes are gendered, and how this operates to confer status and negotiate power, may be shown by comparing Cassatt's *The Bath* with Degas's *The Tub*. Whereas Degas's composition appears to act out the very conditions of looking, embodying it as the absorption of a male gaze in a self-absorbed female body, for Cassatt, looking and nurturing function in sort of a closed loop, as visibly female prerogatives.

The representation of the female body is one of the semester's most recurrent issues. In this context, I recommend three essays, by Carol Armstrong (1985), Carol Duncan (1993), and Carol Duncan and Alan Wallach (1978).

During my second year of teaching, I first began to break rank from the rigors of timeline chronology. Borrowing a bit of Duchampian terminology, I designated a group of classes early in the semester as The Passage from the Nude to Nakedness. We studied Manet's *Dejeuner sur l'herbe* and *Olympia,* several of Degas's bathers, and concluded with a critical analysis of Renoir's *Large Bathers.* Not so covertly, I was polemically setting up Renoir's painting and, to my initial surprise and delight, it seemed to work. My students readily spotted the regressive features of Renoir's approach to representing the female body—so readily, in fact, that I felt obliged to look again, searching for redeeming features in this work.

Rather than vainly trying to redeem the later Renoir, it occurred to me that The Passage from the Nude to Nakedness represented a rather successful experiment in gender-informed pedagogy. I considered that I might make the impact on the Renoir less determined by modifying my designation slightly and expanding its contents chronologically forward and back. Thus, The Passage from the Nude to Nakedness (and Back Again) has become part of my syllabus whenever I teach this course. I envision it as an expandable framework that can and does include at least some of the following works and might suggest others:

1. Ingres's bathers and odalisques, compared with their professed models, the classical nude.
2. Ingres's *Odalisque with Slave* and Gerome's *The Slave Market;* Delacroix's *Death of Sardanapalus* and *Women of Algiers.* With these works, "Orientalism" is introduced and examined in the light of its imagination and colonization of another body, one whose aura of the exotic and mysterious alters the package of traditional meanings carried by the classical nude (see Said, 1978; Nochlin, 1989).
3. The unidealized bodies of Courbet's female bathers and his nude as muse in *The Studio: A Real Allegory.*

4. Seurat's modern studio nude *Les Poseuses,* which meditates on the conditions of artistic enterprise and female labor.
5. Cézanne's "Bather" compositions.
6. Gauguin's Tahitian women, ciphers of erotic availability and spiritual plenitude.
7. Matisse's *Le Bonheur de Vivre* and his Orientalist odalisques from the 1920s.
8. Matisse's *Blue Nude* and Kirchner's *Woman with a Parasol.*
9. Kirchner and Heckel's child models, Franzi and Marcella.
10. Picasso's *Les Demoiselles d'Avignon.*
11. De Kooning's *Women.*
12. "Counter-nudes": male bathers, such as those painted by Bazille and Eakins.

Although the works that I've clustered around this thematic sequence follow a general chronology, admittedly they do leapfrog across conventional art historical time markers. This effect is tonic insofar as it encourages breaking down art history's rigid periodization, according to which a period— Cubism, for example—is constituted by a fixed set of principles that provide a rationale before the fact for all works of art that come within its sphere. Moreover, by extracting works from the undifferentiated flow of a fictive mainstream and from the confinement of periods and "isms," students are stimulated to see these works in terms of broader cultural issues and ideas.

I do not advise that all the above works be incorporated into a single sequence, since their number tends to overwhelm the frame. Some works might well be resituated in the context of their moment or in other contexts, and several works might be studied more than once during a semester. I am not advocating that teachers and students do violence to historical difference, merely that we reconfigure it freshly. The contexts of representation may help us to break ranks more readily, to rethink what we think we already know, to begin to reinvent ourselves as teachers and transform the curriculum.

REFERENCES

Armstrong, C. (1985). Edgar Degas and the representation of the female body. In S. Suleiman (Ed.), *The female body in western culture: Contemporary perspectives* (pp. 223–242). Cambridge, MA: Harvard University Press.

Carlson, C. (1980–81). *Bulletin, 28,* 5 (Oberlin College, Allen Memorial Art Museum).

Duncan, C. (1993). The MoMA's hot mammas. In C. Duncan (Ed.), *The aesthetics of power: Essays in critical art history* (pp. 189–207). Cambridge, MA: Cambridge University Press.

Duncan, C., & Wallach, A. (1978). The Museum of Modern Art as late capitalist ritual. *Marxist Perspectives, 4,* 28–51.

Nochlin, L. (1988). *Women, art, power and other essays.* New York: Harper & Row.

Nochlin, L. (1989). *The politics of vision.* New York: Harper & Row.

Owens, C. (1983). The discourse of others: Feminists and postmodernism. In H. Foster (Ed.), *The anti-aesthetic: Essays on postmodern culture* (pp. 57–82). Seattle: Bay Press.

Said, E. (1978). *Orientalism.* New York: Pantheon.

Said, E. (1989). Representing the colonized: Anthropology's interlocutors. *Critical Inquiry, 15*(2), 205–225.

13

Teaching Psychoanalytic Theory in the Feminist Classroom

Frances Bartkowski

Perhaps there is already an orthodoxy in the teaching of feminist theory. I had already taught two such courses when I began to consider the questions I address here. The first was a course instituted in an existing women's studies program, but one that had never included a course on theory. The second time around it was an established course in the program and one of two required courses. In both cases I incorporated a unit on psychoanalysis. As in other such units on race, socialist feminism, and lesbian feminism, for example, entire discursive practices—with languages and forms of analysis all their own—were being imported for a week or two at a time in order to give students a way of understanding the necessarily interdisciplinary nature of feminist inquiry. In each case I felt the inadequacy of the attempts to maintain the integrity of the feminist questions as well as the loss of subtlety in the presentation of questions of class, race, gender, and psychoanalysis. By now I have taught feminist theory intermittently at four different institutions over a period of 15 years; still I am perplexed and provoked by these complications.

My desire to think pedagogically about the knot of psychoanalysis and feminism stems not only from the fact that this is an area where a form of expertise is being watered down for pedagogical reasons, but also because it

Creating an Inclusive College Curriculum: A Teaching Sourcebook from the New Jersey Project. Copyright © 1996 by Teachers College, Columbia University. All rights reserved. ISBN 0-8077-6282-2 (pbk), 0-8077-6283-0 (cloth). Prior to photocopying items for classroom use, please contact the Copyright Clearance Center, Customer Service, 222 Rosewood Drive, Danvers, MA 01923, USA, telephone 508-750-8400.

is in this unit that I have encountered the greatest resistance from students. The politics that have brought them to a feminist classroom in the first place are such that they are not reluctant to engage their unexamined racist or class-based ideas, nor their homophobia. However, when it comes to their own psychosexual present as rooted in familial history as a gendered subject, there is the apparent belief that they operate in some realm of pure choice. There, ideology does not seem to count. Some of my surprise comes from the fact that although they are willing to work hard to gain a sense of what feminist theory is, this hard work reaches its limit when we arrive at psychoanalysis.

This kind of difficult moment I find useful in any class, and in the feminist class, even more so. This is often the moment when liberal goodwill and the cultural inheritance of individualism can be seen to fall short of what feminism asks us to think. The tension that this demand presents to me as a teaching and writing feminist coalesces with how the teaching of psychoanalytic ideas can all too easily be subsumed by concerns that may leave little behind in the form of radical residue—which returns me to my focus and my task in this imaginary classroom: the disclosure of the subject who does not or cannot know all of what she speaks.

THE PLACE OF HISTORY IN A THEORY COURSE

Among the problems in teaching psychoanalysis is the fact that most students come to such a class replete with received ideas. They have heard about the Oedipus complex, castration, and penis envy, and what's more, they have taken a psychology class where they have already made up their minds about Freud. They also believe that they know why psychoanalysis can serve only as a repressive tool where women are concerned. It is as if in the space of a single class we must replay the history of contemporary feminism from Firestone to Dinnerstein. This is, in fact, one of the ways I have worked in this class; preceding the unit on psychoanalysis was one on early writings in the contemporary women's movement. In one of the institutions where I first taught feminist theory, there was the wish that this course be historical in content and focus. Although I firmly believe that this is important and even necessary, it is nevertheless clear that if the historical aspects of the development of feminist theory are to be given real time and study, a semester is not enough. What is most valuable in unfolding a historical outlook is that it elucidates students' understanding of the workings of ideology so that feminism of the late 19th-century United States could speak forcefully of certain issues, such as protective legislation, but hardly at all of others, such as female sexuality.

Yet I wonder if such frameworks are not more properly those of a history of feminism and not those of a course on theory. It is power that a course on theory must directly address, and to develop a thoroughgoing analysis of questions of power and authority as they permeate feminist issues is no small task for a semester. This is why I think that the better place to begin a course on feminist theory would be with *The Second Sex* (Beauvoir, 1953); indeed, this has become my rule of thumb in recent years. Beauvoir's use of Hegelian dialectics and Sartrean existentialism enables feminist discourse to explore the relations between power and authority that predominate in feminist theory of the 1970s and later. Although we may take Beauvoir's perspective as idiosyncratic where the body is concerned, or too steeped in her Catholic middle history, or too faithful to Sartrean notions of how we experience others, there is no one thinker whose stated goal was to anatomize the situation of the female subject and who has done as much to probe that experience of repeated encounters with the self as cultural construct.

Students invariably find Beauvoir hard work, but work that is worth all the trouble and opens the terrain of feminist theory as a vast one. It demonstrates amply the interdisciplinary nature of women's studies and the political context that remains fundamental to the course itself. Even Beauvoir's Eurocentrism can be marshaled for later discussions of where feminist theory has taken turns that Beauvoir was not in a position to draw out. It is precisely the fact that this is not a polemical work, but rather a diagnostic one, that makes its comprehensive quality stunning both in what it manages to do and in what the absence of historical necessity made it impossible for it to do.

The importance of spending a generous amount of time on psychoanalytic questions has to do with the access it gives us to considering power and authority through language, sexed subjectivity, and the reproduction of familial groups as they are constructed by, around, and for us. If we begin with Beauvoir, then Juliet Mitchell (1974; Mitchell & Rose, 1985) and Nancy Chodorow (1979) are necessary stopping points in the turns this debate takes in the effort to salvage the psychoanalysis that was too hastily thrown overboard. Jane Gallop's (1982; 1990) and Jessica Benjamin's (1988) works further complicate the psychoanalytic traditions from which feminism continues to import the shape of many of its questions about subjectivity, particularly the construction of femininity; that is, whereas Mitchell and Chodorow draw the road maps of neo-Freudian (i.e., Lacanian) psychoanalysis and object-relations theory, respectively, Gallop and Benjamin render those maps topographical. For all their complexity, none of these theorists maps a future, though they all are thinking in the clear service of change. And if, for all these theorists, the family is the basic crucible of gender, none imagines a structure changed as much as it already is in terms of single-parent households—gay, lesbian, and straight—or currently proliferating adoptive and reproductive practices.

If sex is to occupy a place in the list that includes race and class, and is to do so in a meaningful way, then we cannot do without psychoanalytic thought, which offers us ways to navigate the complexities of what sex is as lived reality. Like the multifaceted ways we experience ourselves as members of a race, ethnic group, and class, and how we are placed as to privilege or marginality, so we are signed and learn our signatures as subjects who are becoming women or men. The "or" counts heavily here, because although masculinity and femininity may be only words to denote the borders of a spectrum, for the purposes of everyday life, we are also asked to be definitively men or women. And it is from this position that we learn where we are or may be in relation to lines of power, fields of force in the family, in the schools, and on the streets.

THE RISKS OF PERSONAL EXPERIENCE

The classroom is a predictable site for a situation of collective and individual transference. This is underscored in the feminist classroom, given the personal, interpersonal, and intrapsychic material that surfaces over a semester, no matter the kind of course. And then there is resistance to the methods and issues of psychoanalysis, some of which needs to be marshaled to question a discipline that has historically done a great deal of harm to women and their sense of possibilities in everyday life. But before psychoanalysis can be used oppositionally, against itself, there is much to be learned from the ways it asks us to think about how we are constructed women and men out of female and male—in a world where we *must* occupy such positions, though they may not suit us. It is in order to examine the ill-suitedness of such naming that psychoanalysis offers students some potential byways.

The teacher in the (feminist) classroom, by virtue of being in a position of authority, is already cast in proximity to masculinity, identified as it is with power in our culture. This is a problem that can and must be actively and creatively manipulated for the purposes of dealing with subjectivity, entitlement, and authority and their enactment in language in the classroom. Although this may be true in any classroom, it is true in the feminist theory classroom with its own inflection; here it becomes the area where our place as sexed speaking subjects is under direct interrogation, redoubling its significance and its practice. It is not only the psychosexual material of analysis that students tend to resist; it is also an epistemology based on acts, symptoms, experiences. The access to the signification that such moments breach suggests that we ourselves, not only our writings or our opinions, are subject to interpretation. For many students, the channel to the private that psycho-analysis opens seems to be an invasion, an intrusion in a culture that places a great deal of ostensible value on the inviolability of the private. Here was one of feminism's earliest critiques—bringing into the public the privatized worlds of women's lives—and still we are caught in its grip as part of a di-chotomy that we may wish to preserve.

To enter into a discussion of psychoanalysis in the classroom situates us in a narrative situation; that is, it invokes some of the stories we do not even tell ourselves but are nevertheless stories we all share—the ones we were told again and again so we might properly tell ourselves what it would mean to be girls or boys, women or men. These are the stories of the knowledge of differences, tools for decoding the world and those in it. Where psychoanaly-sis is concerned, the difference that has traditionally mattered the most is anatomical difference and its interpretation into sex, sexuality, and gender. The enterprise of feminist theory is where these conversations, debates, and dialogues on gender, power, and authority coalesce.

The rich and now long debates on language and sexuality have made evident the importance of psychoanalytic thinking within feminist inquiry. The archaeological work of analysis—thinking backward, not developmen-tally—is an indispensable tool in these investigations. Lacanian psychoanaly-sis has come to have the importance it does because of its insistence on the subject *in* language who is also subject *to* language. The arena of the family, whatever its morphology, remains the primary one where our relations to language, power, and authority are staged. Object-relations theory would in-sist on the encounters among and between subjects on this stage.

I spoke earlier of resistance to psychoanalysis in the feminist theory class; among those resistances is that to knowledge, and also to knowledge of our limitations. Using Beauvoir as a starting point is useful because of her emphasis on the burden of freedom. Freedom and resistance need to be accommodated in the feminist classroom. It has been my experience over the years in theory classes that the students who are the most likely, willing, and eager to take on such responsibility are those who have already realized that this hard work is worth doing. And they may know this labor because privi-lege has not been theirs—whether the privilege of skin, class, or heterosexu-ality.

As a result of exploring the rhetoric of desire and the function of lan-guage as a field for our proximity to or distance from power, it also becomes clear how the body remains the medium through which we experience our-selves as gendered. Although language and sexuality exceed the body's forms, psychoanalysis offers routes by which we may interpret the ramifications of early discipline of that medium and its expressions. We ought not to lose sight of the fact that this body is marked by factors other than sex distinctions. It is the task of the feminist theory class to array those perspectives that are necessary for a rich and complex understanding; psychoanalysis is a necessary method in the models we use to broach questions of theory, feminist or other.

REFERENCES

Beauvoir, S. de. (1953) *The second sex* (H. M. Parshley, Trans.). New York: Knopf.

Benjamin, J. (1988). *The bonds of love: Feminism and the problem of domination.* New York: Pantheon.

Chodorow, N. (1979). *The reproduction of mothering: Psychoanalysis and the sociology of gender.* London: University of California Press.

Gallop, J. (1982). *The daughter's seduction: Feminism and psychoanalysis.* Ithaca, NY: Cornell University Press.

Gallop, J. (1990). *Thinking through the body.* New York: Columbia University Press.

Mitchell, J. (1974). *Psychoanalysis and feminism.* New York: Vintage.

Mitchell, J., & Rose, J. (Eds.). (1985). *Feminine sexuality: Jacques Lacan and the ecole freudienne.* New York: Norton.

14

Using Intuition, Emotion, and Personal Story to Teach Multicultural Literature

Sally Hand, Antoinette Liquori, Belkis Petrus, and Ellen Romain

Sally

Teaching an Introduction to Literature course to a special class of adult learners in the fall semester of 1992 gave me an unusual opportunity to demonstrate once again that intuition, emotion, and personal story are effective ways to approach the rational analysis of literature, especially literature of different cultures. I welcomed the chance to start afresh with students who were not exclusively from the United States and who had been away from traditional academic methodology for several years. Although all had strong personal reactions to the literature read, most of them had never formally analyzed literature, and those who had were put off by the impersonality of "critical" analysis. I realized that using intuition, emotion, and personal story would dispel the students' fears, for they would already understand a good deal before moving on to the more formal rational analysis, even if the literature was not from their own culture.

I designed the course to emphasize multiculturalism and to utilize the students' rich life experiences. The text I chose was the anthology *Literature and Society,* edited by Pamela Annas and Robert Rosen, a diversity of literary voices, differing in gender, age, ethnicity, sexual preference, and social class. Not everything worked equally well. The class was too homogeneous and too small. We would have liked more ethnic and gender diversity and enough students to divide into culturally mixed groups of five to eight people, the ideal number for discussion. We did have the benefit, however, of the participation of two men during the semester, John Giaimo, academic counselor for the adult learner program, and Timothy Jameson, an English graduate assistant who taught *Death of a Salesman* while I was in London. At times, the students thought that I went too fast and did not give them enough choice in what literature was discussed. What did work well, however, was my initial approach to the literature through intuition, emotion, and personal story.

For the first time in years, I assigned journals. The three women in the class, who had been out of school from 4 to 12 years, took to the idea of journal writing as something that they were already doing or as an interesting experiment. I stipulated that their journals were to be repositories for their emotional responses to the literature and its relevance, when appropriate, to their own lives and the world around them. In this chapter, each of the three women in the class analyzes a particularly affecting story or poem that helped her assimilate an earlier repressed experience into a richer, fuller understanding of herself and her relation to others and of the literary passage under discussion. Toni, a career woman in her early 20s living in the family home, discusses her identification with her father's struggle to keep the family going during difficult economic times in reading Robert Hayden's poem "Those Winter Sundays" (Annas & Rosen, p. 161). Belle, a Cuban American housewife and mother, analyzes the genesis of her overwhelming reaction to Maxine Hong Kingston's autobiographical story "No Name Woman" (Annas & Rosen, pp. 364–373) in her own wrenching separation in 1966 from her family in Cuba. Ellen, wife and mother and nursing student, describes her resolution of the dual claims of the intuitive and the scientific self in reading the final passage of Pamela Zoline's short story, "The Heat Death of the Universe" (Annas & Rosen, pp. 1156–1167). Finally, we analyze together the nature of the class assignments and the class environment that encouraged intuitive learning.

Toni

"Those Winter Sundays" reminds me so much of my father. From the first time I read this poem, it touched my heart and brought me back to an experience I had as a little girl. My father had lost his job and was out of work for

4 years. During that time we continued to be a happy family. There was no panic. We always made out one way or another. My mother stayed at home with us. Today, if I were in my mom's shoes, I could go out to work and no one would think anything about it, but at that time, a mother was expected to stay home and look after the family while the father looked for work. My brother and sister delivered newspapers and had after-school jobs. My sister had a savings account and bought clothes for herself and for me. I can't honestly recall ever wanting for anything. Our table always had food on it, our backs were clothed, and Christmas was still special. But I didn't fully appreciate the sacrifice. The line "speaking indifferently to him" reminded me of one Christmas when I told my parents I did not like the stereo they had given me and made them feel terrible. I wish I could shake that memory, and my father says that it still makes him feel bad whenever he thinks about it. But as the speaker in Hayden's poem says:

> What did I know, what did I know
> of love's austere & lonely offices.
> (Robert Hayden, "Those Winter Sundays")

At the time I was too young to offer help. Now that I'm old enough, I feel that I'm still not doing enough. Since then my father has gotten us all back on our feet. Even today when my mother and I both work, my father works 7 nights a week. When I get up in the morning, my mom has already gone to work and my father is usually awake and doing the daily housework. Although we know that he works hard, I'll admit that sometimes we take him for granted and we rarely think to thank him. Sometimes I can see the need for a day off in his face. Even on holidays, he is still working around the house. It seems as if he's always working but never catching up; some new expense sets him back. Sometimes I feel guilty for having time to myself. I feel like I'm part of the reason for keeping the ends from meeting. There's my college tuition, high phone bills, and little extras that my paycheck won't cover. The line, "Sundays too my father got up early" sums it all up. Sunday is a day of rest, except for Dad.

Belle

On the advice of Professor Hand, we have been keeping journals on the short stories and poems that we are assigned to read—not so much on the content, but on the emotional chord that they strike. Well, on September 23, Maxine Hong Kingston's "No Name Woman" struck a chord in me! I wrote in my journal that day:

I just finished reading "No Name Woman," and I find myself very sad, almost in tears. I'm mournful for this woman who endured so much and ultimately took her life and her child's. As I'm writing I feel shaky, in my hands and in my heart. Perhaps it's because of my lack of knowledge of Chinese cultures that I find her treatment so horrible. I could never do this, or allow this to be done to my daughter, or my sister! I am glad Maxine Kingston wrote about her aunt, but I'm upset now and I can't write anymore today.

When our class met the next day, we discussed the story and I read a passage aloud. But when I got to the part where the aunt is being cursed and rejected by her family and culture because she is having an illegitimate baby, I had to stop and let someone else in our small group read.

Yet when we decided to write an article about our class experience, I chose to write on "No Name Woman." Why Maxine Kingston's story about her aunt, someone I don't know, brought up such deep emotion in me was unclear at the time. Was there something in my life, past or present, that was brought out by this woman whose existence—even her name—was blotted out from the family memory? Then our teacher mentioned displacement. Oh yes, I know what that is!

I was 4 ½ when my immediate family had to leave Cuba suddenly for the United States in 1966. It was early in the morning on a gray, rainy day. The mood in the house was just as somber. On that last day in Cuba, I cannot recall packing or even loading the car, but I have a vivid memory of our family and the good-byes we said in front of our house that morning. That was when I knew I would not be back. I didn't like this adventure anymore. It wasn't fun and was happening too fast. I was frightened. The cousins I was raised with were like siblings to me. My aunts and uncles gave me so much attention and love. I loved the feeling of belonging to this big, loving family. Now I was being pried away, and there was nothing I could do about it. I was helpless, and my mother couldn't help, for she was devastated.

But what does Maxine Kingston's aunt have to do with me? Is that me feeling alone at the age of 4? I don't think so. I did not know then what a brave and final decision my parents had made. I was 4 and just wanted everything to stay the same. I think it is me feeling my mother's anguish; I was too young to understand but not to "feel" her pain. Kingston's image of the once beloved aunt rejected and banished by her family and the Chinese culture for circumstances beyond her control revived memories of my mother's separation from her beloved home and family in Cuba. Mom must have been 30 then, the age I am now. And I don't know if I could be as brave as she was then. After all, she had lived her 30 years with these wonderful people. All that she was and is today is intertwined with them. I felt her pain when I was 4 and must have put those feelings away in the back of my mind.

Today, as a 30-year-old woman and mother, I am better able to deal with and digest the emotions I felt as a young child. I can understand now the reason for my parents' decision to flee Cuba 26 years ago. I can see it as the act of sacrifice and bravery that it was. Recently, my parents were reunited with their Cuban siblings. Although the love and memories are just as strong, the cultural divide between them after 25 years of separation is almost as great as what my parents experienced in coming to America. Cuba is still a country in turmoil and in a severe economic state. I can only hope for her and her people's liberation soon. But my home and my mother's home is America, and I would not trade America for anything. Thank you, Maxine Kingston, for writing about your aunt and giving her recognition. And thank you, Mom, for everything.

Ellen

As a young mother of two, I know full well the anxiety, frustration, and, yes, confusion of being a wife, mother, lover, and chief bottle washer. Many days, I am left with no room for me. Some days I feel confined to a box of schedules. Other days I feel split between needs and desires, both for myself and for my family. This cramping and stretching leaves me frayed and worn. Bone tired and frazzled, I feel, at times, ready to snap. But somehow, I manage to hold it all together with a fine silver thread. I decided to return to school, not solely as a career move or for monetary gain but as a means of building on something in me that I felt was lacking. I wanted to tone up and shape my intellectual muscles. I felt that this would strengthen that silver thread.

On first reading Pamela Zoline's "The Heat Death of the Universe," I was irritated and troubled. The short story seemed to be a vulture picking at my sore spots. Here was Sarah, a "vivacious and intelligent young wife and mother, educated at a fine Eastern college, proud of her growing family," who felt just as trapped as I did and was even "occasionally given to obsessions concerning Time/Entrophy/Chaos and Death." This frightened me. I wanted to shake off this feeling of entrapment, move on, forget about it. I didn't want to face it. My journal entry shows my denial:

> I hope we move on to a new subject soon. I feel as if the stagnancy of the material is stagnating my mind. I've been there already; I've visited that place; I don't want to live there. I've managed to escape that prison and I don't want to go back. I've moved on in my life; I'm active in

body and mind. I came to school to learn new things, experience new experiences. I'm tired of dredging up the past, picking through the ruins. I want to move forward.

But through the study of this story, I came to realize just what it was that Sarah was trying to tell me. She opened my eyes to the fact that, like her, I was torn between two parts of my own nature: "Sometimes, at extremes, her Body seemed to her an animal on a leash, taken for walks in the park by her Mind." Trying to choose one over the other, intuitive or rational, was tearing me apart. Sarah showed me that I was not a thermodynamically closed system in which expenditure of energy in one part inevitably leads to depletion somewhere else. If both sides of my nature are utilized, they will form a perfect whole whose parts cannot be separated or even separately discerned.

This revelation released me to aim higher than I had ever dreamed possible. I feel like Sarah at the end of the story. Finally emerging from the chaos of her own and her children's making, she throws the last eggs from the carton and serenely watches them arch "like a baseball, hit high against the spring sky, seen from far away . . . higher and higher in the stillness, hesitate at the zenith, then begin to fall away slowly, slowly through the fine, clear air." Science or imagination, concrete or ethereal—must a choice be made? To separate them in me would ultimately cause chaos, leading to "the heat death" of my personal universe.

The experience in this class reaffirms the validity of using intuition, emotion, and personal story to teach multicultural literature. Emotional response as an initial "way in" works especially well in understanding nontraditional and culturally diverse literature. A student "feels" what the literature is about long before she is able to rely on her rational analysis. Furthermore, her initial emotional response gives the student confidence by making her realize that she "knows" more than she thinks she does even though she cannot put it all together. Encouraging students to relate the literature to their personal experience is similar to "method" acting. The student relives a previous emotional experience in order to understand an unfamiliar character or situation. Although the study of multicultural literature is not a social science, a "liberal" (i.e., "progressive") education in the humanities should consider literature in relation to self and society. A primary political issue of the 1990s is the breakdown of nations into separate cultures. The difficulty—which the study of literature can help redress—is how to honor one's heritage in the smaller group while pledging allegiance to the larger whole. One of the things that came out of this course was an appreciation for difference. On the last day of class, Ellen, Toni, and Belle commented that they had enjoyed the diversity of cultures not only in the literature but also in the mutual exchange and celebration of cultural differences among the four of us.

REFERENCE

Annas, P., & Rosen, R. (Eds.). (1990). *Literature and society.* Englewood Cliffs, NJ: Prentice-Hall.

15

Journal Writing as Feminist Pedagogy

Ann L. Saltzman

In her 1982 article on teaching the psychology of women, Sharon Lord delineates 13 principles of a feminist teaching-learning model. Principle 11 reads:

> Providing vehicles outside the class through which students can deal with personal feelings and frustrations, such as journals, dyads, assertiveness training and growth groups, enhances the quality of classroom discussion. (pp. 78–79)

This chapter focuses on the use of the journal in a seminar called The Psychology of Women. In it, I propose that journal writing enhances additional feminist principles noted by Lord:

> *Principle 3:* Every individual in the class is a potential teaching resource. (p. 73)

> *Principle 5:* Effective human behavior in social interactions and within social systems is related to understanding the relationship between the personal and the political. (pp. 74–75)

> *Principle 8:* The subjective, personal experience of women (and men) is valid and important. (p. 77)

Principle 9: The student should ultimately assume responsibility for her own learning and growth. (p. 77)

Principle 10: Cooperation among students in pursuing learning objectives creates a more positive learning climate than does competition. (p. 78)

THE JOURNAL AS CENTRAL

Unlike Lord, I do not use the journal as an "outside-the-group" activity. True, students make journal entries outside of class, but 45 to 55 percent of the student's grade is based on the journal. Thus it is a major evaluative component of the course.

Journal entries are made for each class session and ideally include a summary, analysis, and critique of assigned readings, class discussions, and class process (including the instructor's role). Personal reactions are also encouraged. Frequently students include comments that they were unable to make in class due to either time constraints or anxiety over how others would respond. The journals are rich and reflect the diversity of the students' experiences.

A community journal is compiled of anonymous entries excerpted from individual journals (choosing the most diverse entries available), organized by theme. (Students may indicate in their journals those entries that they do not wish to share even anonymously.) I try to include at least one entry from each student. In this way, the personal experiences of students are validated: these experiences are important enough to appear in print (Principle 8).

Students' experiences are also validated through personal connections with the readings. Their experiences validate theory; theory validates their experiences. An example is the following entry from a student who relates her encounter with psychotherapy to the assigned readings for the day:

> This class concentrated on the different therapies available to people who seek help. . . . Toward the end of class . . . we talked about how it is important for a woman to investigate the different types of therapy until she finds a type that she feels most comfortable with [Task Force on Consumer Issues, 1981]. . . . I saw a psychologist in high school. . . . I do not know what model her therapy was part of or why my parents chose her as opposed to someone else. All I know is that she was terrible. She made me feel like a terrible person. I finally asked if I could stop seeing her after she fell asleep on me. . . . In reference to Stiver's [1985] article on therapists and how much they should care for a pa-

tient, I must say that I found it uncomfortable that she didn't appear to care about me in the least.

The community journal also allows each student to serve as a teaching-learning resource (Principle 3). Three themes may be discerned from students' entries about the community journal. First, reading diverse opinions about the same material fosters new insights into the material. Second, reading others' entries helps students clarify their own reactions:

> I really enjoyed the community journal. . . . Many of the passages were able to explain a feeling that I had but had not been able to verbalize. I think it really increased my understanding of the course content.

Third, reading others' reactions brings home the reality that not all women agree on vital issues. The following entry was written by a student who is a feminist activist and spends most of her time with other feminist activists:

> I think that it is a wonderful idea to have excerpts from different journals. A lot of the things that the other women wrote just didn't get said in class. I particularly found the entries on "images of women" and on "lesbian/lesbian mothering" really interesting because both are controversial topics. Although I don't agree with some of the things (especially some of the comments on lesbianism), it was certainly good for me to read them. I sometimes feel that for me, one of the dangers is losing sight of the "outside world." Living . . . in Womyn's Concerns House . . . I'm sure that just about everyone in the house would write the same things that I've written in the journal. We all have similar views. . . . It's important for me to be reminded of other views, and not completely lose myself in my idealistic, academic world.

This entry, which communicates that differences between and among the women are being noted but not being judged, was included in the next community journal. As noted in the journal entry below, this helps create a sense of community in the classroom. Students view themselves as members of a collective enterprise in which they are working together and not against one another (Principle 10):

> I like the idea of the community journal . . . because it makes me feel more a part of a team than an individual against the class. I like finding out that others have reactions to and opinions of the material that are the same as or different from mine. . . . I love it when other people share experiences that are related to the material we're working on.

As students struggle with course material, they begin to see how women's psychological experiences are shaped by the socioeconomic and political structures of society. Although this awareness is not a direct result of keeping a journal, the journal serves to inscribe this awareness. Further, the community journal offers one more opportunity for this awareness to be articulated, as the following entry about women and eating disorders documents:

> As I sit down to write this journal entry, I cannot help but relate some interesting statistics I have recently come upon. Women own about 1 percent of the world's property, and 10 percent of the world's wages are earned by women; however, two thirds of the world's work is done by women. Any rational person would see some sort of discrepancy between these figures. Why is it that women do so much yet have so little? Why haven't they power enough to say "Stop" or "No more"? The issue really comes down to one of control, and that is how I will make the transition to today's topic of eating disorders. . . . We have discussed in class, in many different contexts, the many types of situations in which women's control (or lack of it) has surfaced. I am not sure how much control anyone really has over his or her life, but it seems to me as if women have less control over the things outside themselves . . . be it property, the job or wage situation, or opportunities for advancement. Women don't have land, but they have their bodies. They can regulate what may come in—how much or how little and how often.

As the semester progresses, women begin to assume responsibility for their own learning and what they will do with that learning (Principle 9). Once again, although the journal may not be the critical causal factor in the development of this responsibility, it provides a written reminder that we must each find a way to continue to learn. The following entry addresses the question of whether the purpose of Psychology of Women is to advocate scholarship about women or to foster advocacy for women in the society (university). The writer recognizes that she is neither a great scholar nor a political activist. Still, she can use the new knowledge:

> For some people in the course, the newfound knowledge . . . represents a forum for advocacy to bring about change in our society. Further, . . . there continues to be material for scholars to research and study. Although both of these activities are very important to the future of the psychology of women, I will personally do something else with the knowledge I've gained in these 3 months. I honestly think I have developed an incredible awareness of the "way things are" and will no longer accept them without questioning. If I cannot change the world by de-

veloping some new therapy or marching on Washington, at least I can help myself better find the person I want to be.

EVALUATING JOURNALS

Finally, Lord's 10th feminist principle notes that "cooperative learning is fostered through the use of a criterion-referenced rather than a norm-referenced evaluation system" (p. 78). To this end, journals are evaluated on whether the writer has demonstrated an understanding of the psychological principles involved, whether all the critical points are addressed, and whether the entry demonstrates an active engagement with the material (new questions are posed, analyses are extended, constructive critiques of the concepts are offered). Students are not judged against one another but on what they are doing with the material under discussion.

SOME WORDS OF CAUTION

Although journal writing provides a rich growth experience for students, the use of journals in the way that I have proposed is a time-intensive endeavor for faculty. It takes time to read and respond to each individual's journal and more time to compile the excerpts. Thus, I would not recommend that faculty adopt my suggestions unless they have relatively small classes. The maximum registration for my seminars in The Psychology of Women is 16.

Further, journals aid faculty in keeping track of classroom process. One learns who is happy with the course, who is unhappy, who is irritated by whom. This information is invaluable for defusing possible group polarizations. However, it is not always easy to hear what students really think and feel. In addition to learning about students' personal problems (e.g., who suffers from an eating disorder), one also learns about students' ideological positions, which may or may not match the instructor's. For example, one learns who is pro-choice and who is anti-choice. I continue to struggle with the correct way to deal with these differences.

REFERENCES

Lord, S. (1982). Teaching the psychology of women: Examination of a teaching-learning model. *Psychology of Women Quarterly, 7,* 70–80.

Stiver, I. (1985, June). Psychotherapy's uncaring language. *APA Monitor,* 5.

Task Force on Consumer Issues in Psychotherapy in the Association for Women in Psychology, Federation of Organizations for Professional Women. (1981). *Women and psychotherapy: A consumer handbook.* Washington, DC: Author.

Syllabi and Narratives

16

Change in Societies: An Interdisciplinary Approach to Teaching Modern History

Lois Fichner-Rathus

In the spring semester of 1994, Trenton State College launched a new course in the history of the modern era, required of all second-semester students. Although the course had had a pilot run a year earlier, its present form was radically different—transformed over the intervening months by a faculty development team committed to the complete integration of gender and diversity issues. The result bespeaks an attempt to teach what is missing from existing history, to teach from a variety of voices.

ABOUT THE COURSE

Change in Societies is one course in a three-course interdisciplinary core sequence required of all students entering Trenton State College in and after September 1993. It is second in the core sequence, preceded by Humanity: Ideas and Ideals and followed by Society, Ethics, and Technology. Change in Societies is a course on the history of the modern era, from the 16th-century Spanish conquest of Mexico to the end of the cold war and the new world (dis)order in our times. Historical change is the overarching theme of the course, and case studies of how change was effected in specific societies at certain moments in time provide the framework for the course. The case studies were selected with two goals in mind: first, to support a history course that is sensitive to issues of gender and multiculturalism, and second, to provide alternative perspectives on historical events that shaped or changed societies. For example, the conquest of Mexico is examined from the points of view of the conquerors and the vanquished; the British presence in Africa is studied from the divergent perspectives of the colonists and the indigenous Africans. The role and plight of women across time and cultures are woven throughout the course, with special attention to changes effected by the women's movement in the United States.

The "delivery system" for course content consists of a mass lecture, held once a week in the college theater, followed by a seminar section that also meets once a week. The case studies are presented in the lecture setting by Trenton State faculty members and some guest lecturers. The seminar sections, in which the material is delved into in greater depth and learning is otherwise facilitated, are taught by full-time and adjunct faculty. The lecture accommodates 500 to 600 students per session and is offered in two sessions on Mondays; seminar sections have a cap enrollment of 25 students and meet at a variety of times over the course of the week.

STUDENT COMPOSITION AND LEVEL

For the most part, the students enrolled in the interdisciplinary core are first-year students, approximately 1,000 in number. The individual courses of the core are also open to students as electives, and some have used Change in Societies to fulfill the general education core requirement for history. Because the course is required of the entire first-year class, the demographics of the course population are the same as the demographics of the class and the college at large. Trenton State College is a liberal arts undergraduate institution of approximately 5,000 students, 60 percent of whom are women.

INCORPORATION OF GENDER, RACE, AND CLASS INTO THE COURSE

The entire course is constructed with consideration of issues of gender, race, and class. One of its two main themes (in addition to how historical change comes about) is the historical and cultural problem of the human family divided against itself. This problem is examined from the perspectives of both unifying elements (universal ideologies, world trade, cultural exchange, and transnational identities) and, perhaps more importantly, divisive ones (conflicts of empire, nation, gender, class, race, and ideology).

In their individual lectures, professors have been mandated to include material on gender and diversity in their presentations of case studies of change. Thus, students are sensitized to the roles of women in these societies as well as the effect—for better or for worse—of societal change on the female population.

In addition, the course outline for Change in Societies features a lecture on American reform movements—including civil rights and labor reform—a lecture on the women's movement, and a slide presentation on politics and protest in contemporary art that focuses on the works of women and artists of color.

STUDENTS' REACTIONS TO THE COURSE

Students' reactions to the course have been mixed. Although most seem to recognize and appreciate the efforts of the course development team to design a history course that respects alternative viewpoints, is enriched by multicultural content, and is sensitive to gender issues, we have had our share of critical commentary. Some students have described the course as one that engages in "white, Western male-bashing," and others have offered the opposite view that our treatment of history is "racist." Still others wonder whether the emphasis on gender and cultural diversity is just a smoke screen that may, in practice, deepen divisions between the sexes and among cultural groups.

Although the course coordinators have met with the relatively few groups of concerned students to explain or defend their position, they have not wavered from their commitment to the syllabus and course outline. Change in Societies has, at its heart, an informed and critical assessment of history. At times the lectures may appear to bend over backward to call attention to gender and cultural diversity. We concur with the position of some historians: When there has been overemphasis on one side, it is necessary to compensate by overemphasizing the other side.

MODIFICATION OF COURSE CONTENT

The desire to construct a course that teaches what is missing from, or deemphasized in, existing history was the guiding principle that led to the course in its current form. Yet the course outline used for the first time in spring 1994 grew from anguished debate over what was important to a history learning experience for first-year students.

The initial course structure was quite different. It was first a two-semester sequence that began with theories of evolution and ended with the collapse of the world order in the late 20th century. It had a heavy Western emphasis and did not include lectures on social and labor reform and the women's movement. Moving to a one-semester course (primarily for financial and logistical reasons) offered the opportunity for a complete reconsideration of the course content. Historians and social scientists on the development team often propounded conflicting views concerning the "responsibility" of teaching history. Most ultimately agreed that the responsibility of teaching history at the close of this century would have to include alternative perspectives.

And so it is that alternative perspectives and consideration of gender and diversity became the foundation of the course. Not only are students introduced to the "monuments" or key moments in world history revolving around the theme of change, but they also come to understand that the same event can be described quite differently depending on the perspective of the witness to that portion of history. It is hoped that they will come to understand that history in general can be written in any number of ways and that their understanding of it must take all vantage points into account; it is important that they move mentally from the notion of "his-story" to the notion of "their-stories." It is hoped that learning to view history critically will translate to their study of other disciplines during their undergraduate tenure.

SYLLABUS FOR CHANGE IN SOCIETIES

Course Description

An examination of historical change in the modern epoch using case studies drawn from world history; topics include the conquest of Mexico, African and Asian responses to imperialism, European revolutions, American social movements, and 20th-century globalism.

Rationale

Having come to live in a global village where change is endemic, we cannot understand human development and behavior without close attention to major sources of change in the making of the modern and postmodern worlds. An approach that compares case studies of change from across the globe—Africa, the Americas, Asia, and Europe—promises to help students cope with endemic change and global challenges of the 21st century.

Central Questions

Topics are structured around ongoing investigation of two major issues:

1. *Change.* The question of how historical change comes about is examined through comparison of various models of change (conquest, challenge and response, revolution, reform, breakdown) in concrete historical circumstances.
2. *"Us and Them."* The problem of the human family divided against itself is examined from the perspectives of both *unifying* elements (universal ideologies, world trade, cultural exchange, transnational identities) and *divisive* ones (conflicts of empire, class, race, nation, ideology).

Topics

Topics are structured to encourage seminar leaders and lecturers to draw comparisons and contrasts:

1. *Conquest and Resistance.* What made Mesoamerica vulnerable to Hispanic conquest? By contrast, what permitted Indonesians to resist the penetration of Dutch culture?
2. *Challenge and Response.* The expansion of the West issued a universal challenge to the non-Western world, but the responses were as different as Africa is from the Middle East.
3. *Revolution and Reform.* The question of how ordinary people change the world, or fail to change it, is addressed through comparison of revolutions (Islamic, 18th-century liberal) and reform movements of the United States (women's rights, labor, civil rights).
4. *World (Dis)order.* What do we make of the 20th-century paradox—humanity united on a global scale as never before, yet every bit as divided between East and West, North and South, rich and poor, Muslim and Christian?

Enrichment

Slide lectures are presented on occasion, in which works of art pertinent to the topic are examined in their social, cultural, political, and historical contexts.

Readings

Selected with the beginning student in mind, readings are to be as enjoyable as they are instructive. Selections are drawn from literature, correspondence, essays, and historical scholarship. Efforts are also made to include a wide range of voices—Western and non-Western, upper and lower class, male and female. Whenever possible, these are put in dialogue with one another (for example, an Aztec account of the conquest of Mexico is contrasted with a Spanish one). (Weekly total: 50 pages; both primary and secondary sources.)

Resources

Seminar leaders are expected to draw creatively on other resources, including television documentaries (for example, *Eyes on the Prize, Seeds of Change*), films (*The Return of Martin Guerre, Revolution*), and short handouts.

SCHEDULE OF CLASSES AND READINGS

Class 1	A Brief Introduction to Change in Societies. Read L. S. Stavrianos, *The World Since 1500: A Global History,* 4th ed. (Englewood Cliffs, NJ: Prentice-Hall, 1982), pp. 83, 155–159, 330–338, 511–522.
Class 2	The Aztec Conquest of Mexico. Read Carlos Fuentes, "The Rise and Fall of the Indian World," in *The Buried Mirror* (Boston: Houghton Mifflin, 1992), and Miguel Leon Portilla, selections from *The Broken Spears* (Boston: Beacon Press, 1962 and 1990).
Class 3	The Spanish Conquest. Read Bernal Dias Del Castillo, excerpts from *The Discovery and Conquest of Mexico* (New York: Farrar, Straus & Giroux, 1956).
Class 4	Traditional Indonesia. Read *Letters of a Javanese Princess,* ed. Hildred Geertz (New York: University Press of America, 1985).
Class 5	Indonesia and the Dutch. Read F. Roy Willis, "The Amsterdam of Rembrandt," in *Western Civilization: An Urban Perspective,* 3rd ed. (Lexington, MA: D. C. Heath, 1981).
Class 6	Traditional Africa. Read Chinua Achebe, *Things Fall Apart* (New York: Ballantine Books, 1959).
Class 7	Art and Belief in Traditional Africa.

Class 8   Africa and the West. Read Olaudah Equiano, "The In-
                   teresting Narrative of the Life of Olaudah Equiano, or
                   Gustavus Vassa, the African," in Richard Barksdale
                   and Kenneth Kinnamon, *Black Writers of America:
                   A Comprehensive Anthology* (New York: Macmillan,
                   1972); and Johann Von Lubelfing, "Johann Von Lu-
                   belfing's Voyage of 1599 to 1600," in Adam Jones, *Ger-
                   man Sources for West African History 1599–1669* (Weis-
                   baden, Germany: Franz Steiner, 1983).

Class 9   Islam and the West. Read Abd al-Rahman Jabarti, *Na-
                   poleon in Egypt: Al-Jabarti's Chronicle of the First Seven
                   Months of the French Occupation*, 1798, ed. Shmuel
                   Moreh (Princeton: Markus Weiner, 1993).

Class 10   Islamic Art.

Class 11   The Iranian Revolution. Read Richard W. Cottam,
                   "The Iranian Revolution," in *Shi'ism in Social Protest*
                   (New Haven, CT: Yale University Press, 1986); and
                   Simin Daneshvar, "Traitor's Deceit," in *Stories by Ira-
                   nian Women Since the Revolution* (Austin: Center for
                   Middle Eastern Studies at the University of Texas at
                   Austin, 1991).

Class 12   The French Revolution. Read Thomas Paine, excerpts
                   from "The Rights of Man," from *The Essential Thomas
                   Paine* (New York: Meridian, 1984); and Edmund Burke,
                   excerpts from *Reflections on the Revolution in France*
                   (Garden City, NY: Dolphin Books, 1961).

Class 13   The Industrial Revolution. Read Kevin Reilly, *The West
                   and the World: A Topical History of Civilization,* pp.
                   335–353, 535–536 (New York: HarperCollins, 1980);
                   Adam Smith, excerpt from *The Wealth of Nations,* ed.
                   Edwin Cannan (New York: Modern Library/Random
                   House, 1937); "The Seneca Falls Declaration of Senti-
                   ments and Resolutions, July 19, 1848," from Henry
                   Steele Commager, *Documents of American History,* 5th
                   ed. (New York: Appleton Century Crofts, 1949); and
                   Karl Marx and Friedrich Engels, "Manifesto of the
                   Communist Party," in *The Marx-Engels Reader,* 2nd

	ed., ed. Robert C. Tucker (New York: W. W. Norton, 1978).
Class 14	American Reform Movements. Read Russell H. Conwell, excerpts from *Acres of Diamonds* (Philadelphia: Temple University, 1959); and Mary Heaton Vorse, excerpt from *Labor's New Millions* (New York: Arno Press, 1969).
Class 15	Politics and Protest in Contemporary Art.
Class 16	The Women's Movement. Read Flora Davis, "The Opening Salvos," in *Moving the Mountain: The Women's Movement in America Since 1960* (New York: Simon & Schuster, 1991); Phyllis Schlafly, "Understanding the Difference," in *The Power of the Positive Woman* (New Rochelle, NY: Arlington House, 1977); and Gloria Steinem, "Words and Change," in *Outrageous Acts and Everyday Rebellions* (New York: Henry Holt, 1983).
Class 17	The Cold War Balance of Terror. Read John Lewis Gaddis, "Toward the Post-Cold War World," *Foreign Affairs,* Spring 1991 (Council on Foreign Relations, Inc.); and Henry Luce, "The American Century," *Life Magazine,* February 17, 1941, pp. 61–65.
Class 18	The New World (Dis)order. Read Joseph S. Nye, "What New World Order?" *Foreign Affairs,* Spring 1992 (Council on Foreign Relations, Inc.); George Bush, "The Possibility of a New World Order—Unlocking the Promise of Freedom," *Vital Speeches of the Day,* May 15, 1991; and William J. Clinton, "Address to the 48th Session of the United Nations General Assembly," September 27, 1993.

17

Africana Women: Two Decades of Evolving Historical Perspectives at Trenton State College

Gloria Harper Dickinson

During the more than two decades that Trenton State College has offered an African American studies course (AAS 280), the instructor, course content, department, and college—indeed the academy and world—have radically changed. Some of this change can be seen by comparing the initial 1973 Trenton State College catalog course description with the 1987 and 1993 revisions:

> 1973, AAS 280   History of the Black Woman
> The experiences of Black women in the United States from 1619 to the present. Contributions Black women have made to American society and the effect of white society upon Black women will be explored.

> 1987, AAS 280   History of the Black Woman
> This course is a cross-cultural survey of the lives and contributions of the women of Africa and of their descendants in North and South America and the Caribbean. Emphasis will be placed upon the elements of African culture that, when impacted by colonialism and/or the Atlantic slave trade, resulted in

similar types of resistance to oppression, and upon analogous cultural expressions among the women of these four locales.

1993, AFAM 280   Africana Women in Historical Perspective
This course is a cross-cultural survey of the lives and contributions of the women of Africa and of their descendants in North and South America and the Caribbean. Emphasis will be placed upon the elements of African culture that, when impacted by colonialism and/or the Atlantic slave trade, resulted in similar types of resistance to oppression, and upon analogous cultural expressions among the women of these four locales.

By appraising the evolution of names, structure, and content of Trenton State College's course on women of African descent, one can derive a modest historical overview of both the steadily increasing number of scholars engaged in diaspora women's studies and the sociopolitical and economic advances and changes among the global community of black women.

EARLY SURVEY COURSES

Structurally and pedagogically, the early 1970s History of the Black Woman imitated that era's Afro-American history survey courses. Both used what University of Washington professor James Banks (1989) calls "Level 1, The Contributions Approach" when defining the four levels of integration of ethnic content. He views these models' focus on heroes, holidays, and discrete cultural elements as the first and most simplistic level of curricular modification and urges further revisions.

Although in accord with the zeal and concerns of the era, the 1973 entry indicates how traditional canonical boundaries delimited the first version of History of the Black Woman. Among the course's restrictive parameters were that it began with the 1619 arrival of African indentured servants in Jamestown, Virginia, thus limiting study to U.S. residents, and that it relied exclusively on historical methodologies. Consequently, after paying 2 weeks' cursory tribute to an African heritage, I, like my predecessor, devoted the remaining 12 weeks to identifying great black "sheroes." Even the excitement surrounding the publication of Gerda Lerner's 1972 documentary history, *Black Women in White America,* turned to dependency. This rich biographical and documentary resource gradually became the axis around which the course design revolved.

In retrospect, it is clear that the original course used the "integrationist approach" that historian Rosalyn Terborg-Penn (1987) views as both the oldest and the most commonly used historical approach. She contends that "the integrationist approach seeks to identify what contributions black women have made to Western culture or looks at how black women have been passively victimized by the mainstream society." She further notes that since Lerner's editorial analysis uses a "white filter," "she [too often] ends up regarding her subjects as victimized black women" (pp. 45–50).

During the second half of the 1970s, as if with a portent of Banks's decade-later definition, scholarship about African American women moved on to "Level 2, The Additive Approach." According to Banks (1989), it is at this level that content, concepts, themes, and perspectives are added to the curriculum without changing its structure. AAS 280 changed in tandem with the interdisciplinary explosion of scholarship. The static catalog entry in no way reflects the massive annual revisions of course content that marked this period.

NATIONALIST THEORY

Unwittingly, the course was also being transformed in accord with the nationalist theory that Terborg-Penn would later define. According to her definition, "Nationalist theory revised the integrationist framework by eliminating the 'white filter' and by seeking to find what black women have done in their own communities or organizations to help themselves and others" (1987, p. 47). Nationalist theory approached the community from the "inside out," and Terborg-Penn cites Jeanne Noble's (1978) *Beautiful, Also, Are the Souls of My Black Sisters* (a text that became central to the Trenton State College course in its late 1970s transformation) as one of the earliest works of this type.

A second 1978 publication, Sharon Harley and Terborg-Penn's edited work, *The Afro-American Woman: Struggles and Images,* also became a key text. These works greatly enhanced the primarily biographical materials on which prior assignments had been based. Consequently, new themes and perspectives were added; the course was reconfigured into three sections:

Part 1. The Facts: A Historical Overview up to World War I
Part 2. The Myths: Moynihan, the Matriarchy, and the "Bad Black Woman"
Part 3. Exploding the Myths—Extending the Facts: Emerging Trends of the 20th Century

INTERNATIONAL AND INTERDISCIPLINARY PERSPECTIVES

By the early 1980s, the international dimensions of the field enhanced its rapidly growing interdisciplinary aspects. Without doubt, Filomena Chioma

Steady's seminal work *The Black Woman Cross-Culturally* (1981) marked the dawning of this "new era." Steady's definition of "an African brand of feminism" was closely followed by Alice Walker's definition of "womanism."[1] And with increasing disregard for conventional disciplinary or geopolitical boundaries, "womanist" scholars and scholarship burgeoned. Throughout the world, Africa's daughters "found their voices," thereby further stretching the boundaries of the "traditional" academic disciplines in which these scholars had been trained and degreed.

The subsequent changes in the course title and description clearly reflect both the impact and the importance of this international explosion of scholarship by and about women of the African diaspora.

It was during the 1980s that scholars progressed to what Banks (1989) calls "Level 3, The Transformation Approach." He says that "at Level 3, the structure of the curriculum is changed to enable students to view concepts, issues, events and themes from the perspective of diverse ethnic and cultural groups" (p. 192). Undeniably, the perspectives of diaspora women in Africa, Latin America, the Caribbean, Europe, and North America are diverse. However, Steady (1981) argues for an entirely new "internal" schema for measuring and assessing women of African ancestry. In her introduction, she identifies eight commonalities that unify diaspora women into a discrete entity. Foremost among these characteristics is an African heritage.

Inspired by Steady's hypothesis, the Association of Black Women Historians sponsored a conference that resulted in the publication of *Women in Africa and the African Diaspora* (Terborg-Penn, Harley, & Benton-Rushing, 1987). The conference and book brought together scholars from diverse disciplines and land masses; few, if any, regarded an internationalized, interdisciplinary "womanist" studies canon as an oxymoron.

By the end of the 1980s, Afro-German, Costa Rican, Afro-French, Afro-Dutch, Peruvian, Ecuadoran, Maori, and black British women had all made their presence known. In anthologies, novels, works of poetry, autobiographies, historical treatises, sociological studies, ethnomusicology, anthropology, jurisprudence, journalism, and countless other disciplines, they have been prolific and profound. Moreover, they have added tremendous credence to Steady's, Terborg-Penn's, and others' assertions with regard to the "connectedness" of diaspora women.

Two outcomes of the aforementioned initiatives were the new course description published in 1987 and the subsequent 1993 name change to African Women in Historical Perspective.

The course now has four areas of concentration—Africa, Latin America, the Caribbean, and Europe and North America. The migrations of diaspora women and the ways in which they preserve and pass on their African culture; cope with new environments; socialize their families; circumvent the restrictions of race, class, and gender; and celebrate their "womanist" characteristics now frame the course. Novels by African, Caribbean, and North American women are among the required readings. Although the growing body of scholarship makes it increasingly difficult to continue to cover all the topics, journals such as *Sage* and *Connections* and books such as *Wild Women in the Whirlwind: Afra-American Culture and the Contemporary Literary Renaissance* (Braxton & McLaughlin, 1990), *Radiance From the Waters* (Boone, 1987), *Daughters of Africa* (Busby, 1992), and *Notable Black American Women* (Smith, 1992) continue to affirm the direction in which this course has evolved.

As diaspora women have found their voices, Trenton State College's course has attempted to keep abreast of new scholarship and a changing world. Although the increased interdisciplinary and global approaches indicated by the syllabus revisions seem in accord with Terborg-Penn's analyses and Banks's stages of multicultural curriculum reform, it was not planned. Rather, the aforementioned changes reflected in the following syllabus are merely illustrative of the growth of diaspora women's studies as an arena of academic inquiry.

SYLLABUS FOR AFRICANA WOMEN IN HISTORICAL PERSPECTIVE

Description

This course is a cross-cultural survey of the lives and contributions of the women of Africa and their descendants in North and South America and the Caribbean. Emphasis will be placed upon the elements of African culture that, when subjected to the impact of colonialism and/or the Atlantic slave trade, resulted in similar types of resistance to oppression and analogous cultural expression among the women of these four locales.

Texts

Ba, Miriama. (1981). *So long a letter.* London: Heinemann.
Emecheta, Buchi. (1974/1983). *Second-class citizen.* New York: G. Braziller.
Giddings, Paula. (1984). *When and where I enter: The impact of black women on race and sex in America.* New York: Morrow.
Hurston, Zora Neale. (1978). *Their eyes were watching God: A novel.* Urbana: University of Illinois Press.
Morrison, Toni (Ed.). (1992). *Race-ing justice, en-gendering power.* New York: Pantheon Books.
Terborg-Penn, Rosalyn, Harley, Sharon, & Benton-Rushing, Andrea (Eds.). (1987).

Women in Africa and the African diaspora. Washington, DC: Howard University Press.

Warner-Vieyra, Myriam. (1987). *Juletane* (B. Wilson, Trans.). London: Heinemann Educational. (Original work published 1982).

Additional Readings

Steady, Filomena. (1981). *The black woman cross-culturally.* (on reserve)
Articles on reserve as assigned.

Book Critiques

Students will be expected to write a 2- to 3-page "reaction paper" for each of the assigned novels. *Do not* retell the story line or plot. Do provide your *reaction* and *opinion*. Support your ideas with examples from the text, assigned readings, and/or other appropriate sources. Paper #1 should compare and contrast African women writers' observations on the adaptability (or lack thereof) of traditional marriage patterns to Euro-American-influenced societies.

Oral History Project

The "oral tradition" has been an integral aspect of the cultural survival of African diaspora people. Women, often the "culture bearers" in these communities, have frequently "talked" their stories rather than "scribing" them. Western technocratic societies often discourage people from taking the time to tell and listen to these stories; too often women's stories are those most easily forgotten or dismissed. Yet their stories are one of our most valuable assets. To aid preservation initiatives, you will be required to complete the following assignment:

Choose a black woman, preferably at least two generations older than yourself, and record her story; use an audio or video recorder.

Step 1. Prepare a list of questions that reflect some of the topics and issues discussed in this class and your readings. Make sure that your questions stimulate detailed responses. Remember, African diaspora women are not likely to be accustomed to being asked about their lives and are likely to dismiss the importance of their experiences.

Step 2. Conduct the interview. Use the supplemental materials on oral history interview techniques to guide you. Allow at least 1 ½–3 hours. Try to select a relaxed setting with few distractions. Request and listen carefully to anecdotal stories, for example, trips "down South" to the Caribbean, dating, political events, childbirth, child rearing, health, discrimination, religion, civil rights activism, group membership.

Step 3. Create an 8-page paper from your findings that includes a summary of this woman's life, some demographic data, and an *analysis* of her experiences that reflects your understanding of the material covered in class. Use references to support and substantiate your analysis and opinion.

COURSE OUTLINE

Week 1	Overview of course
	Afrocentric & Eurocentric scholarship
	The status of the world's women
	Theoretical models for the study of "African feminism"

PART 1—AFRICA

African female origins of humanity:
Review of mitochondrial DNA, linguistic, and archaeological theories, theorists, findings

Week 2	The black woman as a figure in world history:
	Women leaders in ancient Kemet (Isis, Hapshetsut, et al.)
	Sub-Saharan women warriors/chiefs of state
	The black madonna—historical overview/European sites

| Week 3 | Cross-cultural models used to study African diaspora women: |
| | Dr. Filomena Steady's hypothesis regarding eight characteristics common to African diaspora women |

Week 4	The status of African women:
	Varying traditions in eight indigenous African societies
	Contemporary demographic data

THE MARGINALIZATION OF AFRICAN WOMEN

Economic marginality:
Review of literature on African women and work—in-

digenous patterns; contemporary patterns, urban &
rural

Week 5   Psychosocial marginality:
                      Historical overview of female genital mutilation—glob-
                      ally and in Africa
                      Contemporary activism
                      Neocolonial marginalization and resistance movements:
                      The impact of neocolonialism on African women's
                      lives—Angolan, Zimbabwean, and South African wom-
                      en's resistance movements

Week 6   Traditional African women artists:
                      The uses of women's art—visual & fiber artists; potters
                      Artistic marginalization:
                      Biographical data about prominent African women
                      writers
                      Feminist consciousness and African literary criticism
                      Paper due on fictional work by one or more African
                      women

                      PART 2—THE DIASPORA

Week 7   Diaspora women and slavery:
                      Women and slavery in Brazil and the Caribbean—sur-
                      vey history, resistance movements, and cultural continu-
                      ities
                      Antebellum U.S. women:
                      The status of freed black women
                      The status of enslaved women

Week 8   Perspectives on Brazil:
                      18th-century black women's organizations
                      Contemporary sacred and secular
                      organizations—*Candomble* and *Boa Morte*
                      Perspectives on Caribbean women and their literature:
                      The history and current status of Caribbean women—
                      cultural continuities; survey of women writers
                      Paper due on a work of fiction by a Caribbean woman
                      writer

Week 9   Midterm

PART 3—POST–CIVIL WAR NORTH AMERICA

Week 10   Educators and activists:
                F. E. W. Harper, I. B. W. Barnett, Mary McLeod Be-
                thune, M. C. Terrell, Rosa Parks, Fannie Lou Hamer,
                Nannie Burroughs, Marva Collins
                Working women:
                Historical overviews of black women's status, progress,
                struggles, accomplishments in agriculture, nursing, the
                military, domestic work, the professions

Week 11   Women organized for social change:
                Historical overview of black women's role as advocates
                for change in 19th- and 20th-century organizations of
                African American women and Euro-American women
                Women and the civil rights movement:
                Overview of key people and events during the civil
                rights era

Week 12   Politicians, politics, and activism:
                Overview of careers of prominent 20th-century African
                American female elected officials
                Womanists/activists/feminists:
                Survey of theoretical bases of "womanism" and "black
                feminism"
                Discussion of black women's rejection of Euro-
                American feminist models
                Historical overview of the activism emanating from the
                feminist and black feminist movements

Week 13   Visual and fiber artists:
                African antecedents of African American women's artis-
                tic creations
                Biographical sketches of famous 18th-, 19th-, and 20th-
                century artists/artisans
                Black women writers:
                Survey of prominent figures in each of the following
                genres: Slave narratives, fiction, poetry, drama, nonfic-
                tion, journalism, literary criticism
                Due: Critique on a work of fiction written by an Afri-
                can American woman

Week 14   Musicians and entertainers:
                   Historical overview of the participation of black women
                   in the music and entertainment industries
                   Survey of the perpetuation of, and resistance to, stereo-
                   typic images of African American women
                   Profiles of prominent contributors to these industries

Week 15   Male-female relationships, gender discrimination, sex-
                   ual harassment
                   Final Exam

NOTE

1. Alice Walker coined the term "womanist" in *In Search of Our Mothers' Gardens: Womanist Prose* (1983). The term is based on the warning that adult African
American women often direct toward girls whose behavior is deemed too "adult." In
such instances, girls are warned not to be too "womanish." Walker's discomfort with
defining herself as a (black) feminist was shared by many African diaspora women
who have since adopted the term for both scholarly and lay usage.

REFERENCES AND SELECTED BIBLIOGRAPHY

Alexander, Z., & Dewjee, A. (1984). *Wonderful adventures of Mrs. Seacole in many
     lands.* London: Falling Wall Press.
Banks, J. (1989). Integrating the curriculum with ethnic content: Approaches and
     guidelines. In Banks, J. A., & Banks, C. A. (Eds.), *Multicultural education: Is-
     sues and perspectives* (pp. 189–207). Boston: Allyn & Bacon.
Bell, R. P., Parker, B. J., & Sheftall, B. (1979). *Sturdy black bridges.* New York: An-
     chor, Doubleday Press.
Boone, S. (1987). *Radiance from the waters.* New Haven, CT: Yale University Press.
Braxton, J., & McLaughlin, A. (Eds.). (1990). *Wild women in the whirlwind: Afra-
     American culture and the contemporary literary renaissance.* New Brunswick, NJ:
     Rutgers University Press.
Bruner, C. H. (1983). *Unwinding threads: Writing by women in Africa.* London: Hie-
     nemann Educational Books.
Bryan, B., Dadzie, S., & Scafe, S. (1988). *The heart of the race: Black women's lives in
     Britain.* London: Virago Press.
Busby, M. (Ed). (1992). *Daughters of Africa.* London: Pantheon Books.
Bush, B. (1990). *Slave women in Caribbean society 1650–1838.* Kingston: Heinemann.
Christian, B. (1982). *Black feminist criticism.* New York: Pergamon Press.
Collins, P. H. (1990). *Black feminist thought.* New York and London: Routledge.

Davies, C. B., & Fido, E. S. (Eds.). (1990). *Out of the Kumbla: Caribbean women and literature.* Trenton, NJ: Africa World Press.

Davis, A. Y. (1981). *Women race and class.* New York: Random House.

Harley, S., & Terborg-Penn, R. (1978). *The Afro-American woman: Struggles and images.* Port Washington, NY: National University Publications.

Hull, G. T., Scott, P. B., & Smith, B. (1982). *But some of us are brave.* New York: Feminist Press.

Jones, J. (1985). *Labor of love, labor of sorrow.* New York: Vintage Books.

Learner, G. (1972). *Black women in white America: A documentary history.* New York: Pantheon Books.

Noble, J. (1978). *Beautiful, also, are the souls of my Black sisters.* Englewood Cliffs, NJ: Prentice-Hall.

Opitz, M., Oguntoye, K., & Schultz, D. (Eds.). (1992). *Showing our colors: Afro-German women speak out.* Amherst: University of Massachusetts Press.

Smith, J. C. (Ed.). (1992). *Notable black American women.* Detroit: Gale Research.

Steady, F. C. (1981). *The black woman cross-culturally.* Cambridge: Schenkman.

Sterling, D. (1984). *We are your sisters.* New York: W. W. Norton.

Stuckey, S. (1987). *Slave culture.* New York: Oxford University Press.

Terborg-Penn, R. (1987). African feminism: A theoretical approach. In R. Terborg-Penn, S. Harley, & A. Benton-Rushing (Eds.), *Women in Africa and the African diaspora* (pp. 45–50). Washington, DC: Howard University Press.

Terborg-Penn, R., Harley, S., & Benton-Rushing, A. (Eds.). (1987). *Women in Africa and the African diaspora.* Washington, DC: Howard University Press.

Walker, A. (1983). *In search of our mothers' gardens: Womanist prose.* New York: Harcourt Brace Jovanovich.

Washington, M. H. (1987). *Invented lives, narratives of black women 1800–1960.* New York: Anchor Press.

18

Immigrant Women in the New World: African and Caribbean Communities and Cultures

JoAnn Cunningham

COURSE PURPOSE AND CONTENT

The purpose of this course is to provide an in-depth study of the Caribbean immigrant women who reside in the inner cities and suburbs of the United States from Florida, up the eastern seaboard, and into the Boston area. The course was designed as a result of the recognized need for students to understand the Caribbean women who have had a significant impact on the population demographics in this country; to have knowledge of and appreciate the marvelous diversity of women in America; to have knowledge of the origin countries of Caribbean women; to understand U.S. immigration legislation and policies that affect the lives of so many immigrant women; to appreciate the role that immigrant women play in the economic structure of the United States; and to explore any existing correlations between immigrant legislation and economic trends in the United States and between economics in the countries of origin and economics in the United States.

It is important for students to understand the role that race, class, and gender play in the study of Caribbean immigrants to the United States for a number of reasons. First, women constitute a substantial proportion of Caribbean immigrants. Second, women constitute the majority of the numerous refugees around the world. Third, it has been established that the migration experience of women differs from that of their male counterparts. Fourth, the study of the historical origins of Afro-Caribbeans clarifies the identity of many Caribbean women.

The focus of the course is on Barbadian, Afro-Cuban, Haitian, and Jamaican or Dominican women (women from the Dominican Republic alternate with Jamaican women every other semester). These groups were selected based on the significant number of immigrant women from such groups who have migrated into the United States.

Films on the Caribbean are used to bring about a visual awareness of the intense situations existing in much of the Caribbean. A film on Cuba entitled *A Portrait of Cuba* describes the successes and failures of the Cuban revolution. Four films on Haiti are used: *Haiti* describes Haitian culture, *Bitter Cane* examines Haiti's current economic structure and its origins, *This Other Haiti* examines the activities of the peasant movement under the leadership of a Haitian woman, and *Haitian Children in the Dominican Republic* describes the lives of Haitian children brought to the Dominican Republic to work in the sugar cane fields as free laborers. *Jamaica in Review* describes social and political events in Jamaica; the film is updated each year the course is taught. *Sugar Cane Alley* portrays the strength of a Martinique woman within a colonial and racist environment.

This course is designed for upper-level students. The only prerequisites are that a student have an interest in the plight of immigrant women in the United States, an interest in the changing face of America and why the changes are occurring, and a desire to learn the cultural, sociopolitical, and economic factors surrounding Caribbean immigrant women within the migration process.

The course has been taught at both Rutgers University and William Paterson College within the Departments of Africana Studies and African, African American, and Caribbean Studies. The course was revised in the transition from Rutgers to William Paterson as a result of ongoing research on Caribbean women immigrants in the United States.

ASSIGNMENTS: DESCRIPTION AND PURPOSE

1. *Participation in class discussions.* Students should plan ahead and be prepared to discuss readings in class. When students are prepared, the discussions are exciting and become a real learning experience. The terms and concepts that are not understood in the readings are explained during the

discussions. The purpose of having discussions rather than all lectures is to allow students to express their opinions and become involved in the teaching and learning process.

2. *Two examinations.* The two examinations will cover lectures, readings, terms and concepts, map information, and films.

3. *Research paper on women and migration.* Students must select a paper topic on a group of women immigrants or refugees from the Caribbean or some other part of the world. The topic should be one that they will enjoy researching. All topics must be approved by the instructor to ensure that there is enough information for a paper to be generated from the particular topic. The purpose of the research paper is to motivate students to do research in the library, use computers, and familiarize themselves with materials on migration to the United States. A format for the paper will be provided. Papers must reflect the theories, concepts, and materials covered in the lectures and required readings.

EVALUATION

Students will be evaluated in the following areas:

1. Attendance and participation in class discussions
2. Ability to grasp theories, legislation, terms, concepts, and facts as demonstrated on two examinations
3. Ability to write a theoretical and analytical research paper on women immigrants from one of the Caribbean groups (or on women from outside the Caribbean)

STUDENT RESPONSE TO THE COURSE

Students' responses to this course have been diverse, to say the least. There are differences between the responses of students from the Caribbean and those of non-Caribbean students. The Caribbean students tend to grasp the material more readily and bring some knowledge of the migration process to the class. Stereotypes and negative images are expressed by all students. Students bring to class information about Caribbean immigrants living in proximity to them and their different cultural factors (religion, language, food, music) and behaviors. Students also express concern about the impact of the immigrant population on the U.S. job market and about immigrants' use of social services.

The course always ends with expressions of a deeper understanding among students of different backgrounds. Students say that the course helps reduce conflict and misconceptions and helps bring about better race relations.

COURSE OUTLINE

BARBADIANS AND HAITIANS

Week 1	Course introduction Glossary of terms and map Immigration law (terms and concepts) Paper discussion
Week 2	Discussion/readings: Marshall (1981)—Afterword (p. 311) by Washington Marshall (1981)—chaps. 1,2
Week 3	Discussion/readings: Marshall (1981)—chaps. 3,4 Article: Barry et al., "Barbados" (1984)
Week 4	Discussion/readings: Article: Marshall, "Black Immigrant Women in Brown Girl, Brownstones" (1981) Article: Barry et al., "Haiti" (1984)

HAITIANS

Week 5	Discussion/readings: Ferguson (1987)—chaps. 1, 2, 3 Film: *Bitter Cane*
Week 6	Discussion/readings: Ferguson (1987)—chaps. 4, 5 Haitian migration patterns Films: *Haiti* and *Haitian Children in the Dominican Republic*
Week 7	Discussion/readings: Articles: Miller, "The Closed Golden Door" (1984), and French, "Haiti's New Dawn" (1981) Ferguson (1987)—chap. 6 Film: *This Other Haiti* Exam 1

CUBANS

Week 8   Discussion/readings:
                  Article: Barry et al., "Cuba" (1984)
                  Film: *Portrait of Cuba*

Week 9   Discussion/readings:
                  Cuban migration patterns
                  Film: *Racism Among Black and White Cubans in South
                  Florida*

Week 10   Discussion/readings:
                  Article: Bryce-LaPorte, "Black Immigrants: The Experi-
                  ence of Invisibility and Inequality" (1972)
                  Paper discussion

JAMAICANS

Week 11   Discussion/readings:
                  Article: Barry et al., "Jamaica" (1984)
                  Jamaican migration patterns

Week 12   Discussion/readings:
                  Article: Bonnett, "The New Female West Indian Immi-
                  grants: Dilemmas of Coping in the Host Society"
                  (1990)
                  Film: *Jamaica in Review*

Week 13   Exam 2
                  Discussion/readings:
                  Article: Bonnett, "The New Female West Indian Immi-
                  grants: Dilemmas of Coping in the Host Society"
                  (1990)

Week 14   Discussion/readings:
                  Problems encountered by immigrant women in their at-
                  tempts to resettle (lecture)
                  Paper discussion

Week 15   Research shared

REQUIRED TEXTS AND ARTICLES

Texts

Ferguson, J. (1987). *Papa Doc, Baby Doc: Haiti and the Duvaliers.* New York: B. Blackwell.

Marshall, P. (1981). *Brown girl, brownstones.* Old Westbury, NY: Feminist Press.

Articles

Barry, T., Wood, B., & Preusch, D. (1984). Barbados. In *The other side of paradise: Foreign control in the Caribbean* (pp. 268–283). New York: Grove Press.

———. (1984). Cuba. In *The other side of paradise: Foreign control in the Caribbean* (pp. 264–267). New York: Grove Press.

———. (1984). Haiti. In *The other side of paradise: Foreign control in the Caribbean* (pp. 330–340). New York: Grove Press.

———. (1984). Jamaica. In *The other side of paradise: Foreign control in the Caribbean* (pp. 341–351). New York: Grove Press.

Bonnett, A. W. (1990). The new female West Indian immigrants: Dilemmas of coping in the host society. In R. W. Palmer (Ed.), *In search of a better life: Perspective on migration from the Caribbean* (pp. 139–149). New York: Praeger.

Bryce-LaPorte, R. S. (1972). Black immigrants: The experience of invisibility and inequality. *Journal of Black Studies, 3*(1), 29–56.

French, H. (1981). Haiti's new dawn. *Emerge, 2*(7), 38–43.

Marshall, P. (1981). Black immigrant women in brown girl, brownstones. In D. M. Mortimer & R. S. Bryce-LaPorte (Eds.), *Female immigrants to the United States: Caribbean, Latin American, and African experience* (pp. 3–11). Washington, DC: Research Institute on Immigration and Ethnic Studies, Smithsonian Institution.

Miller, J. (1984). The closed golden door. In *The plight of Haitian refugees* (pp. 79–101). New York: Praeger.

RECOMMENDED READINGS

Buchanan, S. H. (1979). Haitian women in New York City. *Migration Today, 20,* 57–64.

Mortimer, D. M., & Bryce-LaPorte, R. S. (1981). *Female immigrants to the United States: Caribbean, Latin American, and African experiences.* Washington, DC: Research Institute on Immigration and Ethnic Studies, Smithsonian Institution.

Simon, R. J., & Brettell, C. B. (Eds.). *International migration: The female experience.* Totowa, NJ: Rowman & Allanheld.

Smith, E. M. (1976). Women and migration [Special issue]. *Anthropological Quarterly, 49*(1).

Spero, A. (1984, September). *In America and in need: Immigrant, refugee, and entrant women.* Report from Haitian Women's Conference, Miami-Dade Community College.

Sutton, C. R., & Chaney, E. M. (Eds.). *Caribbean life in New York City: Socio-cultural dimensions.* New York: Center for Migration Studies of New York.

19
Women, Culture, and Society: Introduction to Women's Studies

Manijeh Saba

Women's studies critically examines the totality of women's experiences from both historical and contemporary perspectives. Its goal is to unveil, document, restore, and validate the diversities of women's lives, traditions, identities, and voices. It goes beyond challenging limitations of traditional knowledge, methods, and theories by trying to develop a more comprehensive understanding of social life. It further prepares us to go beyond description of the status quo and challenges us to confront and change the social institutions and practices that create and perpetuate systems of oppression.

This course is an introduction to women's studies; hence it includes ideas and topics that express the scope of the field. Although focusing on the present, we use a historical perspective in order to better understand the processes that have shaped our present experiences and to learn the different ways that the interests of women have been defined. Several themes shape this course. First is the idea that although different groups of women share some common experiences, there are aspects of their everyday lives that put them in opposition to one another. We concentrate on class structure and race/ethnic relations to comprehend the sources of antagonism. We focus on the lives of women in the United States and elsewhere, primarily the third world. Second is the significance of global relations in our everyday lives. A global perspective not only shows that the international market economy has connected people of the world but also compels us to see that every individual's action both influences and is affected by the actions of others around the world. Through the study of differences among women we appreciate other traditions and learn new standpoints and successful strategies from those traditions. The third theme pertains to systems of discrimination and domination. In what ways have women been subordinated, and what have been the consequences of their oppression? We also want to know how women have challenged, resisted, and adapted to the devaluation and control of their lives. Finally, we examine the practices and institutions women have created that enable them to survive and evolve.

COURSE REQUIREMENTS

Students are given the following introduction to and explanation of the course:

Critical reading, thinking, questioning, discussing, and writing are essential components of learning in this course. Regular class participation is mandatory. Come to class having read the assigned materials in advance and be prepared to discuss, argue, and perhaps rethink the issues raised. Use the questions appearing at the beginning of each section of the syllabus to help your understanding of the subject and your critical evaluation of the material.

Your final grade will be based on two papers, three exams, and class participation. The first paper is a three-generation ethnographic research, designed to further your understanding of the diversities and complexities of women's experiences throughout history. The focus of your investigation will be one or two themes that have emerged from the course. This project requires that you interview two women of different generations, such as your mother and grandmother, or any other two women who have been significant in your life. The third interviewee is yourself if you are female. If you are male, you will interview a sister, female cousin, or female friend who is close to you in age with a similar class, race, and ethnic experience. When writing the results of the interviews, you will be required to compare the three generations and analyze your findings in light of the course materials. You will be given details of the research design and process later. This paper will be 20% of the final grade. The second paper is based on a liberating "pro-woman" act you have performed during this semester—something you could not have done prior to this course. In a short paper, describe the act. Explain the process that led to the act, others' reactions to it, as well as your own reaction to and experience of it. This paper will be 10% of the final grade.

The exams will be graded based on your ability to integrate the readings, films, lectures, and class discussions. They will constitute 20%, 30%, and 10% of the final grade, respectively. Consistent and meaningful contribution to class discussions is 10% of the final grade.

REQUIRED READING

Required readings include chapters from the following published collections, with additional required readings on reserve.

Rothenberg, P. S. (Ed.). (1988). *Racism and sexism: An integrated study.* New York: St. Martin's Press.
Rothenberg, P. S. (Ed.). (1992). *Race, class, and gender in the United States: An integrated study* (2nd ed. of *Racism and sexism: An integrated study*). New York: St. Martin's Press.
Seager, J., & Olson, A. (1986). *Women in the world: An international atlas.* New York: Simon & Schuster.

RECOMMENDED READING

Boston Women's Health Book Collective. (1984). *The new our bodies, ourselves.* New York: Simon & Schuster.

COURSE OUTLINE

Week 1   INTRODUCTION

Overview of the course and review of ground rules for class discussion

BASIC CONCEPTUALIZATION AND LOCATIONS

Questions to consider: What are prejudice and discrimination? Is it possible for one to be present without the other? What are sexism, racism, and classism? Do these systems have any common characteristics? Can groups of people be privileged and disadvantaged at the same time? How has gender shaped your life? How have race/ethnicity and class influenced the ways that gender shaped your life?

Readings:

Rothenberg, P. S. (1992). Defining "racism" and "sexism." In P. S. Rothenberg (Ed.), *Race, class, and gender in the United States: An integrated study* (pp. 5–8). New York: St. Martin's Press.

U.S. Commission on Civil Rights. (1992). The problem: Discrimination. In P. S. Rothenberg (Ed.), *Race, class, and gender in the United States: An integrated study* (pp. 9–19). New York: St. Martin's Press.

Frye, M. (1992). Oppression. In P. S. Rothenberg (Ed.), *Race, class, and gender in the United States: An integrated study* (pp. 54–57). New York: St. Martin's Press.

Mantsios, G. (1988). Class in America: Myths and realities. In P. S. Rothenberg (Ed.), *Racism and sexism: An integrated study* (pp. 56–69). New York: St. Martin's Press.

Bhasin, K., & Khan, N. (1987). *Some questions on feminism and its relevance to South East Asia.* New Delhi: Kali for Women.

Week 2   SOCIAL CONSTRUCTION OF GENDER

Questions to consider: What does it mean to say that one is not a woman born? How does one learn to be a girl? When were you first aware of being a girl? What has gendered learning meant in your own life? In what ways has your formal education contributed to and/or challenged traditional gender arrangements?

Readings:

Ruth, S. (1990). The origins of female subordination: Theories and explanations. In S. Ruth (Ed.), *Issues in feminism: An introduction to women's studies* (pp. 154–162). Mountain View, CA: Mayfield.

Rich, A. (1986). Notes toward a politics of location. In *Blood, bread, and poetry* (pp. 210–223). New York: Norton.

Shange, N. (1988). is not so gd to be born a girl. In P. S. Rothenberg (Ed.), *Racism and sexism: An integrated study* (pp. 131–132). New York: St. Martin's Press.

Lorde, A. (1986). Man child: A black lesbian feminist's response. In J. B. Cole (Ed.), *All American women:*

Lines that divide, ties that bind (pp. 148–154). New York: Free Press.

Scott, P. B. (1982). Toward a non-racist and non-sexist social science. In G. T. Hull, P. B. Scott, & B. Smith, (Eds.), *All the women are White, all the Blacks are men, but some of us are brave: Black women's studies* (pp. 85–92). Old Westbury, NY: Feminist Press.

Week 3   INEQUALITY AND DIFFERENCE

Questions to consider: How do racism and sexism inter-act with each other? How and why do differences separate people? What purpose does this separation serve? What can women do to work across the lines of race/ethnicity? How might differences enrich and/or strengthen us?

Readings:

Lorde, Audre. (1992). Age, race, class, and sex: Women redefining difference. In P. S. Rothenberg (Ed.), *Race, class, and gender in the United States: An integrated study* (pp. 401–407). New York: St. Martin's Press.

Andre, J. (1988). Stereotypes: Conceptual and normative considerations. In P. S. Rothenberg (Ed.), *Racism and sexism: An integrated study* (pp. 257–262). New York: St. Martin's Press.

Snyder, M. (1992). Self-fulfilling stereotypes. In P. S. Rothenberg (Ed.), *Race, class, and gender in the United States: An integrated study* (pp. 325–331). New York: St. Martin's Press.

Moore, R. B. (1992). Racism in the English language. In P. S. Rothenberg (Ed.), *Race, class, and gender in the United States: An integrated study* (pp. 331–341). New York: St. Martin's Press.

Beuf, A. (1988). The Native American experience. In P. S. Rothenberg (Ed.), *Racism and sexism: An integrated study* (pp. 100–105). New York: St. Martin's Press.

Kumajai, Gloria. (1988). The Asian woman in America. In P. S. Rothenberg (Ed.), *Racism and sexism: An integrated study* (pp. 112–118). New York: St. Martin's Press.

Week 4   POLITICS OF EDUCATION, LANGUAGE, AND
                REPRESENTATIONS

Questions to consider: How are our concepts of one another and ourselves embedded in unconscious language
patterns? How are women represented in traditional art
and literature? What are the implications? How have
women attempted to resist, challenge, or change stereotypical images of themselves?
Readings:
Richardson, L. W. (1977). Gender stereotyping in the
    English language. In L. W. Richardson (Ed.), *The dy-
    namics of sex and gender: A sociological perspective*
    (pp. 5–9) Chicago: Rand McNally.
Brown Parlee, M. (1977). Conversational politics. In
    L. W. Richardson (Ed.), *The dynamics of sex and gen-
    der: A sociological perspective* (pp. 10–12). Chicago:
    Rand McNally.
Baker, R. (1988). "Pricks" and "chicks": A plea for
    "persons." In P. S. Rothenberg (Ed.), *Racism and sex-
    ism: An integrated study* (pp. 280–295). New York: St.
    Martin's Press.
Seager, J., & Olson, A. (1986). The media. In *Women in
    the world: An international atlas* (p. 34). New York: Si-
    mon & Schuster.
Morgan, R. (1990). Know your enemy: A sampling of
    sexist quotes. In S. Ruth (Ed.), *Issues in feminism: An
    introduction to women's studies* (pp. 92–94). Mountain
    View, CA: Mayfield.
Steinem, G. (1990). Sex, lies, and advertising. In *Ms.:
    The World of Women,* July/August 1990.
Rich, A. (1979). Taking women students seriously. In
    On lies, secrets, and silence (pp. 237–245). New York:
    Norton.
Lorde, A. (1990). The transformation of silence into lan-
    guage and action. In S. Ruth (Ed.), *Issues in femi-
    nism: An introduction to women's studies* (pp. 138–
    140). Mountain View, CA: Mayfield.

Weeks 5–7   CLASS, RACE/ETHNICITY, AND GENDER DIVI-
SION OF LABOR

Questions to consider: How do women's work experiences vary by class, race/ethnicity, and age in the United
States? How are these experiences similar and/or different from those of the women in the rest of the world, especially the third world? In what ways does women's domestic labor shape their paid work and vice versa?
What are capitalism and imperialism? How has each of
them connected and/or separated women on the global
level? What, if any, connections exist between women in
the United States and women of the third world? How
can women work across national boundaries to bring
about change?

Readings:

Seager, J., & Olson, A. (1986). Introduction & maps. In
Women in the world: An international atlas (pp. 7–10,
13–20, 28, 34). New York: Simon & Schuster.

Cole, J. B. (1986). Work. In J. B. Cole (Ed.), *All American women: Lines that divide, ties that bind* (pp. 31–
38). New York: Free Press.

National Committee on Pay Equity. (1992). The wage
gap: Myths and facts. In P. S. Rothenberg (Ed.) *Race,
class, and gender in the United States: An integrated
study* (pp. 129–135). New York: St. Martin's Press.

Malveaux, Julianne. (1988). Ain't I a woman: Differences in the labor market status of black and white
women. In P. S. Rothenberg (Ed.), *Racism and sexism: An integrated study* (pp. 76–79). New York: St.
Martin's Press.

Vetter, B. (1989). Bad news for women scientists. *AAA
Observer,* May 5, p. 10.

Colen, S. (1986). With respect and feelings: Voices of
West Indian child care and domestic workers in New
York City. In J. B. Cole (Ed.), *All American women:
Lines that divide, ties that bind* (pp. 46–70). New
York: Free Press.

Fuentes, Ann, and Ehrenreich, Barbara. (1983). *Women
in the Global Factory.* Boston: South End Press.

The cost of "free trade." (1989). *Connexions: An International Women's Quarterly, 30,* 26–27.

The global factory. (1994). *Connexions: An International Women's Quarterly, 44.*

Films: *Maids and Madams; Global Assembly Line*

MOTHERING AND FAMILY

Questions to consider: In what ways have families oper-ated to produce, reproduce, exaggerate, and/or diminish women's equality? What are the major commonalities and differences in women's experiences with family life? If you were to develop a set of public policy recommen-dations concerning women and families, what could they be?

Readings:

Seager, J., & Olson, A. (1996). Families. In *Women in the world: An international atlas* (pp. 6–9, 12). New York: Simon & Schuster.

Glubka, S. (1986). Out of the stream: An essay on un-conventional motherhood. In J. B. Cole (Ed.), *All American women: Lines that divide, ties that bind* (pp. 216–277). New York: Free Press.

Sidel, Ruth. (1992). *Women and children last: The plight of poor women in affluent America* (2nd ed.) (chs. 1–4 and 8–10 and Afterword). New York: Penguin Books.

hooks, bell. (1984). Black women: Shaping feminist the-ory. In *Feminist theory: From margin to center* (pp. 1–15). Boston: South End Press.

FIRST EXAM

Week 8   SEXUALITY AND RELATIONSHIPS

Questions to consider: What is heterosexual privilege? How does power operate in personal relationships? How do race/ethnicity, class, and gender shape sexual re-lationships? What influence does sexuality have on gen-der, class, and racial/ethnic relations? What is a lesbian continuum?

Readings:

Hubbard, R. (1990). The social construction of sexual-ity: Constructing sex differences. In *The politics of women's biology* (pp. 131–140). New Brunswick, NJ: Rutgers University Press.

Rubin, L. B. (1976). The marriage bed. In *Worlds of pain: Life in the working class family* (pp. 134–154). New York: Basic Books.

Espin, O. (1986). Cultural and historical influences on sexuality in Hispanic/Latin women. In J. B. Cole (Ed.), *All American women: Lines that divide, ties that bind* (pp. 272–284). New York: Free Press.

Clarke, C. Lesbianism: An act of resistance. In C. Moraga & G. Anzaldua (Eds.) (1983), *This bridge called my back: Writings by radical women of color* (pp. 128–137). New York: Kitchen Table: Women of Color Press.

Rich, A. (1983). Compulsory heterosexuality & lesbian existence. In A. Snitow & C. Stansell (Eds.), *Powers of desire: The politics of sexuality* (pp. 177–205). New York: Monthly Review Press.

Film: *A Little Respect*

Week 9   SEXUAL POLITICS AND VIOLENCE AGAINST WOMEN

Questions to consider: What are the different kinds of violence against women? Why is it so common? What are the forces that support violence? What can be done about it?

Readings:

Seager, A., & Olson, A. (1986). Domestic disorders. Rape. In *Women in the world: An international atlas* (pp. 3, 37). New York: Simon & Schuster.

Gordon, L. (1988). "Be careful about father": Incest, girls, resistance, and the construction of femininity. In *Heroes of their own lives: The politics and history of family violence* (pp. 204–299). New York: Viking.

Herman, D. F. (1989). Rape culture. In *Women: A feminist perspective* (pp. 20–45). Mountain View, CA: Mayfield.

Davis, A. (1983). The myth of the black male rapist. In *Women, race, and class* (pp. 172–201). New York: Random House.

Chile: The tortured birth of victory. (1987). *Connexions: An International Women's Quarterly, 23,* 16–18, 25–26.

AAWORD. (1983). A statement on genital mutilation. In M. Davis (Ed.), *Third world second sex* (pp. 217–220). London: Zed Press.

Film: *Fear That Binds Us*

THREE GENERATION PAPER DUE

Week 10   WOMEN'S HEALTH AND REPRODUCTIVE RIGHTS

Questions to consider: What are the arguments in favor of a woman's right to choose pregnancy over abortion? What are the opposing arguments? What are the reproductive technologies, and how might they affect women's lives? What is the difference between birth control and population control? What is sterilization abuse?

Readings:

Petchesky, R. (1980). Reproductive freedom. *Signs, 5* (41), 661–685.

Davis, A. (1983). Racism, birth control, and reproductive rights. In *Women, race and class* (pp. 202–221). New York: Vintage Books.

Seager, J., & Olson, A. (1986). Mothers; Abortion; Illness and health. In *Women in the world: An international atlas* (pp. 6, 9, 26). New York: Simon & Schuster.

Reproductive rights: The global fight. (1989, Winter). *Connexions: An International Women's Quarterly, 31.*

Film: *La Operacion*

Week 11   WOMEN'S LIBERATION

Questions to consider: What does it mean to say, "the personal is the political"? Is there a distinctive women's politics? How can women liberate themselves? What roles do class and race/ethnicity play in this process?

Readings:

Rushin, D. K. (1983). The bridge poem. In C. Moraga & G. Anzaldua (Eds.), *This bridge called my back:*

Writings by radical women of color (pp. xxi–xxii). New York: Kitchen Table: Women of Color Press.

Morales, R. (1983). I am what I am. In C. Moraga & G. Anzaldua (Eds.), *This bridge called my back: Writings by radical women of color* (pp. 14–15). New York: Kitchen Table: Women of Color Press.

Combahee River Collective. (1983). A black feminist statement. In C. Moraga & G. Anzaldua (Eds.), *This bridge called my back: Writings by radical women of color* (pp. 210–219). New York: Kitchen Table: Women of Color Press.

Lorde, A. (1983). The master's tool will never dismantle the master's house. In C. Moraga & G. Anzaldua (Eds.), *This bridge called my back: Writings by radical women of color* (pp. 98–101). New York: Kitchen Table: Women of Color Press.

Piercy, M. (1992). The women in the ordinary. In P. S. Rothenberg (Ed.), *Race, class, and gender in the United States: An integrated study* (pp. 449–450). New York: St. Martin's Press.

Allen, P. G. (1986). Angry women are building: Issues and struggles facing Native American women. In J. B. Cole (Ed.), *All American women: Lines that divide, ties that bind* (pp. 407–409). New York: Free Press.

Hohri, S. (1986). Are you a liberated woman? Feminism, revolution and Asian American women. In J. B. Cole (Ed.), *All American women: Lines that divide, ties that bind* (pp. 420–425). New York: Free Press.

LIBERATING ACT PRESENTATION AND PAPER

Week 12   WOMEN'S MOVEMENT, WOMEN'S SOLIDARITY

Questions to consider: How and why do movements for social change begin? What is the relationship between the civil rights movement and the women's rights movement? In what ways did the 1950s set the stage for feminist revolt in the United States? What does the concept of everyday resistance convey to you? What is global feminism? How can women from third world countries and industrialized countries work together to achieve their goals?

Readings:

Seager, J., & Olson, A. (1986). Channels of change. Protest. In *Women in the world: An international atlas* (pp. 38, 39). New York: Simon & Schuster.

Davis, A. (1983). The anti-slavery movement and the birth of women's rights. In *Women, race, and class* (pp. 30–45). New York: Vintage Books.

Davis, A. (1983). Class and race in the early women's rights campaign. In *Women, race, and class* (pp. 46–69). New York: Vintage Books.

SECOND EXAM

Week 13

Readings:

The Equal Rights Amendment (defeated). In P. S. Rothenberg (Ed.), *Race, class, and gender in the United States: An integrated study* (pp. 310–312). New York: St. Martin's Press.

Freeman, J. (1989). The women's liberation movement. In *Women: A feminist perspective* (pp. 543–556). Mountain View, CA: Mayfield.

Women's movements: Thoughts into action. (1986, Winter). *Connexions: An International Women's Quarterly, 19*.

Week 14

Readings:

Mikhail-Ashrawi, H. (1989). Palestinian women: It is possible to agree on principles. *New Outlook,* June–July, pp. 7–9.

Ostrowitz, R. (1989). Dangerous women: The Israeli women's peace movement. *New Outlook,* June–July, pp. 14–15.

Bunch, C. (1987). Bringing the global home. In *Passionate politics: Feminist theory in action* (pp. 328–345). New York: St. Martin's Press.

Morgan, R. (1990). A sampling of feminist proverbs from around the world. In S. Ruth (Ed.), *Issues in feminism: An introduction to women's studies* (pp. 149–150). Mountain View, CA: Mayfield.

THIRD EXAM AND COURSE EVALUATION

ACKNOWLEDGMENTS

Although I developed this version of the course Women, Culture, and Society, its general outline was developed in a collaborative process involving members of the Rutgers University women's studies program and funded by the New Jersey Department of Higher Education. Other participants included Susan Cavin, Judith Gerson, Mary Gibson, Sherry Gorelick, Deborah Gussman, Wendy Hesford, Gwyn Kirk, Jerma Jackson, Carla Jackson-Brewer, Olivia Mitchell-Morris, Joanna Regulska, and Tamar Rothenberg.

20
A Course in the History of Western Sexuality

Adam Knobler

This course in the history of Western sexuality was designed to fill several departmental and campus needs. At Trenton State College, we have initiated a new general education requirement that mandates that all students take an upper-division history course. These courses had to be general enough to give nonhistorians a sufficient overview of a major theme or period in world history, yet detailed enough to give students a thorough understanding of some aspect of history.

My experience at Trenton State and elsewhere of teaching students who are *not* history majors has taught me that, by and large, students have a very antiquated notion of what "history" itself entails. They have been inculcated with the belief that "history" is a chronological study of the public lives of famous people (usually men, usually elite, usually European). As a consequence, they tend to reject history as something without any particular relevance to their own lives. When I have taught Western Civilization, the issue of sexuality has played a prominent role because it *is* so universal—without barrier of class, gender, or race. Students have told me that it is something to which they can easily relate.

The course, as constructed, covers far less material than even one semester of Western Civilization. It examines, chronologically, several points in history—snapshots, if you will—using issues of sexuality as the core theme of investigation. Yet no issue of sexuality concerning, for example, ancient Greece can be fully understood without some basic understanding of the social and political milieu in which it takes place. As a consequence, the course combines historical outline with its study of sexuality, sexual attitudes, and sexual practices. As no satisfactory "sex history" textbook has yet been written, I use Kevin Reilly's splendid *The West and the World* as a broad historical outline in order to give students some firm ground on which they will be able to stand and develop a broader historical consciousness.

In designing this course, I had to take into account several particular needs and concerns I have not faced in the majority of my other courses. First of all, I find myself particularly aware of being a white male instructor dealing with issues of sexuality. One of my concerns has always been whether I can speak of sexual issues, particularly issues of women's sexuality, with sufficient sensitivity. On the plus side, my gender gives me, perhaps, a unique opportunity to bring issues of sexual variance, sexual inequity, and sexual oppression to the attention of the males on this campus, who might not have considered such issues to be of any interest or concern to them.

Trenton State College has a conservative student body; therefore, how does one approach issues of sexuality without risking offending students to the point of legal action? Can one discuss pornography without using pornography in the classroom?

I have also attempted to design a course that discusses sexuality in a way that our student body can relate to. I have seen many course syllabi on the history of sexuality that concentrate on topics of marginality or sexual violence—which are, of course, critical but which might leave students with the impression that sexual relations between individuals are marginal to their own lives. I find this idea oddly self-defeating: the puritanical masquerading as the progressive. As a consequence, I pay particular attention to such issues as courtship and positive attitudes toward sexuality. I do not want to give students the impression that there is something inherently evil or furtive about their own sexuality, as, I fear, our society often implies.

I have also been careful to integrate issues of both male and female sexuality into the course. Too often, I have found that male sexuality—gay sexuality and male as rapist aside—has been disregarded in sex history courses. Again, in an effort not to marginalize anybody in this class, we examine such issues as the construction of masculinity in the Victorian period—with particular attention to the public school ethos of the English elite.

The question has been raised whether sexuality is necessarily a subset of gender relations at all. One of the objectives of the course is, in fact, to raise questions in the minds of students as to exactly what "gender" implies. It is true that in the present Western construction, most of us have been taught that "gender" refers to a dichotomy existing between men and women. However, this course endeavors to introduce students to societies where this bipolar vision does not apply. Prime examples (as noted in the course outline) are some of the traditional Plains Indian peoples in the 19th century. Within these societies, certain individuals who were born as biological males were raised as females. The *berdache*, as they were known, held special places in the society—often as shamans or healers—for it was believed that they combined both male and female characteristics and thus were able to bring a special wisdom to the tribe. As a consequence, they can be considered a third, quite distinct gender.

I have approached many of these issues—my "snapshot" issues, as I call them—in Western civilization classes with a certain amount of success. An advantage of using this overview or snapshot structure is that the subtopics can easily be changed to fit an instructor's own interests and ideas, and I have built flexibility into the syllabus.

SYLLABUS FOR TOPICS IN THE HISTORY OF WESTERN SEXUALITY

This course is designed to introduce students to the role of sexuality in Western history, from the classical to the modern periods. As this is a very broad topic, we examine sexual history through specific examples taken from different periods of time to provide an overview of sexuality, sexual variance, and notions of gender across time.

Readings consist largely of primary sources, supplemented with secondary readings.

Students are required to take a short in-class midterm exam and a take-home final exam and to write a short term paper (8–10 pages). Students must submit a brief (1 page) proposal of their intended topics to the instructor by October 13 and meet briefly with him to discuss feasibility and bibliography. Topics can be of the student's choosing but should cover some comparative aspect of the history of sexuality.

The instructor expects students to take an active role in their education by participating fully in class discussions, asking questions of the instructor and one another, and doing all the assigned readings.

To this end, the final grade will be determined as follows: class participation, 20%; midterm, 20%; final exam, 25%; term paper, 35%.

As there is no single text that sufficiently covers the material for this course, a course packet has been prepared and will be on sale in the History Department. This packet, along with the two volumes of Kevin Reilly's *The West and the World,* is required reading for this course.

Those items in the packet that are to be read for a given segment of the course are identified below with an asterisk (*).

PLEASE NOTE:
This course contains some sexually explicit material as part of the assigned reading (indicated by boldface type and underlining). This material is included because it is necessary for the understanding of the particular topics at hand. If you would prefer not to read this material, please contact the instructor at the earliest possible date so that alternative readings can be assigned. Otherwise, continued attendance in the course will be taken as an agreement on the part of the student to read the material as assigned.

COURSE OUTLINE

Week 1 Class 1	Lecture: Introduction to the course and to the language of sexual discourse
Week 1 Class 2	Lecture: Sexuality in ancient Greece Readings: Reilly, vol. 1, chaps. 6, 7
Week 2 Class 1	Lecture: Male homosexuality and lesbianism in classical Greek society Readings: *K. J. Dover, "Classical Greek attitudes to sexual behavior," *Arethusia,* 6 (1973): 69–73
Week 2 Class 2	Discussion: The poetry of Sappho in its Greek context Readings: *Selections from Sappho
Week 3 Class 1	Lecture: Sexuality in the three major Western faiths Readings: Reilly, vol. 1, chaps. 4, 5; *Peter Brown, *Body and society,* chap. 2
Week 3 Class 2	Discussion: Jews, Christians, Muslims, and sexuality Readings: *Selections from Genesis, Leviticus, Luke, 1 Corinthians, 1 Timothy; selections from Saint Jerome; *Quran* (surahs 2, 4, 24, 33)
Week 4 Class 1	Lecture: Sexuality in the medieval West Readings: Reilly, vol. 1, chaps. 9, 10

Week 4 Class 2	Lecture: Celibacy and sexual modesty in medieval Christendom Readings: *Selections from James Brundage, *Law, sex and Christian society in medieval Europe*
Week 5 Class 1	Discussion: Celibacy and sexual abstinence in religious and secular contexts Readings: *Selections from Jo Ann McNamara, *A new song*
Week 5 Class 2	Lecture: Sexuality in early modern Europe and Puritan America Readings: Reilly, vol. 1, chap. 11; vol. 2, chaps. 1, 5, 6
Week 6 Class 1	Lecture/discussion: Witchcraft and sexuality in Europe and New England Readings: *Selections from the *Malleus Maleficarum*
Week 6 Class 2	Lecture: Libertinage and the "body politic/political body" of ancien régime France Readings: *Selections from Lynn Hunt, *Invention of pornography*
Week 7 Class 1	Discussion: Sade, revolution, and the critics of both Readings: ***Selections from Marquis de Sade, *Justine*;** selections from Angela Carter, *The Sadeian woman*
Week 7 Class 2	Midterm
Week 8 Class 1	Lecture: Sexuality in Victorian England Readings: Reilly, vol. 2, chaps. 3, 5
Week 8 Class 2	Lecture: Sexuality and the Victorian working class Readings: *Jeffrey Weeks, *Sex politics and society,* chaps. 4, 5; selections from Janet Murray, *Strong-minded women*
Week 9	Midterm break

Week 10
Class 1

Lecture: Masculinity and the sexual culture of Victorian elite males
Readings: *Selections from Thomas Hughes, *Tom Brown's school days;* Jeffrey Weeks, *Sex, politics, and society,* chap. 2

Week 10
Class 2

Discussion: Victorian morality
Readings: *Selections from Charlotte Perkins Gilman, *The yellow wallpaper*

Week 11
Class 1

Lecture/discussion: Sexuality and the building of empires
Readings: Reilly, vol. 2, chaps. 7, 8; *Ronald Hyam, *Empire and sexuality,* chaps. 4, 5

Week 11
Class 2

Lecture/discussion: Gender alternatives on the American frontier
Readings: *Selections from Walter L. Williams, *The spirit and the flesh*

Week 12
Class 1

Lecture: Sexuality and sexual issues in contemporary America—an overview
Readings: Reilly, vol. 2, chaps. 11–13; *John D'Emilio and Estelle Freedman, *Intimate matters,* chaps. 13, 14

Week 12
Class 2

Lecture: Courtship in America—a brief postwar history
Readings: *Selections from Beth Bailey, *From front porch to back seat*

Week 13
Class 1

Discussion: Sexuality on American college campuses
Readings: *Selections from Peggy Reeves Sanday, *Fraternity gang rape*

Week 13
Class 2

Lecture: Pornography: free speech or visual rape?
Readings: *Andrea Dworkin, testimony before the Meese Commission

Week 14
Class 1

Discussion: Pornography—an open debate
Readings: ***Selections from Linda Lovelace, *Ordeal***

Week 14   Lecture/discussion: AIDS in America
Class 2   Readings: *Selections from Tony Kushner, *Angels in
                 America;* selections from Randy Shilts, *And the band
                 played on*

Week 15   Lecture/discussion: Sexuality and reproduction
Class 1   Readings: *To be announced

Week 15   Conclusions
Class 2

TEXTS

As I noted in the syllabus itself, I assign only one world history textbook, to
be supplemented with a series of readings, because no one text or set of
source collections quite fits my interests. The textbook I have chosen is Kevin
Reilly's *The West and the World* (2 vols.), which is arranged both chronologically and thematically. Reilly places Western history in a broad global context, and he pays particular attention to issues of gender, race, and class.
I've also chosen the following readings (arranged in the order in which they
are assigned):

K. J. Dover, Classical Greek attitudes to sexual behavior, *Arethusia,* 6(1973): 59–73.
      A good short overview by a classical scholar with a deep knowledge of Greek
      sexual history.
Selections from Sappho in *The Soldier and the lady: Poems of Archilochos and Sappho,*
trans. Mills & Barris. New Rochelle, NY: Elizabeth Press, 1975.
      Perhaps more written about than read, Sappho's poems and the culture of
      Lesbos provide a nice literary introduction to the subject of same-sex relation-
      ships in Greek culture.
Peter Brown, *Body and society: Men, women and sexual renunciation in early Christian-
ity.* New York: Columbia University Press, 1988.
      A masterful study of body image and sexuality in the late Roman and early
      Christian period.
Selections from the Bible and Quran.
      Students should read the texts themselves. One cannot truly understand pre-
      modern Western thought without a fulsome knowledge of the scriptural texts,
      and so it is for sexuality.
James A. Brundage, *Law, sex and Christian society in medieval Europe.* Chicago: University of Chicago Press, 1987.
      This book covers everything from masturbation to multiple partners, as the
      subjects appear in the vast body of legal literature from the Middle Ages. I've

selected the pieces on celibacy, but countless other issues are discussed with clarity and wit.

Jo Ann McNamara, *A new song: Celibate women in the first three Christian centuries.* New York: Haworth Press, 1985.

A nice study of celibate women. Students often forget that celibacy is a sexual choice too.

Selections from the *Malleus Maleficarum* in Alan C. Kors and Edward Peters, eds., *Witchcraft in Europe 1100–1700: A documentary history.* Philadelphia: University of Pennsylvania Press, 1972.

The "Hammer of Witches" was the most influential antiwitch polemic of the Reformation period. As a consequence, it is filled with many lovely tidbits about witches as sexually powerful women. As a text, it can lead to many possible issues for discussion about women and sexual power.

Lynn A. Hunt, ed., *The invention of pornography: Obscenity and the origins of modernity, 1500–1800.* New York: Zone Books, 1993.

A series of essays relating to the development of pornographic literature, especially in ancien régime France. The material is rather explicit but highlights some important issues regarding sexual decadence, libertinage, and the fall of the French aristocracy. (See also Lynn A. Hunt, *Family romance of the French Revolution.* Berkeley: University of California Press, 1992.)

Marquis de Sade, *Justine.* New York: Castle Books, 1964.

I debated about this one but realized that talking about Sade without having students read him was futile. He has engendered so much debate, notably in feminist circles, that I thought that some good discussion would come from it.

Angela Carter, *The Sadeian woman: And the ideology of pornography.* New York: Pantheon, 1978.

A good critique from a marvelous novelist. Too many people rely on Simone de Beauvoir's examination and leave it at that. Andrea Dworkin's critique of him in her book *Pornography: Men possessing women* (New York: Putnam, 1981) could also be used.

Jeffrey Weeks, *Sex, politics and society: The regulation of sexuality since 1800.* New York: Longman, 1989.

A wide-ranging study of sexual ideas of the Victorian period.

Janet Murray, ed., *Strong-minded women: And other lost voices from nineteenth-century England.* New York: Pantheon, 1982.

A source collection of Victorian women's writings. I'm particularly interested in the selections on working-class women and prostitutes in the Victorian period.

Thomas Hughes, *Tom Brown's school days.* London: Dent, 1914.

There is no better introduction to the idealized vision of male bonding in the English public school.

Charlotte Perkins Gilman, *The yellow wallpaper.* New York: Feminist Press, 1973.

What better examination of Victorian morality, the public and private spheres, and sexual oppression in the name of societal norms! I've used this before and the students *love* it.

Ronald Hyam, *Empire and sexuality: The British experience.* Manchester/New York: St. Martin's Press, 1990.

A provocative study of the sexual lure and life of the British colonial empire.

Walter L. Williams, *The spirit and the flesh: Sexual diversity in American Indian culture.* Boston: Beacon Press, 1992.

A marvelous study about gender and gender differences in American Indian culture.

John D'Emilio and Estelle Freedman, *Intimate matters: A history of sexuality in America.* New York: Harper & Row, 1988.

A fine introduction to the sexual history of America—before the AIDS epidemic was in full swing.

Beth L. Bailey, *From front porch to back seat: Courtship in 20th century America.* Baltimore: Johns Hopkins University Press, 1988.

Too many students are under the impression that their parents had absolutely no interest in sexuality. Bailey gives a nice introduction to the history of courtship in the 20th century.

Peggy Reeves Sanday, *Fraternity gang rape: Sex, brotherhood and privilege on campus.* New York: New York University Press, 1990.

A brutal book about a brutal subject. Students (males in particular) need to examine their own sexual behavior and that of their peers, and this is a powerful introduction to one of the grimmer aspects of sexuality on college campuses.

Andrea Dworkin's testimony before the Meese Commission can be found in her *Letters from a war zone: Writings, 1976–1989* (New York: E. P. Dutton, 1989).

This outlines her ideas on pornography in simpler terms than those discussed in her book *Pornography.*

Linda Lovelace with Mike McGrady, *Ordeal.* New York: Bell, 1983.

Very few books overpower the reader in such a visceral way as this unrelenting autobiography of a "porn queen." I chose it because it changed my own view of pornography.

Tony Kushner, *Angels in America: A gay fantasia on national themes.* New York: Theatre Communications Group, 1993–94.

As long as it and its sequels run on stage, much of the discussion of AIDS in popular culture will relate to this play. I thought that students should join in the discussion.

Randy Shilts, *And the band played on: Politics, people and the AIDS epidemic.* New York: St. Martin's Press, 1988.

I have them read this in conjunction with watching the dramatization of it done by HBO.

21
Women in the Middle East: A History Tutorial

Jo-Ann Gross

The course entitled Women in the Middle East is one of several tutorial courses offered in the History Department at Trenton State College. Tutorial courses are small (limited to an enrollment of six) undergraduate seminar-like courses that offer students the opportunity to engage in in-depth research on one topic over one semester. These courses typically emphasize critical analysis, discussion, oral presentation, and written critiques. Each student in the History Department is required to take one tutorial course in order to graduate. A prerequisite of any one of my courses in Islamic history, modern Middle East, or India is required to enroll in my tutorial Women in the Middle East. Most students who take this tutorial are either juniors or seniors and have taken a number of upper-level history courses.

The goal of the course is to expose students to the historical issues concerning the roles of and attitudes toward women in the Islamic societies of the Middle East. The first half of the course is devoted to establishing the main focal points and the diversity of approaches to understanding issues of gender. Three books are discussed in class (see syllabus). After establishing the key questions concerning Islamic legal concepts, social values, and cultural diversity; economic issues of class, labor, and sociopolitical participation; the role of politics and the state; and the current debates concerning modernization, political participation, Islamic revivalism, and feminist ideologies, students choose one topic that they will explore during the second half of the semester. Special attention is paid to providing a variety of sources that include historical narratives and analyses, ethnographic studies, literature, oral history, legal documents (Quran, Islamic law, and hadith), and folklore.

During the second half of the semester, the discussions become more comparative as students begin to see how one issue, such as the political participation of women, may play itself out in very different ways depending on the source, historical context, or cultural milieu. The instructor's role is important in drawing out the comparative concepts and issues and in guiding students to pursue their individual research projects. Special attention is paid to the exposure of popular perceptions and media-sponsored representations of Islamic "fundamentalism" and veiling, for example. Students often find themselves challenged by cultural attitudes or social behavior that is quite alien to their own experiences. As the course progresses, however, students often express their satisfaction in gaining the ability to historically and culturally assess the status and roles of women in the Middle East and to understand, through the eyes of Middle Easterners themselves, the forces at work in the formation of female identity and the realities of everyday life for Middle Eastern women, whether a feminist in Cairo, a Bedouin in the Arabian desert, a fundamentalist in Algeria, or a female saint of medieval Islamic Spain.

SYLLABUS FOR WOMEN IN THE MIDDLE EAST

In this tutorial, historical, ethnographic, and literary sources are used to explore the roles of and attitudes toward women in the Islamic societies of the Middle East. A variety of expressions of female identity expressed by Middle Eastern women themselves are examined in order to understand the divergence among Islamic legal concepts, social values, and personal forms of identity in urban and rural Middle Eastern communities. The role of politics in gender relations and its social and economic dimensions are also addressed in the context of specific contemporary Middle Eastern states.

There are three common readings, after which each student chooses a specific thematic project for the semester. An outline of topics is provided to guide students in choosing a topic. Subsequent to the introductory meeting during the first week of class, the tutorial group meets six times during the semester.

Requirements

Six books (or the equivalent in articles) are read during the semester. Three are common readings, and three are individual readings. Individual readings are chosen by the student in consultation with the instructor. Written reports are required for each of the readings. On a rotating basis, four students make 15-minute oral presentations at each meeting. The other students present major issues or questions for discussion and participate in the discussion and comments.

The following three books are required reading:

Leila Ahmed, *Women and Gender in Islam: Historical Roots of a Modern Debate* (New Haven, CT: Yale University Press, 1992).

Erika Friedl, *Women of Deh Koh: Lives in an Iranian Village* (Washington, DC: Smithsonian Institution Press, 1989).

Deniz Kandiyoti, *Women, Islam and the State* (Philadelphia: Temple University Press, 1991).

Topic Guidelines and Sources

Women and Islamic Fundamentalism

Arat, Yesim, "Islamic Fundamentalism and Women in Turkey," *The Muslim World, 80* (1990), 17–23.

Azari, Farah, ed., *Women of Iran: The Conflict With Fundamentalist Islam* (London: Ithaca Press, 1983).

Hjarpe, Jan, "The Attitude of Islamic Fundamentalism Towards the Question of Women in Islam," in Bo Utas, ed., *Women in Islamic Societies: Social Attitudes and Historical Perspectives* (Atlantic Highlands, NJ: Humanities Press, 1983), 12–25.

Kepel, Gilles, *Muslim Extremism in Egypt: The Prophet and Pharaoh* (Berkeley: University of California Press, 1985).

Mernissi, Fatima, "Muslim Women and Fundamentalism," *MERIP Middle East Report #153,* vol. 18:4 (1988), 8–11.

Tabari, Azar, *In the Shadow of Islam: The Women's Movement in Iran* (London: Zed Press, 1982).

Zakaria, Fuad, "The Standpoint of Contemporary Muslim Fundamentalists," in Nahid Toubia, ed., *Women of the Arab World: The Coming Challenge* (London: Zed Books, 1988), 27–35.

Feminism and the Women's Movement

Ahmed, Leila, "Feminism and Feminist Movements in the Middle East, A Preliminary Exploration: Turkey, Egypt, Algeria, People's Democratic Republic of

Yemen," in Azizah al-Hibri, ed., *Women and Islam* (Oxford: Pergamon Press, 1982), 153–168.

Badran, Margot, "Dual Liberation: Feminism and Nationalism in Egypt, 1870s–1925," *Feminist Issues, 8,* no. 1 (Spring 1988), 15–34.

Badran, Margot, and Meriam Cooke, *Opening the Gates: A Century of Arab Feminist Writing* (London: Virago Press, 1990), 15–34.

Cole, Juan Ricardo, "Feminism, Class and Islam in Turn-of-the-Century Egypt," *International Journal of Middle East Studies, 13* (Nov. 1981), 387–407.

Faruqi, Lois, "Islamic Traditions and the Feminist Movement: Confrontation or Cooperation?" *Islamic Quarterly, 27,* no. 3 (1983), 133–139.

Hatem, Mervat, *Patriarchy and Nationalism in the Middle East* (London: Zed Books, 1987).

Hijab, Nadia, *Womanpower: The Arab Debate on Women at Work* (Cambridge: Cambridge University Press, 1988).

Jayawardena, Kumari, *Feminism and Nationalism in the Third World in the 19th and 20th Centuries* (London: Zed Books, 1986).

Mernissi, Fatima, *The Veil and the Male Elite: A Feminist Interpretation of Women's Rights in Islam* (Reading, MA: Addison-Wesley, 1987).

Mumtaz, Khawa, and Farida Shaheed, *Women of Pakistan* (London: Zed Books, 1987).

Sanassarian, Eliz, *The Women's Rights Movement in Iran* (New York: Praeger, 1982).

Sha'awari, Huda, *Harem Years: The Memoirs of an Egyptian Feminist,* trans. and ed. Margot Badran (New York: Feminist Press, 1986).

Seclusion and Veiling

Ala, Maududi S. Abbul, *Purdah and the State of Women in Islam* (Lahore, Pakistan: Islamic Publications, 1983).

Anderson, Jon, "Social Structure and the Veil: Comportment and the Composition of Interaction in Afghanistan," *Anthropos* (1982), 397–420.

Fernea, Elizabeth, *Guests of the Sheikh: An Ethnography of an Iraqi Village* (New York: Doubleday, 1965).

Jeffrey, Patricia, *Frogs in a Well: Indian Women in Purdah* (London: Zed Press, 1979).

Macleod, Arlene. *Accommodating Protest: Working Women, the New Veiling and Change in Cairo* (New York: Columbia University Press, 1991).

Mernissi, Fatimah, *Beyond the Veil: Male-Female Dynamics in a Modern Muslim Society,* rev. ed. (Bloomington: Indiana University Press, 1987).

Pastner, Carroll McC., "A Social, Structural and Historical Analysis of Honor, Shame and Purdah," *Anthropological Quarterly, 45* (1972), 248–261.

Rugh, Andrea, *Reveal and Conceal: Dress in Contemporary Egypt* (Syracuse: Syracuse University Press, 1986).

Wikan, Unni, *Behind the Veil in Arabia; Women in Oman* (Baltimore: Johns Hopkins University Press, 1982).

Zuhur, Sherifa, *Revealing Reveiling: Islamist Gender Ideology in Contemporary Egypt* (Albany: State University of New York Press, 1992).

Marriage and Sexuality

Doubleday, Veronica, *Three Women of Herat* (Austin: University of Texas Press, 1990).
Farah, Madelain, *Marriage and Sexuality in Islam* (Salt Lake City: Utah University Press, 1984).
Haeri, Shahla, *Law of Desire: Temporary Marriage in Shi'i Iran* (Syracuse, NY: Syracuse University Press, 1989).
Malti-Douglas, Fedwa, *Woman's Body, Woman's Word: Gender and Discourse in Arabo-Islamic Writing* (Princeton, NJ: Princeton University Press, 1991).
Marsot, al-Sayyid Afaf, ed., *Society and the Sexes in Medieval Islam* (Malibu, CA: Undena Publications, 1979).
Mernissi, Fatima, "Virginity and Patriarchy," *Women's Studies International Forum*, 5, no. 2 (1982), 183–192.
Musallam, Basim, *Sex and Society in Islam: Birth Control Before the Nineteenth Century* (New York: Cambridge University Press, 1983).
Smith, W. Robertson, *Kinship and Marriage in Early Arabia* (Beirut: United Publishers, 1973).

Expressions of Female Identity Through Literature: The Life and Works of Nawal el Saadawi

The Circling Song (London: Zed Books, 1989).
Death of an Ex-Minister, trans. Shirley Eber (London: Methuen, 1987).
The Fall of the Imam, trans. Sherif Hetata (London: Methuen, 1988).
God Dies by the Nile, trans. Sherif Hetata (London: Zed Books, 1985).
"Growing up Female in Egypt," trans. Fedwa Malti-Douglas, in Elizabeth Fernea, ed., *Women and Family in the Middle East: New Voices of Change* (Austin: University of Texas Press, 1985), 111–120.
The Hidden Face of Eve: Women in the Arab World, trans. Sherif Hetata (Boston: Beacon Press, 1982).
Memoirs from the Women's Prison, trans. M. Booth (London: Women's Press, 1986).
Memoirs of a Woman Doctor, trans. Catherine Cobham (London: Saqi Books, 1988).
Two Women in One, trans. Osman Nusairi and Jana Gough (London: al-Saqi Books, 1983).
Woman at Point Zero, trans. Sherif Hetata (London: Zed Books, 1983).

Expressions of Female Identity Through Life and Oral History

Abu-Lughod, Lila, *Veiled Sentiments: Honor and Poetry in a Bedouin Society* (Berkeley: University of California Press, 1986).
Abu-Lughod, Lila, *Writing Women's Worlds: Bedouin Stories* (Berkeley: University of California Press, 1993).

Amrouche, Fadhma, *My Life Story: The Autobiography of a Berber Woman*, trans. D. Blair (London: Women's Press, 1988).

Atiya, Nayra, *Khul Khaal: Five Egyptian Women Tell Their Stories* (Syracuse, NY: Syracuse University Press, 1982).

Mernissi, Fatima, *Doing Daily Battle: Interviews with Moroccan Women*, trans. Marjo Lakeland (London: Women's Press, 1988).

Munson, Henry, ed. and trans., *The House of Si Abd Allah: The Oral History of a Moroccan Family* (New Haven, CT: Yale University Press, 1984).

Shaaban, Bouthaina, *Both Right and Left-Handed: Arab Women Talk About Their Lives* (London: Women's Press, 1988).

Women and Islamic Law

Coulson, Noel J., *Succession in the Muslim Family* (Cambridge: Cambridge University Press, 1971).

Coulson, Noel, and Doreen Hinchcliffe, "Women and Law Reform in Contemporary Islam," in Lois Beck and Nikki Keddie, eds., *Women in the Muslim World* (Cambridge: Harvard University Press, 1978), 37–51.

Dwyer, Daisy, "Law Actual and Perceived: The Sexual Politics of Law in Morocco," *Law and Society Review, 13,* no. 3 (1971), 739–756.

Esposito, John, *Women in Muslim Family Law* (Syracuse, NY: Syracuse University Press, 1982).

Hill, Enid, *Mahkama! Studies in the Egyptian Legal System* (London: Ithaca Press, 1979).

Mayer, Ann, "Libyan Legislation in Defense of Arabo-Islamic Mores," *The American Journal of Comparative Law, 28,* no. 2 (Spring 1980), 287–313.

Mayer, Ann Elizabeth, "Law and Women in the Middle East," *Cultural Survival Quarterly, 8,* no. 2 (1984), 49–59.

Mayer, Ann Elizabeth, ed., *Property, Social Structure, and Law in the Modern Middle East* (Albany: State University of New York Press, 1985).

Momeni, Jamshid, "Divorce in the Islamic Context," *Islamic Culture, 60,* no. 2 (April 1986), 1–40.

Najjar, Fauzi, "Egypt's Laws of Personal Status," *Arab Studies Quarterly, 10,* no. 3 (1988), 319–344.

Nelson, Cynthia, and Klause Kock, eds., *Law and Social Change: Problems and Challenges in Contemporary Egypt* (Cairo: American University in Cairo Press, 1979).

Salem, Norma, "Islam and the Legal Status of Women in Tunisia," in Freda Hussain, ed., *Muslim Women* (London: Croom Helm, 1985).

Women in Islamic History

Abbott, Nabia, *A'ishah, the Beloved of Muhammad* (Chicago: University of Chicago Press, 1942).

Abbott, Nabia, "Women and the State on the Eve of Islam," *American Journal of Semitic Languages and Literatures, 558* (1941), 259–284.

Bingham, Marjori Wall, and Susan Hill Gross, *Women in Islam: The Ancient Middle East to Modern Times* (Hudson, WI: Hudson, 1980).

Goldziher, Ignaz, "Women in the Hadith Literature," in S. M. Stern, ed., *Muslim Studies,* vol. 2 (Chicago: Aldine, 1968).

Gursoy-Naskali, Emine, "Women Mystics in Islam," in Bo Utas, ed., *Women in Islamic Societies: Social Attitudes and Historical Perspectives* (Atlantic Highlands, NJ: Humanities Press, 1983), 238–244.

Jennings, R. C., "Women in Early Seventeenth Century Ottoman Judicial Records: The Shari'a Court of Anatolina Kayseri," *Journal of the Economic and Social History of the Orient, 18* (1975), 53.

Keddie, Nikki R., ed., *Women in Middle Eastern History: Shifting Boundaries in Sex and Gender* (New Haven, CT: Yale University Press, 1991).

Peirce, Leslie P., *The Imperial Harem: Women and Sovereignty in the Ottoman Empire* (New York: Oxford University Press, 1993).

Smith, Jane, and Yvonne Y. Yaddan, "Women, Religion and Social Change in Early Islam," in Yvonne Y. Haddad and Ellison Banks Findly, eds., *Women, Religion and Social Change* (Albany: State University of New York Press, 1985), 19–36.

Smith, Margaret, *Rabi'a the Mystic and Her Fellow-Saints in Islam* (New York: Cambridge University Press, 1928).

Stowasser, Barbara, "The Status of Women in Early Islam," in Freda Hussain, ed., *Muslim Women* (New York: St. Martin's Press, 1984).

Women, Politics, War, and Resistance Movements

Awwad, Tawfiq, *Death in Beirut: A Novel,* trans. Leslie McLlughlin (London: Heinemann Educational, 1976).

Bayat-Phillip, Mangol, "Women and Revolution in Iran, 1905–1911," in Lois Beck and Nikki Keddie, eds., *Women in the Muslim World* (Cambridge: Harvard University Press, 1978), 295–308.

Botman, Salma, "Women's Participation in Radical Egyptian Politics 1939–1952," in Magida Salman, ed., *Women in the Middle East* (London: Zed Books, 1987).

Cooke, Miriam, *War's Other Voices: Women Writers on the Lebanese Civil War* (New York: Cambridge University Press, 1987).

Danforth, Sandra, "The Social and Political Implications of Muslim Middle Eastern Women in Violent Political Conflict," *Women and Politics, 4* (1984), 34–53.

Haddad, Yvonne, "Islam Women and Revolution in Twentieth-Century Arab Thought," *The Muslim World, 74,* nos. 3–4 (July–October 1984), 137–160.

Hale, Sondra, "The Wing of the Patriarch: Sudanese Women and Revolutionary Parties," *Middle East Report, 16,* no. 1 (1986), 25–30.

Joseph, Suad, "Women and Politics in the Middle East," *Middle East Report, 16,* no. 1 (1986), 3–7.

Mahjoube, Abdolrahmane, "The Inner Revolution of a Khomeyni Activist," in Monique Gadant, ed., *Women of the Mediterranean* (London: Zed Books, 1984).

Marsot, al-Sayyid, "The Revolutionary Gentlewoman in Egypt," in Lois Beck and
    Nikki Keddie, eds., *Women in the Muslim World* (Cambridge: Harvard Univer-
    sity Press, 1978).
Moghadam, Val, "Revolution, Islam and Women: Sexual Politics in Iran and Afghan-
    istan," in A. Praker, M. Russo, D. Sommer, and P. Yaefer, eds., *Nationalism and
    Sexualities* (New York: Routledge, 1991).
Peteet, Juli M., *Gender in Crisis: Women and the Palestinian Resistance Movement*
    (New York: Columbia University Press, 1991).
Rassam/Vinogradov, Amal, "Revolution Within Revolution: Women and State in
    Iraq," in Timothy Niblock, ed., *Iraq: The Contemporary State* (London: Croom
    Helm, 1982).
Rowbotham, Sheila, *Women, Resistance and Revolution: A History of Women and Rev-
    olution in the Modern World* (Paris: Pavot, 1973).
Senker, Cathy, *Defiance: Palestinian Women in the Uprising* (London: Israeli Mirror,
    1989).
Tucker, Judith, "Insurrectionary Women: Women and the State in Nineteenth Cen-
    tury Egypt," *Middle East Report, 16,* no. 1 (1986), 9–13.

22
Women Artists: Changing the Course of History

Lois Fichner-Rathus

WOMEN ARTISTS AT TRENTON STATE COLLEGE

In the spring of 1992, the Trenton State Art Department featured an experimental course entitled Women Artists in History. The enrollment response was unprecedented for trial courses in the history of art. Trenton State is a liberal arts, undergraduate institution of approximately 5,000 students. Although it offers neither a major nor a minor in art history, it does offer a minor in women's studies. Among its degree requirements is at least one course qualifying as a gender studies course. Women Artists in History was assigned upper-level status, and most students enrolled were juniors or seniors. The prerequisite for the course was Introduction to Art History (a one-semester survey of Western art), but the students who requested that the prerequisite be waived had no difficulty keeping up with the material.

My proposal to offer a course on women and art was met with some suspicion and a great deal of skepticism. The assumption of the departmental administration was that the course "wouldn't go"—in other words, it would appear in the course listings but wouldn't command a large enough enrollment to ever make it to the classroom. The typical cap on enrollment in an upper-level course at Trenton State is approximately 25 students; the cap was never imposed for this course, as it was believed that the course would never fill anyway. The demand for the course was so great that I took in any and all refugees of the registration process. My desire was to run the class not as a strict lecture course but as a seminar. By opening day we numbered 37— whopping, by seminar standards. It was the better part of valor that I decided not to switch my pedagogical method in light of the enrollment figure. I was not sorry. We worked like a well-greased machine or, should I say, like quilters at a bee.

The gender composition of the class was weighted in favor of women; there were 30 women and 7 men. The earliest days witnessed what could be called an obligatory yet good-natured banter that seemed to ease the discomfort of such uneven "sides." Women students had chips on their shoulders, occasionally feigning threats. Male students often felt the need to play devil's advocate or otherwise behave defensively. I watched what was, in its own way, a charming and artful dance around the boundaries. All this didn't last very long. The class quickly united around the work and the issues.

THE COURSE

In my introduction to the students, I explained that the category "women and art" was one of complexity, multiplicity, and contradiction. I explained that the course would address women in art (as portrayed by female and male artists), women artists, and feminism and art history and look at relevant gender issues. I warned them that this course was likely to be different from any other they'd taken; I wanted it to be "woman-like." By this I meant constantly in process, celebratory of difference, and, above all, collaborative.

For the first 5 weeks I lectured on women artists in history, weaving feminist art criticism into a chronological framework. In addition to their text reading (Wendy Slatkin's *Women Artists in History,* 2nd ed., and Whitney Chadwick's *Women, Art and Society*), I assigned articles and text excerpts, as listed in the bibliography at the end of this chapter. The remaining weeks of the semester were divided according to genre and medium: still life, portraiture, "grand" paintings, "little" paintings, sculpture, architecture, public monuments, photography and video, narrative art, collaborative art, feminist art, conceptual and performance art.

During these weeks I employed a seminar format. Students were each assigned one woman artist to research and then gave a 10- to 15-minute class presentation on their research as an introduction to my more detailed discussion of that artist. This exercise was called a "fact-find presentation" and was very well received. Students enjoyed searching for information; they discovered that it sometimes entailed a great deal of effort to find even the most basic biographical facts. They also developed a fascinating intimacy with their assigned artists, referring to them by first name and tirelessly dredging up information that would familiarize their peers with the artists' lives, loves, and personalities. Many students also seemed to adopt defensive or possessive postures, longing to convince the class of the absolute superiority of their artists over others—especially the artists' male contemporaries. Their excitement and good-natured competition was contagious, with each successive presentation becoming longer, more detailed, and more sophisticated. Students enjoyed being engaged in the teaching process, lecturing and fielding questions to the best of their ability.

The topical rather than chronological framework for this material also proved to be very successful. With content as a constant, students became interested in comparing and contrasting artistic approaches among artists and across history. Having been actively involved in teaching, students remained more participatory in the seminar.

COURSE OBJECTIVES

My goal throughout the course, and particularly during these seminar weeks, was to show the students as much work by women artists as I possibly could. I purchased all available slide sets and photographed illustrations from books, magazines, scholarly journals, and exhibition catalogs. I bought whatever I could find in museum shops and borrowed slides from colleagues. I also showed some videotapes—there are many high-quality VHS tapes available on women artists. Students were amazed, absolutely astounded by the sheer number of women's productions they were witnessing. "We had no idea . . ." was the prevailing sentiment, along with "I can't believe we've never seen this stuff! Where are they hiding it?" I also interspersed my lectures and student presentations with discussions of what have become seminal essays in feminist art criticism. These are listed in the bibliography.

With our minds filled with visual images and our hearts filled with a passion and respect for women artists and their struggle, we took a trip late in the semester to the Metropolitan Museum of Art in New York City. Students were to complete an analytical paper on a single work by a woman artist. Some came away gratified that they had found the artist they were looking for. Others put guards and museum workers through their paces by demanding that they indicate where the works by women could be found. All were thrilled by what they saw, though angered and frustrated by the paltry representation of women artists. The class did not travel to the National Museum of Women in the Arts in Washington, D.C.; perhaps we will fit this into our schedule at the next offering of this course.

Happily, I am about to offer this course for a second time, and I plan to deviate very little from the design described above. It's been a year and a half, and my desire to offer the seminar is really more akin to a need, a yearning, maybe even a first-trimester craving. The enthusiasm for this material was one that I have never witnessed in my dozen years of college teaching. Of course, it is time to let them know. How could one believe otherwise?

SYLLABUS FOR WOMEN ARTISTS IN HISTORY

Course Requirements

1. Midterm examination (30% of grade). This exam will consist of an open-book essay.
2. Comprehensive final examination (30% of grade). This exam will consist of traditional slide identification questions as well as compare-and-contrast essays and an essay on gender issues with regard to the arts.
3. Analytical paper (20% of grade). This paper will be 4–6 pages in length and will be based on the observation of a work (or works) of art within a museum setting.
4. Critical thinking exercises and fact-find report (20% of grade). These written and oral assignments must be competently completed and submitted and delivered on time. They will consist of thoughtful responses to gender issues as they relate to art.
5. Mandatory field trip to New York City museum.
6. Readings from sources other than textbook, to be provided in photocopy or placed on reserve in the library.

COURSE OUTLINE

Week 1   Introduction; Prehistory to the Roman Empire:
                    This introductory material addresses representations of
                    women in art, the plight of women and women artists
                    in ancient societies, and the influence of women on the
                    arts.

Week 2   From Earth Goddess to Virgin Mary; Medieval
                    Women:
                    A review of women artists in the Middle Ages, with spe-
                    cial focus on tapestry and manuscript illumination; dis-
                    cussion of images of woman in medieval art, particu-
                    larly those of Eve and Mary. Group discussion of

	Henry Kraus, "Eve and Mary: Conflicting Images of Medieval Woman" (in Broude & Garrad, 1982).
Week 3	The Female Body as Figure; The Nude; Women, Art, and Power: Examination of Renaissance paintings of Adam and Eve with discussion of Margaret Miles, "Female Body as Figure" (in Miles, 1989); discussion of relationships among women, art, and power in visual images from the late 18th to 20th centuries, using Linda Nochlin's *Women, Art, and Power* as a springboard for discussion.
Week 4	The Fallen: Men's Perceptions of Women and Women's Perceptions of Themselves: A survey of images of women in paintings by men and paintings by women.
Week 5	Why Have There Been No Great Women Artists? Still Life and Portraiture Discussion of Linda Nochlin's classic text, "Why Have There Been No Great Women Artists?"; beginning of student "fact-find" presentations on women artists who worked in the genres of still life and portraiture.
Week 6	Grand Paintings versus Little Paintings
Week 7	Sculpture, Architecture, Monuments
Week 8	Midterm exam (open-book essay exam)
Week 9	Women Photographers
Week 10	Narrative Art
Weeks 11–12	Collaboration; Feminist Art
Weeks 13–14	Conceptual Art; Performance
Week 15	Field trip
Exam Week	Comprehensive final exam

BIBLIOGRAPHY

Broude, Norma, and Mary D. Garrard, eds. *Feminism and Art History: Questioning the Litany.* New York: Harper & Row, 1982.

Chadwick, Whitney. *Women, Art and Society.* London: Thames and Hudson, 1990.

Fine, Elsa Honig. *Women and Art: A History of Women Painters and Sculptors From the Renaissance to the Twentieth Century.* Montclair, NJ: Allanheld & Schram/ Prior, 1978.

Harris, Ann Sutherland, and Linda Nochlin. *Women Artists: 1550–1950.* New York: Random House, 1976.

Heller, Nancy. *Women Artists: An Illustrated History.* New York: Abbeville Press, 1987.

Lippard, Lucy R. *From the Center: Feminist Essays on Women's Art.* New York: Dutton, 1976.

Miles, Margaret R. *Carnal Knowing: Female Nakedness and Religious Meaning in the Christian West.* Boston: Beacon Press, 1989.

Nochlin, Linda. *Women, Art, and Power and Other Essays.* New York: Harper & Row, 1988.

Parker, Roszika, and Griselda Pollock. *Old Mistresses: Women, Art, and Ideology.* New York/London: Routledge, 1981.

Pollock, Griselda. *Vision and Difference: Femininity, Feminism and the Histories of Art.* London/New York: Routledge, 1988.

Pomeroy, Sarah B. *Goddesses, Whores, Wives and Slaves: Women in Classical Antiquity.* New York: Schocken Books, 1975.

Robinson, Hillary, ed. *Visibly Female: Feminism and Art: An Anthology.* London: Camden Press, 1987.

Slatkin, Wendy. *Women Artists in History: From Antiquity to the 20th Century,* 2nd Ed. Englewood Cliffs, NJ: Prentice-Hall, 1990.

Witling, Mara R., ed. *Voicing Our Visions: Writings by Women Artists.* New York: Universe, 1991.

23

Teaching Diversity in Western Philosophy and Religion

John Kaltner
Andrea Tschemplik

Feminists have raised questions about sex and gender, and this has led to a reappraisal of important aspects of Western philosophy and religion. Others have questioned prevailing philosophical and theological traditions from specific perspectives on race, class, poverty, and war. Voices calling for liberation can be heard in pulpits and philosophy journals. A variety of issues are discussed in the course New Perspectives in Philosophy and Religion, with an emphasis on how new perspectives may help in understanding and analyzing traditional problems. (from the Upsala College catalog)

PERSPECTIVES ON "PERSPECTIVES"

The course description above was our only road map as we prepared to venture into previously uncharted territory. The two of us were recently hired, and we were the only members of our department currently teaching. We faced the daunting task of constructing a course that had never been offered before at the college, and since *creatio ex nihilo* was not something either of us had any prior experience with, we decided to work together on the project and team-teach the course. Besides, the subject matter intrigued us both, and it seemed to be the type of course that lends itself well to a collaborative effort.

We knew that we were in a unique environment, dealing with the issue of new and different perspectives. All we had to do was look around us. Upsala is arguably the most diverse college in the country, with a student body that is 46% African American, 36.8% white, 9.8% Hispanic, 7.4% Asian, and 10.3% international. Given this distribution, we could expect to have a fairly heterogeneous group of students in our class and could assume that many different perspectives would be represented. This heterogeneity offered the unique opportunity to listen to and experience diversity rather than to simply read about and discuss it.

Despite the exciting prospects this situation promised, we were not naive in our assumptions about the course and its outcome. The simple presence of diversity in our classroom would not guarantee success any more than the attainment of an academic degree indicates intelligence. The real challenge for us was to encourage the adoption and use of new perspectives as analytical and interpretive tools; a simple articulation of new perspectives would not be enough. This would be no easy goal to reach, but we reasoned that a properly structured syllabus and the right readings would make its attainment more likely.

We therefore set ourselves to the task of creating such a syllabus. Three topics would be treated in the semester: gender, poverty, and race, in that order. Under each heading we chose novels, texts, and articles that we were sure would argue persuasively for each perspective, grab the students' attention, and ensure a lively debate in the classroom. We decided against a highly structured delineation of the material that would make each of us "responsible" for a certain portion of it. We agreed that it would be better to keep things open-ended, although we both recognized that there were certain areas in which one of us had more familiarity than the other. Once our work was done, we sat back and eagerly anticipated the start of the new semester, not quite sure what to expect.

Our strategy was to encourage open expression of thoughts about gender, poverty, and race. We did not exempt ourselves from this requirement and hoped that this would create an atmosphere conducive to trust. We encouraged our students to open up by revealing some of our own beliefs and opinions. That was the game plan, but most of the players would not play.

THE MEDIUM IS THE MESSAGE

At the start of the semester, we had not yet determined how our theoretical vision would best be implemented and realized in the classroom context. In other words, the content of the course was set and in place, but the form it would take still remained a mystery. Perhaps the primary reason for this was our firm belief that this was a relatively inconsequential issue. We reasoned that since the topic was timely and the material we had chosen to treat was interesting and, in places, controversial, we would storm out of the gate like gangbusters, hit the ground running, and never look back. The question of the form and structure of the course, therefore, never struck us as a particularly crucial one. By the third week of the semester, we realized what a serious miscalculation this had been on our part.

The format with which we began the semester was a traditional one. One of us was more or less "responsible" for each class period and would begin by presenting some background material to the reading or topic. We would then try to generate discussion by eliciting responses to that day's text, often through the use of leading questions or requests for opinions. This approach failed miserably. It soon became apparent that many students were not taking the reading assignments seriously; the few who were soon became the only voices other than our own heard in the classroom. Many students were reluctant to respond to requests for their views on issues that were based on their personal experiences and required little dialogue with the texts. The environment was quickly taking on all the features of a lecture course and daily looked less and less like the open forum that would allow for a lively exchange of ideas, as we had initially envisioned.

Ironically, part of the reason for this situation was the makeup of the class. The group was so diverse and varied that many felt uncomfortable and were hesitant to speak freely, particularly on a topic that is as potentially volatile as diversity and differences due to gender, class, and race. It was safer to allow the two of us to be the focal point as the recognized "authorities" in the classroom. In retrospect, it is easy to see how the structure of the class—including its physical arrangement, with all facing forward, eyes on that day's facilitator—fed into these feelings and contributed to the situation.

By the third week of the semester, we realized that we needed to take a careful look at things and try to determine why the course was not going the way we had hoped. We were in a situation that many teachers dream about—an environment that allows students to discover that education can be experiential as well as intellectual—yet we were falling well short of the mark. We concluded that the only way to improve things was to totally revamp our approach and method.

We decided that in order to tap into the as yet unexploited resources the group had to offer, we needed to get them to start talking to one another and to stop listening to us. So we broke the class into three smaller groups of five students each, making sure that each group reflected the diversity found in the class as a whole. We explained that this would be the format for the remainder of the semester and that most of the class time would be spent in group work. Approximately two thirds of each period was spent in the discussion groups, with the final one third being used for each group to report back to the entire class on what had gone on in the group discussion. This latter time was also an opportunity for discussion among the groups. The syllabus remained intact, and each day's reading was the starting point and basis for that day's discussion. We stressed the point that although the readings were an important element for the groups, of even more significance was the input each student contributed based on his or her views and personal experiences. Given the heterogeneous nature of each group, the result was bound to be an engaging discussion among people of varied backgrounds and traditions that would be centered on some theme related to the topic of diversity.

Most of the students did not know one another, and we met little resistance when we announced the membership of each group. In a class of 15 students, seven countries were represented: the United States, Puerto Rico, Jamaica, China, Korea, Spain, and Nigeria. This guaranteed ethnic heterogeneity, but since our intent was to achieve as much of a variety of perspectives as possible in each of the groups, we were also attentive to a proper distribution of gender and economic backgrounds. We thus had a kind of *creatio ex plenitudine,* putting them together and making them male and female, foreign and domestic, rich and poor, verbose and shy, honors and basic-skills students.

The results of this new arrangement were immediate and startling. The classroom was suddenly buzzing with activity and discussion as each group grappled with the issues and began the process of developing a corporate identity. We observed and listened in stunned disbelief as this transformation took place. As the focus of authority shifted from us to the groups, our role also underwent a transformation. We now had to decide to what degree we should control or guide the group conversations. We experimented with complete laissez-faire when the readings were explosive; at other times, we provided questions for each group to jump-start the discussions. Occasionally we provided short lectures, which were now given serious attention.

Three times a week, then, we were treated to a vibrant and earnest exchange of ideas. We watched as students who had never volunteered a sentence became vocal leaders of their groups. We saw foreign students who had previously been insecure about their English become more confident in expressing their views. Sometimes the atmosphere in the classroom was so overwhelming that we could not help but smile.

During the first few weeks of this new arrangement, the question of our own role kept us somewhat ill at ease; the transference of power was no easy task for either side. Initially, it seemed that we were expected to provide every service from resource person to referee. We were even asked whether cursing was allowed in the groups. Over time, the groups became increasingly independent, until we began to question what contribution, if any, we were making. The traditional role of teacher as grader remained, as we had to read and evaluate each student's daily written assignment, which was an outline of and reaction to the day's reading. But it was not until the end of the semester that we discovered that we had been performing another function throughout the course of the semester: teacher as midwife. Instead of inseminating them with our ideas, we assisted them in giving birth to their own insights and encouraged them to grow.

We dedicated our last class to evaluating both the content and the method of the course. Overall reaction to group work was very positive, and many students cited the experience of "sanction-free thinking and expression" as an important step toward understanding and analyzing their own perspectives. Most of our students detected a political aspect in their group work, which they described as "the experience of democracy and equality." They explained that they considered this the outcome of recognizing and respecting differences together. In the process of working with the same people throughout the semester, there seemed to develop a "felt obligation" to do readings and prepare assignments, and many commented on the strange experience of a "group conscience." They thus described the transition from education as competitive individualism to education as an interpersonal experience.

In the middle of the semester, we examined articles by feminist theologians (Carol Christ and Judith Plaskow, for example) who emphasized the need for a narrative, the importance of telling one's story and listening to others. We invited our students to use their group work time to tell their stories to one another. This was a risky proposition and required a great deal of trust if it was to be a meaningful exercise. In hushed voices, they told their stories, and some had devastating stories to tell. On the last day of classes, they referred to this experience and mentioned other times when their discussions had led them to talk about themselves. They suggested that although the majority of class time should be devoted to discussing assigned material, some time should be reserved to provide the opportunity for them to get to know one another. We might have been naive, but it came as a shock to us that in most classes, even in a "small college," students don't know and don't talk to one another.

An important aspect of group work is the experience of learning together as friends. It is then possible to say that you don't understand, that you must test your hypotheses against somebody else's views, to speak openly about ideas and to learn to listen and respect others. Only in this context can we take the risk of trying on different perspectives and revealing our own.

SYLLABUS FOR NEW PERSPECTIVES IN PHILOSOPHY
AND RELIGION

Required Books

Toni Morrison, *The Bluest Eye* (New York: Washington Square Press, 1970).
Carol Gilligan, *In a Different Voice* (Cambridge: Harvard University Press, 1982).
Carol Christ & Judith Plaskow (eds.), *Womanspirit Rising* (San Francisco: Harper & Row, 1992).
Leonardo Boff & Clodovis Boff, *Introducing Liberation Theology* (New York: Orbis, 1990).
John G. Neihardt (recorder), *Black Elk Speaks* (Lincoln: University of Nebraska Press, 1979).
James H. Cone, *A Black Theology of Liberation* (New York: Orbis, 1991).

READING SCHEDULE

Classes 1–3   Morrison, *The Bluest Eye*

                  OTHER VOICES: WOMEN ON THE MORAL AND
                  POLITICAL

Class 4   Simone de Beauvoir, *The Second Sex* (New York: Vintage Books, 1974) (excerpts)

Class 5   Alison Jaggar, "Political Philosophies of Women's Liberation," in Richard A. Wasserstrom, *Today's Moral Problems* (New York: Macmillan, 1985)

Classes 6–8   Carol Gilligan, *In a Different Voice*

Class 9   Sara Ruddick, "Remarks on the Sexual Politics of Reason," in Eve Feder Kittay & Diane T. Meyers (eds.), *Women and Moral Theory* (Totowa, NJ: Rowman & Littlefield, 1987)
                  Virginia Held, "Marx, Sex, and the Transformation of Society," in Carol Gould & M. Wartofsky (eds.), *Women and Philosophy: Toward a Theory of Liberation* (New York: G. D. Putnam's Sons, 1976)

Class 10   Sojourner Truth, "Ain't I a Woman?" in Miriam Schneir, *Feminism: The Essential Historical Writings* (New York: Random House, 1994); hooks, "Racism &

Feminism," in Evelyn Ashton-Jones & Gary Olson, *The Gender Reader* (Needham, MA: Allyn & Bacon, 1991.)

Class 11   Sandra Harding, "The Curious Coincidence of Feminine and African Moralities: Challenges for Feminist Theory," in Eva Feder Kittay & Diane T. Meyers (eds.), *Women and Moral Theory* (Totowa, NJ: Rowman & Littlefield, 1987)

OTHER VOICES: WOMEN ON THE SPIRITUAL

Class 12   Clifford Geertz, "Religion as a Cultural System," in W. A. Lessa & E. Z. Vogt (eds.), *Reader in Comparative Religion* (New York: Harper & Row, 1972)

Class 13   Rosemary Radford Ruether, "Motherearth and the Megamachine," and Mary Daly, "After the Death of God the Father," in Christ & Plaskow, *Womanspirit Rising* (San Francisco: Harper & Row, 1992)

Class 14   Sheila Collins, "Reflections on the Meaning of Herstory," and Phyllis Trible, "Eve and Adam: Genesis 2–3 Reread," in Christ & Plaskow, *Womanspirit Rising* (San Francisco: Harper & Row, 1992)

Class 15   Elisabeth Schuessler Fiorenza, "Women in the Early Christian Movement," and Merlin Stone, "When God Was a Woman," in Christ & Plaskow, *Womanspirit Rising* (San Francisco: Harper & Row, 1992)

OTHER VOICES: POVERTY

Class 16   Jonathan Kozol, *Savage Inequalities* (New York: Crown, 1991) (excerpt)

Class 17   Paulo Freire, *Pedagogy of the Oppressed* (New York: Continuum, 1990) (excerpt); Karl Marx, "Wage Labor and Capital," reprinted in Robert C. Tucker (ed.), *The Marx-Engels Reader* (New York: W. W. Norton, 1978)

Class 18   Video: *Romero;* Leonardo Boff & Clodovis Boff, *Introducing Liberation Theology* (New York: Orbis, 1990)

Classes 19–22   Leonardo Boff & Clodovis Boff, *Introducing Liberation Theology* (New York: Orbis, 1990); J. David Pleins, "Is a Palestinian Theology of Liberation Possible?" *Anglican Theological Review,* Spring 1992, 133–43

OTHER VOICES: NATIVE AMERICANS

Class 23   Ake Hultkrantz, "North American Religions: An Overview," in Mircea Eliade (ed.), *The Encyclopedia of Religion,* Vol. 10 (New York: Macmillan, 1987)

Class 24   Video: *The Mission*

Classes 25–26   John Neihardt, *Black Elk Speaks* (Lincoln: University of Nebraska Press, 1979)

Class 27   Article on current social and political situation of Native Americans

OTHER VOICES: AFRICAN AND AFRICAN AMERICAN EXPERIENCE

Class 28   Martin Luther King, Jr., "Letter from a Birmingham Jail," in *Why We Can't Wait* (New York: Signet Books, 1964)

Class 29   Movie: *Malcolm X*

Classes 30–33   James Cone, *A Black Theology of Liberation* (New York: Orbis, 1991)

24

Racism and Sexism in the United States: Introduction to Women's Studies

Arlene Holpp Scala

TEACHING RACISM AND SEXISM IN THE UNITED STATES

In 1989, I was a participant in the International Institute on Peace Education at Teachers College, Columbia University. I attended a workshop on racism presented by an African American woman who began the session with an exercise on discrimination. She handed each of us a circle or a square and then treated us differently according to the shape of the pieces of paper on our desks. The discrimination exercise caused a lot of anger among some of the conferees, especially several white men, and led to an exciting discussion about how discrimination feels.

I was impressed by the exercise and began to use it on the first day of each semester. I prepare paper squares and circles in two different fluorescent colors, and I greet each student at the door. I look them up and down and then hesitate before "deciding" whether they are "circles" or "squares." (I am careful to see that each group is mixed in terms of race and sex.) The students respond good-naturedly but typically look a little confused. When it's time to begin class, I ask either the circles or the squares to move to the back of the room, and I ask the students holding the other shape to move to the front of the room. I then welcome the students up front (I'll call them the "squares") and speak softly to them about how glad I am that they are in my class. I also compliment them on their intelligence, which I say I "noticed" and which allowed me to identify them as "squares." I occasionally glance at the "circles," and eventually I tell them in an unfriendly voice to move further back, preferably against the wall. I tell them that I'll talk to them later. I then change my voice and converse with the favored "squares," asking them how it feels to be among the intelligent. Typically, there are students who acknowledge that they like receiving special treatment.

I continue the exercise for about 15 minutes, rudely addressing the "circles" and offering them a bit of hope if they would "pull themselves up by their bootstraps." Eventually, I give in to student pressure (when I am repeatedly challenged), or else I just tell students in the back to move forward. I tell the class that they just participated in a discrimination exercise. We then talk about how it felt to be either favored or discriminated against. Students who were favored often confess that they liked being "recognized" as superior. Students who were discriminated against talk about how awful they felt and how shocked they were to be treated this way in a class where they thought they wouldn't encounter discrimination from the teacher. I ask students to remember their feelings as we begin our semester's inquiry into discrimination issues. Although it takes some students a couple of class sessions to get over their initial experience, when students anonymously evaluate the course several weeks later and again at the end of the semester, most write that it was a valuable learning experience. One student's anonymous response indicates the pain and value of the exercise: "I feel the exercise was a bit harsh for the first day, but it did allow the class to see just how it is to be treated so unfairly, how it is to be the victim."

Having taught this course for 5 years, I have learned that there is a need for both affective and cognitive learning experiences in a class where issues of systemic oppression are explored. Students are impressed by statistics about income disparities in the United States, but they are also moved by personal accounts in our anthology and by stories told by their peers.

My pedagogical approach draws on Paulo Freire's concept of the teacher-learner community (*Pedagogy of the Oppressed* [New York: Continuum, 1970]), with discussions generated by the concerns of the students in the class following assigned readings. Reader-response theories inform the kind of weekly assignments I require students to work on.

In order to encourage students to connect the issues of racism, sexism, classism, and heterosexism with their own life experiences and observations, I require that students write a response log in conjunction with one of the readings each week. I ask students to summarize the reading and write about their emotional responses and their free associations. It takes some students a few weeks to understand the difference between an emotional response (This reading makes me feel. . . .) and a free association (This reading reminds me of. . . .). Students bring their logs to class and share them in small groups of three or four. They read one another's logs and write responses to their peers' papers in the logs. They then discuss the reading in their groups, using the logs as their jumping-off point. Students spend about 30 minutes in these small groups. I circulate among the groups and sometimes listen in on discussions. We then have a plenary discussion, which begins with a member of each group sharing one of the ideas or issues that emerged in the small-group discussion. Using this reading, writing, and discussion approach guarantees student participation. Recently, a student evaluating the discussion format wrote, "I have never seen a class so talkative."

Speakers and films are very effective when teaching about race, sex, sexuality, and class. For example, when addressing heterosexism, students read an article about gay-bashing, write logs, and engage in small and large group discussions. We also see the film *The Times of Harvey Milk*, which presents some gay history and raises issues about homophobia. The film focuses on the political career of Harvey Milk but also includes images of lesbian women. This film leads to discussions about racism as well as heterosexism and homophobia. It reveals that Dan White was sentenced to only several years in prison for assassinating Milk and another man. A black man in the film tells a reporter that the sentencing is ridiculous and asks what his sentence would be if he killed two men. Typically, this leads to a discussion of racial inequities in the justice system.

I find poetry to be effective when addressing violence against women. An oral reading of Ntozake Shange's poem "is not so gd to be born a girl" is a powerful way to move into the topic of violence against women. The poem encourages an affective response, which I follow up with statistical information about violence against women.

I have noticed that there is a lot of tension in the room when we address racism in a class that is racially diverse. Students tend to be more open (sometimes proud) of their homophobia, and males often take pride in their sexism. But when we address racism, white students go to great lengths to deny and hide their racism, especially against blacks. Responding anonymously early in the semester to a broad question about the class experience, one student wrote, "I sense racist hostility in this class that is being suppressed because people are afraid to say what they really feel."

I think that students need to get in touch with their own racism before we can have a meaningful discussion about racism. Beginning on the first and continuing into the second day of class, students introduce themselves and tell personal stories about their experience with racism. Students interpret the concept of racism broadly and tell stories about many kinds of discrimination, including anti-Semitism, regionalism, ethnocentrism, and sexism. I do not "correct" them because I think that students need to start from wherever they are regarding the issue. This sharing of stories is followed by a discussion of some of the issues that emerged.

By the time we start discussing readings (such as an excerpt from Richard Wright's autobiography), the Howard Beach incident, and more recent events such as the police attack on Rodney King, students start to challenge one another. For example, during one discussion about life in the inner cities, a black student said that he did not want white people coming to his neighborhood and telling him what it means to live in the projects. One white student "heard" the black student say that he did not want whites to come to his neighborhood. When the black student replied that he wasn't opposed to whites coming to his neighborhood but to their coming and telling him about the reality of his life, several white students joined the discussion, chiding the black student for advocating segregation. Other black students joined the discussion and argued that no one was advocating segregation. During this discussion, many students were hearing along racial lines. I encouraged the students to address one another directly, and I later joined the discussion, telling the class what I had heard each student say. (I listen to student discussions with paper and pen in hand, recording as much as I possibly can.) By the time the class was over, the issue was not resolved, but the class session was effective because many white students had let their guard down and allowed themselves to reveal their racism, making the discussion more real. At the next class session, I asked students to write an anonymous response to the previous class. Students commented on the stress that they felt, but they also indicated that the discussion felt "real."

I also work to address racism by asking students to brainstorm for racial stereotypes of African Americans, Latinas and Latinos, Anglo Euro-Americans, Asian Americans, and Native Americans. Students notice that the stereotypes tend to get meaner as the group's skin color gets darker. This exercise also allows us to talk about the classification of Hispanics as a racial group and what that implies about racism and classification systems. The issue of colorism also emerges in the context of this exercise.

I think that it is important for students to address issues of race, sex, sexuality, and class in a manner that engages their feelings as well as their thinking. Also, the pedagogy needs to reflect the goal of student and citizen empowerment. At the state college where I teach, I find it useful to help students come to terms with their working-class roots and realities. When they can find their place in our economic system, they are more likely to understand how oppressive systems function and are perpetuated.

THE COURSE

Required Texts

Paula Rothenberg, *Race, Class, & Gender in the United States: An Integrated Study,* 2nd ed. (New York: St. Martin's Press, 1992).
Suzanne Pharr, *Homophobia: A Weapon of Sexism* (Inverness, CA: Chardon Press, 1988).

Course Description

We are all born into the world as equals. Or are we? Does being black, brown, red, yellow, or white make a difference? How does being born female or male determine the script of one's life? To what extent is one's life determined by the socioeconomic class one is born into? Are we born lesbian, gay, bisexual, or heterosexual, or is sexual orientation learned? Does one's sexual orientation make a difference in terms of human rights and civil rights? What does it mean to be a feminist? Isn't "humanist" a more inclusive term than "feminist"? What do the terms "multicultural" and "multiethnic" mean? Is equality a reality or a myth in the 20th-century United States, or in the United States of the past? Does Columbus Day celebrate a discovery or an invasion? What might we conclude about sex and power when noting that only 6 out of 100 U.S. senators are women? Does a court have the right to take a child away from its mother because the mother is a lesbian? What are some of the racial implications of the case involving the police beating of Rodney King?

The pedagogy of the course reflects the course's content. In other words, as we study systems of oppression and ways to move beyond oppression, we meet as a community of teacher-learners engaging in dialogical education. The pedagogy has been developed by concepts growing out of feminist pedagogy and Paulo Freire's liberatory pedagogy.

Objectives

1. To clarify and analyze the difference between individual prejudices and institutionalized systems of oppression.
2. To investigate the major documents that have determined the de jure and de facto status of women and minorities throughout U.S. history.
3. To understand the connections among all forms of oppression and the economic system in the United States.
4. To investigate several models for social change that seek to eliminate (or at least significantly reduce) racism, sexism, heterosexism, classism, and

other "isms" that undermine the vitality and collective power of a multi-cultural society.

Course Requirements

Students are expected to complete assigned readings on time and to partici-pate in class discussions of provocative and controversial issues. Reactions to readings, films, speakers, class discussions, current events, media programs, and so forth will be the primary focus of class sessions.

Reader-Response Logs and Class Participation. Each week students will write a response to an assigned reading (see calendar). Reader-response logs consist of three parts: a summary of the reading, the student's emotional response to the reading (This reading makes me feel. . . .), and free associa-tions (This reading makes me think about. . . .). If handwritten, logs should be about two pages in length (one page if typewritten). The audience for reader-response logs will be peers working in response groups as well as the instructor. Logs are due at the first class session of each week (one third of grade).

Midterm and Final Essays. These essays will focus on applying critiques of racism, sexism, heterosexism, and classism to current news stories (one third of grade).

Collaborative Project. Students will select topics of interest relating to the course and work in groups of three or more to research and discuss a topic. I highly recommend collaborative projects; however, if it is impossible to meet with peers outside of class, students may do individual projects. Collab-orative projects are presented orally only; individual projects, which will also be presented orally, must be accompanied by a five-page paper. During the second half of the semester, students will present their projects to the class. Some of the topics selected in the past have included date and acquaintance rape, discriminatory graffiti around campus, sexism in children's literature, racist and sexist messages in cartoons, the Ku Klux Klan, AIDS, eating disor-ders, homelessness, lesbian and gay responses to heterosexist society, homo-phobia on campus, racism and sexism in music and music videos, and inter-racial relationships. In the past, students have engaged in primary and secondary research, created videos, brought in guest speakers, created visual artifacts such as posters and montages, and presented discussion-stimulating projects to the class (one third of grade).

Extra Credit. Students may earn extra credit by keeping a journal relating to feelings and thoughts about class discussions, experiences relating to issues discussed in class, news items relating to the course, and so on.

COURSE OUTLINE

(Asterisks indicate reader response log assignments.)

Week 1	Introduction and overview of course "Circles and Squares" discrimination activity Discussion of ground rules (handout) and sharing personal accounts of discrimination
Week 2	DEFINITIONS AND CONCEPTS Readings: "Intro.," Rothenberg, 1–4; "Defining 'Racism' & 'Sexism,'" Rothenberg, 5–8; "The Problem: Discrimination," U.S. Commission on Civil Rights in Rothenberg, 9–19; "Domination and Subordination," Jean Baker Miller in Rothenberg, 20–26; "Racial Formations," Michael Omi and Harold Winant in Rothenberg, 26–36
Week 3	RACISM Readings: "The Ethics of Living Jim Crow," Richard Wright in Rothenberg, 36–45*; "Bias Incident," Howard Blum in Rothenberg, 67–71; "Black vs. White in Howard Beach," Richard Stengel, Joseph N. Boyce, and Mary Cronin in Rothenberg, 71–73; "Act Prohibiting Slaves to Read," General Asembly of North Carolina in Rothenberg, 265; "Three-Fifths Compromise," U.S. Constitution in Rothenberg, 264; "*Plessy v. Ferguson*," U.S. Supreme Court decision in Rothenberg, 297–299
Week 4	SEXISM Readings: "Social Effects of Some Contemporary Myths About Women," Ruth Hubbard in Rothenberg, 45–51; "Gender Issues in College Classroom," Edward B. Fiske in Rothenberg, 52–53; "Nude Pictures Are Ruled Sexual Harassment," Tamar Lewin in Rothen-

berg, 84–86*; "Boys Will Be Boys?" Letty Cottin
Pogrebin in Rothenberg, 78–80; "A War Waged on
Women," Bob Herbert in Rothenberg, 80–82

Week 5   HOMOPHOBIA AND HETEROSEXISM

Readings: "S.I. Man Stabbed Dead: Anti-Gay Bias,"
James C. McKinley, Jr., in Rothenberg, 88–98*; "*Bowers v. Hardwick,*" Rothenberg, 310–312; "Gay/Lesbian
Rights," Arthur S. Leonard in Rothenberg, 313–319
Film: *Times of Harvey Milk*
Gay Speaker

Week 6   RACISM AND COLORISM

Readings: "Aqui No Se Habla Español," Shirley Perez
West in Rothenberg, 86–87; "Black Hispanics," Vivian
Brady in Rothenberg, 183–185; "Blacks and Hispanics,"
Jacqueline Conciatore and Roberta Rodriguez in Rothenberg, 185–189*
First journal collection due, optional

Week 7   ECONOMICS OF RACE, GENDER, AND CLASS
                IN THE UNITED STATES

Readings: "Rewards and Opportunities," Gregory Mantsios in Rothenberg, 96–110*; "Three Realities: Minority
Life in America," Business–Higher Education Forum in
Rothenberg, 110–112; "Middle Class Blacks," Isabel
Wilkerson in Rothenberg, 113–120; "The Poverty Industry," Theresa Funiciello in Rothenberg, 120–128

Week 8   MANY VOICES, MANY LIVES: RACES AND
                ETHNICITIES

Readings: "Racial and Ethnic Minorities," Rothenberg,
145–155; "The Puerto Rican Community in the South
Bronx," Clara Rodriguez in Rothenberg, 166–167*;
"Sun Chief," Leo W. Simmons, Ed., in Rothenberg,
155–156; "*Elk v. Wilkens,*" Rothenberg, 295–297; "Farewell to Manzanar," Jeanne Wakatsuki Houston and
James D. Houston in Rothenberg, 157–161; "*People v.*

Hall," Rothenberg, 275–276; "California Constitution," Rothenberg, 294–295; "*Korematsu v. United States,*" Rothenberg, 300–304

Week 9   Midterm essays due
Film: *Ethnic Notions*
Guest speaker: Prof. Aubyn Lewis, "The African Diaspora and Racism in the United States"

Week 10   Collaborative project work day
Midsemester conferences

HETEROSEXISM AND SEXISM

Reading: pgs. 1–44 in Pharr*

Week 11   Readings: pgs. 45–64 in Pharr;* "Gay Rights: Legal Front," Arthur S. Leonard in Rothenberg, 313–319; "Anti-Gay Stereotypes," Richard D. Mohr in Rothenberg, 351–357

ABLEISM, HETEROSEXISM, AND SEXISM

Readings: pgs. 65–91 in Pharr; "The Case of Sharon Kowalski and Karen Thompson: Ableism, Heterosexism, and Sexism," Joan Griscom in Rothenberg, 215–225*
Second journal collection, optional

Week 12   SEXUAL TERRORISM

Reading: "is not so gd to be born a girl," Ntozake Shange in Rothenberg, 191–192

HATE VIOLENCE

Reading: "Mate Violence," Carole Sheffield in Rothenberg, 388–397*

Week 13   RACISM AND ANTI-SEMITISM

Film: *The Klan*

RACISM, SEXISM, AND LANGUAGE

Readings: "Racism in the English Language," Robert B. Moore in Rothenberg, 331–341*; "The Language of Sexism," Haig Bosmajian in Rothenberg, 341–347; "Beauty and the Beast of Advertising," Jill Kilbourne in Rothenberg, 348–351; "Tyranny of Slenderness," Kim Chernin in Rothenberg, 192–199

Week 14   SEXISM

Film: *Dream Worlds*
Readings: "Age, Race, Class, and Sex: Women Redefining Difference," Audre Lorde in Rothenberg, 401–470; "En Rapport, in Opposition: Cobrando Cuentas as Las Nuestras," Gloria Anzaldúa in Rothenberg, 408–414; "Up Against the Wall," Cherrie Moraga in Rothenberg, 414–417; "Toward a More Caring Society," Ruth Sidel in Rothenberg, 417–431; "Feminism: A Transformational Politic," bell hooks in Rothenberg, 441–448; "Still I Rise," Maya Angelou, 448–449; "The woman in the ordinary," Marge Piercy in Rothenberg, 449–450
Select one reading and write a response log*
Third journal collection due, optional
Collaborative presentations begin

Week 15   Collaborative presentations

Week 16   Collaborative presentations
                   Final essay and course evaluations due

25

Teaching Difference: Two Courses— Homosexuality & Society and AIDS & Gender

Susan Cavin

I inherited the course Homosexuality & Society in the women's studies program at Rutgers University and taught it yearly from 1985 through 1990. The most important lesson I learned from teaching what was once the only Rutgers course to have the word "homosexuality" consistently in its title was this: never make assumptions about who your students are!

I was always surprised by the magnificent range of students interested in the topic. They wore all sexuality stripes and politics: straight, gay, lesbian, bisexual, asexual, unclassified. Although most students came to class with an openness and willingness to learn, there were always a few homophobes and a few radical lesbian or gay activists. The differences in the classroom were vast.

I used the old feminist technique of consciousness-raising to equalize the class and to get everybody's hidden agenda out into the open gradually, doing about an hour of consciousness-raising once every 2 weeks. I chose the discussion topics and then facilitated, always attempting to create a safe space for students to tell the truth about their lives. Gradually, the lesbian, gay, and bisexual students came out of the closet, which made my job easier and is probably what everyone remembers most about a class like this.

Because I also discovered that most of my students knew little about heterosexuality, I found myself teaching about this topic as well. Students come to sexuality classes for various reasons, but they all share a great private need to publicly talk about their own sexuality through ostensibly talking about other people's. A class like this can often be cathartic for all students who have been waiting for a chance to express themselves.

All this student self-awareness is apart from the academic agenda of the professor, who may just want to cover the latest in the field of lesbian and gay studies. But as teachers, we all know that there's always a lot more going on in the classroom than following the syllabus, and the emotional learning and growth I saw in my students throughout this course were more than most of us ever dreamed was possible.

What follows are the syllabi for Homosexuality & Society and for AIDS & Gender. But the enormity of the change, growth, and understanding that resulted from these classes would fill a book (perhaps my next one?).

SYLLABUS FOR HOMOSEXUALITY & SOCIETY

This course explores historical and cross-cultural approaches to lesbian and gay studies. We compare lesbians and gay men to other minority groups and study the rise of lesbian and gay liberation movements in the 19th and 20th centuries, particularly in relation to the first and second waves of feminism. Relevant contemporary topics include the coming-out process; lesbian and gay culture and media; lesbian mothers and gay fathers; lesbian and gay families and communities; theories on the interconnections of sexism, racism, and heterosexism; lesbian and gay nonviolent resistance and organizing; and AIDS. Since this is a women's studies course, we focus primarily on lesbian studies, but not to the exclusion of gay male studies.

A term paper, oral book review, and group history project are required assignments.

Oral Book Review

Read and review one of the books on the list below and give a 10-minute presentation about the book to the class. Summarize the main themes and arguments of the book. Why has the author chosen to address these themes? Choose one chapter for detailed comments.

Book Report Possibilities

Anzaldúa, Gloria. (1987). *Borderlands/La Frontera: The New Mestiza.* San Francisco: Aunt Lute.

Bell, Alan, Martin Weinberg, & Sue Hammersmith. (1981). *Sexual Preference: Its Development in Men and Women.* Bloomington: Indiana University Press.

Boswell, John. (1980). *Christianity, Social Tolerance and Homosexuality.* Chicago: University of Chicago Press.

Faderman, Lilian. (1981). *Surpassing the Love of Men: Romantic Friendship and Love Between Women, From the Renaissance to the Present.* New York: Morrow.

Grahn, Judy. (1984). *Another Mother Tongue: Gay Words, Gay Worlds.* Boston: Beacon Press.

Hoagland, Sarah Lucia. (1988). *Lesbian Ethics: Toward New Value.* Palo Alto, CA: Institute of Lesbian Studies.

Katz, Jonathan. (1976). *Gay American History: Lesbians and Gay Men in the USA: A Documentary.* New York: Crowell.

Kitzinger, Celia. (1987). *The Social Construction of Lesbianism.* Newberry Park, CA: Sage.

Lauritsen, J., & D. Thorstad. (1974). *The Early Homosexual Rights Movement (1864–1935).* New York: Times Change Press.

Lorde, Audre. (1983). *Zami, a New Spelling of My Name.* Trumansburg, NY: Crossing Press.

Marotta, Toby. (1981). *The Politics of Homosexuality.* Boston: Houghton Mifflin.

Pharr, Suzanne. (1988). *Homophobia, a Weapon of Sexism.* Inverness, CA: Chardon Press.

Plant, Richard. (1986). *The Pink Triangle: The Nazi War Against Homosexuals.* New York: Holt.

Ramos, Juanita (Ed.). (1987). *Compañeras, Latina Lesbians: An Anthology.* New York: Latina Lesbian History Project.

Shilts, Randy. (1987). *And the Band Played on: Politics, People, and the AIDS Epidemic.* New York: St. Martin's Press.

(Students may select other books on gay and lesbian topics with the instructor's approval.)

Group History Project

The instructor divides the class into research teams that work in the Rutgers Alexander Library Lesbian/Gay History Archives researching several aspects of lesbian, bisexual, or gay history/herstory at Rutgers University. Each research team gives an oral presentation to the entire class on what gay history they have found in the Rutgers Archive, as well as critically analyzing this data.

Alternative Group Research Project

All students work in their assigned groups as part of a team. Each individual within each group is assigned a specific task. Generally, all students gather all known data on their subjects already written in English. This is a secondary research project, not primary research—meaning that students will not administer a questionnaire to any real group of people, although they might design a questionnaire that they think would be helpful to future researchers in this field. Generally, most of the data will be in the library or at bookstores. Each individual needs to think a lot about the research problem and the literature read, then report his or her ideas and findings to the group and lead several group discussions. Each group submits a group report in both written and oral form to the entire class. Ideally, each individual participates equally in the group, attends all group meetings, and shares the workload.

Students may choose one of the following groups:

1. Homophobia and gender: Are men and women equally biased or unbiased against homosexuals? Are sexism and homophobia (heterosexism) connected? If so, in what ways?
2. How to reduce homophobia on college campuses, particularly at Rutgers. What are other colleges doing in relation to the problem of homophobia?
3. Are homophobic attacks against gay men the same as those against lesbians? Are lesbians and gay men treated similarly or differently by various groups? By men and women?
4. Homophobia by race: Is homophobia similar or different in the Asian community compared with the black community compared with the white community? Are racism and homophobia connected? If so, in what ways? Does individual homophobia vary by the race of the individual homosexual?
5. Homophobia by ethnicity, culture, and nationality: Do Spanish-speaking cultures regard homosexuality in the same way as English-, French-, and Chinese-speaking communities? Is there a difference in the way Haitians vs. Jamaicans regard lesbianism? Does homophobia vary by culture?
6. Homophobia by religion: Study the similarities and differences between Jews, Protestants, Catholics, Hindus, and Muslims on the subject of lesbian and gay men. Are all religions equally homophobic, or are some more or less biased against homosexuality?

Required Texts, Films, and Videos

Texts

Cavin, Susan. (1985). *Lesbian Origins.* San Francisco: Ism Press.
Boston Lesbian Psychologies Collective. (1987). *Lesbian Psychologies: Explorations and Challenges.* Urbana: University of Illinois Press.
Curb, Rosemary, and Nancy Manahan (Eds.). (1985). *Lesbian Nuns: Breaking Silence.* Tallahassee, FL: Naiad Press.
Smith, Barbara (Ed.). (1983). *Homegirls: A Black Feminist Anthology.* New York: Kitchen Table—Women of Color Press.

Films

Pink Triangles, Before Stonewall, The Life and Times of Harvey Milk, Torch Song Trilogy, Choosing Children, Madchen in Uniform, Born in Flames

Videos

Lesbian Soap Opera, Get Your Laws Off My Body, The Families We Choose, Essex Hemphill's *Tongues Untied, Video Against* AIDS, *Testing the Limits*

LECTURE TOPICS

Week 1	Course overview; methodological problems of lesbian and gay studies and terminology
Week 2	Theories and data on prehistoric lesbianism
Week 3	Ancient Western gay history and lesbian herstory
Week 4	Cross-cultural data on preindustrial homosexuality and homosociality
Week 5	Rise of lesbian and gay liberation movement: 19th century
Week 6	20th-century gay liberation and lesbian feminist movements
Week 7	The coming-out process and gay identity

Week 8   Lesbian and gay marriage and family forms

Week 9   Lesbians and gays of color; racism and homophobia

Week 10   AIDS and PWAS (people with AIDS); the politics of homo-
                    phobia

Week 11   Lesbian and gay legal rights and antigay violence

Week 12   Lesbian and gay studies: present and future

Week 13   Theories of lesbian feminist and gay liberation: nonvio-
                    lent social change

SYLLABUS FOR AIDS & GENDER

This course explores a much-neglected topic within the AIDS pandemic: AIDS
and women, looking at race, class, ethnicity, age, sexual orientation, nationality, homelessness, drug usage, sexual partners, sex practices, residence, occupation, and other relevant sociological variables. To date, most AIDS research
in the United States has focused on men, primarily white gay men, as well as
a little research on black and Hispanic intravenous drug users. There is some
question whether this vast amount of medical research on AIDS and men is
entirely applicable to the treatment of HIV among women and children.
Throughout the course, we ponder that question. Some research questions
we study are: How has the AIDS pandemic affected the life chances of women
and children? Which women are currently at higher or lower risk? Which
women are in danger of becoming at higher risk in the future if they are not
educated about safer sex? How can a feminist perspective on health care and
sexual equality be useful in the mobilization to fight HIV? Why are so many
caregivers women? How did heterosexism and homophobia, racism, sexism,
and ageism contribute to misinformation and national paralysis about AIDS
in the 1980s? What contributions can women's studies researchers make to
AIDS research? Each student is expected to read and think critically about
AIDS and gender.

Term Paper

The term paper topic is chosen by the student with the instructor's approval.
The paper must include an original analysis of AIDS and gender, with a solid
review of the literature on the topic.

Group Project

The class is divided into several groups that research, design, and create an innovative AIDS education project aimed at raising the consciousness of and empowering one of the following target audiences to change their behavior:

1. Adult heterosexual women who, because of sexual inequality in their relationships with men, feel unempowered to negotiate safer sex.
2. Gay, straight, or bisexual teenagers of both sexes who feel invincible, that nothing can kill them, and want to experiment sexually without using any precautions. Students must specify which culture these teenagers are from.
3. Children of both sexes who are or could be in danger of incest, sexual molestation, or rape. How can we help them prevent themselves from getting AIDS via forced sexual aggression?
4. Young women are often targets of date rape and sexual harassment. They have not been socialized to forcefully say "no" to males, especially adult males. Often their first heterosexual experiences are not planned. How can they protect themselves against getting AIDS and learn to negotiate when and if they will have safe sex?
5. Closet bisexual men who cannot tell their wives and girlfriends that they've had unsafe sex with high-risk men. How can they be persuaded to come out to their loved ones and learn to use safe sex when they cannot admit to themselves, much less to anyone else, that they've had homosexual relations?

A group project may take the form of a play, video, musical skit, comedy, tragedy, newspaper article to be published in the *Rutgers Targum* (college newspaper), poem, rap song, or dance. Students are encouraged to be creative and smart. They must first figure out the dimensions of the problem, then solve the problem with a creative solution that will reach the target audience intelligently and emotionally.

Required Texts

People with AIDS Coalition Newsline (free newspaper distributed by the instructor).
Richardson, Diane. (1988). *Women and AIDS*. New York: Methuen.
Rieder, Inez, & Patricia Ruppelt (Eds.). (1988). *AIDS, the Women*. San Francisco: Cleis Press.
Sabatier, Renee. (1989). *Panos Dossier: AIDS and the World*. Philadelphia: New Society Publishers.

Recommended Readings

Callen, Michael (Ed.). (1990). *Surviving AIDS.* New York: HarperCollins.

Chirimuuta, R. C., & R. J. Chirimuuta. (1987). *AIDS, Africa and Racism.* London: Free Association Books.

Fettner, Ann G., & William Check. (1984). *The Truth About AIDS.* New York: Holt, Rinehart & Winston.

Kübler-Ross, Elisabeth, & Mel Warshaw. (1987). *AIDS: The Ultimate Challenge.* New York: Macmillan.

Norwood, Chris. (1987). *Advice for Life: A Woman's Guide to AIDS Risks and Preventions.* New York: Pantheon Books.

Patton, Cindy. (1985). *Sex and Germs: The Politics of AIDS.* Boston: South End Press.

Patton, Cindy, & Janis Kelly. (1987). *Making It: A Woman's Guide to Sex in the Age of AIDS.* Ithaca, NY: Firebrand Books.

Peabody, Barbara. (1987). *The Screaming Room.* San Diego: Oak Tree.

Sabatier, Renee. (1988). *Blaming Others: Prejudice, Race and Worldwide AIDS.* Philadelphia: New Society.

San Francisco AIDS Foundation. (1987). *Women and AIDS: A Clinical Resource Guide.* San Francisco: Author.

Shilts, Randy. (1987). *And the Band Played on: Politics, People, and the AIDS Epidemic.* New York: St. Martin's Press.

Sontag, Susan. (1989). *AIDS and Its Metaphors.* New York: Farrar, Straus & Giroux.

LECTURE TOPICS

Week 1	Course overview; Susan Sontag on "AIDS as Metaphor" and AIDS poetry
Week 2	AIDS in the 1990s, guest speaker; film: *Condom Sense*
Week 3	AIDS and women: heterosexual transmission
Weeks 4–6	AIDS and women: lesbians, prostitutes, and women caregivers
Week 7	AIDS children and intravenous-drug-using parents. Videos: *Sex, Drugs & AIDS, Changing the Rules*
Weeks 8–10	Blacks and AIDS in the United States, Haiti, and Africa
Week 11	AIDS health care, social services, and testing; guest speaker from Hyacinth Foundation

Week 12   Hispanics and AIDS in the United States, Caribbean,
                 and Latin America

Week 13   People with AIDS (PWAS) panel; guest speakers

Week 14   AIDS activism: ACT-UP panel

.

26

Teaching Queer: Bringing Lesbian and Gay Studies into the Community College Classroom

Joanne Glasgow
F. David Kievitt

There is no classroom in the country untouched by the presence of lesbians and gays. Nor is there any classroom untouched by the perversion that is homophobia. Historically, Euro-Americans have viewed homosexuality as either sinful or sick. Moreover, there is an almost totally unexamined heterosexism that assumes and even mandates heterosexuality, even as that category remains undefined for most people. It is imperative that all teachers begin to address these issues courageously and honestly for the sake of *all* students.

Our own experience as teachers of introductory courses has taught us that this is precisely the level where we must begin if we are to reach the greatest number of students. At the same time, we are acutely aware that there are indeed difficulties to be faced, especially as heterosexism and homophobia have rarely been considered by the diverse student body that populates the required basic-level courses.

TEACHER POSITIONING

The first, and potentially most daunting, consideration is what we call "teacher positioning." Put simply, many heterosexual teachers are afraid that if they discuss lesbian and gay perspectives, they will be labeled lesbian or gay themselves. And gay and lesbian teachers are often just as afraid to present such perspectives—out of the same fear. Such concerns are real, and there is no easy way to circumvent the problem, if it is a problem, for the individual teacher. The most convenient and often-used route of the nongay teacher is to preface his or her discussions with the phrase, "I'm not gay, but . . ." or "I'm not a lesbian, but. . . ." We believe this to be the worst possible approach to the issue. It invalidates the gay and lesbian perspective, precisely because that perspective is presented as non-normative. It may even, on occasion, signal internalized homophobia or at least encourage such homophobia among students. Labels have power to discredit us only insofar as we allow those labels the very power we seek to diminish.

As for the lesbian or gay teacher, our response would be the same. The additional difficulties such teachers face may stem from internalized homophobia. Often, however, the probable cause is more practical—tenure, promotion, fear of being out to those one would prefer not to be out to, fear for a partner who is closeted, or a more general desire to keep public and private spheres separate. Even if we think that we can safeguard our personal lives or identities, we probably cannot—at least not in the end. Others will have already labeled us, no matter what we teach or what we say.

There is a second fundamental concern: the question of teacher preparation. There will be many student questions that go well beyond the boundaries of the particular subjects under discussion. Put simply, yes, there is a reading list. Some of the works that we have found most useful are included in the bibliography at the end of this chapter.

The third issue that arises for anyone teaching gay and lesbian material is inevitably AIDS. There is a widespread popular linkage between homosexuality and AIDS, which closes the circle again—sin *and* sickness, AIDS as a "specific modality of homosexual pollution" (Butler, 1990, p. 132). Teachers must resist this popular reductionism. Homosexuals are no more defined by AIDS than African Americans are by sickle-cell anemia. No one can or should ignore the very real human costs and suffering in every person in America devastated by this disease, but it is not a specifically gay and lesbian issue, despite the popular linkage.

STUDENT POSITIONING

Another real consideration for teachers undertaking this inclusive approach to course material parallels the first—"student positioning." Again, it is our experience that in introductory courses, most students will never have discussed lesbian and gay issues in an academic framework. Most of them will not even have adequate or appropriate language for the purposes of discussion. Most of them will have gained their (usually limited) knowledge about gays and lesbians from the street, from Oprah, from popular stereotypes, from their families, and from one another.

Many of them will also firmly believe that homosexuality is simply wrong. We frequently hear students say, "It's sinful," referring to the Bible or to the teachings of their particular religion. We find it helpful to point out to students that in a pluralistic society, oppression of one group's rights in order to uphold the religious beliefs of another group is patently indefensible.

Perhaps just as frequent as the term "sinful" is the response that homosexuality is "disgusting." One easy response to this is simply to ask, "Disgusting to whom?" But if we really want to engage the students in a deeper inquiry, we need to recognize that this typical response is probably related to the often unarticulated assumption about the natural versus the unnatural. Since most undergraduates are unfamiliar with the debates concerning natural law concepts, pursuing such ideas would probably be fruitless. A better approach is to try to pry open the meaning of "natural." Often it appears to mean simply the way things always are "if nothing goes wrong." Using cross-cultural and historical evidence, the teacher can easily point out that homosexual behaviors have always been a part of human existence and hence must in some way be a part of nature. What differs is the response of the given culture to this natural phenomenon.

Another classroom obstacle is language. Students often use offensive terms—"fag," "queer," "dyke." There are the inevitable elbow jabs, snickers, laughter, rolled eyes, exaggerated male posturing, and exaggerated female appeals for male approval. Intervention is essential. No matter how nonauthoritarian a teacher may be, certain forms of discourse must simply be stopped. The teacher might repeat the offensive term and ask the students how such language differs from blatant racist, ethnic, and misogynist slurs. Why are homophobic slurs acceptable when other prejudiced speech is not? Intervention also provides an opportunity to introject new language and concepts for students who simply have no adequate level of discourse on this subject.

A second aspect of student positioning concerns the difficult subject of silencing. Many nongay students are afraid to become actively involved in discussion, lest the label stick to them. Equally important is the fact that every classroom in every American college has some lesbian and gay students, many of whom have so identified themselves, many of whom may be struggling with sexual identity. For these students, discussion of gay and lesbian issues may be perceived as a direct threat. Others, although not threatened, are at times concerned that their views are unique, personal, isolated, and perceived as deviant. They are reluctant to speak, especially in a forum where they have usually had to conform to dominant ideologies. Some gay and lesbian students fear speaking as one for the many. The teacher must expect this reluctance and be prepared to fill in the silences.

How this is accomplished depends, as does all good teaching, on several factors: the nature of the course, the nature of the student body, and the nature of the materials available and suitable for the course objectives. Whatever the classroom situation, however, we have found several general principles to be consistently useful.

GUIDING PRINCIPLES

1. The teacher must never assume heterosexuality. Whether the material under discussion is a person (an author, a character, a historical figure, the subject of a case study, a theorist, a philosopher, an artist, a composer, whatever) or a text (a love poem, a diary, a letter, an art object, a treatise on the nature of the self, an analysis of personality, whatever), it is imperative that the teacher not subject the material to a single "take," the lens of heterosexism, the automatic assumption that unless otherwise "proved," all materials are heterosexual. Nor should the teacher require a simplistic, reductionist "proof" that the material exhibits homosexual content—such as proof of explicit genital contact—before the material can be considered "really" homosexual. Such proof is never demanded of presumed heterosexual content. Similarly, teachers should avoid the trap of "explaining" homosexual materials solely or primarily in terms of the causes of homosexuality. As Michael Ruse pointed out, such causal explanations are rarely demanded for presumed heterosexual materials (1988, p. 20). This will be difficult, since many students are fixated on the question What makes someone a homosexual? The teacher can discuss the strenuously competing viewpoints of those seeking biological explanations versus those pointing to sociological and psychological forces. As is evident from the unstable status of all such research, the verdict is not yet in. Hence the question, although interesting, cannot be answered. The teacher might also simply ask, "What makes someone a heterosexual?"

2. The teacher must include in the course syllabus materials that elicit analysis of gay and lesbian experience. As Florence Howe observed with

regard to the inclusion of women's experiences in the curriculum, "In the broadest context of that word, teaching is a political act; some person is choosing, for whatever reasons, to teach a set of values, ideas, assumptions and pieces of information, and in so doing, to omit other values, ideas, assumptions and pieces of information" (1987, p. 282). The deliberate omission of gay and lesbian materials constructs a syllabus that thus politicizes heterosexuality and ignores, disguises, or erases a significant portion of human reality and may potentially ignore or erase a portion of the student body itself. It is not enough to be willing to discuss these topics should they arise (often hoping that they won't). If we are really committed to inclusiveness, we will make sure that these issues do arise.

3. To be effective, the teacher should not introduce this material in a way that isolates it from the rest of the course materials. It is not enough to add a chapter or a unit or a week on lesbian and gay experience to a course that otherwise totally ignores this and other related experiences of "otherness." An inclusive syllabus addresses experiences of gender, race, ethnicity, and class. Lesbian and gay perspectives should be included as part of these other discussions. It has become an axiom of feminist pedagogy that one cannot simply "add women and stir." The same principle applies to gay and lesbian materials.

4. To be effective, the teacher should not, as a rule, introduce these materials at the beginning of a course. For all the reasons outlined in our discussion of teacher and student positioning, later is better. In our experience, students who have already engaged in analyses of racism, sexism, and other oppressive ideological systems are better able to understand the connections between these systems and heterosexism.

5. To be effective, the teacher should present lesbian and gay materials in the context of systemic and institutional oppression. Carter Heyward, one of America's leading theologians, described this institutional oppression:

> Heterosexism is a configuration of relational power in which such events are held together not merely as related but as critical parts of the whole configuration. Each event secures and reinforces the public educational impact of the others. This is how we learn to fear and hate others and ourselves. (1989, pp. 50–51)

What Heyward is elucidating here is the complex web of ideology, stereotype, institutional response, and psychology that operates in a homophobic culture. The teacher may be able to direct attention to those strands of the web that the student can recognize as institutionally oppressive. She or he might offer specific examples, such as the murder of Alan Shipler, the fire-bombing deaths in Oregon of a black lesbian and a gay man, or any gay-bashing from the nightly news. The teacher might then ask students to compare these incidents with other institutional acts of violence. This allows students to see the connections between all oppressive structures, whether racist, sexist, ethnocentric, classist, or heterosexist. But it is especially important for the teacher to explore the structures of heterosexist oppression, since most of our students have never thought about heterosexism before, no matter how much they may have thought about gay and lesbian people.

6. To be effective, the teacher should not confuse an inclusive perspective with mere tolerance. Tolerance is a well-intentioned, often liberal, allowance of difference; it is an acceptance of those whose lives, in whatever way, do not conform to the prevailing norms of the time. Such a stance helps no one—especially not gays and lesbians. It can do more harm than good because the concept of tolerance itself implies that what is tolerated is something that one does not really consider to be equal in value. In the uncompromising words of Audre Lorde, "Difference must be not merely tolerated, but seen as a fund of necessary polarities between which our creativity can spark like a dialectic" (1984, p. 111).

These general principles can, we believe, be adopted in any course. If we remain attentive to Lorde's words and begin to explore that vision of dialectic creativity, everyone will gain. Teachers will expand the boundaries of their traditional disciplines. Nongay students will begin to understand both homosexuality and homophobia, as well as to explore their participation in systems of oppression. Gay and lesbian students will no longer be ignored or made invisible. The end result can indeed be an incredible enrichment of our ways of knowing. We can all participate in the transformation of knowledge, making it more inclusive, more complete, and more just.

BIBLIOGRAPHY

Boswell, John. (1980). *Christianity, Tolerance and Homosexuality: Gay People in Western Europe From the Beginning of the Christian Era to the Fourteenth Century.* Chicago: University of Chicago Press.

Butler, Judith. (1990). *Gender Trouble.* New York: Routledge.

Faderman, Lillian. (1981). *Surpassing the Love of Men: Romantic Friendship and Love Between Women from the Renaissance to the Present.* New York: William Morrow.

Halperin, David M. (1990). *One Hundred Years of Homosexuality.* New York: Routledge.

Heyward, Carter. (1989). *Touching Our Strength: The Erotic Power and the Love of God.* San Francisco: Harper & Row.

Howe, Florence. (1987). *Myths of Coeducation.* Bloomington: University of Indiana Press.

Katz, Jonathan. (1976). *Gay American History.* New York: Crowell.
Lorde, Audre. (1984). *Sister Outsider.* Trumansburg, NY: Crossing.
Rich, Adrienne. (1980). "Compulsory Heterosexuality and Lesbian Existence." *Signs,* 5, 631–660.
Ruse, Michael. (1988). *Homosexuality.* London: Basil Blackwell.
Weitz, Rose. (1992). "What Price Independence? Lesbians, Nuns, Widows, and Spinsters." In Gary Colombo, Robert Cullen, & Bonnie Lisle (Eds.), *Rereading America,* 2nd Ed. (pp. 257–264). Boston: St. Martin's.

27
Women in Technological Cultures

Nancy Steffen-Fluhr
Norbert Elliot

COURSE DESCRIPTION

Institution

New Jersey Institute of Technology (NJIT) in Newark is a public research university with a total enrollment of 7,700. It offers undergraduate and graduate degrees in the Newark College of Engineering, the School of Architecture, the School of Industrial Management, and the College of Science and Liberal Arts. Only 18% of NJIT's students are women.

Sponsoring Department

Science, Technology, and Society, a multidisciplinary degree program offered by the Department of Social Science and Policy Studies

Course Level

Three-credit elective, designed primarily for juniors and seniors

First Taught

Spring 1993

Capsule Course Description

Women in Technological Cultures takes an interdisciplinary and multicultural approach to issues of gender in science and technology. These issues include the current status and problems of women in nontraditional professions; the historical contributions of women in science and technology; images of women in Western and non-Western cultures; theories of gender difference, past and present; the impact of cultural gender coding on the epistemologies of science and technology; and women and third world development.

Course materials include case studies, autobiographical narratives, films, and science fiction as well as historical and sociological analyses. Students demonstrate their command of course readings and concepts in a series of hybrid writing assignments designed to integrate personal narrative and reflection with argumentation and comparative analysis. At the end of the course, students submit portfolios of their best work for final assessment and make oral presentations based on case study interviews they have conducted.

THE STUDENTS

The gender distribution of the students electing this course was predictable: 19 women and 3 men. However, the ethnic diversity surprised (and delighted) us: 6 African Americans, 1 Guyanese, 3 Latinas, 3 Indians and Pakistanis, 1 Chinese. The multicultural focus that we had desired was thus naturally achieved; the students brought it with them into the classroom. Moreover, the differences that so often isolate women from one another at NJIT proved to be a powerful force for group unity—once students accepted that they themselves were the central "subject" of the course and that it was appropriate for them to talk about their experiences and feelings, even negative feelings.

The frank testimony of the African American and third world women about the difficulties and discouragements that they and their mothers had faced was especially moving and encouraged other women to open up and acknowledge some of their own fears and frustrations. Whether discussing math anxiety, subtle forms of discrimination in the classroom, "dumb blonde" stereotypes, or male joking styles, students became adept at crossing the borders of race, class, and custom to achieve a complex group portrait of womanly ways of being.

PROBLEMS AND SOLUTIONS

Student Resistance

Student reaction to the course materials and to the process of personalized, free-flowing classroom discussion was increasingly positive. However, there was some initial resistance—the most predictable of which was a suspicion of any approach that looked too overtly feminist. Equally predictable was the form such resistance took: silence. Silence is bad enough in a Western civilization course, but it can be deadening in the kind of course we designed. Did the silence signal shyness? Hostility? Confusion? Denial? Unread assignments? Some of the African American students, in particular, seemed to hold back, to keep (literally) to the corners and outer borders of the classroom space, especially when white male students tried to monopolize the discussion and hold the floor. The boldness of several of the third world women, however—their willingness to take emotional risks in telling their stories—helped to empower other students to try out their voices as well. When an Indian woman is reminding the class that generalizations about gender are culture bound, seemingly disparate views merge into a third perspective.

Perhaps the most interesting form in which resistance expressed itself was the anxiety many women students felt about sounding negative in their writing or speech. This fear correlated with an initial concern that the course materials were painting a depressing picture of women—stressing problems and injustices and not showing the bright side. We dealt with this, and other forms of resistance, by making them a central subject of the course. Particularly helpful in this regard was the work of Gilligan and Brown (1992) on the perfect girl syndrome—work that produced a powerful "ah ha" response in teachers and students alike.

Maintaining Focus

As we shifted the class between readings that were narrative and evocative and those that were analytic and academic, we had to keep the students focused on the topics at hand. There was, for example, a great deal of discussion about the career of Rosalind Franklin, enough discussion to carry through the early weeks of the course. There was, however, little student discussion about articles such as "Women's Talk in the Ivory Tower"

(Treichler & Kramarae, 1983). Often, the trick was getting the class to speak up regardless of the nature of the reading.

Voiced Writing

Getting students to develop their voices on the page seemed rather difficult at first. The usual authoritarian rules—don't use first person, don't use contractions—simply didn't apply. But neither did free play associated with experiential writing. Our job was to help students interpret what they read and discussed in class in terms of their own voices. The new critical literature on genre blending was very helpful to us here, especially essays of the sort written by Wendy Hesford (1990).

STUDENT GAINS

Critical Thinking

Work by Carol Gilligan helped our students realize that ways of knowing are bound to time and place. Although the scientific method may help ensure objectivity, for instance, it also ensures the absence of dissenting voices. Chief among student gains was the realization that there are diverse ways of knowing that are equally valid and that this diversity can lead, with some luck, to multiple truths. Hackneyed phrases such as "critical thinking" thus took on new meaning: to think critically, one must be prepared to question logic itself.

Thinking and Writing

There were two major kinds of writing assignments in the course. The first, a reaction paper stressing voiced writing, encouraged students to filter the new information they had obtained in the course through their own experiences. The second assignment required that students perform a field study of a woman in the workplace. We helped the students develop concepts of interest and refine interview questions. The stress here was on neither the impersonal rhetoric of the social scientist nor the fetish of the humanist for documentation; rather, we wanted the students to field-test the concepts they had encountered in the course and to construct meaning from their findings.

Students were also required to keep a learning log in which they offered proof that they had both read course materials and thought about them. In some cases, students seemed to use the logs as a place to pose questions and frame positions that would later be addressed in class or in papers. So, in some cases, students used writing as a way of thinking.

At the conclusion of the course, students submitted portfolios of their work. The portfolios included the learning logs, drafts of all papers, and final copies of papers. In essence, we asked the students to make a case for their progress in the course. The portfolios provided a rich source of information about the process of student learning, as well as the kind of authentic judgment of progress and ability that we emphasized in readings and class discussions.

Making Connections

Perhaps the most important gain for students (and teachers) was an enhanced sense of connectedness with other women—both with the living women in the classroom space and with the absent women, past and present, real and fictional, whose stories we read and whose voices we heard. Hearing this complex chorus of other voices helped students find their own voices and helped them place their private experiences in sociopolitical context. This increased connectedness and ability to contextualize brought not only enlightenment but also comfort.

Many students began the course with a relatively fragile sense of self-confidence, expressed often in a reluctance to speak up and out assertively. We focused on this issue directly in reading, discussion, writing, and case study interviews. We brought in women speakers, successful professionals in science and engineering, to act as role models; but we also encouraged our students to become speakers, mentors, and role models themselves. A number of them participated in a series of taped and live teleconferences concerning women in technology, an experience that took them from anxiety to exhilaration. They could do it, and they did.

DETAILED COURSE OUTLINE

Week 1 INTRODUCTION

Discussion topics: Course objectives; course structure

Week 2 MEN AND WOMEN IN SCIENCE: A CASE STUDY

Film: *The Race for the Double Helix*
Discussion topics: Analyze film—barriers to success, stereotyping, gender styles
Readings: Watson, Sayre

Week 3   THE CURRENT STATUS OF WOMEN IN
                SCIENCE AND ENGINEERING

                Discussion topics: The statistics; barriers to entry and
                advancement (overt, covert); stereotypes about gender,
                science, and technology
                Readings: Dupree interview; Keller, "The Wo/Man
                Scientist"; Treichler & Kramarae; Hacker, *Doing It the
                Hard Way*
                Fiction: Del Rey, "Helen O'Loy"; Moore, "No Woman
                Born"

Week 4   THE HISTORY OF WOMEN IN SCIENCE AND
                TECHNOLOGY

                Discussion topics: The absence of women in traditional
                histories; correcting the record: contributions of women
                scientists and engineers; collective contributions of
                women; women, gender, and the "scientific revolution"
                Readings: Glazer & Slater, "Professionalism"; Conway;
                Mendenhall; Glazer & Slater, "Margins"; Gilligan &
                Brown
                Fiction: LeGuin, "Sur"

Weeks 5–6   WOMEN AND NATURE; WOMEN AS NATURE

                Discussion topics: Science, technology, and gender met-
                aphors; technology vs. myth; technology as myth; origin
                stories; the concept of progress; ecofeminism
                Readings: Anderson & Zinsser; Merchant; Dijkstra,
                "Poison Flowers"; Norwood; Keller, "Bacon," in *Reflec-
                tions on Gender and Science*
                Visuals: Analysis of Victorian images of women from
                Bram Dijkstra's *Idols of Perversity*
                Fiction: Hawthorne, "The Birthmark"

Weeks 7–8   THE SOCIAL CONSTRUCTION OF GENDER

                Discussion topics: Changing views of woman's nature;
                science, sexism, and racism: 19th-century theories;
                20th-century theories

Readings: Dean-Jones, Russett, Gould, Fausto-Sterling, Weisman

Weeks 9–10   CHALLENGES TO SCIENTIFIC OBJECTIVITY AND VALUE NEUTRALITY

Discussion topics: The structure of scientific revolutions; bad science vs. good science; radical feminist essentialism; feminist/Marxist critiques of essentialism
Readings: Namenwirth; Keller, *Reflections on Gender and Science* and *Secrets of Life, Secrets of Death;* Harding
Fiction: Mitchison, "Memoirs of a Spacewoman"

Week 11   THE SOCIAL CONSTRUCTION OF TECHNOLOGICAL SYSTEMS

Discussion topics: Value-neutral views of technological change; the impact of technological change on women's lives: historical case studies; alternative strategies for technology assessment
Readings: Cowan, Rothschild, Bush, "Technology, Housework, and Women's Liberation"

Week 12   WOMEN AND THIRD WORLD TECHNOLOGICAL DEVELOPMENT

Discussion topics: Feminism vs. feminisms; sexism, racism, and Western imperialism; the changing status of women
Readings: Shaaban, Bumiller
Fiction: Butler, "Bloodchild"

BIBLIOGRAPHY

Anderson, Bonnie S., & Judith P. Zinsser. (1988). *A history of their own.* New York: Harper & Row.

Bumiller, Elizabeth. (1991). *May you be the mother of a hundred sons: A journey among the women of India.* New York: Fawcett Columbine.

Bush, Corlann Gee. (1983). Women and the assessment of technology: To think, to be, to unthink, to free. In J. Rothschild (Ed.), *Machina ex dea* (pp. 151–170). New York: Pergamon.

Butler, Octavia. (1988). Bloodchild. In P. S. Warrick, C. G. Waugh, & M. H. Greenberg (Eds.), *Science fiction: The science fiction research association anthology* (pp. 499–514). New York: Harper & Row.

Conway, Jill Ker. (1992). Research is a passion with me. In *Written by herself: Autobiographies of American women: An anthology* (pp. 125–129). New York: Vintage Books.

Cowan, Ruth Schwartz. (1979, January). From Virginia Dare to Virginia Slims: Women and technology in American life. *Technology and Culture, 20,* 51–63.

Dean-Jones, Lesley. (1991). The cultural construction of the female body in classical Greek science. In S. Pomeroy (Ed.), *Women's history and ancient history* (pp. 111–137). Chapel Hill: University of North Carolina Press.

Del Rey, Lester. Helen O'Loy. In Norman Spinrad (Ed.), *Modern science fiction* (pp. 58–69). Garden City, NY: Anchor/Doubleday.

Dijkstra, Bram. (1986). *Idols of perversity.* New York: Oxford University Press.

Fausto-Sterling, Anne. (1985). *Myths of gender: Biological theories about women and men.* New York: Basic Books.

Gilligan, Carol, & Mikel Brown, Lyn. (1992). *Meeting at the crossroads: Women's psychology and girls' development.* Cambridge: Harvard University Press.

Glazer, Penina Migdal, & Slater, Miriam. (1987). *Unequal colleagues: The entrance of women into the professions, 1880–1940.* New Brunswick, NJ: Rutgers University Press.

Gould, Stephen Jay. (1981). *The mismeasure of man.* New York: W. W. Norton.

Hacker, Sally. (1989a). *Doing it the hard way: Investigations of gender and technology.* Boston: Unwin Hyman.

Hacker, Sally. (1989b). *Pleasure, power, and technology.* Boston: Unwin Hyman.

Harding, Sandra. (1986). *The science question in feminism.* Ithaca, NY: Cornell University Press.

Hawthorne, Nathaniel. (1988). The birthmark. In P. S. Warrick, C. G. Waugh, & M. H. Greenberg (Eds.), *Science fiction: The science fiction research association anthology* (pp. 1–13). New York: Harper & Row.

Hesford, Wendy. (1990, Spring). Storytelling and the dynamics of teaching. *Transformations, 1,* 6–16.

Interview with Andrea Dupree. (1991). In H. Zuckerman, J. Cole, & J. Bauer (Eds.), *The outer circle: Women in the scientific community.* New York: W. W. Norton.

Keller, Evelyn Fox. (1985). *Reflections on gender and science.* New Haven: Yale University Press.

Keller, Evelyn Fox. (1991). The wom/man scientist: Issues of sex and gender in the pursuit of science. In H. Zuckerman, J. Cole, & J. Bauer (Eds.), *The outer circle: Women in the scientific community* (pp. 227–237). New York: W. W. Norton.

Keller, Evelyn Fox. (1992). *Secrets of life, secrets of death: Essays on language, gender, and science.* New York: Routledge.

Le Guin, Ursula. (1985). Sur. In S. M. Gilbert & S. Gubar (Eds.), *The Norton anthology of literature by women* (pp. 2008–2022). New York: W. W. Norton.

Mendenhall, Dorothy Reed. (1992). From an unpublished memoir. In J. K. Conway (Ed.), *Written by herself: Autobiographies of American women: An anthology* (pp. 171–199). New York: Vintage Books.

Merchant, Carolyn. (1983). Mining the earth's womb. In J. Rothschild (Ed.), *Machina ex dea* (pp. 99–117). New York: Pergamon.

Mitchison, Naomi. (1962). *Memoirs of a spacewoman.* New York: Berkeley.

Moore, C. L. (1988). No woman born. In P. S. Warrick, C. G. Waugh, & M. H. Greenberg (Eds.), *Science fiction: The science fiction research association anthology* (pp. 154–188). New York: Harper & Row.

Namenwirth, Marion. (1986). Science seen through a feminist prism. In R. Bleier (Ed.), *Feminist approaches to science* (pp. 18–41). New York: Pergamon.

Norwood, Vera. (1993). *Made from this earth.* Chapel Hill: University of North Carolina Press.

Rothschild, Joan (Ed.). (1993a). *Machina ex dea.* New York: Pergamon.

Rothschild, Joan. (1993b). Technology, housework and women's liberation: A theoretical analysis. In *Machina ex dea* (pp. 79–93). New York: Pergamon.

Russett, Cynthia. (1989). *Sexual science: The Victorian construction of womanhood.* Cambridge: Harvard University Press.

Sayre, Ann. (1975). *Rosalind Franklin and DNA.* New York: W. W. Norton.

Shaaban, Bouthaina. (1988). *Both right and left handed: Arab women talk about their lives.* London: Women's Press.

Treichler, Paula A., & Kramarae, Cheris. (1983, Spring). Women's talk in the ivory tower. *Communication Quarterly, 31,* 118–132.

Trescott, Martha Moore. (1990). Women in the intellectual development of engineering: A study in persistence and systems thought. In G. Kass-Simon and P. Farnes (Eds.), *Women of science: Righting the record* (pp. 147–181). Bloomington: Indiana University Press.

Watson, James. (1968). *The double helix.* New York: Mentor, NAL.

Weisman, Leslie Kanes. (1992). *Discrimination by design.* Urbana: University of Illinois Press.

28

Environmental Science: A Syllabus with Transformation Strategies

Sara L. Webb

Like most scientific subjects, environmental science has little obvious gendered content. Thus at first glance it is unclear what relevance feminism and women's studies have to the teaching of this discipline, with its objective geological and botanical underpinnings. However, a course experience is much more than primary informational content. Pedagogy and secondary content, such as examples, are valuable tools for transforming science courses to achieve the important goals of attracting and retaining women in science.

This chapter describes my college course Advanced Environmental Science, in which I seek to meet three major objectives: (1) to make science engaging through connected learning; (2) to provide role models, mentoring help, and inclusive language that unequivocally includes women in the world of science; and (3) to empower women with confidence-building skills for research, writing, and analysis.

FORGING CONNECTIONS

Only when students forge connections do they truly learn, beginning to construct knowledge by moving beyond the passive receipt of information that is quickly forgotten after exam time. In addition, by relating information to students' experience, we stimulate not only learning but also the enthusiasm that is so important for attracting uncommitted students to scientific study. Feminist scholarship suggests that women are especially responsive to pedagogy that places scientific information in a personal and social context (Harding, 1986; Rosser, 1990), although all students will benefit from such an approach.

Connection is a pedagogical theme in Advanced Environmental Science, woven into the course in three ways. First, students make interpersonal connections: all meet with me frequently (see Role Models and Mentoring), and all must contact environmental officials while researching their projects. Second, students are encouraged to link academic and real-world problems; they frequently refer to current newspaper items and read essays that depict the human concerns on both sides of each issue. Third, interdisciplinary perspectives are offered and reinforced through a requirement that both science and policy be treated in course writings. The separation of knowledge from policy has been criticized from the feminist perspective that argues for connecting academia with society's problems (Rosser, 1990). This separation is clearly seen in ecology, where scientists rarely enter the policy arena and where applied ecology has traditionally been a low-status subfield. Through their own inquiry, students often discover for themselves the chasm between the state of our scientific knowledge and the policies in place for environmental protection.

GOOD PEDAGOGY

Students who are marginally committed to science are most in need of excellent teaching (Quina, 1986; Rosser, 1990; Tobias, 1990). Thus we must not forget the basics of good teaching as we broaden our epistemology and scrutinize our assignments for bias. Teaching well requires institutional support because it takes an enormous amount of time. Classes must be small and teaching loads manageable so that we can offer frequent and prompt feedback, be available for questions and mentoring, and teach through writing assignments and discussion. Other fundamentals include an organized course framework, explicit expectations of students, and clear explanations with examples, preferably drawn from students' experiences in the real world. Good pedagogy also means breaking away from a traditional focus on memorizing information. Students are best served when we broaden our instructional goals beyond facts to the process and skills of learning: writing, discussing, and critical thinking.

FEMINIST PEDAGOGY AND SCIENTIFIC OBJECTIVITY

Feminist scholarship suggests other strategies for teaching well and engagingly (Schuster & Van Dyne, 1985; Rosser, 1986, 1990). Several concepts already mentioned have their roots in a feminist vision of inclusive, dynamic teaching: teaching through connection, forging interdisciplinary linkages, broadening the epistemology by teaching through student writings, and showing the human side of controversies. It is also essential to tend to classroom dynamics, where subtleties can lead women to disengage. Research has shown that male and female students still receive differential treatment from the podium (Rosser, 1990; American Association of University Women, 1992).

Feminist theory poses another, more controversial challenge to science teachers by calling into question the concept of scientific objectivity. Some feminist philosophers argue that scientific agendas and findings are grounded so firmly in social context that truly neutral objectivity is elusive or impossible (Bleier, 1984; Harding, 1991).

Even those convinced that science can be objective must agree that environmental issues have spawned an enormous body of biased science, much of it funded by pro-development organizations or government agencies that have an economic or political stake in downplaying environmental risk. Thus environmental science is an excellent discipline for teaching about bias and subjectivity in scientific research. We are obligated in the name of good teaching to help our students recognize how scientific findings often reflect the values and funding sources behind them. The acid rain controversy is the example that I press into service in Advanced Environmental Science. Recent government reports on acid rain were misleading in part because of political forces and in part because of a common line of illogic that antienvironment factions often follow: A failure to *find* causal linkages is treated as evidence that there *is no* causal linkage (details in Webb, 1995).

Parallel scenarios have played out around many environmental issues. Pairs of opposing articles are valuable pedagogical tools for helping students sharpen their skills of weighing evidence and detecting bias. For example, see the supplementary readings on global warming in the syllabus.

ROLE MODELS AND MENTORING

Alongside a stimulating syllabus, we must provide women with examples of women scientists and with mentoring relationships if we hope to draw them into science careers. We can look to historical figures such as Rachel Carson, who single-handedly brought the hazards of pesticides to public attention

(Hynes, 1989). We can also bring in female guest speakers (Rosser, 1986) to break the stereotype of the scientist as male. With support from the Booth Ferris Foundation, Drew University has invited visiting scientists for extended visits for both formal class presentations on science and informal discussions about careers, graduate school, and life; thus these visitors serve as temporary mentors in some cases. We can also use assignments to induce students to contact other scientists—women and men—and hence further broaden their exposure to diversity.

The importance of mentors to women in the sciences cannot be overstated. As Sandler (1993) points out, the mentoring relationship need not be lifelong but can be valuable under a variety of rubrics. During the semester, I serve as mentor to all my students as I guide them through their projects, taking the opportunity to discuss with them their individual interests and aspirations. The one-on-one contact permitted by a small class size is very valuable. In the many departments that lack women faculty members, men can obviously mentor women, although the role model problem still needs to be addressed in these situations.

INCLUSIVE LANGUAGE

As anyone who teaches environmental science can attest, students love to blame the male of the species for all our ills ("man has destroyed the rain forest"). "Man" is a false generic; despite its second dictionary definition, the word does not evoke women along with men (Miller & Swift, 1991). In my experience, in the environmental arena, this usage distances women from environmental problems and weakens the sense of empowerment that we all need to resolve these problems. Thus I insist that my class eliminate the word "man" from its overused position as proxy for the entire human race in their writings and presentations. Texts should be carefully screened for this linguistic error.

BUILDING SKILLS

My third transformation objective toward attracting women to science is to build skills as an explicit component of the course. In environmental science, appropriate skills include writing, speaking, searching the scientific literature (including government documents), and information interviewing. Other science courses can likewise incorporate quantitative, statistical, computer, and field or laboratory research techniques.

Building skills is different from expecting students to acquire skills incidentally. For example, writing proficiency can be built by starting with small assignments and proceeding to larger papers, with plenty of feedback along the way. This differs from the common "sink or swim" approach that assigns a large term paper without previous groundwork. Meanwhile, students' comprehension of subject matter is deepened when learning is made active through writing, speaking, and seeking information.

It stands to reason that inexperienced and educationally disadvantaged students will benefit most from a structured program of skill development. Do women have special needs in this regard? The answer is yes for some skills, for those women students who tend to avoid courses with quantitative earmarks. All students benefit when skills are integrated into the fabric of content-oriented courses.

In Advanced Environmental Science, skills are built through several activities. A news analysis assignment gives students confidence speaking briefly and informally in front of the class. Through short essay assignments, students begin to hone their writing skills, including documentation, with detailed feedback from me. Only after all this practice does the large project lead students to write a longer paper and present a longer, more formal speech. Meanwhile, students learn to pick up the phone and call officials for information, a life skill of value when seeking jobs, grants, and graduate school opportunities. Finally, library research techniques are explicitly taught through sessions with librarians and, for on-line literature searching, with me. Within an inclusive climate for connected learning, these activities convey confidence-building life skills in the hope that more women will enjoy science and succeed in its pursuit.

ECOFEMINISM AND DEEP ECOLOGY

Clearly my course takes only one of many possible approaches to teaching about the environment, with a strong focus on the scientific basis of environmental problems. Other approaches might incorporate stronger philosophical, ethical, or activist themes.

Ecofeminism and deep ecology are unusual philosophical movements that call for reexamination of both our spiritual relationship with nature and our exploitation of nature. Both movements relate only remotely to the science of ecology. Advanced Environmental Science touches lightly on the deep ecology perspective when we discuss reasons for preserving species and biodiversity; the textbook by Miller distinguishes values that relate to human benefit from those values that do not. I have not incorporated ecofeminism into my course because ecofeminism's analogy between the exploitation of nature and the exploitation of women seems flawed to me. Like some other feminists who are scientists, I question the essentialism that underlies this philosophy, and I hesitate to introduce the spiritual into a science course after battling "creation scientists." Ecofeminism also paints an equilibrial vision of nature that contrasts sharply with modern scientific understanding about the complexity and chaos of nature. For more discussion of deep ecology and ecofeminism, see Webb (1995). Certainly environmental studies can be inter-disciplinary in many directions.

SYLLABUS FOR ADVANCED ENVIRONMENTAL SCIENCE

The Course

Advanced Environmental Science, Drew University Biology Department, a nonlab three-credit one-semester course

The Students

15–20 junior and senior science majors; typically 55–70% female, 5–10% students of color

Grading

50% essay-style exams; 50% written and oral assignments

Textbook

Miller, G. T., Jr. (1985). *Living in the Environment.* Belmont, CA: Wadsworth.
    Frequent new editions; avoids sexist language; treatment somewhat one-sided (pro-environment).

Supplementary Readings

McPhee, John. (1971). *Encounters with the Archdruid.* New York: Farrar, Straus & Giroux. This book reveals the complexity and human side of three environmental conflicts in beautifully written essays: "A Mountain," "A River," and "An Island."
Brief articles about current environmental controversies; specifics vary from year to year for up-to-date coverage. Recent topics and assignments include:
Global Warming: Two diametrically opposed viewpoints are presented in:
Brookes, Warren T. (1989, December 5). The global warming panic. *Forbes,* 96–102.
Schneider, Stephen H. (1989, September). The changing climate. *Scientific American,* 70–79.

Pollution in Eastern Europe:
World Resources Institute. (1992). *World resources 1992.* Washington, DC: World
    Resources Institute. Chap. 5, Central Europe.
Ozone Depletion:
Kerr, Richard A. (1992). New assaults seen on earth's ozone shield. *Science, 255,*
    797–798.
Appenzeller, Tim. (1991). Ozone loss hits us where we live. *Science, 254,* 645.
Wetland Preservation:
 Alper, Joseph. (1992). War over the wetlands: Ecologists vs. the White House. *Sci-
    ence, 257,* 1043–1044.

Assignments

News Analysis. Students take turns presenting current newspaper articles
about environmental problems to the class. This activity builds student
comfort with speaking in front of a group and forges linkages between the
course's academic content and real-world problems, serving as connective
tissue by providing illustrations for later lectures and discussions.

Short Essays. Brief but fully referenced essays are assigned on controversial
topics, with students required to present all sides of each issue. Recent topics:
Dams—Pro and Con, Global Warming, Wilderness Preservation. These assignments induce students to synthesize information from diverse sources,
capture and review primary informational content in preparation for exams,
and gain practice with writing and documentation in preparation for the
larger written project; toward this end, I provide prompt and detailed feedback, identifying writing problems for each student to work on with subsequent assignments.

Major Project. Each student chooses an environmental problem to investigate. The steps of this project are built into the course, with firm deadlines
for topic proposals, on-line literature searching, and detailed written outlines.
This structure helps students produce wonderful work; it prevents procrasti-
nation and those terrible last-minute papers that I once thought inevitable.
This major project incorporates required multidisciplinary investigation of
both scientific and political aspects of the topic; scheduled one-on-one progress meetings with the professor, for guidance and to head off procrastina-
tion, which can result when students are overwhelmed by a large project;
required phone or personal contact with scientists or government officials
to connect the environmental problem to real people and to get students
comfortable calling strangers; a library training session with a library faculty
member to introduce searching concepts and government documents; on-line
literature searching with the professor; a written, fully documented research

paper; and formal oral presentations to the class after informal "news analysis" presentations have broken the ice.

Class Sessions

Lectures are presented during 60 to 70% of all class meetings, often illustrated with slides. Guest lecturers are invited at least once or twice to expose students to diverse role models.

Films are heavily utilized as powerful visual learning aids. For maximum pedagogical value, each film is best preceded by contextual remarks and followed by a review of major points. Screening and selecting films is a time-consuming but important ongoing part of course preparation in this discipline; some films in this syllabus will be out of date by the time this book is published. When possible, I choose films that depict women in active roles (e.g., Susan Solomon leading the ozone expedition to Antarctica in *Hole in the Sky*). Also worthy is the Race to Save the Planet series (CPB/Annenberg Project), which is used elsewhere in the curriculum.

Discussions are held on occasional topics. For example, the first session is devoted in part to risk assessment, using small-group discussions to compare student opinions with a risk ranking prepared by the Environmental Protection Agency's Science Advisory Board ("Reducing Risk: Setting Priorities and Strategies for Environmental Protection." Report SAB EC-90–021, NTIS, 1990). By starting the course in a discussion motif, one can help create an open classroom atmosphere in which students know that questions and comments are always welcome.

Student presentations of "news analysis" occur during half our class meetings, and the final weeks of the course are devoted to project presentations by students as they take over the podium entirely.

Topics Covered

No single course in environmental science can do full justice to all relevant topics. I emphasize advanced ecological principles, basic geology, current controversies, and those topics to which my own research pertains.

COURSE OUTLINE

	TOPIC	READINGS AND WRITINGS
Class 1	Environmental risks	Miller, chap. 13: Water Resources

Class 2	Water conservation	McPhee, Pt. 3. "A River"
Class 3	Soil conservation	Miller, chap. 12: Soil Resources
Class 4	Food resources	Miller, chap. 14: Food Resources
Class 5	Film: *Will the World Starve?* (NOVA series)	Miller, chap. 13: Land Resources
Class 6	Forest and rangelands, USA	Essay #1 due: Dams: Pro and Con
Class 7	Wilderness and open space	
Class 8	Deforestation: tropical forests	Miller, chap. 10: Deforestation
Class 9	Film: *Battle for Wilderness* (American Experience series)	
Class 10		Exam #1
Class 11	Endangered species	Miller, chap. 16: Plant/ Animal Resources
Class 12	Biological invasions	Miller, pp. 161–162: Genetic Engineering
Class 13	Bioremediation & risks	Project topic due
Class 14	Air pollution	Miller, chap. 21: Air Pollution Meet this week with professor to discuss your project plans
Class 15	Greenhouse effect	Miller, chap. 11: Climate Change

Class 16	Global warming: biotic effects	Brookes: Global warming panic Schneider: Changing climate
Class 17	Ozone depletion	Essay #2 due: Global Warming
Class 18	Film: *Hole in the Sky* (NOVA series)	Appenzeller; Kerr: Ozone
Class 19	Acid rain: causes and effects	
Class 20	Acid rain: political case study	
Class 21	Energy and mineral resources	Miller, chap. 18: Nonrenewable Energy Miller, chap. 19: Mineral Resources
Class 22	Nuclear energy	McPhee, Pt. 1: "A Mountain"
Class 23	Renewable energy sources	Miller, chap. 17: Perpetual/Renewable Energy
Class 24		Exam #2
Class 25	Water pollution	Miller, chap. 22: Water Pollution
Class 26	Water pollution, continued	Written project outline due
Class 27	Pesticides	Miller, chap. 23: Pesticides
Class 28	Film: *The Insect Alternative* (NOVA series)	

Class 29	Hazardous waste	Miller, chap. 20: Risk, Human Health
Class 30	Pollution in central Europe	World Resources Institute: chap. 5: Central Europe
Class 31	Urbanization	Miller, chap. 9: Populations, Urbanization
Class 32	Land use planning	McPhee, Pt. 2: "An Island"; Miller, pp. 132–143: Coastal Zone
Class 33	Environmental protection laws	Miller, chap. 25: Politics & Environment
Classes 34–39	Project presentations (attendance required!)	
Class 40		Exam #3 during finals week

CONCLUSIONS

Environmental science courses can be transformed to encourage and train all students through attention to secondary content and pedagogy. My course for advanced undergraduates is only one model, itself constantly changing as problems arise. I offer several strategies toward the goal of attracting and retaining women in science. I strive to create an engaging experience for all students by forging connections to real-world problems, to real people, and across disciplinary boundaries. Feminist theory offers a framework from which to counter the fragmentation of knowledge and scrutinize scientific objectivity in the politicized environmental arena. It is imperative to ensure inclusive language, provide diverse role models, and offer mentoring opportunities. Advanced Environmental Science is also designed to build skills for success in the course and thereafter. With structured guidance and movement from modest to major assignments, students can make astounding progress with speaking and writing skills while simultaneously mastering subject matter more effectively through active learning. All students benefit when skills for communication and research are explicitly taught as part of course content, eliminating a "sink or swim" approach to student projects.

Ongoing institutional support is needed to ensure small class sizes and manageable faculty workloads that permit the frequent feedback, learning through writing, and personal mentoring interactions that characterize a supportive learning environment for women and indeed for all students.

NOTE

This chapter is condensed from S. L. Webb, Female-friendly environmental science: Building connections and life skills, in S. V. Rosser (Ed.), *Teaching the majority* (New York: Teachers College Press, 1995).

BIBLIOGRAPHY

American Association of University Women (AAUW). (1992). *How schools shortchange girls.* Washington, DC: Educational Foundation and National Education Association.

Bleier, R. (1984). *Science and gender: A critique of biology and its theories on women.* Elmsford, NY: Pergamon.

Harding, S. (1986). *The science question in feminism.* Ithaca, NY: Cornell University Press.

Harding, S. (1991). *Whose science? Whose knowledge?* Ithaca, NY: Cornell University Press.

Hynes, H. (1989). *The recurring silent spring.* New York: Pergamon.

Miller, C., & Swift, K. (1991). *Words and women, updated.* New York: HarperCollins.

Quina, K. (1986). *Teaching research methods: A multidimensional feminist curricular transformation plan* (Working Paper No. 144). Wellesley, MA: Wellesley College Center for Research on Women.

Rosser, S. V. (1986). *Teaching science and health from a feminist perspective: A practical guide.* New York: Pergamon.

Rosser, S. V. (1990). *Female-friendly science.* New York: Pergamon.

Sandler, B. R. (1993). Mentoring: Myths and realities, dangers and responsibilities. In D. C. Fort (Ed.), *A hand up: Women mentoring women in science* (pp. 271–279). Washington, DC: Association for Women in Science.

Schuster, M., & Van Dyne, S. (1985). *Women's place in the academy: Transforming the liberal arts curriculum.* Totowa, NJ: Rowman and Allanheld.

Tobias, S. (1990). *They're not dumb: They're different: Stalking the second tier.* Tucson, AZ: Research Corporation.

Webb, S. L. (1995). Female-friendly environmental science: Building connections and life skills. In S. V. Rosser (Ed.), *Teaching the majority.* New York: Teachers College Press.

29

Integrating Feminism into the Nursing Curriculum: Experiences in Required and Elective Courses

Susan Boughn

Although there may be no other professional group more in need of being "feminized" than nursing, there is probably no other that is more resistant to it. Ironically, many nursing professors came of age in the 1960s and are more feminist than their students, who came of age in the conservative Reagan-Bush era. For the most part, the present student population is comfortable with its choice of an occupation that has been clearly designated as "women's work." It will therefore be difficult to feminize nursing education, but it is not impossible. It can be done and it should be done in order to produce professionals who are able to establish a power position in their own industry for the benefit of both themselves and their patient-clients.

This chapter presents two education strategies for integrating feminist thinking into nursing curricula. One strategy is to integrate feminist and gender issues into traditional nursing curricula, and the other is the more straightforward strategy of including an elective course, a feminist women's health course called Women's Health, in the nursing program.

Why is it important for feminist and gender issues to be part of nursing education? Feminist education empowers women students. Most nursing stu-

Creating an Inclusive College Curriculum: A Teaching Sourcebook from the New Jersey Project. Copyright © 1996 by Teachers College, Columbia University. All rights reserved. ISBN 0-8077-6282-2 (pbk), 0-8077-6283-0 (cloth). Prior to photocopying items for classroom use, please contact the Copyright Clearance Center, Customer Service, 222 Rosewood Drive, Danvers, MA 01923, USA, telephone 508-750-8400.

dents are women; therefore, nursing students would benefit. Empowered pre-professionals become powerful professionals. Powerful professional nurses can empower their patient-clients. Powerful health care consumers empower themselves and their families.

Nurses are integral to one of the most powerful and massive industries in the United States, the American health care system. The health care industry is second only to the retail industry. Projections from the U.S. Commerce Department are that health care costs in 1994 will reach $1.06 trillion, approximately 15% of the gross national product ("Findings and Forecasts," 1994). Within this complex industry is the nursing profession. The over 2.2 million registered nurses represent the largest professional group within the industry ("Nursing Facts," 1993). This profession provides vital knowledge, skill, and service to the health care–consuming public. They carry the American health care system on their overworked and underpaid shoulders. Further complicating this picture is the continuing serious shortage of nurses. The U.S. Department of Labor recently predicted that an additional 765,000 registered nurses will be needed by 2005 ("Forecast," 1994).

These projections, coupled with the fact that the health care system is in crisis, clearly call for nursing education that creates powerful nurses. This means that nurses must be educated to be autonomous, independent self-initiators who are able to take measured risks and to manage and lead other workers. These characteristics are necessary so that nurses can first take care of themselves and then take care of the health care–consuming public. For example, nurses must be educated to align with their profession, which is almost 97% female, and with their patients. Historically, nurses were trained to align with the medical establishment and health care institutions at the expense of both themselves and their patients. Feminist principles must be part of nursing education. Feminism and gender-related issues teach female and male students to value women, to respect work done by women, and to embrace equality of treatment and equity in rewarding women for their contributions to society. Most important, feminist education teaches women students to develop voice, to create meaning about the lived experience of being female, and to contest, resist, and assert in response to inequities. These concepts are highly compatible with the needs of nursing students. Nursing students are ripe for feminist education.

INTEGRATING FEMINIST AND GENDER ISSUES

Integrating feminist and gender issues throughout a nursing curriculum is a challenging process since all curricular changes must go through a complex and lengthy evaluation. Historically, the rationale for careful control of curricular content has been that all content taught in a nursing curriculum must be grounded in the philosophy, theoretical framework, and goals and objectives of the established program. This practice must be vigilantly followed to ensure internal consistency of all program content and concepts. This is a criterion required for accreditation by the National League for Nursing. However, in the past few years, the new leadership of the league has called for a "curriculum revolution" that makes women's issues more central. The door for introducing feminist concepts into nursing education has been opened.

In the School of Nursing at Trenton State College, under the leadership of Dean Marcia Blicharz, the faculty has undertaken a curriculum revision that takes advantage of the window of opportunity provided by the National League for Nursing. In this new curriculum, for the first time in the school's 25-year history, gender issues are given formal sanction in a course description. The course involved is titled Professional Role Development I: Caring Within the Learner Role. The course description states that the course examines "the concepts of caring, power and empowerment, autonomy, and advocacy and activism as related to nursing using the models of Watson, Benner and Rogers." Watson and Benner are well-known feminist nurse-leader-scholars who are proponents of the feminist ideals of caring, empowerment, advocacy, and activism. The terms "socialization, self-development, and gender issues" appear in the course description. For the first time in the school's history, there is a formal course objective that, however gently stated, shows an intention to address women from a feminist perspective: to "explore the relationship between women's history as consumers and as providers to women's current roles as consumers and providers in the health care system, using the concepts of caring, power and empowerment, autonomy and advocacy." It is within this window of opportunity that gender issues and feminist concepts can make their formalized entry into the nursing curriculum.

A feminist perspective naturally emerges when presenting the history of the development of nursing in America in the early 1900s. A video developed by the National League for Nursing titled *Nursing in America: Through a Feminist Lens* introduces students to their own professional history from a feminist perspective. This documentary reveals that in the 1800s, schools of nursing were freestanding, autonomous schools, separate from hospitals. Nursing students learn that it did not take long for doctors, who owned and ran the hospitals, to realize that they could secure cheap labor in the form of nursing students if they created schools of nursing within the hospitals. An often overlooked fact is that throughout the first half of the 1900s, thousands of "schools of nursing" were created in hospitals all over the country for the purpose of promoting the medical profession at the expense of the nursing profession.

At the end of the professional role development course, students completed anonymous quantitative (Likert scale) and qualitative (written narrative) evaluations. Students revealed that they had a very positive response to the course; they felt empowered.

> I have been challenged to *think,* to support my opinions, and to express my ideas. I felt myself physically fighting the internal changes in my viewpoints. Thank you for challenging me like *no one* has done before! . . . You encourage power and empowerment, and you are power in action.

> This course began as a nightmare and ended on a very enlightening note. It was the first time I was asked to think about my values and ideals in regard to nursing. That bothered me a great deal because I was shocked that a professor would have the nerve of challenging my beliefs. It [the class] ended up to be most enjoyable and to be a period of immense growth as a student and nurse and as a person as a whole.

Women students are hungry for courses that make them central. They deserve to have a fundamental issue acknowledged: that of being a female as related to being a nurse. It is dishonest and disrespectful to neglect to examine the impact that being composed largely of females has had on the nursing profession's success in securing respect, decent working conditions, and pay equity.

DESIGNING AND TEACHING AN ELECTIVE FEMINIST WOMEN'S HEALTH COURSE

I developed and teach a feminist women's health course titled Women and Health: Power, Politics and Change, which is offered as an elective to nursing and non-nursing majors through the School of Nursing and the women's studies program at Trenton State College (Boughn, 1991). The course examines, from a feminist perspective, women's health issues as they are related to the concerns of women consumers and providers. Although pathophysiology is included, the course goes beyond the standard medical and scientific model–based content often found in nursing curricula today. All health care issues are addressed from the lived experience of being female and are integrated with the psychosociological concerns of women. Obstetric and gynecologic problems are examined from a pro-woman position, focusing on the right of consumers to be informed, to make choices, and to accept responsibility for their informed choices. Topics include informing consumers of the various settings, providers, and conditions for their childbirth experiences; violence against women (e.g., sexual harassment, sexual assault, battering, incest); female sexuality and reproductive freedom; drugs and surgery specific to women; myth and reality (e.g., premenstrual syndrome, dysmenorrhea, postpartum depression syndrome); breasts (e.g., historical, commercial, pathophysiologic issues); and superwoman syndrome and the impaired nurse. The goals of the course are to provide a body of knowledge about women's health problems needed to empower women health care providers and to increase autonomy-related attitudes and behaviors in women students as manifested by a regard for self, women, and nurses and activism and advocacy for self and others.

To accomplish these goals, the course employs a variety of teaching and learning strategies, including lectures, audiovisuals, role-playing, case studies, surveys of student populations (including analysis of data and use of descriptive statistics to present findings), class discussions, formal oral presentations by students, scholarly writing by students, letter writing to legislators, and debate. Students have a lot of power and responsibility in the course. For example, grades are awarded based on teacher, peer, and self-evaluation.

Students complete quantitative and qualitative questionnaires to evaluate their response to the content and processes presented in the course. Analyses of quantitative data based on a questionnaire that measures autonomy-related attitudes and behaviors in women students reveal statistically significant changes ($p < 0.001$) in the students (Boughn, 1994). Some examples of qualitative data in the form of student narratives follow. Students revealed that they had positive responses to the course. They felt empowered, challenged, and changed.

> I *loved* this class . . . I gained significant knowledge and empowerment from the course . . . *excellent,* worthwhile experience . . . I would recommend it to all women.

> This class was very enlightening and a great learning experience. The instructor introduced many, many topics unknown to me that will be invaluable to me in my life. I hope now I can use some of this valuable information and enlighten other women. My main goal is to stand up for what I believe in.

If the power of a movement is measured by the backlash it generates, then the course (as a microcosm of the world) experienced its own backlash, as revealed in the following comment by a male student in the class. Although he deliberately elected to take a women's health course clearly identified as a feminist course (in the course catalog and course outline), one has to wonder why. Strangely, this student was also earning a minor in women's studies.

> I see this [the feminist] movement as a manipulative political group seeking to enact radical, liberal political ideologies for their own personal benefit and reasons under the guise of defending the trodden masses of women from a cold, insensitive male bureaucracy.

Nursing students must be empowered throughout nursing education if they are to survive and thrive in the American health care system, which is under close scrutiny for reform. The American Nurses Association has been urged to advocate changes in nursing education and curricula to "reflect the changes we're about to face" (Mikulencak, 1993). Nursing students who have been taught from a pro-woman perspective in the women's health course score significantly higher on scales designed to measure autonomy-related attitudes and behaviors in women nursing students (Boughn & Wang, 1994). However, historically, student nurses have not been educated to be proactive during periods of reform in their own industry. Traditionally, nurses have assumed a reactive position to changes in the health care system. This mentality has benefited neither nurses nor health care consumers. However, this passiveness has enabled other industries (e.g., the medical establishment and the insurance and pharmaceutical industries) to benefit as health care has evolved. The teaching of feminist principles using feminist pedagogy empowers women students. It does so by giving facts and information about the lived experience of being female in our society and by having students engage in debate and verbal confrontation. Feminist teaching enables students to create meaning with their teacher for making change and to learn the skills of resisting, contesting, and asserting. These skills are necessary for the empowerment of nurses, which ultimately will enable nurses to empower their patient-clients for the betterment of our society.

REFERENCES

Benner, P. (1984). *From novice to expert.* Menlo Park, CA: Addison-Wesley.

Boughn, S. (1991). A women's health course with a feminist perspective: Learning to care for and empower ourselves. *Nursing and Health Care, 12,* 76–80.

Boughn, S. (1994). An instrument for measuring autonomy-related attitudes and behaviors in women nursing students. *Journal of Nursing Education.*

Boughn, S., & Wang, H. (1994). Introducing a feminist perspective to nursing curricula: A quantitative study. *Journal of Nursing Education, 33,* 112–117.

Findings and forecasts. (1994). *American Journal of Nursing, 3,* 77.

Forecast: 765,000 new jobs by 2005. (1994). *American Journal of Nursing, 4,* 75.
Mikulencak, M. (1993). Staff nurses speak out on reform. *The American Nurse* (March), 2.
Nursing facts. (1993). *Nursing and Health Care,* 14, 156.
Rogers, M. (1993). Models of nursing. In S. Leddy & M. Pepper (Eds.), *Conceptual basis of professional nursing* (pp. 167–169). Philadelphia: J. B. Lippincott.
Watson, J. (1988). *nursing: Human science and human care.* New York: National League for Nursing.

30
Guiding the Learning Experiences of Young Children: A Course in Early Childhood Education

Blythe F. Hinitz

Guiding the Learning Experiences of Young Children is the sophomore-level practicum course in early childhood education at Trenton State College. It consists of two college classroom meetings and one field-based 3 1/2-hour laboratory period per week for 14 weeks, followed by a written final examination. Among the topics covered in this course, as described in the college catalog and the course syllabus, are the needs of young children; the significance of experience to development; the importance of the environment; the role of the teacher; basic principles and practices of teaching young children; historical background; and diversity, including multicultural, peace, and gender-equity education.

Included among the course objectives are the following. Upon completion of the course, students will be able to:

1. Identify group behavior of preschool children
2. Describe major materials and equipment necessary for the optimum development of young children

3. Demonstrate educationally effective use of early childhood manipulative materials in a group setting
4. Describe program goals, objectives, schedules, and staffing patterns
5. Construct plans for activities that reflect an understanding of the significance of play in early childhood growth
6. Demonstrate procedures in guidance strategies with young children in indoor and outdoor settings
7. Describe a coherent sequence of historical occurrences in early childhood education and their relationship to today's practices in the field of early education
8. Understand the history and implications of Public Law 94–142 and other related federal and state legislation (for children with special needs) for early childhood education
9. Demonstrate the incorporation of diversity education into the curriculum and program of the early education center

EXCERPTS FROM THE SYLLABUS FOR GUIDING THE LEARNING EXPERIENCES OF YOUNG CHILDREN

The course content includes the following topics, which are related to the theme of this volume:

1. The environment, including the organization of physical space indoors and outdoors, facilities, equipment, materials, and responding to multicultural and gender issues
2. Physical development, including gross and fine motor development and related activities and materials
3. Health and safety issues, including related state regulations
4. Diversity, including multicultural, global, and peace education; nonsexist education; and gender and lifestyle issues
5. Play and sociodramatic play
6. Children's literature and language arts, including books, stories, and related classroom activities
7. Creative arts
8. Historical perspective

COURSE REQUIREMENTS

1. Readings in required texts.
2. Participation in each college class and laboratory field experience and completion of related written assignments. These assignments include two

classroom floor plans, a facility checklist, a teacher role interaction tally sheet, a running record, answers to questions on rules and routines and classroom communication, and 10 sets of observation and participation (activity plan) sheets.
3. Two term papers, one of which is a research paper on classroom environments and facilities for 3- and 4-year-olds.
4. Two formal written examinations.
5. Four written anecdotal observations of one selected child.
6. Optional assignment: Read one book by Barbara Sprung on nonsexist early education and write a brief summary and reaction paper.

THE INSTITUTION AND THE STUDENTS

The School of Education at Trenton State College trains personnel for teaching, counseling, and management and administrative responsibilities in educational institutions. The undergraduate major in early childhood education prepares students to teach in programs for children aged birth to 11 years, with a primary emphasis on ages 2 to 8 years. Guiding the Learning Experiences of Young Children is a required course for early childhood education majors and is preceded by a one-credit introductory course and followed by courses in child development and curriculum and teaching (junior and senior practicum blocks). The majority of students in this course are female. There have been a total of three male students in the course over the past 10 years. There is a wide range in students' prior experiences. Some students are graduates of 2-year (vocational) programs in early childhood education and hold associate's degrees. Others have only baby-sitting or high school home economics course experiences to draw on at the beginning of the semester. Some of the class members are returning to college after years away from school spent working, raising their own children, or both. The majority of the students in the class during the past 10 years have been Caucasian. Approximately 10% of the students have been people of color, primarily African American and Hispanic. During the same period, approximately 5% of the students have come from the college's Equal Opportunity Fund program that admits promising low-income and inner-city youth who are deemed to have potential.

DIVERSITY INFUSION

Background

A grant received from the New Jersey Department of Higher Education in 1989 was used to develop and field-test modules in multicultural education.

The modules were fully implemented in 1990 in this course and other early education courses. In 1992, I attended the summer seminar held by the New Jersey Project. Following this intensive immersion experience, content related to nonsexist early education was infused into our early childhood courses. During the first academic year, these efforts met with limited success, as described below.

Draft Objectives for the Infusion of Nonsexist Content

Concept and attitude formation begin in the earliest years, so it is important that early childhood educators have the knowledge, understanding, and skills to provide a nonsexist education for the young children they teach. To this end, the following objectives were drafted:

1. The college students will demonstrate an awareness of gender issues through their responses (oral and written) to classroom presentations by the professor, their participation in class discussions, and the questions they ask.
2. The college students will develop nonstereotypical definitions of gender roles and demonstrate these definitions through their practices and language usage in early childhood classrooms.
3. The college students will foster children's healthy gender identity by helping children to clarify the relationship between biological identity and gender roles (female, male, androgynous).
4. The college students will be able to plan and organize a physical environment that fosters diversity, a bias-free environment that is nonsexist.
5. The college students will demonstrate through discussion and classroom practice knowledge of bias-free curricula, including nonsexist curricula.
6. The college students will foster equality of development for both sexes, as demonstrated by their lesson and activity plans, their choices of books and materials, and their classroom participation.

Implementation

In the college class (lecture and workshop section), the professor uses a series of questions and answers dealing with diversity issues as a motivational technique. Derman-Sparks's (1989) ideas regarding antibias teaching are also shared. Suggestions regarding appropriate teaching techniques and for recognizing personal biases are considered. In the area of curriculum, books on developmentally appropriate practices and antibias curriculum are included. The professor presents principles to follow in setting up a classroom in which diversity is valued. These principles incorporate statements articulated in the literature regarding environments that are free of bias in the areas of culture, ethnicity, gender, and handicapping condition. For example, the placement of the block and dramatic play areas in close proximity can encourage non-sexist play. Widening the spaces between pieces of furniture and equipment can facilitate independence by children and adults who use wheelchairs and other devices to assist their movement within the classroom. The use of non-sexist and antibias terminology is encouraged. Selection of children's books and materials with diverse content is demonstrated. Other examples of lecture and discussion topics are sensitive holiday celebrations and techniques in peace education and conflict resolution with young children.

In preparation for the field practicum, college students participate in workshops on reading books and telling stories to children. Students are required to bring to class two books that they believe fit the criteria for a book that would be useful in multicultural education for a 3- or 4-year-old. Selected books from personal and college sources are displayed, discussed, and demonstrated. Examples include bilingual books (mostly Spanish and English) and many volumes from Lollipop Power (a women's publishing collaborative). The session on telling stories may include folktales and flannel-board presentations. There are also creative arts demonstrations and participation opportunities, including diverse singing and creative movement experiences. Students are required to teach an activity using multicultural content in their field placement classrooms with children. They may choose to read a book, tell a story, or guide an art project or a music, dance, or creative movement experience. Students must write and use a participation sheet that details their planning, teaching, and self-evaluation of the activity. The cooperating teacher is asked to evaluate the presentation of the activity and the children's responses. Another aspect of the field practicum portion of this course is a series of observations in a local Head Start program.

Assessment Tools Used

> Report on reading in journals (optional reading assignment)
> Participation in college class discussion
> Terminology used in participation sheets (activity plans) and lesson plans
> Vocabulary used in actual classroom interactions (informal) and lessons (formal)
> Examination questions—short-answer and essay

STUDENT REACTIONS, TEACHING PROBLEMS, COURSE MODIFICATION

In general, student reaction to the course content in the areas of special needs, multicultural, global, peace, and nonsexist education and gender and lifestyle issues has been positive. The students are motivated by the introductory questions because they are often unable to answer many of them or deal appropriately (at that point) with the common situations they represent. Students are interested in these topics and make a concerted effort to include related understandings in their research papers and field assignments.

This content is, however, only a small portion of the total content of the course. Due to limitations imposed by the state teaching certification requirements, the course cannot carry more than two semester hours of credit. For this reason, assignments are designed to either include these content areas along with others (the multicultural activity requirement in the field placement, for example), or be optional extra credit (the reading and paper on Barbara Sprung's work). Aspects of this content are also incorporated throughout the course and referred to specifically, when relevant.

One of the recurring problems is students' failure to incorporate gender-free terminology in lesson plans, written assignments, and teaching. This matter is always brought to the students' attention. It was, however, instructive to find that a recent early childhood curriculum guide includes the following quote in the section on the family and the community (italics added): "Children need to learn that all kinds of workers—lawyers, *seamstresses,* computer programmers, migrant workers, secretaries, doctors, *clergymen,* pilots, bus drivers, construction workers, sanitation workers, nurses, teachers, butchers—make a community that serves everyone" (Mitchell & David, 1992). This quote points up the fact that we have a long way to go before appropriate terminology will be second nature, even to those who care about it.

WHAT STUDENTS GAIN

As a result of the infusion of the content discussed above, students are challenged to become antibias teachers. They have access to the printed materials, media, and hands-on experiences that will assist them in incorporating such ideas and content into their personal lives as well as into their teaching. One purpose of studying education at the higher education level is to open oneself to new ideas, philosophies, and ways of thinking. It is only through this exploration that the content information and techniques will have meaning. This opening to, and trying out, of new ideas and techniques provides the basic rationale for the infusion of diversity studies into early childhood education courses.

REFERENCES

Booth-Butterfield, M. (1981, Summer). The cures we don't question: Unintentional gender socialization in the day care facility. *Day Care and Early Education, 8*(4), 20–22.

Carlsson-Paige, N., & Levin, D. E. (1990). *Who's calling the shots? How to respond effectively to children's fascination with war play and war toys.* Philadelphia: New Society.

Clay, J. W. (1990, March). Working with lesbian and gay parents and their children. *Young Children, 45*(3), 31–35.

Cohen, M. D. (Ed.). (1976, February). Overcoming sex-role stereotypes [Special issue]. *Childhood Education, 52*(4).

Corbett, S. (1993, March). A complicated bias. *Young Children, 48*(3), 29–31.

Derman-Sparks, L. (1989). *Anti-bias curriculum: Tools for empowering young children.* Washington, DC: National Association for the Education of Young Children.

Hinitz, B. F. (1992). *Teaching social studies to the young child: A research and resource guide.* New York: Garland.

Jenkins, J. K., & Macdonald, P. (1979). *Growing up equal: Activities and resources for parents and teachers of young children.* Englewood Cliffs, NJ: Prentice-Hall.

Kessler, S., & Swadener, B. B. (Eds.). (1992). *Reconceptualizing the early childhood curriculum: Beginning the dialogue.* New York: Teachers College Press.

Mitchell, A., & David, J. (Eds.). (1992). *Explorations with young children: A curriculum guide from the Bank Street College of Education.* Mt. Rainier, MD: Gryphon House.

Sadker, M. (1977). *Now upon a time: A contemporary view of children's literature.* New York: Harper & Row.

Sadker, M. (1979). *Beyond pictures and pronouns: Sexism in teacher education textbooks.* Washington, DC: U.S. Department of Health, Education and Welfare, Office of Education.

Sadker, M. (1982). *Sex equity handbook for schools.* New York: Longman.

Schultz, S. B., & Casper, V. (1992). *Tentative trust: Enhancing connections between gay and lesbian parents and the schools.* New York: Bank Street College of Education.

Sprung, B. (1975). *Non-sexist education for young children: A practical guide.* New York: Citation Press.

Sprung, B. (Ed.). (1978). *Perspectives on non-sexist early childhood education.* New York: Teachers College Press.

Sprung, B. (1983a). Beginning equal: The project on nonsexist childrearing. *Day Care and Early Education, 11*(2).

Sprung, B. (1983b). Rearing and educating children for the twenty-first century. In H. Nuba (Ed.), *Resources for early childhood* (pp. 481–486). New York: Garland.

Waxman, S. (1976). *What is a girl? What is a boy?* Los Angeles: Peace Press.

Wickens, E. (1993, March). Penny's question: "I will have a child in my class with two moms—What do you know about this?" *Young Children, 48*(3), 25–28.

Zolotow, C. (1972). *William's doll.* New York: Harper & Row.

31

Beyond Math Anxiety: Developmental Mathematics

Laura Hepburn Rawlins

As a developmental mathematics instructor, I am challenged by two related and recurring issues. The first is the exceptionally high proportion of women who lack confidence in their mathematical ability. The second is their skeptical attitude toward the relevance of the subject matter in their lives. This chapter offers practical strategies to deal with these issues. In particular, it addresses the most common manifestations of such impediments to learning, which include anxiety, boredom, and low performance levels. Because of the detrimental effect that anxiety has on performance, an essential component of my pedagogy is to explore ways to alleviate this phenomenon.

An approach that was devised during a study conducted at Sussex County Community College involved a math anxiety workshop (Rawlins, Miller, & Linden, 1992). During this session, students addressed their feelings toward math and math-based classes. Students responded orally and in writing to a series of prompting statements designed to stimulate exploration, recognition, and expression of their feelings toward learning mathematics. Topics raised included elementary and high school experiences, stereotyping, and responses to specific math-related activities, as well as issues of anxiety and motivation.

This was followed by a reaction paper assignment that included a discussion of their math autobiographies. Also, they identified their biggest barriers to, and rewards in, learning mathematics. In this process, students validated one another's experiences and, in some cases, verbalized better strategies. The women's rate of improvement on the New Jersey Basic Skills College Placement Retest was significantly higher in this group than in all other groups. For the men in the group, improvement was noted but was not significant.

According to Domarin (1990), we are reminded that most mathematics curricula, and even most mathematics, are masculine constructions. Domarin describes the climate of mathematics classrooms as aggressive and competitive, where students are driven by external reinforcement. Conversely, providing an atmosphere that encourages internally generated motivation requires deemphasizing the student's performance in relation to others.

This leads us to the second issue, that of personal relevance. When teaching algebra, I frequently hear, "Why do I need this class?" The evasive answer, "It's a thinking skill," is unfair. Students need to experience for themselves how it relates to their lives. A study by Brush (1980) revealed that as girls progressed through high school and into college, they found mathematics harder and less accessible. At higher course levels, their anxiety increased; they failed to see the utility in studying mathematics and felt generally discouraged and bored.

Whether or not the ability to reason mathematically is intrinsically valuable, one cannot deny that as society becomes more technologically oriented, the pressure to be mathematically literate increases dramatically. Today, 60% of American women work outside the home (Jeweler & Gardner, 1993). However, this figure does not reflect how technically prepared women are.

Past studies of gender differences and mathematics show that women are both outnumbered and outperformed by men (Fennema & Behr, 1980; Raffalli, 1994). Women have been shown to be less interested than men within a mathematics class environment (Brush, 1980). Also, studies show that as girls and women progress through school, they experience lower self-esteem and higher anxiety levels than do boys and men (Fennema & Behr, 1980; Mincer, 1994).

The causes of this vary. Some studies cite incidents of girls being given less instructional contact than boys (Leindhardt, Seewald, & Engel, 1979; Mincer, 1994). Others assign blame to less obvious factors, such as the instructor's body language and lack of patience with girls and women (Jeweler & Gardner, 1993; Mincer, 1994). Regardless, as women are "squeezed out" of the mathematics curriculum, a subtle yet powerful filtering system evolves that separates women and limits their personal choices, including college education, employment, and advancement.

In an attempt to connect the students personally to what they are doing—that is, the almost mechanical manipulation of algebraic symbols—I have devised two activities that require students to draw upon personal experience. I intend to incorporate the first of these activities—a research project—into all my developmental courses this semester. Students will be assigned to research a career, preferably one that they themselves are considering, and write a brief summary of the following:

- Mathematical skills needed
- Mathematics courses at Sussex County Community College that provide the necessary instruction
- Relationship of the above to the individual's expectations in present course work

The effectiveness of this activity in relating subject matter to individual interests will be assessed through a questionnaire at the completion of the semester.

The second activity designed to relate subject matter to self culminates from a pedagogy that is not new. Felix Klein, a German mathematician who played a pivotal role in formulating the American mathematics curriculum of the early 20th century, believed that psychological factors must be considered when designing methods of presentation. He espoused an approach that interrelates mathematics with other subjects, and he argued that applied problems had the power to motivate students (Hanna, 1983). This approach is endorsed by the Harvard Consortium and is applied throughout its text *Calculus* (Hughes-Hallett, Gleason, et al., 1992).

Consequently, I have included an activity that asks students to design word problems themselves for given algebraic expressions. The results have been surprisingly creative. Students of all types find ways to channel their interests and experiences into a variety of abstract expressions. Students solve and critique one another's work and, in so doing, discover a multitude of ways in which algebra is personally relevant, practical, and applicable to the real world. In fact, two returning women students chose to enter their problems into a national contest. One problem was accepted and will be published in three mathematics and algebra textbooks published by Saunders College Publishing Company.

These activities are illustrated in the following sample assignment and course outline excerpt. They are designed to confront the issues of anxiety, boredom, and weak performance, which are more prevalent among women mathematics students. By narrowing the gender gap in attitude and performance, I hope to broaden the outlook and potential of all students.

COURSE OUTLINE FOR BASIC ALGEBRA

The following segment of a Basic Algebra course outline includes both the application assignment and the reaction paper assignment. Only the reaction paper assignment was incorporated into the classes that were involved with the above-mentioned study.

Purpose of the Course

This is a developmental course in elementary algebra. It is designed to emphasize the critical thinking skills needed in problem solving. In particular, you will develop and apply mathematical reasoning and logic to a variety of algebraic problems that arise both in the text and in real life. Upon successful completion of this course (i.e., a C or better) and the New Jersey Basic Skills Placement Test, you will be prepared to enter College Algebra I.

Class Structure

Student Participation. You are encouraged to participate in class discussions and problem solving.

Math Journal. Each week, a series of computational and discussion exercises will be assigned to be turned in. These are designed to strengthen your understanding and to provide you with feedback on your progress. All hand-in work should be kept in a folder; this is your math journal. Journal entries will be collected every Monday. No late journal entries will be accepted.

Reaction Paper. Prior to midterm you will be given an assignment entitled "A Look Inside." This consists of a series of prompting statements and questions designed to encourage you to reflect back on your experience in studying mathematics. Your responses to these statements and questions form the resource from which you will write a brief math autobiography. One hour will be allotted to reading excerpts from these papers and discussing how your self-observations could be helpful in the future.

Assignments. You are expected to complete all assignments. Make note of questions or problems you have in your journal and bring them up in class.

Application Paper. You will be given the assignment of researching a career and identifying the necessary skills that apply to this profession. A brief paper summarizing your findings will be due during the sixth week of the course.

Cooperative Learning. Throughout the course you will spend time working in small groups. During this period, feel free to discuss questions that you have and to provide input on those questions raised by other group members.

SAMPLE ASSIGNMENT: A LOOK INSIDE

How motivated we are to study mathematics may well be the most influential factor in determining our level of success. Motivation is defined as "an inner urge that prompts a person to action with a sense of purpose." The words "inner urge" here suggest that this attitude or desire originates within us. Consequently, exploring our feelings—what they are and where they come from—enables us to recognize their influence on our ability to learn. The following discussion and writing activities are designed to prompt an exploration of these inner forces that impact so greatly on our performance.

Discussion Activity

Complete the following statements, and feel free to share your responses during our class discussion.

1. I would describe my elementary school experience of learning math in the following way:
2. I would describe my high school experience of learning math in the following way:
3. Most people who are successful in mathematics are:
4. When in a math class, I generally felt:
5. If I did not understand what was being taught, I would usually:
6. Overall, my performance in math class usually made me feel:
7. In signing up for a math class, I am most concerned about:
8. My most memorable experience in a math class is:
9. If I were to take another math class, it would be because:
10. My feelings about taking a diagnostic or placement test are:

Reaction Exercise

One step in exploring our feelings about studying mathematics is to write a math autobiography. Therefore, use your responses to the 10 items above to write a short (3–4 typed pages) paper that discusses the following:

1. Reflect back to a previous math class in which you felt most discouraged to learn. Recall specific experiences that gave you negative feelings about

yourself or the subject. How old were you? What were you thinking and feeling? Who else was with you? What did those people say or do?

2. Reflect back to a previous math class in which you felt most encouraged to learn. Recall specific experiences that gave you positive feelings about yourself or the subject. How old were you? What were you thinking and feeling? Who else was with you? What did those people say or do?

3. Compare these experiences by completing the following sentences: (a) I discovered that my biggest barrier to success in math is . . . . (b) I discovered that the most rewarding part of doing math is . . . .

4. Considering your responses, what steps could make you a more effective learner in the future?

BIBLIOGRAPHY

Brush, L. R. (1980). *Encouraging girls in mathematics: The problem and solution.* Cambridge, MA: Abt Associates.

Domarin, S. K. (1990). Teaching mathematics: A feminist perspective. In T. J. Cooney & C. R. Hirsch (Eds.), *Teaching and learning mathematics in the 1990s.* Reston, VA: National Council of Teachers of Mathematics.

Fennema, E., & Behr, M. J. (1980). Individual differences and the learning of mathematics. In R. J. Shumway (Ed.), *Research in mathematics education.* Reston, VA: National Council of Teachers of Mathematics.

Hanna, G. (1983). *Rigorous proof in mathematics education.* Ontario: Ontario Institute for Studies in Education.

Hughes-Hallett, D., Gleason, A. M., et al. (1992). *Calculus.* New York: John Wiley & Sons.

Jeweler, A. J., & Gardner, J. N. (1993). *Your college experience: Strategies for success.* Belmont, CA: Wadsworth.

Leindhardt, G., Seewald, A. M., & Engel, R. (1979). Learning what's taught: Sex differences in education. *Journal of Educational Psychology, 4,* 432–439.

Mincer, J. (1994, January 9). Boys get called on. *The New York Times,* p. 27.

Raffalli, M. (1994, January 9). Why so few women physicists? *The New York Times,* pp. 26–28.

Rawlins, L. H., Miller, N., & Linden, R. (1992, November). *Performance and attitude—a function of behavioral contracting or instructor support in the developmental classroom?* Presentation at the annual New Jersey Association of Developmental Education Conference, Jamesburg, NJ.

32
Curriculum Transformation in Calculus I

Diane Kalish
Beva Eastman

Our aim is to support the incorporation of new technologies and learning styles into our teaching in order to widen the circle of participating mathematicians. We would like to counteract the subtle pressure and not so subtle propaganda foisted upon us by society that mathematics is a white male domain. Mathematics will become more accessible to women and people of color when teachers broaden their approach to the subject.

We examine curriculum transformation in Calculus I, which is often a turning point in a student's decision to continue in a mathematics career. Calculus, with its emphasis on infinite rather than discrete processes, is different in concept from previous courses.

William Paterson College is a public college of about 6,000 undergraduates and 3,000 graduate students, most with New Jersey residency. The Mathematics Department has a faculty of 16, including 5 women. The college usually graduates 25 math majors each year. The intended audience for the calculus courses offered at our college is science, mathematics, computer science, and business majors, as well as all other students interested in obtaining a knowledge of the methods and techniques of calculus. The prerequisites are 2 years of high school algebra and trigonometry or precalculus.

The traditional course is taught primarily as a lecture course, with microcomputers incorporated for classroom demonstrations to illustrate concepts, student assignments to enhance those concepts with hands-on experience, and the solving of problems that are not usually attempted because of the amount of computation involved. The usual evaluation of students is through four in-class examinations, short quizzes or graded homework assignments at the discretion of the instructor, and a common cumulative final exam.

Following are the course description, course objectives, and course contents as they appear in our departmental file.

TRADITIONAL SYLLABUS FOR CALCULUS I

Course Description

Limit and continuity of functions, derivatives, differentiation of algebraic and trigonometric functions, applications (including related rates and optimization), differentials, antiderivatives, integration, definite and indefinite integrals, fundamental theorem of calculus, numerical integration, applications (areas between two curves).

Course Objectives

To teach calculus techniques and methods related to limit, continuity, differentiation, and integration. To illustrate applications of those techniques to problem solving in science, mathematics, business, computer science, and other related areas.

Course Content

Limit. Informal definition of limit, computation of limits, sandwich theorem, special limits, limits involving infinity, continuous functions, formal epsilon and delta definition of limit.

Differentiation. Slopes, tangent lines, derivatives, rules for differentiation, velocity and other rate of change, review of trigonometric functions, derivatives of trigonometric functions, chain rule, implicit differentiation, fractional powers, linear approximations and differentials, Newton's method.

Applications of Derivatives. Related rates of change, maxima and minima, mean value theorem, curve sketching using the first and second derivatives, graphing rational functions, asymptotes, optimization, antiderivatives, initial value problems, mathematical modeling.

Introduction to Integration. Finite sums, definite integrals, the fundamental theorem of calculus, indefinite integrals, integration by substitution, numerical integration, areas between curves.

TRANSFORMING THE TRADITIONAL COURSE

The above course is the traditional calculus course offered at many colleges with a standard curriculum. Curriculum transformation in mathematics has been slow to take place. A quick perusal of an old calculus book will reveal that most of the computational problems at the end of each chapter are of an impersonal, technical nature, devoid of interest to most students. Should women or men appear in the problem, they are often cast in stereotyped sex roles.

We define curriculum transformation at this point to mean that in each assignment, a variety of tasks is given in order to allow for the different learning styles of *all* students. However, by introducing new types of assignments, the traditional methods for evaluating students must be expanded. This might include a portfolio that consists of writing assignments, special projects, and individual work that is assessed by both the student and the teacher.

The following paragraphs contain suggestions for curriculum transformation, with sample assignments provided. First, there is the visual approach. Previously, without technology, we could look at only a limited number of graphs. Technology allows us to look at almost any graph we can name. Several of us have already successfully used MathCad or Mathematica. Our Mathematics Department voted this semester to change the curriculum to use an integrated approach with Mathematica. This means that assignments that were once limited to textbook examples can now be changed, with the students creating and analyzing their own functions. Students can now solve interesting problems that previously involved boring, lengthy calculations. They can also explore new concepts and formulate their own individual ideas on problem solving, since creativity is one of the most important goals in mathematics.

Writing within the mathematics classroom has been used successfully in many ways—from keeping a journal about the ideas and applications in the course to writing assignments on specific topics. Writing is important not only to teach students how to explain their analyses to a layperson but also to give the students an opportunity to explore and understand their own style of learning and problem solving.

The textbooks are changing, but we feel adamant that "she/he" should be used in the introduction and exposition. The use of a personal direct conversational style would surely engage the students' attention more easily. Numerous "word problems" and mathematical modeling applications need to be broadened or rewritten. For example, most texts stress the classical applications of acceleration and velocity. We should explain the historical development of these problems and include more applications from the social and behavioral sciences. Examples need to be taken out of the personless abstract mode and placed within the realm of the human.

Along with changes in the texts and assignments, the instructor must always be aware that students have varied ways of learning mathematics. Presentations of new concepts should include visual and verbal explanations as well as formal symbolic ones, each helping to illuminate the others. Since men are often more outspoken than women in the classroom, and hence may tend to dominate the discussion of a lesson, it would be wise to encourage small groups of students to work collaboratively on problems. Many studies have shown that teachers of mathematics have higher expectations of their male students. This translates into a greater positive reaction to the men in the classroom—a behavior that is most often unconscious on the part of the instructor. Greater self-awareness will help instructors modify and eventually eliminate such biased treatment of the sexes. From the low numbers of Ph.D.s awarded to people of color, it is also clear that instructors must extend their self-awareness in the encouragement and treatment of all students.

SAMPLE ASSIGNMENTS

These sample assignments are only a beginning in terms of transforming the calculus curriculum. Various projects, such as the Harvard project or the Berkeley project, have made changes in this direction. We encourage teachers of mathematics to experiment and to find methods of their own to transform the curriculum.

Limits

Technology helps students begin to experience the idea of a limit.

1. An intuitive approach would be to explore sequences of numbers that may or may not "close in on" a number called the limit, with the following writing assignment: Describe in your own words what is happening in the

sequences that allows us to decide if a sequence has a limit or not. Then translate these ideas of limits of sequences into mathematical terms.
2. A continuation of the above is: Choose any sequence that "approaches" or "closes in on 3." Pick a function defined about the number 3 and substitute the values of the chosen sequence into the function to obtain a new sequence. Does this new sequence also have a limit? Use several linear functions, rational functions, trig functions, or any other functions you like. (Note: This assignment works well in a small collaborative group setting.)
3. *Project:* One of the joys of using Mathematica is that it has an extensive library of packages. Thus, ideas that were once separated out by course are now readily accessible. Using the Continued Fraction Package, choose an irrational number and generate the continued fraction approximation correct to at least 4 decimal places.

Continuity

1. Formulate and graph your *own* polynomial function for each of the following conditions:
   a) discontinuous at 1 point
   b) discontinuous at 2 points
   c) discontinuous at n points, where n is any finite number
2. Write a brief paragraph about how to define a function that is discontinuous at a countable set of points.

Differentiation

1. Formulate and graph your *own* function for each of the following conditions (*when possible*):
   a) where the derivative does not exist at 1 point
   b) where the derivative does not exist at 2 points
   c) where the derivative does not exist at n points when n is any finite number
   d) in part (a), was your function continuous at that point?
   e) where the derivative exists at a point but the function is not continuous
2. Write a brief paragraph that would define a function where the derivative does not exist at a countable set of points.
3. Many of the applications can simply be rewritten. For example, velocity problems can be considered using Olympic skiing and swimming. Instead of a block of wood sliding down an inclined plane, an Olympic skier can travel down the slope at $s = 16t^2$ feet in t seconds. Then, the question How

long does it take the block to attain a velocity of 50 feet per second? is changed to How long does it take the skier to attain a velocity of 50 feet per second? This is followed with an analysis of the mathematical model as it applies to a skier.

4. *Project:* One way to find the time of the month when a woman ovulates is for her to take her temperature daily throughout a menstrual cycle. The result of graphing these data yields a sine function. Can you use the derivative to solve the problem?

5. Newton's method is used by many of the symbolic computer algebra systems to locate roots. The following group of assignments can be used to demonstrate the use of different technologies: To estimate π to five decimal places, locate a root of $f(x) = \tan x$ by

    a) using Newton's method and a scientific calculator with $x_0 = 3$

    b) using a graphing calculator to graph $f(x) = \tan x$ and zoom in on the root at $x = \pi$

    c) using the Mathematica Solve command with $x_0 = 1$, $x_0 = 2$, and $x_0 = 3$

Compare the methods and results obtained.

Related Rates Problems

Related rates problems can easily be rewritten. One way is to create a detective series with Hazel Axelrod and Morty MacDonald. Thus, "the 13-foot ladder that starts to slide away" turns into Hazel climbing down a rope from the second floor as the suspect runs from the building. The "dinghy pulled toward a dock" becomes Hazel, who has been thrown overboard, being pulled by a life preserver thrown by Morty. Two different vehicle rates become Morty and Hazel in a helicopter chasing a car across the desert. What is even more fun is to have students rewrite the problems using their imaginations.

Mean Value Theorem

A typical mean value theorem application is as follows: Show that for any numbers a and b, $|\sin b - \sin a| \le |b - a|$. This problem can be expanded to a writing assignment that asks students to explain their proof or problem-solving method.

Asymptotes

Project: The behavior or limit of rational functions (as $x \to \pm \infty$) can be approximated through their asymptotes. Create your *own* polynomial function of at least 5th degree that serves as an asymptote for a rational function. Write a brief paragraph explaining the relationship of these two functions.

Integration

1. Using computers, find the area of approximating rectangles whose height is a functional value, and then repeat this process by increasing the number of rectangles.
2. Compare methods of calculating Reimann sums using various types of technology.
3. Since most texts present only simple bounded shaded area problems, use the Mathematica commands to find the area between two polynomials of at least 5th degree.

Applications

One assignment that is very successful is to ask students to look at the application problems in a section of the text and to analyze how the problems apply to their lives. If they do not find any relevance, ask them to rewrite one problem so that it is pertinent.

33

The Social Analysis of Difference

Rhoda K. Unger

Courses on women and gender in various academic disciplines have prolifer-
ated over the past 20 years. Nevertheless, their focus on sex and sexism has
produced problems as well as positive change. Like many others, I believe
that our most urgent problem in developing courses in this area is to incorporate categories such as ethnicity, social class, and sexual orientation (and
probably others that have not yet been clearly identified as group rather than
individual labels) into our course syllabi. As I have attempted to do so, however, I have discovered that integrating gender is not as simple a matter as I
had once supposed.

GETTING STARTED

First of all, I discovered that there are several ways that one can integrate
ethnicity, class, and so forth into the curriculum. The most obvious way to
do so is to consider the lives of women who are not white, middle-class, or
well-educated (see Yoder & Kahn, 1993, for a discussion of how this may be
achieved in psychology). One problem with this approach is that, by definition, little research has been done on those women who have been excluded,
and students may perceive such attempts as tokenism and pay little attention
to so-called peripheral findings. Students of color may be particularly sensi-

Creating an Inclusive College Curriculum: A Teaching Sourcebook from the New Jersey Project. Copyright © 1996 by Teachers College, Columbia University. All rights reserved. ISBN 0-8077-6282-2 (pbk),
0-8077-6283-0 (cloth). Prior to photocopying items for classroom use, please contact the Copyright
Clearance Center, Customer Service, 222 Rosewood Drive, Danvers, MA 01923, USA, telephone 508-
750-8400.

tive to the low ratio of studies of marginalized women as compared with the dominant group. They need to be assured that this disparity is a consequence of biased scholarship (cf. Reid, 1993) rather than instructor bias.

Research on people of color has, in addition, usually involved explicit or implicit comparisons with normative, culturally dominant groups (Reid, 1988). If the instructor does not take great care to explain theoretical biases as well as confounding variables, some students may use the information provided to confirm stereotypic assumptions about the nature of people who are less privileged than themselves. This is especially likely to occur in psychology, where behavioral characteristics in ethnically diverse populations are portrayed as the problems of individuals rather than as an outcome of social dynamics. Neither the strengths of such populations nor alternative coping strategies have been given much attention.

Although I believe that naming the excluded and giving them the power to name themselves are important tools for feminist teaching, they are only the first step in integrating gender. I would prefer to examine gender more as a verb than as a noun (see West & Zimmerman, 1987; Unger, 1988a). I believe that it is possible to construct a course that focuses on gender as a process rather than on people who have a particular sex or gender. Paradoxically, such a course deemphasizes the importance of sex and sex differences by showing the other kinds of group differences that are said to exist (see Unger, 1992). At the same time, it demonstrates what sex, race, sexual orientation, and so on have in common in terms of social processes that shape people's lives.

A few years ago, I had the opportunity to put these ideas into practice by developing a course for our all-college honors program. These courses cannot duplicate any already existing courses at the college. They are small seminars that must be interdisciplinary in nature. This was a unique opportunity for me to pursue my personal, political, and pedagogical objectives. The course called the Social Analysis of Difference is compatible with my theoretical emphasis on social construction (Unger, 1989, 1990); it allows me to discuss aspects of power without being forced to rank order forms of oppression, and it appears to be less threatening than a course on either race or sex to students who do not identify with any one particular marginalized group. I have also found that an analysis of the similarity of the sociocultural processes that define and determine various groups is a particularly useful teaching tool (see Unger, 1988b).

PURPOSE AND STRUCTURE OF THE COURSE

The purpose of this course is to analyze the many ways in which difference is defined, used, and experienced at various levels in our society. Differences are explored mainly in terms of race and sex, since these are the most common distinctions used by both scholars and society. However, other factors that have been relatively neglected, such as class and culture, are also examined.

The course begins with an introductory discussion on the dilemma of individual and group differences. I have found that a short story by Kurt Vonnegut entitled "Harrison Bergeron" produces good class participation. The story involves a society that attempts to eliminate all differences by handicapping those who excel; for example, good athletes have weights hung on them, attractive people wear grotesque masks, and intelligent people receive bursts of noise to destroy their concentration. Questions that may be discussed include: Is it possible to make people equal? Is it fair? How are the needs of individuals and those of society reconciled? This latter theme can be reiterated throughout the course.

Following the initial discussion, the course is divided into four major parts. In the first part of the course, we explore how physical differences have been used by biologists and physical anthropologists to define racial and sexual categories. This section focuses primarily on similarities between theories about race and sex that have been used in the past and those that are popular today.

Unfortunately, it is quite easy to find current material that emphasizes biological determinism. The first time I taught the course in 1992, a major cover story in *Time* stressed sex-related differences in the brain. I was able to incorporate this story into the course by having students read the article and criticize it. Their critique was facilitated by required reading in the history of science and the sociology of knowledge (Gould, 1981, and Russett, 1989, are particularly valuable resources; see syllabus). Current media attention to the purported genetic and neural bases of sexual orientation could also be useful.

Our students' critical thinking skills can also be enhanced by asking them to analyze definitions of race and sex. Students need to recognize the historical and cultural context of such definitions. The analysis of the political and economic factors that influence apparently contradictory definitions appears to be helpful in enhancing understanding. For example, students are intrigued to learn that during apartheid, South Africans classified Chinese as "colored" and Japanese as "white." Because it is less threatening than "reality," speculative fiction is also a useful vehicle to help students learn to deconstruct "what is known." I have found Ursula Leguin's "Left Hand of Darkness" as well as some of her shorter fiction to be both readable and effective.

Students, like many people in our society, are reluctant to challenge the authority of science. At the conclusion of the first part of the course, students write papers discussing the evidence for or against the relationship between scientific theories about group differences and political ideology. The issue of whether science is objective and value-free may also be addressed as a debate in the classroom.

The second part of this course examines theories about the causes of group differences in outcomes. For example, both sex- and race-related differences in cognitive performance have been attributed to evolutionary adaptation by sociobiologists and to interpersonal processes by social constructionists. Students seem to find the similarity between explanations of race and sex quite illuminating.

It is relatively easy to induce college students to discuss data on putative group differences in cognitive performance, such as on the SATs. However, they appear to have more difficulty discussing how one's perspective may influence which questions are asked and which are ignored. An analysis of scholarly explanations for the relative achievement of Asian Americans, Anglo Americans, and African Americans and for women versus men is helpful in this regard. I focus on social psychological mechanisms such as situational and dispositional explanations and stable or unstable causality. I have also had some success using fictional material such as Tillie Olsen's "I Stand Here Ironing" to introduce the potential confounds of culture and social class.

The third part of this course focuses on the personal implications of difference. We discuss how information about difference is conveyed in terms of stereotypes and interpersonal behaviors. We also discuss whether difference has different implications at different stages of life; for example, adults are more free to change their circumstances and choose their associates than are children.

In this part of the course, we also look at issues of multiple or interactive differences, such as being a black or a Latina woman. A particularly important issue is whether individuals have to choose between which form of oppression to address. A number of essays in Toni Morrison's book (1992; see syllabus) on the Anita Hill–Clarence Thomas controversy are particularly valuable resources for discussion of this issue.

The final part of this course deals with the issue of how theories about the sources of difference influence the social remedies offered to deal with them. We look at whether sources of difference are seen as problems of the individual or problems of society and how this influences educational policies and legal mechanisms such as protective legislation, divorce laws, and affirmative action. The concept of "separate but equal" is discussed from an individual as well as a societal perspective.

I conclude the course with a take-home final that requires students to address the question of individual responsibility and social causality. They discuss an article that they read just before the course ended—Hochschild's (1991; see syllabus) paper on the politics of the estranged poor. The article sets out a dialogue between an extremely liberal and an extremely conservative point of view in terms that are comprehensible for students from a variety of disciplines. I end the course with this paper because I want students to recognize that no one position is completely without problems.

SOME CONCLUDING COMMENTS

I have now taught this course twice and would be glad to do so again, although it is not without its frustrations. Because I tried to be as inclusive as possible, no one source of difference ever received the amount of attention I thought it deserved. One solution is to encourage my students to take additional courses involving multicultural perspectives.

Because of the breadth of the course in terms of both content and discipline, it has been impossible to find an acceptable textbook, and I have been forced to use materials from a large number of sources. There seems to be no good solution to this problem, especially since course packs are no longer supportable without a great deal of advance planning to obtain permissions from authors and publishers. My solution has been to use a number of relatively inexpensive paperbacks and modules. Some of these are now available through a new database publishing program developed by McGraw-Hill called Primis.

It is important not to be too prescriptive about the content of the course. A number of current anthologies include excellent personal accounts, and some choices may be left to the students. Part of the excitement in the course is provided by analysis of the news media, and I recommend that instructors keep an eye out for current sources. Unfortunately, these are not hard to find.

SYLLABUS FOR SOCIAL ANALYSIS OF DIFFERENCE

Required Texts

Gould, S. J. (1981). *The mismeasure of man*. New York: Norton.
Madden-Simpson, J., & Blake, S. M. (1990). *Emerging voices: A cross-cultural reader*. New York: Holt, Rinehart & Winston.
Morrison, T. (Ed.). (1992). *Race-ing justice, en-gendering power*. New York: Pantheon Books.
Rothenberg, P. S. (1988). *Racism and sexism*. New York: St. Martin's Press.
Russett, C. E. (1989). *Sexual science*. Cambridge: Harvard University Press.
Unger, R., & Crawford, M. (1992). Modules from *Women and gender: A feminist psychology*. New York: McGraw-Hill.
Assorted handouts as indicated in the course syllabus.

Part I

In the first part of this course, we explore how physical differences have been used by biologists and physical anthropologists to define racial and sexual categories. We focus, in particular, on the similarities between past theories and findings and those that are popular today.

COURSE OUTLINE

Week 1   Introduction to the subject, with an emphasis on the various levels at which difference may be analyzed
                          The dilemma of difference
                          "Harrison Bergeron" by Kurt Vonnegut (handout)

Week 2   Scientific definitions of race: the past and present
                          Harris, M. (1988). Race, human variation, and the forces of evolution. In *Culture, people, and nature,* 5th ed. (chap. 6). New York: Harper & Row (handout)
                          Gould, chaps. 2, 3

Week 3   Scientific definitions of sex: the past
                          Russett, chaps. 1, 3

Week 4   The construction of sex and gender
                          Unger & Crawford, "The multiple components of biological sex" and "Does the brain have a sex?"

Project 1. Write an 8–10-page paper discussing the evidence for or against the relationship between scientific ideas about group differences and political ideology. Discuss the question of whether science is objective and value-free.

Part II

We examine theories about the causes of group differences, with a particular emphasis on evolutionary theory and sociobiology on the one hand and social constructionism on the other. We look at how terminology is used and how it influences our causal explanations. An important aspect of this part of the course is the issue of which questions are asked and which are ignored. Factors that influence which findings are given public visibility and which are ignored by the media are also explored.

COURSE OUTLINE

Week 5	The IQ controversy Gould, chap. 5 Madden-Simpson & Blake, reading by Agueros

Week 6	Gender and cognitive differences
	Unger & Crawford, "The meaning of difference" and
	  "Gender and cognitive abilities"
	Madden-Simpson & Blake; readings by Smith and by
	  Brand

Week 7	Culture and class: the neglected variables Russett, chap. 2 Gould, chap. 4 Rothenberg, pp. 54–69 Madden-Simpson & Blake, story by Olsen
Week 8	Midterm

Part III

We discuss how information about being different is conveyed. Difference has different implications at various stages of life, such as childhood and adulthood. We also look at the issue of multiple or interactive differences, such as being a black or a Latina woman. Do individuals have to choose between what forms of oppression to address? Are forms of social stigma a matter of an individual's choice? We consider the issue of how social interactions may label and maintain so-called marginalized behaviors and how societal values influence what is defined as socially problematic behavior.

COURSE OUTLINE

Week 9	Images of difference
	Rothenberg, pp. 257–279
	Unger & Crawford, "Images of women and men" and
	  "Gender stereotypes as social demands"
	Madden-Simpson & Blake, readings by Bosmajian and
	  by Naylor (p. 197)

Week 10   Doing race and gender: the self-fulfilling prophecy
                           Unger & Crawford, "Gender, status, and 'power'"
                           Madden-Simpson & Blake, reading by Staples

Week 11   Blaming the victim
                           Rothenberg, pp. 324–348
                           Madden-Simpson & Blake, reading by Naylor (p. 14)

Week 12   The double jeopardy of race and sex
                           Morrison, readings by Marable, Williams, and Painter

Project 2. Write a short paper (5–6 pages) on the personal meaning of
difference. You may write an essay or a work of fiction. You may even do an
art project if you so choose. The subject of this project may be drawn
from some aspect of your own life or that of a close relative or friend.
Address the issue of whether a difference is always seen as a deficiency.
You may also address the question of who is or was seen as responsible
for the difference.

Part IV

How do theories about the sources of differences influence the social remedies offered to deal with them. We look at whether sources of difference are
seen as problems of the individual or problems of society. Thus, we examine
programs of "remedial" education as well as the idea that it is possible to
have separate but equal schools. We also look at laws such as protective legislation, divorce laws, and affirmative action.

COURSE OUTLINE

Week 13   When is a difference important?
                           Gould, chap. 6
                           Hubbard, R. (1990). The political nature of human na-
                               ture. In D. L. Rhode (Ed.). *Theoretical perspectives on
                               sexual difference.* New Haven, CT: Yale University
                               Press (handout)

Week 14   Group differences and the law
                           Rhode, "Definitions of difference" (handout)
                           Rothenberg, pp. 242–251
                           Madden-Simpson & Blake, reading by Houston &
                               Houston

Week 15 Group differences in outcomes
Rothenberg, pp. 88–97, 125–130, 139–147, 157–164
Madden-Simpson & Blake, reading by Baldwin
Unger & Crawford, "Women and work" and "Gender dynamics in the workplace"

Week 16 Dealing with clashing paradigms
Hochschild, H. (1991). The politics of the estranged poor. *Ethos, 101,* 560–578

Take-Home Final. Discuss the various viewpoints expressed in Hochschild's article in terms of their advantages and disadvantages for the individual and society. Indicate where you stand and why.

REFERENCES

Reid, P. T. (1988). Racism and sexism: Comparisons and conflicts. In P. A. Katz & D. A. Taylor (Eds.), *Eliminating racism* (pp. 203–221). New York: Plenum.

Reid, P. T. (1993). Poor women in psychological research: Shut up and shut out. *Psychology of Women Quarterly, 17,* 133–150.

Unger, R. K. (1988a). Psychological, feminist, and personal epistemology: Transcending contradiction. In M. Gergen (Ed.), *Feminist thought and the structure of knowledge* (pp. 124–141). New York: New York University Press.

Unger, R. K. (1988b). The psychology of social issues: Commonalities from specifics. In K. Quina & P. Bronstein (Eds.), *Teaching about a psychology of people* (pp. 184–191). Washington, DC: American Psychological Association.

Unger, R. K. (Ed.). (1989). *Representations: Social constructions of gender.* Amityville, NY: Baywood.

Unger, R. K. (1990). Imperfect reflections of reality: Psychology and the construction of gender. In R. Hare-Mustin & J. Marecek (Eds.), *Making a difference: Representations of gender in psychology* (pp. 102–149). New Haven, CT: Yale University Press.

Unger, R. K. (1992). Will the real sex difference please stand up? *Feminism and Psychology, 2,* 231–238.

Unger, R. K., & Crawford, M. (1992). *Women and gender: A feminist psychology.* New York: McGraw-Hill.

West, C., & Zimmerman, D. H. (1987). Doing gender. *Gender & Society, 1,* 125–151.

Yoder, J. D., & Kahn, A. S. (1993). Working toward an inclusive psychology of women. *American Psychologist, 48,* 846–850.

34
Integrating the New Scholarship into Introductory Psychology

Toby Silverman

William Paterson College of New Jersey requires a course in racism and sexism as part of its undergraduate curriculum. When I first began my teaching career, there was no such requirement, and I often felt that the perception among students was that there were two forms of psychology—the one taught by regular faculty, and fringe lunatic psychology taught by me. After the introduction of our racism and sexism requirement, I began noticing a significant change in student acceptance of the material. I no longer have to spend a lot of time convincing students that the issues of race, gender, class, and sexuality are indeed part of mainstream psychology. My efforts at curriculum transformation also receive support from other faculty engaging in similar dialogues within their own fields.

I teach the undergraduate introductory psychology course, which serves both psychology majors and students from other departments. My day students are mostly first-year students and sophomores, working- and middle-class commuters. The night class serves a mostly adult population (over age 25).

OBJECTIVES

For all students, the objective is the same: to integrate issues of race, gender, class, ethnicity, sexual orientation, and so forth into a core psychology course.

TEXTS

I try to use texts that integrate these issues throughout the book rather than consign the material to separate chapters. I have used Carole Wade and Carol Tavris's book successfully for several years (*Psychology,* 2nd ed. New York: Harper & Row, 1990). Two years ago I switched to David Myers's latest book (*Psychology,* 3rd ed. New York: Worth, 1992) because it makes extensive use of multicultural materials. I intend to switch again to a text by John Dworet- zky (*Psychology,* 5th ed. St. Paul, MN: West, 1994) because it incorporates the scholarship from the Stone Center, which I believe is doing cutting-edge work in psychology. For instructors who prefer traditional texts but want to learn more about the recent scholarship, the American Psychological Associ- ation has a number of fine resources. Phyllis Bronstein and Kathryn Quina have edited a book that includes recent scholarship on many of the subfields taught in a traditional course (*Teaching a psychology of people: Resources for gender and sociocultural awareness.* Washington, DC: American Psychologi- cal Association, 1988). One of the more recent books that the organization offers is edited by Jacqueline Goodchilds (*Psychological perspectives on hu- man diversity in America.* Washington, DC: American Psychological Associa- tion, 1991).

SUPPLEMENTAL MATERIALS

I still need to supplement the text with other lecture topics. Most of the traditional introductory psychology texts devote a considerable amount of space to the concept of "self." Notably absent is a discussion of the "self-in- relation" theory from the Stone Center of Wellesley College. I have been excited by their theories since reading the work of Jean Baker Miller (*Toward a new psychology of women.* Boston: Beacon Press, 1976). The Stone Center formulations, originally published in a series of working papers, are much more widely available now that they have published in the mainstream (Judith V. Jordan, Alexandra G. Kaplan, Jean Baker Miller, Irene P. Stiver, & Janet L. Surrey. *Women's growth in connection: Writings from the Stone Center.* New York: Guilford Press, 1991).

BEYOND TRADITIONAL "SELF" PSYCHOLOGY THEORY

The typical models of "self" development presented in introductory psychology textbooks are those of Freud, Jung, Adler, Horney, Erikson, and Maslow. All use some variation of the concept of separation-individuation as a hallmark of adult development. The central belief is that each man is an island unto himself, and each of these theorists (with the notable exception of Karen Horney) equates maturity with independence, autonomy, separation, and individuation. The white male, who is the model in all these theories, depends on many other people for growth and development while promulgating the notion that he is a self-made man—independent, autonomous, individuated, and separate.

The Stone Center model, in contrast to "self" theories, uses the concept of the "self-in-relation." This theory proposes that we do not develop a separated, individuated, or independent self. We develop in the context of relationships. Relationships can be between two parties, within a family, or to larger social and political entities. We discuss what relationships mean and the popular mythology that in male-female pairs, the woman pulls toward the relationship and the man tries to isolate himself. Recent Stone Center formulations by Stephen Bergman and Janet Surrey (*The woman-man relationship: Impasses and possibilities,* Working Paper No. 55. Wellesley, MA: Stone Center, 1993) have centered on men's development, with the isolation viewed as a form of relational dread. This relational dread is experienced by men when women ask them to take the emotional temperature of their relationships.

In dealing with the topic of gender differences in depression, for example, I add the Stone Center model to provide an alternative perspective. For example, I discuss the work of Seligman on "learned helplessness." Women learn early on that they are "helpless"; this feeling is associated with elevated levels of depression. Poverty is likewise associated with depression. Women and other minority group members more frequently fall into the category of the poor, which contributes to elevated depression rates. Victims of violence experience elevated depression rates. Traditional theories use the concept of "loss" as central to depression. Those who lose their mothers prior to age 11 are considered to be especially vulnerable to depression. The "loss" of self-esteem is correlated with depression. Alexandra Kaplan of the

Stone Center has extended the concept of loss to include the sense of "loss" women experience in their relationships with men. Women frequently report feeling "at a loss" in attempting to interact with significant male partners.

I frequently draw the students' attention to the impact of language. Jean Baker Miller frequently uses the word "empower." Traditional definitions of "power" preclude what women do. Women do not exercise power in the sense of control or domination; they do help others to grow and develop, however, and "empowering" others should be part of the definition of power. I find that I spend a large amount of class time dealing with language issues—who defines what is "normal"? Traditional psychological theories label women as dependent. This is due primarily to our tendency to define behavior on a bipolar line—with independence at one end and dependence at the other. There is a general failure to recognize that dependence-independence is really a continuum and that the context often defines how one behaves in a particular situation. Feminists have pondered over using pejorative labeling to describe what females do. Why are women labeled "field dependent" and men "field independent"? It might be just as accurate to label women as "field sensitive" and men as "field insensitive." The diagnostic category "dependent personality disorder" is used almost exclusively for women. There is no parallel "independent personality disorder" category. Independence, autonomy, and separation are more apt to be associated with the concept of mature adult development, as exemplified by the "self" theories, whereas caring, nurturing, and cooperating are seen as limiting one's personal development. Thus, language can be used to define female characteristics as inferior or pathological.

BEYOND TRADITIONAL MORAL DEVELOPMENT THEORY

Although I also use the basic text's discussion of moral development, I spend a lot of time adding different perspectives, specifically the work of Carol Gilligan and John Snarey. Most of the textbooks include Gilligan's work (*In a different voice: Psychological theory and women's development.* Cambridge: Harvard University Press, 1982) but devote more space to Lawrence Kohlberg's model of moral development. I discuss the issue of sampling bias. If Kohlberg threw out all data from women, how can we apply his model to women? Is Gilligan's "caring" orientation diametrically opposed to Kohlberg's "justice" orientation? Snarey's work on moral development includes the variable of culture (Cross-cultural universality of social-moral development: A critical review of Kohlbergian research. *Psychological Bulletin, 97* [1985], 202–232). His research demonstrates that we in America use an individual model for decision making; in other cultures, the collective good is used in defining what is moral. Although many texts discuss Carol Gilligan's research on moral development, almost none discuss her work on female development. Along with a number of her colleagues, Carol Gilligan has studied the drop in achievement and self-esteem in girls (*Making connections: The relational worlds of adolescent girls at Emma Willard School,* Cambridge: Harvard University Press, 1990; Women, girls and psychotherapy: Reframing resistance [Special issue], *Women and Therapy, 11* [3/4]). The girls in these studies can clearly name their own experience and articulate their understanding of the world up to about ages 9 to 11. After that, Gilligan and her researchers found a silencing of the girls' own experience in favor of an archetypically male view of the world.

I try to weave issues of race, class, gender, and sexual orientation into my ongoing lecturing. When we discuss parenting issues, I show a videotape of two gay males at home with their daughter. I ask the students to respond with a paragraph after viewing the tape. I try to get them to understand that diversity is not a bad thing. Perhaps there are very few laws of behavior that apply to humans generically. What we do spend a lot of time doing is discussing how the variables of race, gender, sexual orientation, and ethnicity interact to produce a wide variety of behaviors that are generically human.

SYLLABUS FOR INTRODUCTORY PSYCHOLOGY

Overview

Psychology is the study of behavior and mental processes. We will be studying a wide variety of subjects under these headings.

Text

David G. Myers. *Psychology,* 3rd ed. New York: Worth, 1992.

Attendance

Required.

Exams

Three multiple-choice or essay exams (your choice). Bring a no. 2 pencil and Scantron sheet with you.

Grades

A traditional grading system will be used (A = 90–100, and so on).

Note

Please! If you are having difficulty with any part of this course, come and see me during my office hours or call me to schedule an appointment at a different time. This also applies to students requiring assistance under the Americans with Disabilities Act.

COURSE OUTLINE

	READING (Chap. in Myers)	Topic
Week 1	1	What is psychology?
Week 2	2	Biological roots of behavior
	3	The developing child
Week 3	4	Adolescence and adulthood
Week 4	5	Sensation
	6	Perception
Week 5		Exam 1
Week 6	7	States of consciousness
	8	Learning
Week 7	9	Memory
Week 8	10	Thinking and language
Week 9	11	Intelligence

	READING (Chap. in Myers)	Topic
Week 10		Exam 2
Week 11	14	Personality
Week 12	15	Psychological disorders
Week 13	16	Therapy
Week 14	17	Stress and health
Week 15	18	Social psychology
Week 16		Exam 3

35

Introduction to the Psychology of Women

Karen G. Howe

COURSE CHARACTERISTICS

The course objectives of Psychology of Women include enabling students to understand the complex interactions of biological, psychological, and social factors influencing women's development and behavior. Students become able to critically evaluate traditional psychological theories and consider less biased ways to study women. They become able to identify many aspects of the social construction of gender and to consider the ways in which gender, race, and class interact. Students develop an awareness of the similarities and differences among women from various multicultural contexts and develop an appreciation for their diversity. The classroom environment is a nonthreatening and comfortable one that allows for and encourages an exchange of ideas regarding course material and the application of that material to one's own experiences. The various writing assignments also encourage students to examine their personal values.

The students in my Psychology of Women course are usually female; each term I have from zero to three males in each section of the course. Students come from a variety of majors. The course is an upper-level one that counts for a psychology major or minor, for a women's studies minor, as a general elective, or as a general education option. Since the course is popular and has limited enrollment, almost all the students tend to be seniors or juniors. This works out well, since the seniors are at a crossroads regarding their futures, and much of the course material is directly relevant to the important decisions they will be making.

The theme of the "social construction of gender" is woven throughout the course as it examines society at large, psychological theories, and specific aspects of women's development and behavior. I am always struggling with how to most successfully incorporate multicultural and diversity issues in the course and am never quite satisfied with the results. I try to incorporate these themes in discussions of course material throughout the semester, as does the text, and continually point out the white, middle-class bias in the field. I use a variety of videos that include visual representations of diverse groups and also have specific discussions that focus on these issues. I am currently using a book of readings by African American women, assigning these readings throughout the term so that there is a continuing discussion of these themes. Finally, I make a special effort to encourage students from various backgrounds to speak up in class, at the same time trying to avoid making them spokespeople for their groups as a whole.

IMPACT

"This course has changed my life" is a comment I have heard from female students for the 14 years I have been teaching Psychology of Women. Student reaction to the course has been extremely positive on both intellectual and personal levels. They learn critical thinking skills and gain experience in challenging existing perspectives. Other faculty members report that Psychology of Women students bring up issues and biases in other courses and are eager to share course material.

Students report that the course allows them to more clearly see the effects of gender socialization and sexism on their own development and interpersonal relationships. They have greater understanding of their various relationships with males, other females, and mothers—and often report improvements in those relationships. Many students feel that they have increased feelings of self-esteem, derived partly from their awareness of the "personal is political" theme of feminism. They appreciate other women more: women in general, women friends, women from backgrounds and ethnic groups different from their own. They develop more confidence in the possibility of change in their social reality after they see the strong influence of the social context on women and themselves. They usually develop clearer and more specific future goals for themselves and understand the sources of the role or achievement conflicts they experience. This increased awareness of their own motivations also gives them a greater feeling of control over their lives, and they report more assertive, confident, and sometimes activist behavior. Although the students don't always get positive feedback for this new assertiveness, they recognize it is important for their personal development. Most of the students develop more positive views toward feminism as a social movement and are more willing to identify themselves as feminists at the end of the course.

The male students also report positive reactions. These include greater appreciation of women and a deeper understanding of the factors influencing female behavior. In addition, male students develop an awareness of and discomfort with their own sexism and stereotyping, as well as that of society as a whole. Most of the male students also report having very constructive conversations with friends, mothers, and girlfriends.

There are, however, sometimes students (male or female) who exhibit resistance to course material and discomfort in the class. Early on in the course, they make comments or convey nonverbally their disagreement with course themes or their denial of the existence of sexism and racism in the society. Often they want to spend time discussing men's problems with stereotyping, "reverse discrimination," pressures on males, and so forth. Although these students can be difficult, my experience is that in almost every case such students eventually work through the resistance and come to understand it. Often they are much more enthusiastic by the end of the course. I think several factors encourage the overcoming of this resistance. One is the passage of time; as the weeks go by and issues are discussed, certain themes keep coming up and are hard to ignore. As these students continue to hear class discussions, they find examples in their own lives that validate the course material. In addition, when they keep journals for the term project, they have an opportunity to explore their resistance on a continuing basis and to apply course material. Such "black-and-white" concrete evidence helps them "see" course material and move beyond their denial and defensiveness.

The student resistance just described is probably the major problem in teaching the course, and it doesn't last all semester. Another facet of teaching Psychology of Women that can become problematic is the level of emotional and time commitment required of the instructor. I get very involved with the course and the students, putting much time and energy into preparations and handouts and responding extensively to a lot of written work by the students. I also spend a great deal of time talking with students outside of class. However, these facets are also part of what makes teaching this course such a rewarding professional experience for me. The rewards are many: the pleasure in empowering students and seeing their gains on intellectual and personal levels, and also the more personal interactions with students. I have

been to a number of weddings, have had a baby named after me, and corre-
spond with many former students for years after they graduate.

SYLLABUS FOR PSYCHOLOGY OF WOMEN

Readings

Unger, Rhoda, & Mary Crawford. *Women and Gender: A Feminist Psychology.* New
York: McGraw-Hill, 1992. (*Text*)
Steinem, Gloria. *Outrageous Acts and Everyday Rebellions.* New York: New American
Library, 1983. (*GS*)
Bell-Scott, Patricia, and others (Eds.). *Double Stitch: Black Women Write About
Mothers and Daughters.* New York: HarperCollins, 1991. (*DS*)

COURSE OUTLINE

Week 1	Introduction to the course
	Readings: Introductions to *DS* & *GS*; *Text,* intro & chap. 1
Week 2	Social construction of gender: Introduction to noncon- scious ideologies in society, language, socialization
	Readings: *Text,* chap. 7; handouts; *GS:* "Words & Change," "Marilyn," "I Was a Playboy Bunny"
Week 3	Cultural images of women: Examination of stereotyp- ing, myths and stereotypes of women in media, society, language
	Readings: *Text,* chap. 4; various articles
Week 4	Understanding women—theoretical perspectives: Criti- cal examinations of early psychoanalytic theories
	Readings: *Text,* chap. 2; *GS:* "If Men Could Men- struate"
Week 5	Social context perspective: Focus on theories with so- cial context perspective (Horney, Miller, etc.)
	Readings: Handouts; *Text,* chap. 2; *DS:* "Thursday Ladies"; *GS:* "Jackie Reconsidered," "Networking," "Sisterhood"
	Exam

Week 6	Beauty and appearance issues: Examination of social factors and psychological effects of beauty quest Readings: *Text,* chap. 9; *GS*: "In Praise of Women's Bodies," "Politics of Food"
Week 7	Sex, love, romance: Social construction of sexuality, women and relationships, lesbian identity and relationships Readings: *Text,* chaps. 9, 10; *DS*: "Mom de Plume," pp. 103–105
Week 8	Doing gender: The social construction of interpersonal behavior and "sexual politics"; gender/status/power issues Readings: *Text,* chap. 5; *GS*: "Men & Women Talking"; *DS*: "Family Tree," "Something Domestic"
Week 9	The diversity of women: Interrelationships between gender, class, race issues Readings: *DS:* assorted readings; handouts; articles
Week 10	Women's roles, work, achievement issues: Role expectations and conflicts, internal and external barriers to achievement, comparison of white and black women's experiences Readings: *Text,* chap. 12; *DS*: "Meaning of Motherhood in Black Culture . . ."; *GS*: "Time Factor," "Importance of Work" Exam
Week 11	Violence against women: Sociocultural factors and psychological effects of various forms of violence Readings: *Text,* chap. 14; *DS*: "Daughter Survives Incest"; *GS*: "Erotica vs Pornography," "Real Linda Lovelace"
Week 12	Motherhood and mother-daughter relationships: Social construction of motherhood, mother-daughter dynamics Readings: *Text,* chap. 11; *GS*: "Ruth's Song"; *DS*: "Power of Names," "Successions," "In Search of Our Mothers' Gardens"; other poems

Week 13   Aging issues for women: Double standard of aging, bio-
                   logical and sociocultural factors involved, research
                   problems
                   Readings: *Text,* chap. 13

Week 14   Mental health issues for women: Psychological disor-
                   ders, traditional and feminist therapies
                   Readings: *Text,* chap. 15
                   Exam

Assignments and Projects

Each semester, in addition to three exams, I assign a project and several of
the following written assignments, which I have designed to be thought-
provoking ways for students to apply course material to themselves and society.

1. *Integrative term project.* Students can write a *paper* or keep a *journal.* The
   paper involves analyzing an account of a woman's life with a range of
   course concepts. The *journal* involves writing twice a week and integrating
   academic material with personal reflections, reactions, examples.
2. *Cultural images of women.* Students create a collection of magazine ads
   and analyze them, integrating various myths, stereotypes, and other
   course themes regarding the representation of women in the culture.
3. *Discovering Marilyn Monroe.* Students read Gloria Steinem's *Marilyn:
   Norma Jeane* and apply course concepts to her life.
4. *Mother biography.* Students interview their mothers and write their biographies as well as analyze their own reactions to the assignment, using
   relevant course material.
5. *Social construction of male-female relationships.* Students find popular
   songs and/or fairy tales and analyze them with course material regarding
   love, sex, romance, appearance, relationship, and beauty issues.
6. *Appreciating diversity.* Students read various poems and essays from
   Double Stitch and reflect on questions addressing issues of diversity.

36
The Psychology of Women of Color: Culture, Acculturation, and the Definition of Self

Ruth L. Hall

COMPOSITION AND LEVEL OF THE STUDENTS

Ideally, The Psychology of Women of Color (WOC) should be offered as a 300-level course and is best suited for upperclass students. The course can easily be adapted to an honors or a graduate format as well. To ensure representation and a racial mixture of students, WOC should be offered as an interdisciplinary course. The class size should be limited to 15.

Students should have taken at least one course in psychology, sociology, anthropology, or African American, Asian American, Latino/a, or Native American studies. A course in the psychology of women is also preferable.

COURSE DESCRIPTION

Women of color have long been overlooked in the literature on the psychology of women, the literature on and of people of color, and the literature addressing self-concept, self-esteem, and coping styles. This course addresses the issues and dynamics unique to African American, Asian American, Latina, and Native American women. A special emphasis is placed on the following: the definition of self (coping styles, identity development, and self-perception), the role of culture in self-concept (including gender identity and gender roles), racial identity, and the impact of biculturalism and of acculturation of the self (i.e., the dissonance created and its resolution). In addition, the impact of oppression on self-concept and the internalized "isms" (e.g., racism, classism, sexism, heterosexism) are identified as compromising constructs in the formation of the self.

The class assignments are threefold. Each student interviews an older woman of color and is required to write a formal paper based on the interview. The students also make oral presentations of their papers to the class. In addition, the class is subdivided into four groups with each group responsible for a 20-reference annotated bibliography on one of the four racial groups. Since the number of citations that address Native Americans is small, this annotated bibliography is supplemented with citations that address biracial women and lesbian or bisexual women of color. Third, each group makes an oral presentation of the fiction readings assigned for their racial group. The intent of this assignment is to generate discussion and to encourage students to critically examine one group of readings in particular.

COURSE OBJECTIVES

1. To develop students' in-depth knowledge of the psychology of women of color, particularly in terms of feminist epistemology, self-concept, coping styles, racial identity, gender identity, and ego strengths in a cultural context
2. To assess the applicability of theories of identity development and self psychology in relationship to women of color
3. To enhance the students' familiarity with the current major research and theories on the psychologies of women of color
4. To examine basic research principles and biases used in assessing women of color, including the roles of biculturalism, acculturation, oppression, and internalized oppression
5. To integrate material and knowledge gained from courses in psychology and courses addressing cultural differences
6. To make effective use of library resources, obtain primary source data addressing women of color, and develop an annotated bibliography of the contemporary literature addressing women of color
7. To develop the students' ability to criticize, evaluate, and compare research data in the field of psychology, the psychology of women, and the psychologies of people of color
8. To formulate a scholarly project in both written and oral formats

TEACHING PROBLEMS

1. Students who have not taken any psychology courses may not grasp some of the psychological concepts discussed in the course and may need supplemental readings suggested by the instructor.
2. At present, there is no comprehensive text on the psychology of women of color. The professor must gather material from a variety of sources to complement the texts selected for the course. Having a number of articles on reserve in the library is extremely useful (bulk packs are costly), and the reserve articles allow the professor to incorporate the most current literature on the psychology of women of color. The 1994 text *Women of Color and Mental Health: Integrating Race, Gender and Culture into Treatment* by Comas-Diaz and Greene can be adapted to the undergraduate classroom.
3. Films, videos, and fictional material are also beneficial in presenting a comprehensive portrayal of women of color. The inclusion of this material is, in part, a response to the dearth of psychological literature on women of color. Films such as *Like Water for Chocolate, Dim Sum, The Joy Luck Club, The Color Purple,* and *El Norte* are excellent choices and can be easily integrated into the course. Public television frequently has specials that address women of color as well.
4. The inclusion of guest speakers representing the four racial groups, biracial women, and lesbians of color can serve as a means to enhance the understanding of the diversity of women of color.
5. Anglo students who take woc, contingent on their stage of white racial identity (Helms, 1990), may find it difficult not to be the focus of the course material and challenging not to objectify women of color. This course may be their first experience not operating from a position of privilege. As such, the role of privilege should be addressed as part of the learning experience. The dynamic of privilege can be challenging for the professor if the students feel the need to focus on their exclusion rather than focusing on women of color.
6. If there is a disproportionate number of one racial group in the class, the professor must ensure that the discussions include all racial groups.

SYLLABUS FOR THE PSYCHOLOGY OF WOMEN OF COLOR

Texts

Comas-Diaz, Lillian, & Greene, Beverly (Eds.). (1994). *Women of color and mental health: Integrating race, gender and culture into treatment.* New York: Guilford Press.

Giovanni, Nikki. (1994). *Racism 101*. New York: William Morrow.
Locke, Don C. (1992). *Increasing multicultural understanding: A multicultural model.*
    Newbury Park, CA: Sage.
Madison, D. Soyini (Ed.). (1994). *The women that I am: The literature and culture of
    contemporary women of color.* New York: St. Martin's Press.
Reserved readings library (see partial list of suggested references).

Recommended Readings

Delany, Sarah, Delany, A. Elizabeth, & Hearth, Amy Hill. (1993). *Having our say:
    The Delany sisters' first 100 years.* New York: Kodansha International.
Root, Maria P. P. (1992). *Racially mixed people in America.* Newbury Park, CA: Sage.

Course Requirements

Interview. Each student is to interview an older woman of color (50+ years of age) and to integrate questions that we raise in class, as well as additional questions you may wish to address. You are required to write a paper of approximately 10–12 pages in length based on your interview and to present your paper to the class. Your paper must integrate course material and is to be a referenced paper.

INTERVIEW WITH OLDER WOMAN OF COLOR

1. Draw a genogram. Your genogram should include age, marital status, (grand)children, employment, education, disability, and any other relevant data (e.g., inherited diseases). We will discuss additional information in class.
2. Include your perception of her racial and gender identity. Use the minority identity scale for the former and the gender identity scale for the latter.
3. Using the cultural criteria discussed for each racial group as a foundation, indicate the role of cultural values (e.g., family, religion) and traditions in the life of your interviewee.

Ask the following questions:

1. What is unique about being an Asian/black/Latina/Native American/biracial/lesbian woman?
2. What are some of the positive and negative aspects about being an Asian/black/Latina/Native American/biracial/lesbian woman?
3. What has had a greater impact on your life: being a woman or being Asian/black/Latina/Native American/biracial/lesbian?

4. How has your sense of yourself as an Asian/black/Latina/Native American/biracial/lesbian woman changed over time?
5. How has your sense of yourself as a woman changed over time?
6. What role have hair, skin color, or other clearly racial features played in your life?
7. What role has your body image played?
8. What has been the role of internalized racism, sexism, classism, and so on in your life?
9. What is your attitude toward other racial minorities and toward the dominant group in America?
10. How do you take care of yourself emotionally (e.g., stress management) and physically (e.g., exercise)?

Joint Projects—Annotated Bibliography; Fiction Assignment. Each student will be a member of one of four groups, representing the racial groups covered in the course. Each group will be responsible for the development of a 20-reference annotated bibliography of scholarly journals, books, or book chapters for its racial group. Since there are not many references for Native American women, this group will access sources on Native American women as well as lesbians of color and biracial women. All references must be psychological, sociological, ethnographic in nature. Suggested topics for the articles include bicultural acculturation, self-concept, identity, coping styles, racial and gender identity, culture and tradition, oppression, and relationships. The annotations are to be approximately 100 words in length and written in your own words. Copies of the completed lists will be made available to all class participants. Your annotations must be accompanied by the article itself or the first page of a book chapter. All references *must* be from 1986 to the present. They *must* be in APA style.

Your group will also be responsible for a class overview of the fiction assignment for your racial group. Broadly speaking, your group will answer the following questions as they pertain to your book.

DISCUSSION FORMAT FOR FICTION ASSIGNMENT

1. How are cultural values (e.g., family, religion, relationships, names, children, the elderly, marriage, gender roles, the expression of feelings, food, traditions, holidays) and culture (art, music, dance, literature, entertainment) reflected in your readings? What references and connections are made with one's homeland (e.g., Africa, China)? How are education, sexuality, and women's independence portrayed?
2. What did your book reveal about the history of your racial group?
3. What role, if any, does being bilingual play?

4. Using our readings, what variations of racial, ethnic, and minority identity, gender and feminist identity, and sexual orientation are represented in your book?
5. How is oppression manifested (e.g., racism, sexism, heterosexism, differently abled, classism, ageism, internalized "isms")?
6. What is the feeling about the majority culture? Other ethnic minority groups? How are interfaith, interracial relationships and friendships handled? How are homosexuality and disability portrayed?
7. How do the characters cope with stress? What stressors are placed on this racial group?
8. How are acculturation, assimilation, biculturality, immigration, refugee status, and generation in United States portrayed?
9. Did the book alter some of your stereotypes and assumptions about this racial group?
10. What stories did you particularly like?

COURSE OUTLINE

	TOPIC	READING
Week 1	Introduction/overview: Multiculturalism	Espin & Gawelek
Week 2	Identity development	Phinney
Week 3	Latina women (group presentation)	Vazquez-Nuttall et al.
Week 4	Latina women (film or speaker)	
Week 5	Asian American women (group presentation)	True
Week 6	Asian American women (film or speaker)	
Week 7	African American women (group presentation)	McNair
Week 8	African American women (film or speaker)	

Week 9	Native American women (group presentation)	LaFromboise
	Bibliography due	
Week 10	Native American women (film or speaker)	
Week 11	Biracial women of color (film or speaker)	Root
Week 12	Lesbians of color (film or speaker)	Lourde
Week 13	Interview presentations	
Week 14	Interview presentations and wrap-up Paper due	

Note: The chapters in Comas-Diaz and Greene (1994) for each racial group should be included during the weeks that the racial group will be discussed. The same format should be followed for the inclusion of the Locke (1992) and Madison (1994) texts.

SUGGESTED RESERVE READINGS

Espin, Oliva M., & Gawelek, Mary Ann. (1992). Women's diversity: Ethnicity, race, class, and gender in theories of feminist psychology. In L. S. Brown & M. Ballou (Eds.), *Personality and psychopathology* (pp. 88–107). New York: Guilford.

Helms, Janet (Ed.). (1990). *Black and white racial identity: Theory, research and practice.* New York: Greenwood Press.

LaFromboise, Theressa. (1990). Changing and diverse roles of women in American Indian cultures. *Sex Roles, 22,* 455–476.

Lourde, Audre. (1987). There is no hierarchy of oppressions. *Interracial Books for Children Bulletin, 14*(7/8), 9.

McNair, Lily D. (1992). African American women in therapy: An Afrocentric and feminist synthesis. *Women and Therapy, 12*(1/2), 5–19.

Phinney, Jean S. (1990). Ethnic identity in adolescents and adults: Review of research. *Psychological Bulletin, 108*(3), 499–514.

Root, Maria P. P. (1990). Resolving "other" status: Identity development of biracial individuals. In L. S. Brown & M. P. P. Root (Eds.), *Diversity and complexity in feminist therapy* (pp. 185–205). New York: Haworth Press.

True, Reiko H. (1990). Psychotherapeutic issues with Asian American women. *Sex Roles, 22*(7/8), 477–486.

Vazquez-Nuttall, Ena, Romero-Garcia, Ivonne, & De Leon, Brunilda. (1987). Sex roles and perceptions of femininity and masculinity of Hispanic women: A review of the literature. *Psychology of Women Quarterly, 11*(4), 409–426.

37

Advanced Studies in the Psychology of Women

Ann L. Saltzman

The following syllabus is designed for a 13-week seminar called The Psychology of Women that meets twice a week and is offered in alternate years. Historically, psychology students have studied "mainstream psychology" in which either gender is not considered as a variable or women's "place" in that psychology is problematic. Thus, I set three goals for the seminar: (1) to acquaint students with research by, for, and about women; (2) to explore the relationship between the psychology of women and mainstream psychology; and (3) to facilitate the transfer of knowledge to both students' personal lives and their future involvement in the study of psychology. With regard to this last goal, I urge students to return to their mainstream courses and to "make trouble": ask what a particular body of research has to say about women; advocate for more inclusive syllabi; bring a woman-focused perspective.

The course is structured so that students enter the dialogue between two research approaches within the psychology of women. The first, which tends to rely on quantitative methodologies, emerges from an "individual differences" tradition that has, in the past, "documented" women's deficiencies. When claimed by feminist psychologists, this tradition focuses on gender similarities; women's and men's behaviors and experiences are shown to be

more alike than they are different. The required course text, Janet Hyde's
Half the Human Experience: The Psychology of Women, 4th ed. (Indianapolis: D. C. Heath, 1991) represents this approach.

The second research orientation is more "woman focused"; it concen-
trates on women's experiences without concern about how they compare with
men's. Psychologists adopting this approach tend to utilize qualitative and
clinical methodologies. It is represented in the syllabus by a required set of
audiotapes (The Seventh Annual Women in Context Conference, "Women
and Self-Esteem: Exploring the Forces That Enhance and Diminish the Self,"
Topeka, KS: Menniger Foundation, 1990) as well as numerous assigned
articles.

The course is conducted as a colloquium; dyads and triads of students
take turns facilitating discussions of assigned readings. They are also required to keep a session-by-session journal in which they address the issues
raised by these readings and class discussions. The journals, which constitute
the major written requirement of the course, are reviewed and responded
to by the instructor three times during the semester. Finally, students must
complete an empirically based project on a topic of interest. They are encouraged to work collaboratively and to choose a methodology that best suits
their research question. Project findings are shared in both oral and written
forms.

COURSE OUTLINE

Session 1   Introduction to the course

Session 2   Why a psychology of women?
                       Required readings:
                       Hyde, chap. 1
                       Brown, A., Goodwin, B., Hall, B., & Jackson-Lowman,
                           H. (1985). A review of psychology of women text-
                           books: Focus on the Afro-American woman. *Psychol-
                           ogy of Women Quarterly, 9*(1), 29–38
                       Gannon, L., Luchetta, T., Rhodes, K., Pardie, L., & Se-
                           grist, D. (1992). Sex bias in psychological research:
                           Progress or complacency? *American Psychologist,
                           47*(3), 389–396
                       Weisstein, N. (1968). Psychology constructs the female.
                           In V. Gornick & B. K. Moran (Eds.), *Woman in a sex-
                           ist society* (pp. 207–224). New York: Basic Books

UNIT I
THE POWER/STATUS CONTEXT OF WOMEN'S
LIVES

Session 3

Images of women and nonconscious ideologies
Required readings:
Hyde, chap. 2, pp. 38–40
Bason, S. (1991). The hairless ideal: Women and their body hair. *Psychology of Women Quarterly, 15,* 83–96
Rothenberg, P. (1988). *Racism and sexism: An integrated study.* New York: St. Martin's Press ("The prison of race and gender: Stereotypes, ideology, language social control," pp. 252–254)
Schwartz, A. (1988). *A woman with body hair.* Unpublished manuscript
Films: *Still Killing Us Softly: Advertising's Image of Women* (produced and distributed by Cambridge Documentary Films, Cambridge, MA) and *Keltie's Beard: A Woman's Story* (distributed by Filmmakers Library, New York, NY)

Session 4

Language—a tool for social control
Required readings:
Hyde, chap. 4, pp. 98–106
Baker, R. (1988). "Pricks" and "chicks": A plea for "persons." In Rothenberg, pp. 280–295
Dick and Jane as victims: Sex stereotyping in children's readers. (1975). Princeton, NJ: Women on Words and Images (excerpts)
Moore, R. B. (1988). Racist stereotyping in the English language. In Rothenberg, pp. 269–279

Session 5

Gender as a status variable—male as normative
Required readings:
Hyde, chap. 2, pp. 59–61
Broverman, I. K., Vogel, S. R., Broverman, D. M., Clarkson, F. E., & Rosenkrantz, P. S. (1972). Sex-role stereotypes: A current appraisal. *Journal of Social Issues, 28*(2), 59–78
Feinman, S. (1981). Why is cross-sex role behavior more approved for girls than boys? A status characteristic approach. *Sex Roles, 7*(3), 289–300

Session 6   The impact on women's self-esteem
                     Required readings:
                     Hyde, chap. 3, pp. 82–83, 85–86
                     Audiotape (from required TapeSet):
                     Lerner, H. G. *Struggles with authenticity, competence
                        and self-regard in women's key relationships.* Tape 1,
                        side A, 65–530

Session 7   Gender and race as status variables
                     Required readings:
                     Hyde, chap. 9
                     Chan, C. S. (1988). Asian-American women: Psychologi-
                        cal responses to sexual exploitation and cultural ste-
                        reotypes. In L. Fulani (Ed.), *The psychopathology of
                        everyday racism and sexism* (pp. 33–38). New York:
                        Harrington Park Press
                     Grady Truely, W. (1991, May/June). The needs of Afri-
                        can American girls. *National NOW Times, 23*(4), 4
                     Audiotape (from required TapeSet):
                     Wilson, S. B. *From Aunt Jemima to Nefertiti: African-
                        American women and the self-esteem trap.* Tape 1, side
                        B, 318–540 (end of tape)

Session 8   Sexual orientation as a status variable
                     Required readings:
                     Hyde, chap. 13, pp. 286–290
                     Lorde, A. (1988). I am your sister: Black women
                        organizing across sexualities. In Fulani,
                        pp. 25–30
                     Rich, A. (1980). Compulsory heterosexuality and les-
                        bian existence. In C. R. Simpson & E. S. Person
                        (Eds.), *Women: Sex and sexuality* (pp. 62–91). Chi-
                        cago: University of Chicago Press
                     Weitz, R. (1989). What price independence? Social
                        reactions to lesbians, spinsters, widows and nuns.
                        In J. Freeman (Ed.), *Women: A feminist perspec-
                        tive* (pp. 446–456). Mountain View, CA:
                        Mayfield
                     Audiotape (from required TapeSet): Reinke, K. *Lost &
                        found: A journey to lesbian esteem.* Tape 1, side B,
                        000–280.

UNIT II
DEVELOPMENTAL PERSPECTIVES

Session 9

Psychoanalytic theory
Required readings:
Hyde, chap. 2, pp. 24–36; chap. 6, pp. 124–127; chap. 13, pp. 292–294
Lewis, H. B. (1989). Is Freud an enemy of women's liberation? Some historical considerations. In T. Bernay & D. Cantor (Eds.), *The psychology of today's woman: New psychoanalytic visions* (pp. 7–8, 20–26, 30–33). Cambridge: Harvard University Press

Session 10

Guest speaker: Louise Taylor, a student of the late Dorothy Dinnerstein, speaks on Dinnerstein's theory of masculinity and the male need to control women

Session 11

Social learning and cognitive theories
Required readings:
Hyde, chap. 2, pp. 42–51, 55–59, 61–62; chap. 6, pp. 128–130; chap. 13, pp. 294–295
Bem, S. (1983). Gender schema theory and its implications for child development: Raising gender aschematic children in a gender schematic society. *Signs, 8*(4), 598–616
Hale, J. (1980). The black woman and child rearing. In L. Rodgers-Rose (Ed.), *The black woman* (pp. 79–87). Beverly Hills, CA: Sage
Film excerpts from *The Pinks and the Blues,* NOVA Series (1980), produced by WGBH

Session 12

Gilligan—the importance of attachment/connection
Required readings:
Hyde, chap. 2, pp. 51–55
Gilligan, C. (1982). *In a different voice: Psychological theory and women's development.* Cambridge: Harvard University Press, chap. 2, pp. 24–63
Audiotape: Gilligan, C. (1991, March 9). *Joining the resistance: Psychology, politics, girls and women.* Talk given at 16th National Conference of Association for Women in Psychology

Session 13   Adolescent identity formation: Achievement
                    Required readings:
                    Hyde, chap. 6, pp. 131–136; chap. 7, pp. 148–171

Session 14   Adolescence: Menstruation
                    Required readings:
                    Hyde, chap. 11, pp. 230–244
                    Chalmer, J., & Solin, F. (1988). Turning 12: Becoming a
                        woman. *Lilith, 21,* 17–18
                    Golub, S. (1983). Menarche: The beginning of men-
                        strual life. In S. Golub (Ed.), *Lifting the curse of*
                        menstruation: A feminist appraisal of the influence of
                        menstruation on women's lives (pp. 17–36). New York:
                        Harrington Park Press
                    Powers, M. N. (1980). Menstruation and reproduction:
                        An Oglagla case. In C. R. Stimpson & E. S. Person
                        (Eds.), *Women: Sex and sexuality* (pp. 117–128). Chi-
                        cago: University of Chicago Press

Session 15   Adulthood I: Love, marriage, and family
                    Required readings:
                    Hyde, chap. 6, pp. 136–142
                    Belle, D. (1982). The stress of caring: Women as provid-
                        ers of social support. In L. Goldberger & S. Breznitz
                        (Eds.), *The handbook of stress* (pp. 496–505). New
                        York: Free Press
                    McAdoo, H. P. (1980). Black mothers and the extended
                        family support network. In Rodgers-Rose, pp.
                        125–144
                    Russo, N. F., & Sobel, S. B. (1981). Sex differences in
                        the utilization of mental health facilities. *Professional*
                        Psychology, 12(1), 7–19
                    Audiotape (from required TapeSet): Safier, E. *Staying*
                        connected. Tape 2, side B, 247-end

Session 16   Choosing children
                    Required readings:
                    Brown, L. S. (1989). New voices, new visions: Toward a
                        lesbian/gay paradigm for psychology. *Psychology of*
                        Women Quarterly, 13(4), 445–458
                    Film: *Choosing Children,* a film about lesbian parenting
                        (produced and directed by Debra Chasnoff and Kim

Klausner; distributed by Cambridge Documentary
Films, Cambridge, MA)

Session 17

Adulthood II: Work and generativity
Required readings:
Hyde, chap. 8, pp. 174–191
Daniels, P. (1981). Dream vs. drift in women's careers:
The question of generativity. In B. Goldman & B.
Forisha (Eds.), *Outsiders on the inside: Women and
organizations* (pp. 283–302). New York: Prentice-
Hall
Daniels, P. (1977). The birth of the amateur. In P. Dan-
iels & S. Ruddick (Eds.), *Working it out* (pp. 55–70).
New York: Pantheon Books
Pleck, J. H. (1977). The work-family role system. *Social
Problems, 24,* 417–427
Repetti, R., Matthews, K. A., & Waldron, I. (1989). Em-
ployment and women's health: Effects of paid employ-
ment on women's mental and physical health. *Ameri-
can Psychologist, 44*(11), 1394–1401
Scarr, S., Phillips, D., & McCartney, K. (1989). Working
mothers and their families. *American Psychologist,
44*(11), 1402–1409
Audiotape (from required TapeSet): Ault-Riche, M.
Sharing laundry consciousness. Tape 2, side B,
000–245

Session 18

Finding our mothers
Required readings:
Herman, J. D., & Lewis, H. B. (1989). Anger in the
mother-daughter relationship. In Bernay & Cantor
pp. 139–163
Howe, K. G. (1989). Telling our mother's story: Chang-
ing daughters' perceptions of their mothers in a wom-
en's studies course. In R. K. Unger (Ed.), *Representa-
tions: Social Constructions of Gender* (pp. 45–60).
Amityville, NY: Baywood
Marshall, N. (1991). *Personal reflections on crossing
the class line* (Working Paper No. 228). Wellesley,
MA: Wellesley College Center for Research on
Women

UNIT III
WOMEN AND MENTAL HEALTH

Session 19   Depression
                      Required readings:
                      Hyde, chap. 6, pp. 142–143; chap. 11, pp. 244–247; chap.
                          14, pp. 306–310
                      Carrington, C. H. (1980). Depression in black women:
                          A theoretical appraisal. In Rodgers-Rose, pp.
                          265–271
                      Lewis, H. B. (1987). *Sex and the superego: Psychic war
                          in men and women.* Hillside, NJ: Lawrence Erlbaum
                          Associates; chaps. 13, 14, 16 (pp. 185–220, 236–255)
                      Weissman, M., & Klerman, G. L. (1981). Sex differ-
                          ences and the epidemiology of depression. In E. How-
                          ell & M. Bayes (Eds.), *Women and mental health* (pp.
                          160–195). New York: Basic Books

Session 20   Obesity and eating disorders
                      Required readings:
                      Hyde, chap. 14, pp. 312–319
                      Chernin, K. (1981, October 11). How women's diets re-
                          flect fear of power. *Sunday New York Times Maga-
                          zine,* pp. 38, 40, 42–44, 46, 50
                      Mazur, D. C. (1981). A starving family: An interac-
                          tional view of anorexia nervosa. In Howell & Bayes,
                          pp. 240–247
                      Polivy, J., & Herman, C. P. (1985). Dieting and binging.
                          American Psychologist, 46(2), 193–201
                      Stuart, R. B. (with Jacobsen, B.). (1979). Sex differences
                          in obesity. In E. Gomber & V. Franks (Eds.), *Gender
                          and disordered behavior* (pp. 241–256). New York:
                          Brunner/Mazel
                      Wooley, S. C., & Wooley, O. W. (1980). Eating disorders:
                          Obesity and anorexia. In A. M. Brodsky & R. Hare-
                          Mustin (Eds.), *Women and psychotherapy* (pp. 135–
                          158). New York: Guilford Press

Session 21   Women and psychotherapies
                      Required readings:
                      Hyde, chap. 14, pp. 319–333
                      Comas-Diaz, L. (1988). Feminist therapy with His-

panic/Latina women: Myth or reality. In Fulani, pp. 39–61

Gilbert, L. A. (1980). Feminist therapy. In Brodsky & Hare-Mustin, pp. 245–265

Hare-Mustin, R. T., & Marecek, J. (1988). The meaning of difference. *American Psychologist, 43*(6), 455–464

Task Force on Consumer Issues in Psychotherapy in the Association for Women in Psychology. (1981). *Women and psychotherapy: A consumer handbook.* Washington, DC: Federation of Organizations for Professional Women

Session 22   The politics of diagnosis
Film: *Diagnosis Today: Women and Mental Health* (produced by The Parasol Group, New York, NY)
Required readings:
Caplan, P. J., & Gans, M. (1991). Is there empirical justification for the category of "self-defeating personality disorder"? *Feminism and Psychology, 1*(2), 263–278
Landrine, H. (1989). The politics of personality disorder. *Psychology of Women Quarterly, 13*(3), 325–339

Sessions 23–25   Student presentations

Session 26   Questions that remain
Required readings:
Hyde, chap. 17, pp. 396–406

38
Advanced Women's Studies:
Psychoanalysis and Feminist Theory

Frances Bartkowski

What follows is a tentative schedule for a 14-week course with one 3-hour meeting per week. I envision this as a course for those who have done substantial work in women's studies already and who are prepared to take on the task of theorizing about gender and its problematic categories.

Where I have indicated selections from certain anthologies or entire books, I leave the specificity of which chapters or essays to include an open question, depending on the makeup of the class and the tenor and direction of discussions as they develop. I outline discussions for only 12 of the 14 weeks of the semester so as to leave room for the inevitable but unpredictable breaks and gaps in the semester's work. The weekly work I schematize below is somewhat densely packed, and, therefore, some expansion from one week into the next will be a likely consequence.

COURSE OUTLINE

Week 1   Simone de Beauvoir, *The Second Sex,* the chapter on
psychoanalysis and "The Formative Years"
Joan Riviere, "Womanliness as Masquerade"
Karen Horney, selections from *Feminine Psychology*

Week 2   Freud, *Three Essays on the Theory of Sexuality,* "Female
                Sexuality" and "Femininity"
                Juliet Mitchell, *Psychoanalysis and Feminism,* selected
                chapters

Week 3   Juliet Mitchell and Jacqueline Rose, introductions to
                Feminine Sexuality
                Jane Gallop, chapters from *The Daughter's Seduction*

Week 4   Melanie Klein, "Early Stages of the Oedipus Complex"
                D. W. Winnicott, "Mirror-role of Mother and Family in
                Child Development"
                Jessica Benjamin, *Bonds of Love,* selected chapters

Week 5   Freud, "Fragment of an Analysis of a Case of Hysteria
                ('Dora')"
                Charles Bernheimer and Claire Kahane, *In Dora's Case,*
                selected essays

Week 6   Jane Gallop, *Thinking Through the Body,* "Phallus-
                Penis: Same Difference"
                Judith Butler, *Bodies that Matter,* "The Lesbian
                Phallus"
                Freud, "Some Psychical Consequences of the Anatomi-
                cal Distinction Between the Sexes"

Week 7   Freud, "On Narcissism: An Introduction"
                Freud, "The Dissolution of the Oedipus Complex"
                Luce Irigaray, *This Sex Which Is Not One,* selected
                essays

Week 8   Julia Kristeva, "Motherhood According to Giovanni
                Bellini"
                Jacques Lacan, *Encore*
                Stephen Heath, "Difference"

Week 9   Michele Montrelay, "Inquiry Into Femininity"
                Monique Wittig, "The Straight Mind"

Week 10   Shulamith Firestone, *The Dialectic of Sex,* selected
                chapters

Dorothy Dinnerstein, *The Mermaid and the Minotaur,* selected chapters
Nancy Chodorow, *The Reproduction of Mothering,* selected chapters

Week 11   Naomi Schor, "This Essentialism"
               Jane Gallop, selections from *Thinking Through the Body*

Week 12   Diana Fuss, *Inside/Out,* selected essays
               Eve Sedgwick, *The Epistemology of the Closet,* introduction

SELECTED BIBLIOGRAPHY

Beauvoir, Simone de. (1953). *The second sex* (H. M. Parshley, Trans.). New York: Knopf.
Benjamin, Jessica. (1988). *The bonds of love: Feminism and the problem of domination.* New York: Pantheon.
Bernheimer, Charles, & Claire Kahane (Eds.). (1985). *In Dora's case: Freud, hysteria, feminism.* New York: Columbia University Press.
Bonaparte, Marie. (1973). *Female sexuality.* New York: International Universities Press, 1973. (Original work published 1953)
Butler, Judith. (1990). *Gender trouble: Feminism and the subversion of identity.* New York: Routledge.
Butler, Judith. (1993). *Bodies that matter: On the discursive limits of "sex."* New York: Routledge.
Chasseguet-Smirgel, Janine. (1981). *Female sexuality: New psychoanalytic views.* London: Virago.
Chodorow, Nancy. (1979). *The reproduction of mothering: Psychoanalysis and the sociology of gender.* London: University of California Press.
Dinnerstein, Dorothy. (1976). *The mermaid and the minotaur: Sexual arrangements and human malaise.* New York: Harper & Row.
Firestone, Shulamith. (1970). *The dialectic of sex: The case for feminist revolution.* New York: Morrow.
Freud, Sigmund. (1953). The dissolution of the Oedipus complex. In *Standard edition* (*SE*), London: Hogarth Press, Vol. 19, pp. 173–179.
Freud, Sigmund. (1953). Female sexuality. In *SE,* Vol. 21, pp. 223–243.
Freud, Sigmund. (1953). Femininity. In *SE,* Vol. 22, pp. 112–135.
Freud, Sigmund. (1953). Fragment of an analysis of a case of hysteria ("Dora"). In *SE,* Vol. 7, pp. 1–122.
Freud, Sigmund. (1953). On narcissism: An introduction. In *SE,* Vol. 14, pp. 67–102.
Freud, Sigmund. (1953). On the universal tendency to debasement in the sphere of love. In *SE,* Vol. 11, pp. 177–90.

Freud, Sigmund. (1953). Some psychical consequences of the anatomical distinction between the sexes. In *SE*, Vol. 19, pp. 243–258.

Freud, Sigmund. (1953). Three essays on the theory of sexuality. In *SE*, Vol. 7, pp. 123–245.

Fuss, Diana (Ed.). (1991). *Inside/out*. New York: Routledge.

Gallop, Jane. (1982). *The daughter's seduction: Feminism and psychoanalysis*. Ithaca, NY: Cornell University Press.

Gallop, Jane. (1990). *Thinking through the body*. New York: Columbia University Press.

Heath, Stephen. (1978/1979, Winter). Difference. *Screen, 19,* 4.

Horney, Karen. (1967) *Feminine psychology*. London: Routledge and Kegan Paul.

Irigaray, Luce. (1985). *Speculum of the other woman* (Catherine Porter, Trans.). Ithaca, NY: Cornell University Press.

Irigaray, Luce. (1985). *This sex which is not one* (Catherine Porter, Trans.). Ithaca, NY: Cornell University Press.

Klein, Melanie. (1928). Early stages of the Oedipus complex. *International Journal of Psychoanalysis, 9,* 167–180.

Kristeva, Julia. (1980). Motherhood according to Giovanni Bellini. In *Desire in language: A semiotic approach to literature and art* (Thomas Gora, Alice Jardine, & Leon S. Roudiez, Trans.). New York: Columbia University Press.

Lacan, Jacques. (1975). *Encore*. Paris: Seuil.

Mitchell, Juliet. (1974). *Psychoanalysis and feminism*. New York: Vintage.

Mitchell, Juliet, & Jacqueline Rose (Eds.). (1985). *Feminine sexuality: Jacques Lacan and the école freudienne*. New York: Norton.

Montrelay, Michele. (1978). Inquiry into femininity (Parveen Adams, Trans.). *m/f, 1,* 65–101.

Riviere, Joan. (1929). Womanliness as masquerade. *International Journal of Psychoanalysis, 10,* 303–313.

Schor, Naomi. (1989). This essentialism which is not one: Coming to grips with Irigaray. *Differences, 1*(2), 38–58.

Sedgwick, Eve Kosofsky. (1990). *The epistemology of the closet*. Berkeley: University of California Press.

Winnicott, D. W. (1971). Mirror-role of mother and family in child development. In *Playing and reality*. London: Tavistock.

Wittig, Monique. (1980, Summer). The straight mind. *Feminist Issues, 1*(1), 103–112.

39
Philosophy of Science Syllabus

Lynn Hankinson Nelson

COURSE INFORMATION

The field of philosophy of science has long focused on the epistemology of science: how theories are generated, the relationship between our theories and evidence, the nature and strength of the evidence available to us, and the nature of scientific revolutions. These questions are central to the course.

But the course also focuses on questions that are relatively new to the field. Philosophers long approached science as an autonomous entity, detached (at least when things were going as they should) from the social and political contexts within which it is practiced. The assumption that science is somehow autonomous of so-called common sense and political context has come to seem far less warranted in the last 3 decades. This has been due in part to research in the history of science, social studies of science, and feminist science critiques that indicate strong relationships between science and social context; it has also been due to a renewed interest among philosophers and others in the "context of discovery," an area virtually ignored in earlier philosophy of science. We begin with a survey of the kinds of issues now of interest in the field, then focus on traditional epistemological questions, and finally consider the interplay of the two. Evolutionary theory serves as our case study.

COURSE REQUIREMENTS

As a 300-level course, the class is organized as a seminar. Each student is responsible for outlining the main points of two readings (a sign-up sheet will be circulated).

Formal writing requirements are two topic papers (one for each of the two topics of the course), a major paper (8–10 pages), and a collaborative project that serves as the final exam.

Attendance and participation in all classes are required.

The "weighting" of these requirements is to be determined by each student, with no requirement counting less than 10% or more than 30% of the final grade.

TEXTS

There is no single text appropriate for the course. Accordingly, I have ordered several. You may share these texts (they are also in the library, and used versions are available in the bookstore).

Philip Appleman, ed., *Darwin: A Norton Critical Edition,* 2nd ed. (New York: W. W. Norton, 1970).
Alan Chalmers, *What Is This Thing Called Science?* (St. Lucia: University of Queensland Press, 1982).
Stephen Jay Gould, *Mismeasure of Man* (New York: W. W. Norton, 1981).
Lynn Hankinson Nelson, *Who Knows: From Quine to a Feminist Empiricism* (Philadelphia: Temple University Press, 1990).

SCHEDULE OF READINGS AND DISCUSSIONS

Codes: *NCE:* Appleman, *Darwin: A Norton Critical Edition; WIT:* Chalmers, *What Is This Thing Called Science?; MOM:* Gould, *Mismeasure of Man; WK:* Nelson, *Who Knows: From Quine to a Feminist Empiricism;* H: Supplementary handouts

TOPIC I
A SURVEY OF ISSUES

Meeting 1   Introduction: Philosophy of science

Meetings 2, 3   Views of the epistemology of science
                    Sheldon Glashow, "Articles of Faith" (H)

NAS, "On Being a Scientist" (H)
Chalmers, "The Inductivist View of Science" (*WIT*)
Selection from Nelson (*WK*)

Meetings 4, 5   Science and the citizen
                  Wade, "The Ultimate Revolution: Man-Made Evolu-
                  tion" (*NCE*)
                  Wilson, "Sociobiology" (*NCE*)
                  Gould, introduction and "American Polygeny . . . Be-
                  fore Darwin" (*MOM*)

Meeting 6   Scientific revolutions
                  de Beer, "Biology Before the *Beagle*" (*NCE*)
                  Millhauser, "In the Air" (*NCE*)
                  "Argument over a Woman: Science Searches for the
                  Mother of Us All," *Discover,* Aug. 1990 (H)

Meeting 7   Falsificationism—an alternative to inductivism
                  Chalmers, "Falsificationism" (*WIT*)
                  Popper, Postscript to *Objective Knowledge* (H)

Meetings 8, 9   Alternatives to inductivism and falsificationism
                  Chalmers, "Kuhn: Theories as Paradigms" (*WIT*)
                  Selection from Kuhn, *Scientific Revolutions* (H)
                  Nelson, "Quine: Science (Almost) Without Boundaries"
                  (*WK*)
                  Quine, "Posits and Reality" and "The Scope and Lan-
                  guage of Science" (H)

                  TOPIC II
                  A CASE STUDY—EVOLUTIONARY THEORY

Meeting 10   Introduction, Darwin's *The Origin of Species* (*NCE*)

Meetings 11–13   Chapters 1–4 of *The Origin* (*NCE*)

Meetings 14, 15   Applying the theories of science to Darwin (inductiv-
                  ism, falsificationism, Kuhn, and Quine)

Meetings 16, 17   Evolution and humanity
                  Introduction and Chapters 1 and 3 of Darwin, *The De-
                  scent of Man* (*NCE*)

Meetings 18, 19 Science and society—gender
Darwin, "On Sexual Selection" (*NCE*)
Nelson, "Androcentrism and Science: Man the Hunter and Woman the Gatherer" (*WK*)
Hubbard, "Have Only Men Evolved?" (H), E. O. Wilson, "Sex" (H)

Meetings 20, 21 Science and society—race
Darwin, variation among "the races of man," *The Origin* (*NCE*)
Loehlin et al., "The Context of the Race-IQ Question" (*NCE*)
Herrnstein, "I.Q." (*NCE*)
Chomsky, "The Fallacy of Richard Herrnstein's IQ" (*NCE*)

Meeting 22 Science and society—class
Carnegie, "The Gospel of Wealth" (*NCE*)
Hofstadter, "The Vogue of Spencer" (*NCE*)

Meeting 23 Biological determinism
Wilson, "Sociobiology" (*NCE*)
Gould, "Biological Potentiality vs. Biological Determinism" (*NCE*)
Nelson, "A Question of Evidence" (H)

Meeting 24 The status of evolutionary theory
Gould, "Evolution as Fact and Theory" (H)

Meeting 25 Implications
Gould, "A Positive Conclusion" (*MOM*)
Lewontin, selection from *Biology as Ideology* (H)
Nelson, "Science Communities" (*WK*)

Meeting 26 What is this thing called science?

40

Teaching About Elder Women: Wallflowers at the Women's Studies Dance

Roxanne Friedenfels

One of the goals of feminist teachers is integrating the voiceless and invisible into the curriculum. But only a whisper is heard from elder women, who remain largely absent from our courses. Ageism in women's studies is strong. As Barbara Macdonald (1989) asked, "how [is it] possible that the last thirty years of women's lives have been ignored in women's studies?" In the generally lively dance that is women's studies, women over age 50 are the wallflowers.

The integration of elder women into the curriculum is at the same stage that the integration of women of color was in the early 1980s. Based on Schuster and Van Dyne's (1985) stages of integrating women into the curriculum, modified to focus on elder women, most women's studies courses are at stage 1: invisible (elder) women. An examination of 49 introductory women's studies syllabi collected by the National Women's Studies Association showed that fewer than half had any material on women over age 50. Of those that did, most had only one or two articles. Women's studies theory courses were even less likely to contain material on elder women or the life courses of women. Only a small number of us have searched for missing (elder) women (stage 2) or examined (elder) women as a subordinate group (stage 3). Fewer still have studied elder women on their own terms (stage 4). Stage 5—(elder) women as a challenge to the discipline—constitutes substantially changed course goals and conceptions. Finally, stage 6 is a fully transformed, balanced curriculum.

The need to convince people that the last 30 years of women's lives need to be included in our courses confronts us in many places—in the lack of courses on elders, in the failure to include material on long-living women in the courses that do exist, in the lack of material on women over age 50 in women's studies courses, and in the invisibility of long-living women in the media and in many of our lives. I suggest five reasons that we should begin the journey to stage 6.

WHY INTEGRATE ELDER WOMEN INTO THE CURRICULUM?

1. *An increased number of elders will change society.* Increased numbers of elders constitute an unintentional social change, with various unintended consequences. Elders, defined here as people aged 50 and over, will also be key agents of intentional change in the years to come, whether through their positions in government, schools, and other societal institutions or through the collective efforts of organizations such as the Older Women's League. Our curriculum should prepare students to understand and participate in the discussions and decisions that will be part of this era of change.

Changes in the demographic makeup of U.S. society are especially significant with regard to the old (people 65 and over). The percentage of people in this group has been steadily increasing and will continue to do so. In 1970, people 65 or over were 9.8% of the population; by the year 2000, they will be over 12% of the population (Hess, 1985). By the year 2040, they could approach 20% of the population (Butler, 1994). The more inclusive group of people who are 50 and older (elders) has increased more slowly but will begin growing rapidly in the late 1990s, when the huge baby boom cohort starts turning 50.

The problems of elders are the problems of women. This is numerically true. Women in their 50s slightly outnumber men of the same age, a tendency that becomes increasingly pronounced and reaches across races and ethnicities. By the ages of 80 to 84, there are almost twice as many women as men. It is also socially true that the problems of elders are the problems of women. Social issues that especially affect long-living women include poverty, Social Security, lack of insurance coverage (with women of color less likely than Caucasian women to have adequate wages, pensions, and insurance coverage), Alzheimer's disease, and elder abuse (Barrow, 1992). Caretaking looms large as a present and future issue for unpaid elder women who are caretakers, for paid professionals, and for disabled elders who need caretaking. There is increased pressure for elder women to do caretaking, even as rising numbers of them hold paying jobs. Finally, many more women than men end up in nursing homes, often receiving substandard care. The growing numbers of elder women suggest a need to rethink these issues and find solutions.

But although the problems associated with living a long time may be the problems of women, so too may the future be transformed by elder women. They will constitute an ever greater proportion of the population and be more educated and politicized than in the recent past. Their involvement in the social movements of the 1960s, 1970s, and 1980s; their release from child care; and the greater strength of personality that many elder women experience (Gutmann, 1987) all bode well for future activism around issues of women's aging.

Why integrate elder women into the curriculum? Because changes in the number and character of the elder population will transform society as we know it. Longevity will both yield wider options and create new societal problems (Riley, 1985). Understanding, creativity, and empathy for the aged and aging will be needed in this transformation.

2. *Women's bodies are changing.* If we are not yet old, we will probably become old. If we are not yet middle-aged, we will probably become middle-aged. Only the unlucky ones will never get past youth. But elder women's chances of a low quality of life are much greater than elder men's, and women experience ageism sooner and more acutely than men. The reach of the media means that no woman is immune, though ageism undoubtedly varies in form and intensity by race, ethnicity, and class (variations that remain largely unstudied).

Many women have denied their age and, with it, their aging. Western societies have a particular dislike of the old female body, a dislike women have internalized as individuals. Negative images of women's aging are deeply entrenched in our culture and need to be examined for women's personal liberation.

With the revulsion toward aging female bodies comes the denial of the sexuality of elder women. Although this is somewhat true for both men and women, it is especially true for women, and it applies earlier. The media portray middle-aged men and even men aged 65–75 in (usually heterosexual) partnerships. Women over 35 are less likely to be portrayed in such relationships. In real life, of course, middle-aged and old women often have partners, but at a lesser rate, if they are heterosexual, than men do. The pattern is reversed for lesbians and homosexual males—with elder lesbians being more likely than elder gay men to have partners (Kelly, 1977)—but the general view that elder women are asexual still applies. Although most women remain sexually active with self or others, some are inactive—partly because they think that others believe that elder women are asexual, or should be. Women both internalize the revulsion and experience it in others' reactions to them.

Elder women's lack of life partners also means that illness is more catastrophic for them than for long-living men. They are less likely to be able to remain at home while ill and are less assured of constant loving care. They make more visits to doctors than elder men but may be badly served by them. Recent studies suggest that doctors do not treat some of elder women's physical problems aggressively but overuse other procedures (Podolsky & Silberner, 1993). A comparison of the relatively conservative treatment of prostate cancer with the epidemic of hysterectomies (Doress & Siegal, 1987) suggests that women's bodies are treated with less respect than men's by the mostly male medical establishment.

Why integrate elder women into the curriculum? Simply, for women themselves.

3. *Our courses don't encourage students' personal and academic development as fully as they could.* As many of us do in our everyday lives, our curricula deny that aging exists. We teach not only a partial curriculum but also a distorted curriculum, because elder women are left out. If our courses do not make it possible for us to listen to elder women, we fail to adequately prepare younger students for their future, and we deny students over 50 the chance to think fully about the social forces affecting them. Students who will work with elder clients as doctors, nurses, social workers, psychiatrists, and therapists are poorly prepared.

Women taking courses that integrate the voices of elder women will be able to better consider the implications of holding paying jobs or working solely at home; of marrying, cohabiting with men, forming lesbian partnerships, or remaining alone; of having some, one, or no children. Menopause will be less strange and frightening; the likely continuities and changes in sexual desire and practice will be known, as will the possible liabilities and rewards of doing elder care. They will have had the opportunity to think about social programs such as Social Security and national health insurance in the context of an abundance of information about the life courses of women. They will be able to look at these issues through a multiplicity of lenses, understanding how race, ethnicity, and class interact with age and gender. Each student will reach her own conclusions, but I think that few students will hold entirely the same views when the last 30 years of women's lives are included in the curriculum, or think about their own lives in quite the same way.

Why integrate elder women into the curriculum? For the academic and personal development of our students.

4. *For the development of our disciplines.* Elder women are almost invisible in our theory, research, and teaching. Our disciplines, including women's studies, suffer as a result. Consider the assertion, made to one of my students by another professor, that most women's marital satisfaction declines over time. This is partly true, but satisfaction increases again in the postretirement years, then declines once more when the husband or wife develops serious health problems (Barrow, 1992). There are several reasons for this pattern, but the point is that if we do not study the entire life course, our knowledge and understanding will be incomplete and biased. The age homogeneity of many women's studies classes contributes to this problem. If our classes included the shared experiences and interpretations of elder students, our writing and thinking would broaden and our disciplines would better reflect—and critique—the world in which they are embedded.

Women's studies programs also need to hire elder women and to encourage their hiring in other departments and programs. Women completing their degrees later in life often have difficulty finding jobs—one of a number of reasons for the dearth of research and theory on elder women. The "aging in place" of female academics who were hired at younger ages doesn't end the "gender gap" in numbers of professors, and women trained later in life may have quite different perspectives on gender and the life course—shaped in part by the greater discrimination they experience. Their inclusion might well have a significant impact on feminist research and theory.

Why integrate elder women into the curriculum? To expand and enrich our various disciplines, including our common one of women's studies.

5. *For the solidarity of women.* Women's studies grew out of the women's movement. But as long as many young, middle-aged, and (sometimes) even old women accept the stereotypes of elder women—that they are old-fashioned, ugly, and either incompetent or competent only in grandmotherly skills—the women's movement suffers. The stereotypes encourage us to see elder women as good grandmothers, meddling mothers and mothers-in-law, shuffling bag ladies, and ugly wicked witches. Women's studies courses need to analyze these pernicious ideas about elder women that are embedded in fairy tales, jokes, cartoons, and films. Materials, assignments, and speakers that expose students to self-accepting, self-loving elder women will counter the stereotypes and increase young women's acceptance of elder women in the movement. We must also be careful not to substitute new stereotypes. To suggest that elder women are necessarily wise, spiritual, or strong is to make them icons, not women. Such idealization separates women rather than enabling them to work together.

Moving toward solidarity also means exploring how young women have benefited from making elder women "other" (Copper, 1988). It is not men alone who have done this. Exploring this complicity will be painful.

Some younger women believe that their youth makes them superior to elder women. Some take elder women's jobs, lovers, or husbands. Some exploit elder women as workers, mothers, and grandmothers. Some talk past elder women as if they were air, walk past them as if they were ghosts. Some treat elder women, in short, as the social dead.

Solidarity means exploring all these issues in the curriculum, and it means new ways of interacting among women. It is self-love, an ethic of care, and sisterhood based on recognizing one another's powers and needs. It means elder women dancing at the women's studies dance.

Why integrate elder women into the curriculum? To nurture the root of women's studies, which is the women's movement. In continuing to recognize women's connections to the women's movement, we further the efforts toward justice and the liberation of women.

Vision: They are dancing dances from Asia, Africa, Latin America, and Europe. They dance in circles, in lines, separately, together, on tables, with wheelchairs and canes, theatrically, in trance, in costume and without. They dance. In rhythms and styles different from younger women, they dance. In rhythms and styles the same, they dance. Startling in their diversity, growing lovely (Baker, 1980), they dance, filling the dance floor of women's studies, wallflowers no more.

Why integrate elder women into the curriculum? As another leap toward the learning of the future, a learning that will reflect and embrace all our lives.

SYLLABUS FOR SOCIOLOGY OF AGING

The following syllabus integrates gender materials into a basic sociology of aging class. Some readings are multicultural, and some cover class issues. Although the focus is sociological, some of the sources would also be appropriate for political science, psychology, anthropology, or English courses.

Course Description and Goals

This course introduces you to the key concepts, main theoretical perspectives, and important substantive issues of the sociology of aging. Among the central issues explored are gender differences in aging and the experiences of elder women; course credit is available for both sociology and women's studies. The course helps you explore your own feelings about aging and examines public policy as it has been applied to aging.

Journal Keeping

You need a notebook or folder in which to keep a journal. The journal's purpose is to give you a chance to think sociologically on a regular basis and to critically explore the course readings and the similarities and differences in the perspectives of the authors. It will also help you explore your own feelings and changing perspectives on aging. You will do 10 journal entries over the semester, spread out over four due dates. You may choose the topics for which you make entries. Each entry should be at least two pages long and cover two to three of the assigned articles. On days when we have a film, field trip, or speaker, you may substitute discussion of that event for one article.

Please keep all journal entries together in the folder or notebook. I may want to refer back to earlier entries. Women's studies students should focus especially on the readings about women and gender differences.

Your journal grade is one third of your final grade.

Exams

There are two essay exams, with a choice of essay questions. Each exam is worth one third of your grade, for a total of two-thirds of your final grade. The second exam is *not* cumulative; it covers only the material in the second half of the course.

Discussion and Attendance

Thoughtful and regular class participation can improve your grade. More than three unexcused absences from class will lower your grade.

Readings

The following books may be purchased at the university bookstore:

Barrow, Georgia M. (1992). *Aging, the individual, and society.* St. Paul, MN: West.
    This is a basic introductory (gender-integrated) textbook on aging.
Hess, Beth, & Markson, Elizabeth (Eds.). (1991). *Growing old in America.* 4th ed. New Brunswick, NJ: Transaction.
    This is a wide-ranging collection of sociological articles on aging.
Lyell, Ruth Granetz (Ed.). (1980). *Middle age, old age: Short stories, poems, plays, and essays on aging.* New York: Harcourt Brace Jovanovich.
    This book integrates sociological views of aging with those of the writers; for each story or poem there are "sociological notes." This material will help you explore some of your own feelings about aging and the problems that many long-lived people must face.

Myerhoff, Barbara. (1978). *Number our days.* New York: Dutton.
This book is an insightful and sensitive case study of the elderly of the Aliyah Senior Citizens' Center in southern California.

We will also read parts of the following books:

Alexander, Jo, et al. (Eds.). (1986). *Women and aging: An anthology by women.* Corvallis, OR: Calyx Books.
Arber, Sara, & Ginn, Jay. (1991). *Gender and later life.* Newbury Park, CA: Sage.
Butler, Robert. (1975). *Why survive?* New York: Harper & Row.
Copper, Baba. (1988). *Over the hill.* Freedom, CA: Crossing Press.
Doress, Paula Brown, et al. (1987). *Ourselves, growing older.* New York: Simon & Schuster.
Enright, Robert B., Jr. (Ed.). (1994). *Perspectives in social gerontology.* Boston: Allyn & Bacon.
Fishman, Walda Katz, & Benello, C. George (Eds.). (1986). *Readings in humanist sociology.* Dix Hills, NY: General Hall.
Formanek, Ruth. (1990). *Meanings of menopause.* Hillsdale, NJ: Analytic Press.
Grau, Lois (Ed.). (1989). *Women in the later years.* New York: Haworth Press.
Hooyman, Nancy R., & Kiyak, H. Asuman. (1988). *Social gerontology.* 3rd ed. Boston: Allyn & Bacon.
Julty, Sam. (1979). *Men's bodies, men's selves.* New York: Dell Press.
Kübler-Ross, Elisabeth. (1975). *Death.* Englewood Cliffs, NJ: Prentice-Hall.
Markides, Kyriakos S., & Mindel, Charles H. (1987). *Aging and ethnicity.* Newbury Park, CA: Sage.
Minkler, Meredith, & Estes, Carroll L. (1991). *Critical perspectives on aging.* Amityville, NY: Baywood.
Pifer, Alan, & Bronte, Lydia. (1986). *Our aging society.* New York: W. W. Norton.
Rossi, Alice S. (1985). *Gender and the life course.* New York: Aldine.
Sang, Barbara, et al. (Eds.). (1991). *Lesbians at midlife.* San Francisco: Spinsters Book Co.
Saul, Shura (Ed.). (1983). *Aging: An album of people growing old.* 2nd ed. New York: John Wiley & Sons.
Shield, Renee. (1988). *Uneasy endings.* Ithaca, NY: Cornell University Press.
Williamson, John B., Evans, Linda, & Powell, Lawrence A. (1982). *The politics of aging.* Springfield, IL: Thomas.
Zarit, Steven, H. (1977). *Readings in aging and death.* New York: Harper & Row.

CALENDAR AND ASSIGNMENTS

Week 1   Introduction (no journal entries) and overview
                   Film: *Lifequest*
                   Barrow: Chapter 1, Aging in America; Chapter 13, The
                       Minority Elderly

Hess & Markson: Hess, B., "Growing Old in America
in the 1990s," pp. 5–22

Week 2   STEREOTYPES

Barrow: Chapter 2, Stereotypes and Images
Hess & Markson: Cole, T., "The Specter of Old Age,"
pp. 23–37; Turner, B., & Turner, C., "Through a
Glass Darkly: Gender Stereotypes for Men and
Women Varying in Age and Race," pp. 137–150
Arber & Ginn: Chapter 3, Ageism and Cultural Stereo-
types of Older Women, pp. 36–49

LIFE CYCLES

Barrow: Chapter 3, The Life Cycle
Fishman & Benello: Rader, V., "Social Construction of
Life Cycles Crises," pp. 47–69
Lyell: West, J., "Sixteen," pp. 131–136
Copper: "On Becoming Old Women," pp. 73–75

Week 3   HISTORICAL AND CROSS-CULTURAL
PERSPECTIVES

Pifer & Bronte: Rossi, A., "Sex and Gender," pp.
111–139
Zarit: Kessler, J. Braun, "Aging in Different Ways," pp.
147–151
Barrow: Chapter 15, Aging in Other Cultures

THEORY

Barrow: Chapter 4, Theoretical Frameworks
Williamson, Evans, & Powell: Chapter 7, Power in Fam-
ilies
Markides & Mindel: Chapter 2, Theoretical Perspec-
tives and Methodological Issues
Journals Due

RELATIONSHIPS

Week 4   Barrow: Chapter 5, Social Bonds: Family and Friends
                Markides & Mindel: Chapter 5, Family Structure and
                    Family Relations
                Hess & Markson: Wolf, R., & McCarthy, E., "Elder
                    Abuse," pp. 481–501
                Silent Pioneers (film)
                Saul: Almvig, C., "Coming Out—At Last," pp. 132–134
                Hooyman & Kiyak: "Gay and Lesbian Partners in Old
                    Age," pp. 228–230

Week 5   Hess & Markson: Ikels, C., "Delayed Reciprocity and
                    the Support Networks of the Childless Elderly," pp.
                    441–456; Lopata, H. Znaniecka, "Which Child?" pp.
                    39–49
                Lyell: Anderson, R., "I Never Sang for My Father," pp.
                    55–110

ELDER CARE

Barrow: Chapter 6, The Old-Old and Caregiving
Hess & Markson: Wagner, D., "Eldercare: A Workplace
    Issue," pp. 377–387; Rosenthal, C., et al., "Is Parent
    Care Normative?" pp. 427–440
Sang et al.: Warshow, J., "Eldercare Is a Feminist Is-
    sue," pp. 65–72

Week 6   Midterm Exam

WORK AND RETIREMENT

Barrow: Chapter 7, Work and Leisure: The Right to
    Choose
Markides & Mindel: Chapter 8, Work, Income, and
    Retirement
Hess & Markson: Szinovacz, M., "Women and Retire-
    ment," pp. 293–303; Vinick, B., & Ekerdt, D., "The
    Transition to Retirement," pp. 305–317

Week 7   OLD AGE DEPENDENCY, SECURITY, AND
              POVERTY

              Hess & Markson: Evans, L., & Williamson, J., "Old
                 Age Dependency in Historical Perspective," pp. 525–
                 530; Morgan, L., "Economic Security of Older
                 Women," pp. 275–292
              Minkler & Estes: Dressel, P., "Gender, Race, and Class:
                 Beyond the Feminization of Poverty in Later Life,"
                 pp. 245–252
              Barrow: Chapter 8, Finances

              MORE ON ECONOMICS AND INDEPENDENCE

              Driving Miss Daisy (film—will be shown on university
                 cable in the evening)
              Hess & Markson: Eisenhandler, S., "The Asphalt Iden-
                 tikit," pp. 107–120
              Journals Due

              PLACES TO LIVE

Week 8   Barrow: Chapter 9, Living Environments
              Lyell: Winslow, T., "Grandma," pp. 35–49; Ferber, E.,
                 "Old Man Minick," pp. 20–34

              A CASE STUDY: THE ELDERS AT THE ALIYAH CENTER

              Myerhoff: Chapters 1, 5, 6, 7

Week 9   Tour of Pine Acres Nursing Home

              Read the following in preparation for the tour:
              Minkler & Estes: Harrington, C., "The Nursing Home
                 Industry," pp. 153–164
              Shield: "Separation and Adaptation," pp. 124–140
              Alexander et al.: Rust, L., "Another Part of the Coun-
                 try," pp. 137–147

MENTAL HEALTH

Barrow: Chapter 10, Mental Health
Lyell: Winslow, T. Samter, "The Odd Old Lady," pp.
 298–307
Saul: Saul, S., "An Open Letter to a Young Doctor," pp.
 130–132
Butler: Chapter 14, Growing Old Absurd

Week 10   ALZHEIMER'S DISEASE

There Were Times, Dear (film)
Hess & Markson: Gubrium, J., "The Social Preservation of Mind: The Alzheimer's Disease Experience,"
 pp. 151–168
Doress et al.: Sarton, M., "Mourning to Do," p. 389

PHYSICAL HEALTH AND CHANGE

Barrow: Chapter 11, Physical Health and Sexuality
Hess & Markson: Ansello, E., "The Intersecting of
 Aging and Disabilities," pp. 207–218
Formanek: Bowles, C., "The Menopausal Experience,"
 pp. 157–171
Julty: "Changes in Body Processes of Older Men and
 Women," p. 269

Week 11   EXPERIENCING PHYSICAL ILLNESS

Zarit: Dahlberg, C., "Stroke," pp. 229–233
Sang et al.: Lorde, A., "Two Excerpts From 'A Burst of
 Light: Living With Cancer,'" pp. 265–268
Kübler Ross: Mauksch, H., "The Organizational Con-
 text of Dying," pp. 7–24
Lyell: Beernink, K. D., "Gino Spinelli: Acute Lympho-
 cytic Leukemia," pp. 295–296
Journals Due

DEATH

Visit to Madison Memorial Funeral Home

Read the following before the visit:
Barrow: Chapter 14, Death and Dying
Markides & Mindel: Chapter 7, Death and Dying

Week 12   Doress et al.: Chapter 29, Dying and Death
                   Hess & Markson: Rosenfeld, J., "To Heir Is Human,
                       Updated," pp. 531–538; Baker, P., "Socialization
                       After Death," pp. 539–551
                   Zarit: Caine, L., "Crazy Lady," pp. 270–271

DISPELLING AGEISM: SOCIAL POLICIES

Enright: Butler, R., "Dispelling Ageism: The Cross-
    Cutting Intervention," pp. 3–10
Grav: Olsen Faulkner, A., & Micchelli, M., "The Aging,
    the Aged, and the Very Old: Women the Policy Mak-
    ers Forgot," pp. 12–19
Markides & Mindel: "Ethnicity and Utilization of Ser-
    vices," pp. 224–227
Hess & Markson: Quadagno, J., "Generational Equity
    and the Politics of the Welfare State," pp. 341–351

Week 13   ELDER POWER

                   Speaker from the Older Women's League (OWL)
                   Barrow: Chapter 16, Senior Power
                   Hess & Markson: Meyer, M. Harrington, "Organizing
                       the Frail Elderly," pp. 363–376

VISIONS

Butler: Chapter 13, Loosening Up Life
Rossi: Riley, M. White, "Women, Men, and the Length-
    ening Life Course," pp. 333–347
Hess & Markson: Reinharz, S., "Creating Utopia for
    the Elderly," pp. 589–601
Journals due
Final exam

REFERENCES

Baker, Karla. (1980). Let me grow lovely. In Ruth Granetz Lyell (Ed.), *Middle age, old age.* New York: Harcourt Brace Jovanovich.

Barrow, Georgia. (1992). *Aging, the individual & society.* St. Paul, MN: West.

Butler, Robert. (1994). A generation at risk: When the baby boomers reach golden pond. In Paul Brezina, Charles Selengut, & Robert Weyer (Eds.), *Seeing society: Perspectives on social life.* Needham Heights, MA: Simon & Schuster.

Copper, Baba. (1988). *Over the hill: Reflections on ageism between women.* Freedom, CA: Crossing Press.

Doress, Paula, & Laskin Siegal, Diana. (1987). *Ourselves, growing older.* New York: Simon & Schuster.

Gutmann, D. L. (1987). *Reclaimed powers: Toward a new psychology of men and women in later life.* New York: Basic Books.

Hess, B. B. (1985). Aging policies and old women: The hidden agenda. In Alice Rossi (Ed.), *Gender and the life course.* New York: Aldine.

Kelly, J. (1977). The aging male homosexual: Myth & reality. *The Gerontologist, 17,* 328–332.

Macdonald, Barbara. (1989). Outside the sisterhood: Ageism in women's studies. *Women's Studies Quarterly, 17,* 6–11.

Morales, A. L., & Morales, R. (1986). *Getting home alive.* Ithaca, NY: Firebrand Books.

Podolsky, Doug, & Silberner, Joanne. (1993, January). How medicine mistreats the elderly. *U.S. News & World Report,* pp. 72–79.

Rich, Cynthia. (1990). Ageism: Why is revulsion over old people's bodies socially acceptable? *Broomstick,* March/April.

Riley, Matilda. (1985). Women, men, and the lengthening life course. In Alice S. Rossi (Ed.), *Gender and the life course.* New York: Aldine.

Schuster, M. R., & Van Dyne, S. R. (1985). Stages of curriculum transformation. In M. R. Schuster & S. R. Van Dyne (Eds.), *Transforming the liberal arts curriculum.* Totowa, NJ: Rowman & Allenheld.

41
Teaching the Sociology of Women and Work

Laura Kramer

I have found teaching the Sociology of Women and Work more rewarding and more challenging than just about any other course I have taught. It is rewarding because much of the feminist sociological scholarship of the last 2 decades has focused on work or the work-family interface. We have a wide choice of readings using gender as a central explanatory dimension. Further, many studies of work actually focus simultaneously on gender and either ethnicity or social class.

STUDENT ATTITUDES

Students bring a high level of interest to the course. As paid or unpaid workers, they have often observed patterns in their workplaces and tried to make sense of, or construct explanations for, those patterns. Students are impressed if you show them that you know what "really" goes on and intrigued—even if not persuaded—by new contextualizations and interpretations of their experiences. The key is to "hook" the students by dealing with what is familiar in ways that they find illuminating and then moving, with that excitement intact, into the macrosocial and the more theoretical areas of the subject.

Students are more likely to consider themselves expert in this course than in others (for example, a demography course). Their willingness to challenge what they read by "experts" can be useful for motivating interest in epistemological issues. Having assigned Joan Acker's feminist sociology of knowledge early in the semester, I return to it as discussions bring out a student's assumptions about how we "know." Students who have had other women's studies courses often help in such discussions.

My experiences are certainly strongly affected by local circumstances (e.g., my students are likely to have had a lot of paid work experiences). However, I suspect that most people teaching "college aged" students in the United States share what I consider to be the most frustrating aspect of my course: students' lack of historical knowledge. How can we assess theoretical approaches to the field if we are unfamiliar with the existence and shape of changes and constancies over time? How are we to assess the social policy implications of contemporary scholarship when we don't know about previous policies and their impacts?

Students also challenge us with their preference for sweeping generalizations about realities and categories of people (except for the ones they belong to, which take a more sophisticated approach). Student diversity (in race, ethnicity, class, and age) means that someone has usually read the assignment closely and critically because it is about a group she or he identifies with. With the authoritative support of an assigned reading that challenges popular oversimplifications, that student is more apt to participate in class.

CONTEMPORARY RESOURCES

I find films invaluable. They motivate curiosity about history: *Hearts and Hands, Union Maids, Wilmar Eight, The Life and Times of Rosie the Riveter.* Documentaries about related social movements (e.g., *I Am Somebody,* about a southern hospital workers' union struggle) communicate a sense of intensity that is often lacking in disembodied readings. Feature films are wonderful; not only are they entertaining, but their simplified view of reality can be subjected to student critique. Examples include *Norma Rae, Nothing But a Man,* and *A Woman Under the Influence.*

Contemporary news stories provide an essential pedagogical tool; students are familiar with them, or can become so when you alert the class to an issue. When news accounts describe the principals by race, gender, and class characteristics simultaneously, discussions can focus on the interplay among these dimensions (often missing in historical accounts). For example, during the American Airlines flight attendants' strike in November 1993, students could address issues of service workers—mainly white women—

whose economic situation was working class even though they were sur-
rounded by upper-middle-class accoutrements. Students can be assigned to
write a paper in which they critique news accounts of a current issue.

Finally, government documents permit students to bring the statistical
descriptions in assigned readings up to date and to focus on groups and
occupations of particular local interest. If we hook them with qualitatively
rich and stirring accounts of past experiences and struggles, our students
may appreciate these as one avenue for testing popular and scholarly explanations of the intertwined stratification related to sex, race, and class.

REQUIRED TEXTS AND ASSIGNMENTS

Amott, Teresa L., & Julie A. Matthaei. (1991). *Race, gender, & work.* Boston: South
     End Press.
Statham, Anne, Eleanor M. Miller, & Hans O. Mauksch (Eds.). (1988). *The worth of
     women's work.* Albany, NY: State University of New York Press. (SM&M)
Stromberg, Ann Helton, & Shirley Harkess (Eds.). (1988). *Women working.* Mountain
     View, CA: Mayfield. (S&H)

COURSE OUTLINE

Week 1   INTRODUCTION

                      S&H: 5–9
                      Acker, "Women and Work in the Social Sciences"
                      (S&H: 10–24)
                      Film: *Hearts and Hands*

Week 2   HISTORICAL AND CONTEMPORARY DESCRIP-
                      TION: THE UNITED STATES

                      Anderson, "A History of Women's Work . . ." (S&H:
                      25–41)
                      Spitze, "The Data on Women's Labor Force Participa-
                      tion" (S&H: 42–60)
                      Smith and Tienda, "The Doubly Disadvantaged:
                      Women of Color . . ." (S&H: 61–80)

Weeks 3, 4   MAJOR THEORETICAL APPROACHES

                      Stevenson, "Some Economic Approaches to the Persis-
                      tence of Wage Differences . . ." (S&H: 87–100)

Coverman, "Sociological Explanations . . ." (S&H: 101–115)
Sokoloff, "Contributions of Marxism and Feminism . . ." (S&H: 116–131)
Film: *Union Maids*

Weeks 5, 6   SOCIAL PROCESSES AND INSTITUTIONS

Ireson & Gill, "Girls' Socialization . . ." (S&H: 132–148)
Wilkie, "Marriage, Family Life, and Women's Employment" (S&H: 149–166)
Taylor, "Women in Organizations" (S&H: 166–182)
Christensen, "Sex Discrimination and the Law" (S&H: 329–347)
Film: *The Life and Times of Rosie the Riveter*

Weeks 7–9   HISTORICAL BACKGROUND: WORK AND WORKER ACTIVISM AMONG MAJOR U.S. ETHNIC GROUPS

Amott & Matthaei, Chapters 3–8
Film: *Salt of the Earth*

Weeks 10–13   VARIETIES OF OCCUPATIONS

MALE-DOMINATED ELITE WORK

Reskin & Phipps, "Women in Male-dominated Professional and Managerial Occupations" (S&H: 190–205)
Statham, "Women Working for Women" (SM&M: 225–243)

FEMALE-DOMINATED PROFESSIONS

Stromberg, "Women in Female-dominated . . ." (S&H: 206–224)
Corley & Mauksch, "Registered Nurses, Gender, and Commitment" (SM&M: 135–149)
Rothman & Detlefs, "Women Talking to Women" (SM&M: 151–165)
Spencer, "Public Schoolteaching" (SM&M: 167–186)
Collins, "Women at the Top . . ." (SM&M: 187–201)

SALES AND SERVICE WORK

Gutek, "Women in Clerical Work" (S&H: 225–240)
Film: *The Wilmar Eight*
Berheide, "Women in Sales and Service . . ." (S&H:
241–257)
Connelly & Rhoton, "Women in Direct Sales"
(SM&M: 245–264)
Glenn, "A Belated Industry Revised: Domestic Service
Among Japanese-American Women" (SM&M: 57–75)
Romero, "Day Work in the Suburbs" (SM&M: 77–91)
Hood, "The Caretakers" (SM&M: 93–107)
Film: *I Am Somebody*
Martin, "Think Like a Man . . . Occupational Dilem-
mas of Policewomen" (SM&M: 205–223)

INDUSTRIAL WORK AND SKILLED TRADES

O'Farrell, "Women in Blue-collar . . ." (S&H: 258–272)
Fernandez Kelly & Garcia, "Invisible . . . Hispanic
Women in the . . . Electronics Industry" (SM&M:
265–290)

INVISIBLE WORK/INVISIBLE EXPERIENCES

Berk, "Women's Unpaid Labor" (S&H: 287–302)
Schneider, "Invisible and Independent: Lesbians' Experiences . . ." (S&H: 273–286)
Miller, "Some Peoples Calls It Crime" (SM&M:
109–132)

Week 14   SOCIAL POLICY AND THE FUTURE

Steinberg & Cook, "Policies Affecting Women's Employment in Industrial Countries" (S&H: 307–328)
Harkess, "Directions for the Future" (S&H: 348–360)
Needleman & Nelson, "Policy Implications" (SM&M:
293–307)

42

Transforming the Legal and Social Environment of Business Courses

Elaine D. Ingulli

STUDENTS

Richard Stockton College describes itself as a liberal arts college whose primary mission is undergraduate education. As is typical of state colleges, it is populated by many first-generation college students from the area (southern New Jersey). The student body is almost evenly divided by gender.

There is no college-wide core curriculum, although all students are required to take a distribution of courses from the interdisciplinary general studies program, as well as traditional courses "at some distance" from their major courses of study. The other 50% of their course work is in ("program") or near ("cognate") their major programs of study.

At Stockton, as at most institutions, undergraduate business majors are required to take at least one law course that introduces them to the major legal concepts and processes that underpin the relationships of business, government, and individuals. The Legal and Social Environment of Business is the required business law class for most business majors at Stockton (i.e., finance, marketing, and management majors). It also attracts a sprinkling of criminal justice and political science majors and others who view themselves as prelaw. Although designated a junior-level course, the class almost always includes students from every class level, including junior-year transfer students from community colleges. During the past 5 years, enrollment has varied from 15 to 35 students in each section.

In my syllabus, I describe my course objectives as introducing legal concepts and language; exploring the legal, ethical, and policy implications of the government regulation of business; and developing critical thinking, reading, writing, and oral communication skills. My unspoken goals include sensitization to issues of race, class, and gender subordination and conflict.

TEXTS

When I first started teaching this course in 1985, I used various standard "legal environment" textbooks, most of which include some 30-odd chapters, each covering a topic that would be an entire course in law school. I selected a chapter or two a week and taught such topics as an introduction to legal procedure (litigation and alternatives to litigation), kinds of law (torts, contracts, property law, criminal law), constitutional law (usually the Interstate Commerce Clause of the U.S. Constitution), employment law (including union-management relations, equal opportunity laws, unemployment compensation), and antitrust law and securities regulation. This survey approach to law was never satisfactory to me, and I gradually began to teach from larger and larger packets of handouts.

Since 1990, I have been teaching from a book I coedited with Terry Halbert, *Law and Ethics in the Business Environment* (St. Paul, MN: West, 1990). Our intention in designing the book was to provide a structure for a course that focuses on a few selected topics and explores each topic in greater depth than do standard texts. Thus, I have abandoned the survey approach and adopted in its place one that acknowledges that we attempt to generalize about the law and its relationship to business through the study of sample topics. Classes are highly participatory, with discussions most often revolving around close textual reading and an exploration of the political, policy, and social implications of various laws that impact on business.

Assigned readings include the case law and statutory readings that dominate most business law texts as well as interdisciplinary articles, including explicitly feminist works by leading feminist scholars. When studying economic equity in the workplace, for example, the class reads in the textbook excerpts from the civil rights laws; the leading Supreme Court decisions on affirmative action and minority set-asides; a defense of affirmative action by Deborah Rhode, a feminist legal scholar; a piece on status hierarchies and occupational segregation by feminist social scientists Barbara Reskin and Patricia Roos; and an excerpt from the controversial "Mommy-Track" proposal by Felice Scwartz. The text is supplemented by handouts that include copies of the Family Leave Act. When we discuss the *Santa Clara County* affirmative action case, I usually read aloud to the class from a chapter of Susan Faludi's *Backlash* (New York: Crown, 1991) that describes the personal background of the first woman to be hired as a road dispatcher in Santa Clara and the aftermath of her Supreme Court victory. One of my goals is to focus on topics that are marginalized or covered only superficially in most courses and texts. For example, the text and the class treat sexual harassment as a chapter-length topic. (Typically, textbooks cover sexual harassment in a few pages in a chapter on employment law.)

My own work in curriculum transformation began about the same time I began work on *Law and Ethics* and has continued since. I find myself constantly updating and revising the course to incorporate additional material on race, gender, and class. This is done by using supplementary readings that update the law (e.g., handing out the Americans With Disabilities Act and the Family Leave Act) and provide fresh perspectives on the topics. For example, I require students to read chapters from a book edited by Toni Morrison, *Race-ing Justice/En-gendering Power* (New York: Pantheon Books, 1992), for insight into the gender and race implications of the sexual harassment charges brought by Anita Hill. Supplementary materials also allow me to add coverage of discrimination on the basis of sexual orientation. In the fall of 1993, for example, the class debated the wisdom and impact of laws similar to Colorado's Amendment 2, which would have outlawed local ordinances prohibiting discrimination based on sexual orientation. The textbook includes only one case on HIV testing at the end of the chapter titled "Privacy in the Workplace." Passage of the Americans with Disabilities Act and the continuing controversy over HIV testing of health workers has led me to expand my coverage of this topic, using current newspaper articles and court cases.

PERSONAL EXPERIENCE AND "MODEL OPINIONS"

A major pedagogical change wrought by my exposure to women's studies and the literature on curriculum transformation is a sustained effort to bring my students' personal experiences into the classroom. The use of journals gives the students a chance to reflect on readings, react to class discussions, and integrate their own experiences with the legal materials we are studying. I collect, read, and comment in the journals until I am satisfied that each student knows what a satisfactory journal is. After that, I read and comment as often as students wish to interact with me in that way. I encourage them to clip and comment on current news articles and to raise questions that can be discussed in class.

I have experienced little resistance to the topics I teach or to my classroom approach to such topics. Most classes are lively and controversial, and student reaction is generally positive. I am avowedly feminist and antiracist in the classroom and do nothing to hide my opinions on any subject. I do, however, take great pains to assure my students that they are free to adopt their own political opinions and that they will not be penalized for disagreeing with me. Since much of the course revolves around controversial topics, there are always some skeptics. One technique I use to demonstrate my sincerity is to discuss a typical writing assignment in which students are given a choice of hypothetical scenarios and asked to write a judicial opinion deciding the case. I put "model opinions" from previous classes (based on different scenarios) on reserve in the library. I am careful to provide "A" models that include an opinion favoring the plaintiff and an opinion favoring the defendant for each topic. In that way, I am able to point to the models when I explain that grades depend on the quality of one's argument (reasoning, support for it, understanding of the law), not which side one takes in a particular case or argument. Similarly, by emphasizing that I find dissenting judicial opinions more compelling than majority opinions in some cases, I try to communicate respect for diverse views. Although student evaluations of the class are not uniformly positive, the most common complaint is that students lack interest in "the law," not those aspects of the law that I have chosen to teach.

I have met considerable resistance to the journal requirement. Students find it burdensome, and many do not invest much time in their journals (despite the potentially adverse effect on their grades). I continue to insist on journal use because class preparation and participation are far superior from students who keep serious journals.

The syllabus that follows is a variation of the one I hand out to students. After each section, there is an annotation entitled "Gender, Race, Class Integration." These paragraphs do not appear in the syllabus I distribute to the class but were written as guidance to other faculty members who are interested in the transformation of business law courses.

SYLLABUS FOR LEGAL AND SOCIAL ENVIRONMENT OF BUSINESS

Required Reading

Text. *Law and Ethics in the Business Environment,* T. Halbert & E. D. Ingulli, Eds. St. Paul, MN: West, 1990.

Supplementary Readings. Selected additional materials are available in the bookstore, including a glossary, the U.S. Constitution, new statutes, and recent court decisions.

Background Readings. I have placed a dozen standard legal environment textbooks on reserve in the library. Throughout the semester, I will suggest chapters in standard texts that might be useful to read to supplement class discussions and readings from our text. These texts also provide useful background for papers.

Ground Rules

Preparation for Class. Unless otherwise indicated, there will be *a reading assignment for every class.* Reading should be done *prior* to class as preparation for class discussions. The best preparation for both class and the written assignments is to take notes on the reading *prior to class.* Your notes might include case briefs, summaries of the reading, questions, insights, problems, reactions.

Journal Keeping. My purpose in requiring you to keep a journal is to encourage you to become more active and critical readers and to reflect on both the readings and the class discussions. Journals also give me an opportunity to give individualized feedback on the subjects we are studying, to correct misinformation, and to learn from you.

TENTATIVE COURSE OUTLINE

Week 1	I. GETTING STARTED
	Topic: Introduction to the course, the law, the legal system, and legal reasoning: Sources of American law; litigation process; appellate courts
	Required reading: Chapters on the American legal system, court system, legal reasoning (library reserve)
	Mandatory attendance (one class): Intro to library resources and legal research taught by Stockton librarian
Week 2	II. LAW AND ETHICS
	Topic: Law and ethics: The duty to rescue
	Reading: Text, chap. 1; *Tanja H. v. Regents of the University of California,* 228 Cal. App. 3d 434 (1991)

Gender, Race, Class Integration. Chapter 1 of the text begins to explore the relationship between law and ethics by means of the Anglo-American legal doctrine that there is no legal duty to rescue another. Although somewhat marginal to the legal environment of business, the topic introduces a major theme of the course: the idea that every law has policy, social, economic, and ethical implications.

Cases in the text do not explicitly raise issues of gender, race, or class. However, one case involved a suit against a supermarket brought by a woman who had been mugged in the parking lot. Discussion of the obligation to provide a reasonably safe place for shoppers necessarily includes consideration of gender and class aspects of safety and responsibility. I incorporate a supplemental case in which a woman who was the victim of gang rape in a college dorm brought an unsuccessful suit against the college, charging that it breached a duty of care by not fully enforcing its own rules against alcohol use by minors. The case provides an opportunity to discuss date rape.

Weeks 3, 4   III. EQUAL PROTECTION

Topic: The right to equal treatment: Discrimination, sexual harassment, new civil rights laws
Reading: Civil Rights Act of 1964 (Title VII); Text, chap. 8; *Stockton Student Handbook,* college policy on sexual harassment; Americans with Disabilities Act
Background reading: Agency-principal law; administrative agency law; equal employment opportunity; discrimination

Gender, Race, Class Integration. I begin teaching this topic by first describing my own experiences with sexual harassment and then asking students to describe theirs. This provides a basis for exploring the legal issues raised in the chapter of the text, which focuses entirely on sexual harassment. Issues of race are incorporated by use of racial harassment analogies. The last case in the chapter involves a consensual sexual relationship between a female graduate student and a female undergraduate. The case is a good vehicle for discussing issues of sexual orientation. We also look specifically at our college rules on sexual harassment—clearly marginal to the issue of the legal environment of business but central to students' lives—and at sexual harassment policies from students' own workplaces.

Although near the end of the text, this chapter is taught early in the semester so that I give it great weight in students' minds and I am certain to get to it. It also becomes a reference point for discussions throughout the semester. Since the chapter involves the civil rights laws, EEOC regulations, and case law interpreting both, it also serves as a concrete example of central themes of the course: how government regulates business and the relationship between the courts, the legislature, and government administrative agencies.

After the chapter, I teach the Americans with Disabilities Act—a law passed since the book went to press—as another example of new legal protection for the rights of those who have been subordinated in American society.

Weeks 5, 6   IV. DUTY OF LOYALTY

Topic: The duty of loyalty: Termination at will and whistle-blowing
Reading: Text, chap. 2; N.J. Conscientious Employee
   Act; National Labor Relations Act
Background reading: Torts, contracts, labor law

Gender, Race, Class Integration.   This topic is about a long-standing rule of American law that unless it specifically provides otherwise, an employment contract is "at will," permitting employees to quit when they please and employers to fire them when they please. That rule has been eroded by civil rights statutes that prevent discharge based on race, sex, and so forth; the National Labor Relations Act, which encourages and protects union organizers and members; and a doctrine called "wrongful discharge," which protects whistle-blowers and other workers who are fired in violation of a clear mandate of public policy. Discussions of labor history and the power imbalance between large companies and employees provide an opportunity to raise issues of class, as do readings on communications within corporations and comparison between Japanese and American management techniques.

Weeks 7, 8   V. RIGHT OF PRIVACY

Topic: The right to privacy: Drug testing in the workplace; HIV testing
Reading: Text, chap. 3; handouts on HIV testing
Background reading: Constitutional law (Fourth
   Amendment—search and seizure); tort law (right to
   privacy); civil rights law (Rehabilitation Act of 1973)
Required journal entry: Assume your assigned role for
the debate/legislative hearing we will hold on a proposed bill to require HIV testing of all health workers.

Write the best possible arguments to defend the position that a person in that role is likely to take. Critique those arguments from your perspective as a business law student. Explain any legal or ethical concerns that either support the position taken or might prevail over that position.

Gender, Race, Class Integration. This chapter explores the legal issues connected to workplace drug testing and includes readings on the function of privacy in our lives. After discussing the chapter, the class participates in a mock legislative hearing. Students are assigned to role-play either legislators or witnesses (e.g., ACLU lawyer, AMA member, dentist, parent of young children). The "hearing" (which may take one or two class sessions) engenders lively discussion of issues of privacy, public health, safety, and the political, economic, and social consequences of certain policies for persons of various backgrounds. Inevitably, race, class, sexual orientation, and disability issues are raised and discussed.

Weeks 8, 9   VI. PRODUCT AND ENVIRONMENTAL SAFETY

Topic: Product and environmental safety
Reading: Text, chap. 7
Background reading: Torts (negligence, nuisance, trespass); environmental law; product liability

Gender, Race, Class Integration. The chapter provides an overview of a variety of environmental law issues, including use and abuse of pesticides, radiation dangers, Superfund cleanup, and global warming. Related issues that can be explored with supplementary readings include: (1) the use of Native American lands to store toxic waste and Native American views on the environment; (2) first world–third world conflicts over development and environment; (3) controversies over environmental causes of illnesses such as breast cancer.

Weeks 10, 11   VII. WORKPLACE SAFETY

Topic: Safety in the workplace
Reading: Text, chap. 6; *Johnson Controls,* 886 F.2d 871
    (7th Cir. 1988)
Background reading: Occupational safety and health
    (OSH Act and OSHA); labor relations (National Labor
    Relations Act and NLRB); corporate criminal law
    (white-collar crime)

Gender, Race, Class Integration. This segment of the course focuses on the laws requiring employers to provide a safe workplace—and the failures of government regulatory efforts to ensure such safety. Readings in the text include the case brought against the Kerr-McGee nuclear plant by the estate of Karen Silkwood and cases involving criminal charges brought against employers who recklessly exposed workers to mercury and other hazards.

I have used several techniques to further integrate issues of race, class, and gender. One is the showing of *Global Assembly Line,* a 1-hour film that integrates issues of workplace and environmental safety, unionizing, and gender and class exploitation. Another is to role-play a legislative hearing or debate on what steps companies can, should, or cannot take to protect workers from reproductive hazards in the workplace. Personal narratives on workplace safety and reproductive rights are also useful. Susan Faludi, *Backlash* (New York: Crown, 1991), has some interesting material on fetal protection policies that can be assigned or read aloud.

Weeks 11, 12   VIII. ECONOMIC EQUITY

> Topic: Economic equity: Affirmative action; comparable worth; occupational segregation; family-centered employment policies
> Reading: Text, chap. 9; Family Leave Act
> Background reading: Constitutional law (equal protection); equal employment opportunity; affirmative action; comparable worth; Pregnancy Discrimination Act

Gender, Race, Class Integration. This chapter focuses entirely on issues of race, class, and gender: minority and female set-aside programs for government contracts; affirmative action; comparable worth; occupational segregation; Pregnancy Discrimination Act; maternity leave laws.

Text materials are easily supplemented by statistical materials from current reports that demonstrate income, education, and job disparities based on gender, race, and ethnic background. I usually begin this chapter by handing out a packet of such statistics and asking students to try to explain them based on readings. This inevitably leads to a discussion of occupational segregation, intentional and unintentional discrimination, the role of unions, the differential valuing of various kinds of work, and subtle forms of discrimination.

Week 13   IX. TRADE SECRETS

                     Topic: Trade secrets; covenants not to compete
                     Reading: Text, chap. 4

Week 14   X. OWNING INFORMATION

                     Topic: Owning information: Insider trading; Freedom
                     of Information Act; Plant Closing Act
                     Reading: Text, chap. 3

BACKGROUND READING FOR INSTRUCTORS

Ingulli, Elaine. (1991). Transforming the curriculum: What does the pedagogy of in-
    clusion mean for business law? *American Business Law Journal, 28,* 605–647.
Ingulli, Elaine. (1992). Toward a more inclusive vision of legal studies in business: An
    annotated bibliography of resources. *The Journal of Legal Studies Education,
    10,* 219–244.
Lindgren, J. Ralph, & Nadine Taub. (1993). *The law of sex discrimination.* 2nd ed. St.
    Paul, MN: West.
Rhode, Deborah L. (1989). *Gender and justice.* Cambridge: Harvard University Press.
Thomas, Claire Sherman. (1991). *Sex discrimination in a nutshell.* 2nd ed. St. Paul,
    MN: West.

43

Curriculum Transformation for Basic English Composition and Introduction to Literature: A View from the Trenches

Crystal V. Bacon

The answer to simple curriculum transformation lies in change. We must begin somewhere, especially when we consider the great need that most core curricula and the students for whom they are designed have for the inclusion of other than a white, male, Eurocentric, middle-class, heterosexual perspective. For simplicity, let us call this perspective feminist. If we simply begin to revamp our courses from semester to semester, adding readings and assignments that come our way through a variety of networks and periodicals, the task will accomplish itself quietly and thoroughly. For teachers of English Composition at the community college level—generally a two-pronged course in basic composition followed by a semester of writing about literature—there are a few simple steps that can lead to this much needed transformation.

As a junior faculty member on the campus of a small, suburban community college, I find myself teaching two valuable staples for curriculum transformation: English Composition I and II. What follows is an overview of techniques from the trenches, suggestions that may enable others to effect a fairly painless transformation of core curriculum in liberal arts.

BASIC ENGLISH COMPOSITION

Anthologies

Let's start with College Composition I. The place to begin is with your reader. There are so many good ones available. Many of them offer integrated readings by women and men of color from other than U.S. cultural backgrounds and address issues of personal economics beyond the confines of the middle class. In the past, I was quite happy with *Readings for Writers* by Jo Ray McCuen and Anthony C. Winkler (New York: Harcourt, 7th ed., 1992). Each chapter includes something called "Issues for Critical Thinking," a collection of three essays posing a pro, con, and more or less neutral viewpoint on such topics as legalized abortion, nuclear weapons, surrogate motherhood, and women's liberation, to mention a few. I am often at odds with the selections, but they have never failed to provide for excellent in-class discussion, in-depth journal entries, and impassioned papers. I later discarded that text in favor of *Our Times/2* edited by Robert Atwan (New York: Bedford/ St. Martin's, 1991). This text offers chapters on adolescence, physical appearance, rock: music or menace, hate comedy, gay outing, TV, and sex stereotypes. One article that I found especially fresh was Barbara Ehrenreich's "The Wretched of the Hearth." Originally appearing in *New Republic,* this article is especially interesting to discuss along lines of rhetorical analysis and content. After Allan Bloom's display of his psychosexual qualms about Mick Jagger, Michael Jackson, and Prince in the pseudoscholarly yet drastically uninformed chapter on rock music from *The Closing of the American Mind,* Ehrenreich on Roseanne as a left-wing radical feminist was a good counterpoint from which to evaluate feminist theory at work in popular culture. Atwan covers a variety of perspectives with excellent articles taken from many periodicals both in and out of the mainstream. We no longer suffer a dearth of anthologies for feminist composition courses.

Library Research and Current Affairs

Presently, I have abandoned a text altogether in favor of a selection of topics that students must research in the library. They must locate at least three articles, each from a different perspective, on the given topic. A sampling of one semester's topics is Racism on College Campuses, Acquaintance Rape:

How Do We Define It? The Environment: Can Government Save It? Gender Equality: Where Do We Stand? and Animal Experimentation: Are There Alternatives? These topics provide a good forum for writing argument and analysis, the crux of the college composition course.

I also keep an informal collection of pertinent news articles that catch my eye in the daily paper and various magazines. I have a piece by Barbara Ehrenreich called "The Warrior Culture" from *Time;* some interesting statistics about the dollar value of housework from the Wages for Housework Campaign and an editorial regarding the "white, male-dominated, conservative bastion" of the Supreme Court, both from the *Philadelphia Inquirer;* a chart depicting the percentage of nonwhite elected representatives in relation to available seats in 10 states; and some valuable statistics and anecdotes about the experiences of young black men and women on a variety of college campuses from the *Wall Street Journal.* I am easily able to replace and update these pieces regularly. They make wonderful motivational devices with which to start class discussions, and they show my students that issues of race, class, and gender are universal and not just part of my highly specialized and, to their way of thinking, somewhat hysterically myopic worldview. It also helps them to read in a different light the newspapers and magazines that come into their homes.

Course Structure

In both of these basic courses, one of the most crucial areas for transformation is the structure of the course itself. This semester I abdicated more power in this area than ever before and found it to be satisfying to both me and my students. The students are responsible for working more or less independently in the library, researching the topics assigned and locating their sources. During class meetings, which alternate week to week with research sessions, the students work in small groups discussing the topics, their findings, and their writings in progress. My job is to circulate and eavesdrop, suggest cross-pollination, and work one-on-one with those students who really need my time. These changes decentralize the classroom and the learning situation, improving students' learning, writing, and often self-esteem.

In the midst of all this valuable eye-opening information, we also address style, purpose, thesis, and rhetorical technique. Each student is responsible for keeping a journal in which they write on the topic, compile their photocopied articles, summarize, identify the thesis and main points, and write on what they learned from their readings. After 16 weeks, students come away with a portfolio of some 15 pieces of prewriting and five polished essays of argumentation and analysis.

INTRODUCTION TO LITERATURE

If your school is like mine, you find a handful—maybe between 10 and 25%—of your Composition I students joining you in Composition II. This poses a number of interesting considerations. Those who go on to other faculty members take a considerable amount of information about gender, race, and culture. Even in a worst-case scenario—a class in which they read nothing but "classics"—they cannot help but recognize the absence of women or people of color from the syllabus. Whether they'll mention this is purely speculation, but their awareness is a place to begin.

Another scenario regards those who come from more "traditional" Composition I settings. My experience has been that those students often comment on the feminist perspective in my Composition II course. These comments generally stem from the syllabus, which is highly representative of women writers, and from outside readings, which are often either feminist literary criticism or criticism of feminist literature. Having had no exposure to feminist pedagogy, these students are often made uncomfortable by what they read. This is a highly desirable effect. It is also a place where the veteran students can come in handy. It is always invaluable when a student addresses a peer's ignorance, innocence, or discomfort, providing a much more evidently safe environment for learning. This is all highly unscientific, of course, but it happens to me every semester and with good results.

Anthologies

Text is not quite as easy a place to begin the quiet revolution in English Composition II. There are a plethora of anthologies, but they are so similar that occasionally price seems to be the deciding factor. What these anthologies offer are the scope and sheer number that an introductory text ought to present. What these books have in common is a slowly developing awareness of our desire for multicultural literature that meets our exacting standards. You can find Walker, Hong-Kingston, Garcia-Marquez, Oates, Bambara, and Erdrich in most standard texts. It is important to remember what *Introduction* to Literature means; this course is a point of departure. Students can read only so much if they're also going to write a fair number of high-quality critical essays and do a research paper. Also, like Composition I, Composition II is a course that can use stimulating outside readings and in-class discussion, all of which yields a greater awareness of the larger worldview associated with a liberal education.

Assignments, too, can go far in applying breadth to your students' thinking. Critical essays on short stories can probe relationships between the genders and among the races, ages, and classes while analyzing tone or character or even setting. Pairing more traditional readings with those by less traditional writers offers a perfect scenario for comparison and contrast. The readings suggest various truths to be ferreted out. For example, my students often start out feeling highly unsympathetic toward Louise Erdrich's character Fleur, a Native American woman whose adherence to the "old ways" results in a number of cataclysms, including her gang rape by some of the slimiest white men in the canon. I've even heard male students say that she "deserves" to be raped for "teasing" the men who rape and impregnate her. She's a witch, a demon; she's evil. When we talk about what they know about Native Americans in general and Chippewa in particular, however, they don't have much to offer. What they know is largely historicized myth gleaned from TV and movies. Given that each class dealing with fiction begins with a few informal comments by students on background or criticism on the authors (usually originating in the volumes of *Contemporary Literary Criticism*), they know enough about Erdrich to try to answer some important questions. How does she think Chippewa women were perceived by European settlers? What informs the narrator's view of Fleur's "keeping the old ways"? What role does Christianity play? What is Fleur's purpose for being in the story? What is she beyond her character? In answer to each of these questions, my final comment is usually something like, "That would make a great paper topic." The same is true of drama and poetry. The possibilities abound.

Course Structure

In Introduction to Literature classes, I no longer select the poems, stories, and plays to be read for analysis. We all read the teaching apparatus chapters on the elements of the various genres, but instead of my assigning 20 poems, eight stories, and three plays as I did as recently as last semester, I hold the students responsible for making their own individual selections. They must apply the elements of criticism to the works they read, and we spend four class periods discussing these readings. Contrary to the traditional structure of other classes, we sit in a circle (which takes an unnatural amount of prodding to accomplish), and students talk to their classmates about their elementary analyses of the readings. Through this approach, I am learning quite a bit about students' personalities and learning styles. They are often frustratingly reticent or certain of their inability to say anything enlightening or "right." The peer discussion, however, seems to give them the forum for exploring greater openness.

OVERCOMING RESISTANCE

The most common complaint that I hear from my colleagues both at home and at conferences and seminars is that they don't have much time to read and learn new works by new—or noncanonical—writers. This is at best a feeble excuse. Whoever said revolution would be easy? We all find time to read what interests—or agrees with—us. There is no better antidote to impending burnout than learning. When we put ourselves into the positions of students and remove our safe mantles of authority and scholarship, we inevitably improve the quality of learning for our students. They are more compelled, more encouraged, to make sense of what they read when there are no easy, ready-made answers. In the 5 years that I have been teaching at my institution, I have come to know Louise Erdrich, the Tao, volumes of Latin American writers, Rumi, Gilgamesh. Necessity has brought me to new names, unknown criticism, and foreign customs. I often admit to my students that "I'm not an expert on this . . . I haven't studied this . . . I went to the library and found . . ."—all of which seems to increase their willingness to learn what they never considered necessary to know.

Tennessee Williams created a wonderfully wise character in Blanche DuBois, whose criticism of Stanley Kowalski is pertinent here. "Thousands and thousands of years have gone by and there he is still swillin' and hulkin' in his cave, last vestige of the ice age, Stanley Kowalski." Now, although your colleagues might neither swill nor hulk, nor really date back to the ice age, you could probably find better things to do with your time than to pickax your way through their frozen consciousness to attempt to get their approval on your Erotic Poetry by Lesbians and Gays of Color course. We find ourselves confronted by a tidal wave of backlash. Nobody in the opposition knows what "PC" really means, but they're sure that they don't want it in their schools. Most persons on the street—and in the classroom—don't think about transformation and canon; they think about vacations and compact discs. What happens usually happens without anyone's permission. Some of us got good and mad, and we made some valuable changes.

What matters is that the powers that have appointed themselves the arbiters of truth are up in arms because transformation *really does* mean tearing down the university. It means reconstructing hundreds of years of fascinating but limited history and literature and pedagogy itself. It means taking power to construct an inclusive reality—one that does not systematically excise 90% of the human race. It's time to dig in. The change you make is only as good as the risk you take.

44

Revisiting Freshman Composition: Opening Up the Traditional Curriculum

Mary Cross

Without changing the content of a composition course, an instructor can, with two strategies, radically alter its effects on student understanding of race, class, and gender diversity: first, by introducing narrative into the course, and second, by teaching students to read and write *against* the text— in the current lingo, teaching them to deconstruct traditional perspectives. These strategies, used with any first-year-student reader, can open up the standard curriculum to new horizons.

Academic discourse, in its historically hidebound mode, offers a version of reality and authority that needs to be confronted. Such writing also tends to shape thinking, excluding the personal and subjective. It is "author-evacuated" prose, as Peter Elbow (1988) points out, in its "rubber-gloved" way smoothing over difference and the dialogic in favor of institutionalized language and style (p. 145). One of Elbow's most important points is that, even as we offer students the most eloquent literary models for reading, we refuse them the opportunity to write in this way (p. 137).

Narrative—long a taboo in composition courses, giving rise to the dread "What I Did on My Summer Vacation" essay—is a way of giving voice to the diversity that lives in our classrooms, opening up the curriculum to perspectives long denied it. Letting students tell their individual stories in the genre most familiar to them—indeed, often the *only* one familiar to them—allows difference into a course that is most often concerned with turning out a homogeneous product. Telling stories, students reveal not only the ways their individual experiences and perceptions differ but also the things they have in common. Moreover, narrative gives students a personal stake in writing. Perhaps for the first time, it suggests that writing can be a valid form of self-expression.

We can help students uncover the hidden perspectives in traditional texts by teaching them to read and write against the stratified systems and ideologies these texts contain. My method is not to teach students to be "normal" readers but to challenge that stance and show them how different readings—and readers—can emerge from the same text. I want students to question what they generally regard as the authority of the writer or expert. And, in the process, I want them to write against what they read by writing about the questions or difficulties they have with the text. Inevitably, this focus means that they have to pry loose and unpack—that is, deconstruct— the author's assumptions in some way. What they write then becomes theirs, carrying their own fresh stamp of race, class, and gender perspective.

One can use selections in any first-year-student reader to put these two strategies into play. The point is not essay content or information but the instructor's tactical approach, allowing students to tell their own stories and showing them that their own questions about or problems with a reading are valuable and necessary, revealing the race, class, and gender exclusions that, deliberately or unconsciously, the text may make.

PERSONAL NARRATIVES: FIRST STEPS FOR BEGINNING WRITERS

The first of the strategies I propose—that of using narrative in composition courses—has long been excluded from the first-year writing curriculum. Narrative's order is chronology, its voice often the first person, its style idiosyncratic. Narrative tends to blur the boundaries of the canonic genres, so neatly categorized and closed off in their safe little hierarchies. It doesn't resemble the classic essay in tone or content. It is subjective, not objective in the much-touted way of academic prose. Yet it's heartening to realize that there are some academic theorists (of the white, male, European persuasion) on whom I can draw in support of narrative in the composition curriculum. As James Kinneavy (1980) writes:

> A democracy which ignores expression has forgotten its own roots. The ignoring, by the disciplines of speech and English, of the very kind of discourse by

which an individual or group can express his personal or its societal aspirations, is certainly a symptom, if not an effect, of the impersonality of the university machines of the present day. (p. 396)

Mikhail Bakhtin (1981) makes the same point. Our "public" language, he writes, is stratified into a system, a "correct" or socially sealed off and artificially unified language that speaks a belief system, leaving an enormous gap between accepted forms of expression and the reality of languages and cultures. The solution, Bakhtin says, is to rescue individual style from the institutional and tap into the "concrete social context of discourse," determined not from without but from within (p. 300). This is the "dialogic," the "diversity of speech" that arises from opening up discourse to the "alien word" (p. 279).

Student storytelling puts the "alien word" back into the curriculum where it belongs, voicing fresh perspectives on old ideologies. Personal narratives, assigned as commentary on course readings, are beginning writers' first steps into the world of issues and arguments that college opens to them. They reveal the ways the students are or are not included in the discussion and give them back their right to be heard. From these written narratives, and the classroom "dialogic" they inevitably inspire, can come more structured second and third written versions to argue a point of view, using the original story for support.

DECONSTRUCTION: LEARNING TO READ BETWEEN THE LINES

A second strategy for opening up the composition curriculum comes in the wake of deconstruction, that teasing out of *différence* that marked feminist readings long before Jacques Derrida gave it a name. It has always seemed to me that a composition teacher's major goal is to teach students to read between the lines and arm themselves, in a commodity culture, with a knowledge of how language can operate to cloud reality. Deconstruction, loosely applied, *is* a method of reading between the lines, looking for the ways that a text contradicts or undermines itself, whether by what it says or by what it doesn't say. My trial run with this strategy was conducted several semesters ago with a group of first-year honors students and the Bartholomae and Petrosky (1993) text *Ways of Reading,* which, as its title suggests, is a how-to guide on what to do with a text, with good readings and assignment ideas that give instructors plenty of leeway in shaping the course.

We began the class with two essays from Roland Barthes's *Mythologies,* "Wrestling" and "Striptease," a couple of surprising takes on two very gendered activities. A woman reading either one immediately sees through it; she can't help but read against it, deconstructing its assumptions and ideology. The women in the class did this readily, and the discussion, rereading, and papers that emerged from these essays began the process of turning students' own basic assumptions upside down. They were surprised at the ease with which a different reader (female) could locate the problematic moments in the text and surprised that they were being allowed to question the text in the first place.

But students are resistant to examining their own assumptions so closely, and they are stubborn about admitting other points of view. In their reading, they were asked to locate parts of the text that they either didn't understand or didn't agree with. In writing, they were asked to explore these problematic moments, questioning both their own and the writer's point of view, and to try to find ways that the argument didn't hold up. In other words, they were asked to stand outside the text, a stance they initially found uncomfortable. One way to pry them loose is to have them first write a narrative of their reading, noting honestly the hard places and the questions they had as they went along.

Thanks to the selections in the Bartholomae and Petrosky (1993) anthology, we were able to read a number of essays in thematic sequence. Essays by Mark Crispin Miller and Simon Frith helped uncover ways of reading against cultural "norms" projected by the media. As students began to read between the lines of advertisements and MTV, they eventually picked up on the ideologies embedded in these cultural materials and could enumerate the ways that they and other consumers are urged to "buy" into them. Another reading sequence focused on the concept of entitlement as both the affluent and the underprivileged reader might conceive of it. Students said that they'd never looked at their own sense of entitlement before; they were surprised at how much they took for granted and how they were able to locate contradictions and gaps in essays by Robert Coles and John Edgar Wideman that seemed to have escaped the authors themselves.

We did another sequence on education, using Paulo Freire's essay "The 'Banking' Concept of Education," among others, to begin questioning concepts of public education. Finally, we read and wrote about a group of essays by women writers, including Virginia Woolf, Alice Walker, and Adrienne Rich, investigating and questioning the feminist stance to discover its problematic moments. Beginning and ending with a female point of view on some of these cultural issues was especially revealing and successful for a course designed to unpack traditional assumptions.

Student writing in this class was extraordinarily fresh. Students were asked to tackle the essays from a personal point of view, using "I" and focusing on their own problems with the text. Personal narrative was an important part of the writing they did in response to the readings. Although they did not learn strategies of deconstruction as Derrida might have taught them, they did learn to locate the "warring forces of signification," which Barbara Johnson (1980) defined as at the heart of deconstruction (p. 5).

I was actually surprised at the alacrity with which students undertook to read and write against the text. I think part of that was the sense of discovery they felt in exploring a new intellectual territory (deconstructing a text is a lot like playing detective). Their ability to take arguments apart and reconstruct them grew, opening up their reading to new angles and shifting personal stances. Even if students felt uneasy about the newly relative way they were asked to view the world, they realized that they could no longer return to their old, unthinking assumptions. The black-and-white world that first-year students tend to clutch had gradually blurred to gray, then burst into a rainbow of new perspectives—not a bad result for one semester at the beginning of their college lives, and not a bad way to open up the traditional composition course to its multicultural 21st-century future.

COURSE OUTLINE FOR ENGLISH 101

Week 1	Introduction Ways of reading *Ways of Reading* Assignments: (1) Roland Barthes, "The World of Wrestling" and "Striptease." Write a narrative describing a cultural ritual from your own experience. (2) Mark Crispin Miller, "Getting Dirty" and "Cosby Knows Best." (3) Notes toward essay one: Interpret your narrative of a cultural ritual by reading against it. What does it "ritualize"? Is there a hidden agenda? How would Barthes write about it?
Week 2	Draft of essay one due Assignments: (1) Notes toward essay two; (2) Simon Frith, "Rock and Sexuality"
Week 3	Finished essay one due Assignments: (1) Drafting essay two; (2) Jane Tompkins, "Indians: Textualism, Morality, and the Problem of History"—take notes for essay three
Week 4	Draft of essay two due Assignments: (1) Bring notes toward essay three for discussion; (2) In class, write a narrative of your own childhood understanding of an "other"

Week 5	Finished essay two due Assignment: John Berger, "Ways of Seeing"
Week 6	Draft of essay three due Ways of seeing: Interrogating works of art Art museum trip
Week 7	Finished essay three due Assignments: (1) In-class writing; (2) Paulo Freire, "The 'Banking' Concept of Education"
Week 8	Draft of essay four due In-class assessment of writing
Week 9	Finished essay four due Assignment: Robert Coles, "Entitlement"
Week 10	Draft of essay five due Assignment: John Edgar Wideman, "Our Time"
Week 11	Draft of essay six due Assignment: Harriet Jacobs, "Incidents in the Life of a Slave Girl"
Week 12	Draft of essay seven due Assignments: (1) Adrienne Rich, "When We Dead Awaken: Writing as Re-Vision"; (2) Essay eight, reevaluating Coles's theory of entitlements
Week 13	Finished essay eight due Assignments: (1) Virginia Woolf, "A Room of One's Own," and Alice Walker, "In Search of Our Mothers' Gardens"; (2) Notes toward essay nine

BIBLIOGRAPHY

Bakhtin, Mikhail. (1981). Discourse in the novel. In *The dialogic imagination.* Austin: University of Texas Press.

Bartholomae, David, & Anthony Petrosky. (1993). *Ways of reading.* 3rd ed. Boston: Bedford Books of St. Martin's Press.

Elbow, Peter. (1988, Winter). Reflections on academic discourse: How it relates to freshmen and colleagues. *College English, 53,* 87–95.

Johnson, Barbara. (1980). *The critical difference: Essays in the contemporary rhetoric of reading.* Baltimore: Johns Hopkins University Press.

Kinneavy, James L. (1980). *A theory of discourse.* New York: W. W. Norton.

45

Integrating Race and Gender into the Second-Language Curriculum

José A. Carmona

We, second-language educators, tend to believe that because we are teaching certain aspects of culture in our classes, we are also integrating race and gender into our curricula; in fact, we are only barely addressing the issues. The mere use of culture in the classroom is not enough to make our students aware of the complicated issues that evolve around race and gender. These statements may seem general and powerful, but they are the conclusion of having to reexamine not only what I do in the classroom but also my own prejudices and biases in addressing these issues. Although at times we need to address these issues right up front, there are other subtle ways of making sure that we are giving our students a fair exposure to racial and gender differences without causing chaos or creating resistance from them in our classrooms. Therefore, this chapter addresses two things: the need to reexamine ourselves as well as our own curricula, and specific approaches I have used in the classroom in order to enhance both the English as a second language (ESL) and the Spanish for non-native speakers curricula.

During the latter part of May 1991, I decided to attend the New Jersey Project summer institute, where I was exposed to a series of debates that made me reexamine my own curriculum. It was then that I realized how little I had done in terms of my previous course revisions. I had incorporated gender into my ESL courses to a degree, but my Spanish courses were still lacking revision. I decided to use some of the same approaches I was using in ESL in my beginning and intermediate Spanish courses. I was not assuming that these two distinct fields follow the same theories and ways of teaching but that there are similarities within their pedagogy and that we, as educators, can and should take advantage of the strategies that can be transferred from one to the other. In fact, Eugene Eoyang (1988) declares that teachers of English and foreign languages "have more in common, both intellectually and pedagogically, than they recognize. Only ethnocentrism keeps them apart."

REEXAMINING THE SPANISH CURRICULUM

The first thing I looked at within my Spanish courses was the use of language in the exercises, both written and oral, conducted in class as well as in examinations. Sure enough, most names used were masculine. Moreover, the use of masculine personal pronouns, such as *el* and *ellos,* and the preference for male gender words, such as *profesor* and *abogado,* were predominant. Therefore, my quest was to balance my classes with the use of female gender words. Although this daily use of masculine words in the classroom was not done purposely, the problem comes from the prejudice embedded within our unconscious. Paula Rothenberg (1991) made reference to this during her introductory speech at the New Jersey Project summer institute: "We are always looking at the world with somebody's eyes . . . we have internalized racism, sexism, etc." She describes this phenomenon as "unintentional racism," which means that even teaching race and gender studies for a long time doesn't make one immune to one's "unconscious ideology."

In addition to revising language use in the classroom, I had to change the cultural aspects presented in the beginning and intermediate courses. In these Spanish courses, I usually give a research assignment about Latin American writers. Each student has to select an author from a list and go to the library to research the author's life. Because of their lack of linguistic ability in the target language, the students do the research in English. They then introduce their authors in short class presentations. I thought that it was a great idea; the students were learning about Vargas Llosa, Fuentes, Garcia Marquez, Cabrera Infante, Borges, and Sor Juana. It was a great list of well-known men and one woman, but where were the other women? Then I realized that I didn't know much about the "other" Latin American women writers; in fact, during my 4 years of college, I had read novels only by famous male writers. Indeed, one of my favorite courses, taught by an adjunct professor, was the only course that dealt with such equally famous women writers as Gertrudis Gomez de Avellaneda (Cuba), Delmira Agustini (Uruguay), Gabriela Mistral (Chile), and Alfonsina Storni (Argentina/Italy). The impressions of these women's works have remained with me forever, for I was guided through the lives of "silenced voices." I now read and incorporate into this assignment the literature of many women I hadn't previously considered: Isabel Allende (Chile), Rosario Castellanos (Mexico), Elena Poniatowska (Mexico), Luisa Valenzuela (Argentina), Rosario Ferre (Puerto Rico), and Lydia Cabrera (Cuba). Most recently, I have discovered and enjoyed the works of Sandra Cisneros (Chicana), Julia Alvarez (Dominican), Nicholasa Mohr (Nuyorican), and Carolina Hospital (Cuban American).

A STRATEGY FOR INTEGRATING THE ESL CURRICULUM

Since the ESL curriculum is already crowded with "things we must teach," the best approach to integrating it is to tie in new material with the required text. For example, to introduce a grammar lesson, an instructor can discuss the works of one or two of the women mentioned above in which this particular grammatical point is clearly expressed.

In my search for authentic materials to supplement my text, I came across a fall 1990 special issue of *Time* entitled "Women: The Road Ahead." In this issue, I found a series of short articles under the heading "World Trouble Spots" from which I developed a 2-day project. This unit plan has been used within the four levels of ESL classes at Hudson County Community College; of course, it takes into consideration the abilities of students at different levels.

First, the class is divided into groups, according to the number of students present. When working in groups, the students feel more comfortable dealing with a longer, sometimes threatening-looking piece of work. An article is assigned to each group to be read and understood, summarized, presented to the class, and developed into a final project (more detailed information is found in the unit plan that follows). The students were shocked by these articles in such a way that they began to share many intimate anecdotes from their own or others' lives. At the end of 2 days, they had learned more about the unfair treatment of women around the world and in their lives than if I had mentioned it in passing while covering one of the chapters in the textbook. Indeed, it is a learning experience not only for the students but also for me, since they are bringing their own insights and solutions to these problems and sharing them openly with one another. Not all their "unconscious ideologies" have been exposed, but I believe that through the examination of these cases as well as the sharing of opinions, they are on the road to self-examination.

COMMENT

Having proposed several strategies for integrating the Spanish and ESL curricula, I would like to reiterate that only through the reexamination of our language and teaching style can we become more in touch with our own "unconscious ideologies" and at the same time begin destroying the stereotypical myths of our society by becoming positive role models. In closing, I would like to leave the reader with this thought by Audre Lorde (1988):

> Certainly there are very real differences between us of race, age, and sex. But it is not those differences between us that are separating us. It is rather our refusal to recognize those differences, and to examine the distortions which result from our misnaming them and their effects upon human behavior and expectation. . . . It is a lifetime pursuit for each one of us to extract these distortions from our living at the same time as we recognize, reclaim, and define those differences upon which they are imposed. (p. 446)

UNIT PLAN FOR INTEGRATING GENDER AND MULTICULTURAL EDUCATION IN THE ESL CURRICULUM

Unit Title

Women in Trouble in the World

Length

2 days

Groups

Each lesson/unit must include a minimum of three racial groups and be gender/handicap fair.

    Native American
    Asian American
    African American
    Hispanic American
    European American
    Other cultures/groups
    Female
    Male
    Handicapped

Goal

The students will develop a sensitivity toward the treatment of women as well as the cultural differences among the peoples of the world and one another.

Instructional Objectives

Students will

1. Identify the problems faced by women in the United States and in the world
2. Increase their appreciation for other cultures even if they do not agree with the customs
3. Form, express, and share their own opinions in the class
4. Design a final project to be presented to the class
5. Use the English language while reading, writing, and speaking within each group

Teaching Procedures and Student Activities

1. The students are divided into small groups, each of which is given a magazine article.
2. The students read the article and discuss it with the group.
3. The students select three representatives from the group, although everyone must participate in all group decisions.
4. One student writes a summary of the article and presents it to the class.
5. A second student compiles the opinions of each person in the group about the article and presents them to the class.
6. A third student compiles five questions that everyone in the group has about the article and presents them to the class.
7. A final group project must be handed in to the teacher on the second day, compiling all the information mentioned above.

Enrichment

1. The students interview someone from a different culture about the role of women.
2. The students share an example of mistreatment of women as seen in their everyday lives.
3. The students research the life of a woman from their own cultural or ethnic background. The person selected may be famous or a member of the student's family.

Evaluation Procedure

1. Class presentations by individual groups
2. Final group projects
3. Projects developed out of the enrichment mentioned above

Instructional Materials

World Trouble Spots. *Time,* Fall 1990.

BIBLIOGRAPHY

Eoyang, Eugene. (1988, June 18–20). *Taking the "foreign" out of foreign language teaching.* Paper presented at Association for the Development of Foreign Languages Seminar West, Boulder, CO.

Lorde, Audre. (1988). Age, race, class, and sex: Women redefining difference. In Paula S. Rothenberg (Ed.), *Racism and sexism: An integrated study* (pp. 352–359). New York: St. Martin's Press.

Rothenberg, Paula. (1988). Integrating the study of race, gender, and class: Some preliminary observations. *Feminist Teacher, 3*(3), 37–42.

Rothenberg, Paula. (1991, May 5). Rethinking reality: Learning to see the squirrels. Presented at New Jersey Gender Project summer institute.

World trouble spots. (1990, Fall). *Time, 136* (19), 39–40.

46

Nineteenth- and Twentieth-Century Literature: Centering the Margins

Margaret Roman

In June 1991, I had the good fortune to attend the New Jersey Project's summer institute just as I was in the planning stages for a senior seminar for English majors to be given the following fall semester. There was a great deal of discussion at the institute about who and what was considered marginal by the canonical curriculum that was in place in our institutions of higher learning. Paula Rothenberg at one point used the expression "centering the margins" when she was discussing curriculum transformation, and I thought, That's it! The theme for my senior seminar would be centering the margins, and I would invert the present canonical structure and make the writers who generally appear on the periphery the central core of the course.

I wanted my students to attempt to answer several questions during the course of the semester: What are the criteria for good and "classic" literature? Is good literature synonymous with "the classics"? What writers are included in the canon, who is on the periphery, and who is left out? Why are these choices made and by whom? What is lost or gained by these choices for a student of literature?

BUILDING A CASE FOR INCLUSIVE LITERATURE

The class readings were structured as an argument. I wanted to build a case for inclusion. I began with the most obvious and palatable—Nobel Prize winners in literature of whom we had never heard. These were writers who had been given the canonical stamp of approval but still were not represented in our curriculum. We studied the poetry of Gabriela Mistral, Yasunari Kawabata's *Snow Country,* and poetry selections and the play *The Madmen and the Specialist* by Wole Soyinka. The class was somewhat startled, and students themselves brought up issues of race and ethnicity as possible motives for exclusion. We spoke of ethnocentrism. I mentioned that one argument academics give for not teaching these works has to do with what is lost in translation. However, I remarked that that has never stopped us from reading *Crime and Punishment* and *Madame Bovary.* We discussed the problems with translated texts and proposed ways that these concerns could be addressed.

Gender was the central issue in our discussion of the work of Sarah Orne Jewett. Although she is now included in every survey text for American literature, she was once ignored in favor of the sentimental, contrived stories of Bret Harte as the leading example of regionalist writing during the rise of American literary realism. Why were her writings, lauded by William Dean Howells and Henry James for their substance, buried? How did Jewett's stories compare with "The Luck of Roaring Camp" by Harte, which the students had read?

Who is American, and what constitutes American literature? We spent the next 4 weeks reading ethnic literature. The issue of class was discussed at length. I used the text *The American Mosaic,* edited by Barbara Roche Rico and Sandra Mano (Boston: Houghton Mifflin, 1991), because the writings are placed in their historical context, which is helpful to students. They also read Anzia Yesierska's *The Breadgivers* and N. Scott Momaday's Pulitzer Prize–winning *The House Made of Dawn.* Reading these two novels helped students flesh out the shorter selections in the text on early immigrants and American Indians by both Yesierska and Momaday, getting more of a sense of their respective literary styles.

For the remainder of the class, we studied writings with which the students were familiar, but from perspectives that they had not entertained before. We studied Virginia Woolf's *Orlando* as lesbian fiction. Short selections of lesbian fiction were introduced the next week, as well as the poetry of Audre Lorde. I paired the text *Six Women's Slave Narratives,* edited by Henry Louis Gates (New York: Oxford University Press, 1988), with Margaret Atwood's *The Handmaid's Tale.* At the summer institute, Susan Van Dyne of Smith College had suggested reading *The Handmaid's Tale* as a 19th-century slave narrative. I found Charles Davis and Henry Louis Gates's book *On*

Slave Narratives (New York: Oxford University Press, 1985) useful for this section.

Finally, we discussed the relativity of truth via Isabel Allende's *Eva Luna* and William Faulkner's *Absalom, Absalom.* These readings produced wonderful class discussions about how race, class, and gender might contribute to each author's presentation of relative truth. Of course, questions of what reality is and what truth is also surfaced at this time, providing a wonderful conclusion to a course whose theme questions the dimensions of authentic literature.

In addition to providing an inclusive course content, I made an effort to have pedagogy reflect inclusiveness. I wanted students to have some input into grading, and I wanted them to feel that they possessed knowledge. Together, the class and I determined the number and nature of the formal papers. The class especially appreciated the nongraded response papers that began each class, and those responses set the framework for the class discussion that followed. We always sat in a circle.

In teaching this course, I encountered two problematic areas. Because of the nature of the material, some racist attitudes surfaced. Students asked, "If the early immigrants, who were poor, could make it in this country, why can't black and Hispanic people do it?" and "Why can't they speak English?" However, I am glad that these uncomfortable situations arose, because at least these questions and attitudes could be addressed. I also had to remind students not to generalize about groups of people based on a few reading selections.

The benefits far outweighed the problems, however. Students remained vitally interested in the newness of the material and the questions posed. I believe that the course empowered them to think deeply and critically. I asked them to write me letters at the end of the course, and they were uniformly positive. One student wrote, "I am no longer content simply to say, 'that's the way it is'; now I am looking at motives and underlying causes." Another wrote, "I learned to appreciate different cultures and people, and to look at things with an open mind. This class has really broadened my horizons." Although this course was designed for senior English majors, it would also serve well as an honors program course, a capstone course, or even an introduction to literature course. I am presently adapting some of this material to be used in my other courses because of the vital experience I shared with my students.

SYLLABUS FOR NINETEENTH- AND TWENTIETH-CENTURY LITERATURE: CENTERING THE MARGINS

Rationale

When we read "literature," there are always writers on the periphery whom we include from time to time but who are not central to our studies. In so doing, these writers are reduced by the very nature of their placement. I would like to put these marginal writers at the center of our studies for this semester, and I would like to pose several questions that you should be able to answer partially by the end of the course: Who decides what literature is important as well as what is not as important? What are the criteria for good and great "literature"? Who is included, who is on the periphery, who is left out? Why? What is lost or gained by these choices?

Our readings will form a sort of pastiche, organized so that you will be able to read from a number of perspectives that you probably haven't entertained before. The list is taken from 19th- and 20th-century writings. The list is not by any means meant to be conclusive. If anything, I hope it does away with margins to give you a more open-ended approach to writers and their writings.

Requirements

In addition to the readings, you will be required to write two 4–5-page papers and one 8–10-page research paper. You will also have 13 opportunities (one for each class period) to make informal written responses to our readings. These are required but ungraded. They will be written in class at the beginning of each session (15 minutes). They will serve as a basis for class discussion and for your paper topics.

READINGS

Week 1	Gabriela Mistral (poetry selections)
Week 2	Yasunari Kawabata, *Snow Country*
Week 3	Wole Soyinka, *The Madmen and the Specialist;* poetry
Week 4	Sarah Orne Jewett, *The Country of the Pointed Firs*
Week 5	Early immigrant writing (chap. 1: *American Mosaic*) Anzia Yesierska, *The Breadgivers*
Week 6	Puerto Rican and Chicano writing (chaps. 4, 7: *American Mosaic*)
Week 7	Chinese, Japanese, and Native American writing (chaps. 2, 5, 8: *American Mosaic*)
Week 8	N. Scott Momaday, *The House Made of Dawn*

Week 9   Virginia Woolf, *Orlando*

Week 10   Woolf, Sackville-West continued (short selections)

Week 11   *Six Women's Slave Narratives*

Week 12   Margaret Atwood, *The Handmaid's Tale*

Week 13   William Faulkner, *Absalom, Absalom*

Week 14   Isabel Allende, *Eva Luna*

47

Gender, Narrative, and Interpretation in Literature and Film

Jim Hala
Wendy K. Kolmar

Gender, Narrative, and Interpretation in Literature and Film is an upper-level, team-taught seminar offered in the English Department and cross-listed with women's studies. The texts for the course are chosen principally from contemporary American literature and popular cinema. We normally offer the course during a 6-week intensive summer session and have now taught the course three times in succession. The class meets three times a week for 2½ hours (longer on the Wednesday night film showings).

OBJECTIVES

In the course, we attempt to change the way our students "read" both films and literary texts. Our purpose is, first, to make students increasingly aware of the construction of perspective and point of view in the texts we study and to introduce them to the idea that cinematic and fictional "reality" is always a construct. We hope to move students from traditional textual and thematic modes of reading both literary and film texts to a more semiotic mode.

A second objective of the course is for students to understand the role of the reader or audience (themselves) in the creation of narrative meaning. Robert Scholes's (1982) concept of "narrativity" helps students understand the ways in which the viewer or reader participates in the construction of narrative and perspective. Each text constructs (assumes) a reader (viewer), but every viewer is also complicit in constructing the perspective of the text.

Our third objective is to have students see that not only do films always have a constructed perspective, but that particularly in cultural products such as Hollywood films, the perspective is consistently that of the dominant culture. Using the feminist film theory of E. Ann Kaplan (1983a) and Laura Mulvey (1989), among others, we suggest that the perspective of dominant cinema is inevitably gendered, that the gaze is male, white, heterosexual, and middle class. Against this dominant perspective, we set off such texts as Louise Erdrich's *Tracks* (1988), Margaret Atwood's *The Handmaid's Tale* (1986), and Marleen Gorris's film *A Question of Silence,* in which the perspective is defined explicitly and is defined as not-white or not-male or both. Through these texts, we want to lead students to ask: Is the gaze (inescapably) male? Or is a female spectatorship possible in popular literature and film?

The approach to reading and the concepts we attempt to teach students in this course are fundamental to women's studies and carry over into the other courses we both teach. Students come to understand that every cultural product—literary text, film, advertisement, photograph, song lyric, and so forth—embodies the perspective of its producer. That perspective is inevitably defined by the producer's social location. Therefore, as critical readers and viewers, their task is to tease out and deconstruct that perspective.

PEDAGOGICAL CHALLENGES

The course consistently presents us with three pedagogical challenges. First, students are hesitant to admit their own complicity in the creation of narrative structures that place women (or poor and working-class people, people of color, lesbians and gays) in the objective position. Even those students who are well aware of gender and other biases in economic, professional, and public policy spheres are often reluctant to fully acknowledge that dimension in their own leisure-time activity of viewing films.

Second, students come to the course steeped in visual culture, but they are not trained to look in a critical way and have almost no vocabulary for talking about what they see. We have to teach students the rudiments of film criticism, beginning with the idea that a camera is *not* an impartial recorder of reality. That is, they must first understand that the process of making sense out of the sutured pieces of a film narrative is learned. They then learn that, although the culture has already made them visually literate in a passive way, they must learn to become visually literate in an active, critical sense.

The third hurdle is the considerable amount of rather dauntingly theoretical material that students must grasp in order to engage in a discussion of the complex issues we raise in the course. We try to introduce the theoretical readings in such a way that they build on one another, but we have to devote considerable class time to explicating the vocabulary and theoretical points in a number of the articles.

COURSE STRUCTURE

The first night of the course presents the methodology of the course in miniature. We show the students a number of brief film clips arranged to invoke first their awareness of gender stereotypes in mainstream film (images of women). Then we move them from that awareness to an analysis of how those stereotypical images are created. Clips of Cinderella, Jessica Rabbit in *Who Framed Roger Rabbit,* and Julia Roberts in *Pretty Woman* are useful here. Our responses to the students' observations attempt to move them from seeing only the stereotypes to considering the gendered construction of images on the screen—the films invite the audience to participate in the act of watching women. We see Marilyn Monroe on the beach in *Some Like It Hot* from Tony Curtis's thickly bespectacled perspective; we peep with Anthony Perkins through a hole in the wall of the Bates Motel at Janet Leigh in *Psycho.* With this, we introduce the idea that the audience, too, is complicit in this watching.

The first session ends with an assignment: Students are to read the first two chapters of Giannetti (1990), which discuss basics of camera angles, lighting, and so on. Each student is also asked to bring to class next week a clip of her or his own choosing that illustrates one of the techniques Giannetti discusses.

With Hitchcock's *Rear Window,* the first film we show, we expand our discussion of watching and of voyeurism. John Berger's *Ways of Seeing* (1977) introduces the notion of visual comprehension as a socially determined construct. Tania Modleski's (1988) revisionist essay on *Rear Window,* "The Master's Dollhouse," although admitting the issues of voyeurism and the construction of perspective, suggests that Grace Kelly's character in the film makes a conscious effort to subvert to her own purposes the conventions of voyeurism. By presenting these two very different readings of the first film in the course, we suggest to students that there is more than one way to "read" a cinematic representation.

Week two problematizes the audience's participation in the creation of seemingly coherent narration. With their self-reflexive, disjunctive narratives, Thomas Pynchon's *The Crying of Lot 49* (1976) and Jim Jarmusch's film *Mystery Train* both invite students to examine the process through which readers and viewers construct meaning. Robert Scholes's (1982) essay on narrativity further explicates the process, discussing how what the camera does not show in Pakula's *The Parallax View* is as important in the processing of meaning as what it does show.

Week three presents students with the issue of perspective in relation to ethnicity through the example of Native American history. Erdrich's *Tracks* (1988) provides multiple perspectives on a single sequence of events, whereas Kevin Costner's *Dances with Wolves* is used to ask the thorny question of whether the dominant culture can present alternative histories without aggrandizing them in the process. The choice of film here is problematic. Clips from traditional Westerns (e.g., *Stagecoach, Broken Arrow*) can illustrate stereotypes without the necessity of showing full-length features of this sort. There are films such as *Black Robe* that are credited with being more authentic representations of native cultures; however, we choose to show either *Little Big Man* or *Dances with Wolves* precisely because we can highlight the issue of a dominant culture's representations of a marginalized culture. How do the marginalized view their own portrayal by the dominant culture, even in narratives that purport to be "sympathetic"? Robert Stamm's (1991) essay explicates this issue from a Bakhtinian perspective, and Trinh T. Minh-Ha's (1989) essay—which refuses to participate in linear, rationalist discourse—shows students just how accustomed they are to a particular culturally determined form of (re)presentation and just how alienated they become when that form is absent.

In the following week, we examine narratives in which the marginalized take over their own representation. The indeterminacy and subjectivity of the narrative in Atwood's *The Handmaid's Tale* (1988) is contrasted with linearity and closure imposed on the narrative in Schlondorff's film version. In the same week, Gorris's film *A Question of Silence* presents the class with its first look at a feminist film narrative. Does it avoid the kind of gendered spectatorship Mulvey (1989) identifies in all narrative film? Does the film create a female point of view as its dominant perspective? Gentile's (1990) essay looks at the production and promotion of Gorris's film, thus introducing consideration of the larger cultural institutions in which narratives are embedded.

In week five, picking up on the discussion of *A Question of Silence,* we further explore the idea of a gynocentric narrative. What might a narrative driven by female desire look like? Judy Grahn's *Mundane's World* (1988) eschews linearity, has multiple points of view, and consistently demonstrates its own narrative premises, whereas Susan Seidelman's *Desperately Seeking Su-*

san and Bob Raphaelson's *Black Widow* show as subjects women engaged in a process of constructing meaning or truth. Using essays by Jackie Stacey (1990), Laura Mulvey (1989), and E. Ann Kaplan (1983a), we now begin to discuss psychoanalytic theories of language, representation, and film. Again, the questions arise: Does Madonna's eclectic cross-dressing in *Desperately Seeking Susan* suggest a female eroticism unconstrained by conventional gender roles? *Black Widow* portrays two women who come to identify strongly with each other and who develop a powerful attraction for each other as a result of that identification; yet each is forced by cultural circumstances to attempt to destroy the other. Can this be taken as a comment on the suppression of female desire? Can a film take up this topic without succumbing to the cinematic conventions of voyeurism and subject-object hierarchies? Are these films, at least in part, construing their audience as female?

By week six, most students have some understanding of the issues and theories involved in the question of narrative perspective and dominance. At this point, we try to urge that understanding into realms that, for many students, are intimidating. First, we use Soderbergh's *Sex, Lies, and Videotape,* which reprises most of the issues raised by *Rear Window,* as a way of bringing together all the issues of the course. Students realize that when James Spader's character smashes all his tapes and video equipment, he is finally emerging from his privileged-but-limited, self-protected position as a subject-watcher and is pursuing a reciprocity with the "other."

Finally, we show a lesbian film, most often Donna Deitsch's *Desert Hearts.* Here again, the choice of film is problematic, both in terms of theoretical concerns and in terms of availability and accessibility. We have tried Sayles's *Lianna,* Towne's *Personal Best,* as well as *Desert Hearts.* See Jane Gaines's (1990) essay for a discussion of the problems involved with each. Through the film, we explore the possibility of a narrative film that is constructed solely from the standpoint of female desire. Marilyn Frye's (1983) powerful essay on the cultural invisibility of lesbians suggests that such representations of lesbian desire as *Desert Hearts* can never be acknowledged, cannot be "seen" in a patriarchal culture. Gaines's (1990) essay extends the discussion by asserting that psychoanalytic theories of cinematic pleasure and films that refuse to participate in conventional modes of visual narrative are elitist and homophobic to the extent that they deny women pleasure at the sight of or identification with other women's bodies.

We have learned to anticipate students' homophobic responses at this point. To counter these responses, we draw on the understanding they have developed that the passive acceptance of representation from a single, subject perspective necessarily exploits the object of representation. If the class insists that homosexual behavior is beyond the ken of cultural representation, then they are admitting Frye's point that the culture refuses to "see" lesbians and gays, and the point about the power of dominant perspective is still made. If the class finds the love scene in *Desert Hearts* unsettling, then are they tacitly accepting the premises of the psychoanalytic critics who insist that all pleasure in cinema is derived from a male, heterosexual voyeurism? If they do not accept this psychoanalytic view, then Gaines's (1990) essay asks why not show women loving women (or men, men), and once again, they confront the issue of dominance in representation.

In presentations on the last night of the course, students analyze the construction of perspective in a film of their choice, showing clips and using the questions and critical approaches we have developed together. Here, we often get some sense of the course's effectiveness as students lament that they cannot "just watch a movie for fun" anymore. They have become aware of the ways in which gender, race or ethnicity, class, and sexuality shape all texts, and their reading and viewing of texts has consequently changed— which was, after all, one of the objectives of the course.

SYLLABUS FOR GENDER, NARRATIVE, AND INTERPRETATION IN LITERATURE AND FILM

Texts

Atwood, Margaret. (1986). *The handmaid's tale.* Boston: Houghton Mifflin.
Berger, John. (1977). *Ways of seeing.* Harmondsworth, England: Penguin.
Erdrich, Louise. (1988). *Tracks.* New York: Henry Holt.
Erens, Patricia (Ed.). (1990). *Issues in feminist film criticism.* Bloomington: Indiana University Press.
Frye, Marilyn. (1983). To be and be seen: The politics of reality. In *The politics of reality.* Trumansburg, NY: Crossing Press.
Gaines, Jane. (1990). Women and representation: Can we enjoy alternative pleasure? In Patricia Erens (Ed.), *Issues in feminist film criticism* (pp. 75–92). Bloomington: Indiana University Press.
Gentile, Mary. (1990). Feminist or tendentious: Marlene Gorris's *A question of silence.* In Patricia Erens (Ed.), *Issues in feminist film criticism* (pp. 395–404). Bloomington: Indiana University Press.
Giannetti, Louis. (1990). *Understanding movies.* 5th ed. Englewood Cliffs, NJ: Prentice-Hall.
Grahn, Judy. (1988). *Mundane's world.* Freedom, CA: Crossing Press.
Kaplan, E. Ann. (1983a). Is the gaze male? In *Women and film: Both sides of the camera.* New York: Routledge.
Kaplan, E. Ann. (1983b). Silence as female resistance in Marguerite Duras's *Nathalie Granger.* In *Women and film: Both sides of the camera.* New York: Routledge.
Modleski, Tania. (1988). The master's dollhouse: *Rear window.* In *The women who knew too much.* New York: Routledge.

Mulvey, Laura. (1989). Visual pleasure and narrative cinema. In *Visual and other pleasures*. Bloomington: Indiana University Press.

Pynchon, Thomas. (1976). *The crying of lot 49*. New York: Perennial Library.

Scholes, Robert. (1982). Narration and narrativity in film and fiction. In *Semiotics and interpretation*. New Haven, CT: Yale University Press.

Stacey, Jackie. (1990). Desperately seeking difference. In Patricia Erens (Ed.), *Issues in feminist film criticism* (pp. 367–377). Bloomington: Indiana University Press.

Stamm, Robert. (1991). Bakhtin, polyphony, and ethnic/racial representation. In Lester Friedman (Ed.), *Unspeakable images: Ethnicity and the American cinema*. Urbana: University of Illinois Press.

Trinh, T. Minh-Ha. (1989). The language of nativism: Anthropology as a scientific conversation of man with man. In *Woman, native, other: Writing postcoloniality and feminism*. Bloomington: Indiana University Press.

Procedures

This course will be conducted through discussion involving both the whole class and smaller groups. Each Wednesday we will see a film or films and have some preliminary discussion immediately afterward. Each Thursday, we will discuss that film, along with one or more theoretical or critical essays. Mondays will be given to discussions of novels.

Requirements

> Four typed response papers (1–2 pages each) on the assigned novels (checked, not graded)
>
> Selection and presentation of film clips to illustrate one or more of Giannetti's technical points (checked, not graded)
>
> A collaborative presentation of an essay read by the class (checked, not graded)
>
> A 2-page proposal for your final paper, due the third week of the course (graded)
>
> Participation in a small group that will be responsible for discussion of a film not seen by the class (graded)
>
> A final paper of 7–10 pages, due in the last week of class (graded)

COURSE SCHEDULE

Class 1   Introduction

Class 2   Alfred Hitchcock, *Rear Window* (1954)

Class 3	Discussion of *Rear Window* Essays: Giannetti (chaps. 1, 2); Modleski; Berger Class examples of Giannetti's technical points
Class 4	Discussion of Pynchon, *The Crying of Lot 49*
Class 5	Jim Jarmusch, *Mystery Train* (1989); Alan Pakula, *The Parallax View* (1974)
Class 6	Discussion of *Mystery Train* and *Parallax View* Essays: Giannetti (chap. 4 and pp. 296–304), and Scholes
Class 7	Discussion of Erdrich, *Tracks*
Class 8	Kevin Costner, *Dances with Wolves* (1990)
Class 9	Discussion of *Dances with Wolves* Essays: Giannetti (pp. 357–361), Trinh T. Minh-Ha, and Stam
Class 10	Discussion of Atwood, *The Handmaid's Tale*
Class 11	Marleen Gorris, *A Question of Silence* (1982) Paper proposal due
Class 12	Discussion of *Question of Silence* Essays: Gentile in Erens; Kaplan
Class 13	Discussion of Grahn, *Mundane's World*
Class 14	Double bill: Susan Seidelman, *Desperately Seeking Susan* (1985); Bob Raphaelson, *Black Widow* (1987)
Class 15	Discussion of *Desperately Seeking Susan* and *Black Widow* Essays: Stacey in Erens; Mulvey; Kaplan
Class 16	Double bill: Soderbergh, *Sex, Lies, and Videotape* (1989); Donna Deitsch, *Desert Hearts* (1985)

Class 17   Discussion of *Sex, Lies, and Videotape* and *Desert Hearts*
            Essays: Gaines in Erens; Frye

Class 18   Group presentations
            Papers due

New Jersey Project Staff 1986–1995

Project Director

Paula Rothenberg, William Paterson College, 1989–present
Carol H. Smith, Douglass College, Rutgers University, Institute for Research on Women, 1986–1989

Assistant Directors and Faculty Fellows

Mia Anderson, Bergen Community College, Assistant Director, 1994–present
Naomi Miller, Sussex County Community College, Assistant Director, 1993–1994
Margaret Roman, College of Saint Elizabeth, Assistant Director, 1992–1993
Barbara Seater, Raritan Valley Community College, Assistant Director, 1991–1992
Isa Tavares Maack, Essex County College, Assistant Director, 1990–1991
Constance Murray, New Jersey Institute of Technology, Associate Director, 1989–1990; Faculty Fellow, 1988–1989
Wendy Kolmar, Drew University, Assistant Director, 1989–1990
Ferris Olin, Douglass College, Rutgers University, Associate Director, 1986–1989
Corann Okorodudu, Rowan College, Faculty Fellow, 1988–1989
Judith Johnston, Rider University, Faculty Fellow, 1986–1987

ALANA (African, Latina, Asian, and Native American) Network for Women of Color in Higher Education

Charley Flint, William Paterson College, Coordinator, 1989–present

Regional Coordinators

Ellen Friedman, Trenton State College, Spring 1992, 1992–1993,
Irma Lester, Brookdale Community College, 1993–1994, 1990–1991
Bill Olson, Upsala College, 1993–1994
Elaine Ingulli, Richard Stockton College, 1993–1994
John Hillje, Rider University, Spring, 1992–1993
F. David Kievitt, Bergen Community College, 1992–1993
Tamara Richardson, Ocean County College, 1992–1993
Sylvia Baer, Gloucester County College, 1989–1992
Elaine Foster, Hudson County Community College, Spring 1992
Jean Palmegiano, Saint Peter's College, Fall 1991
Barbara Seater, Raritan Valley Community College, Fall 1991
Isa Tavares Maack, Essex County College, 1990–1991
Lorraine Mayfield-Brown, Montclair State University, 1989–1990
Dori Seider, Mercer County Community College, 1989–1990

Student Awards Competition Judges

1994–1995

Carmen Whalen, Rutgers University–New Brunswick, Chair

Floresta Jones, Brookdale Community College

Godwin Ohwerei, Jersey City State College

Laura Winters, College of Saint Elizabeth

1993–1994

Linda Williamson Nelson, Richard Stockton College, chair

Wendy Kolmar, Drew University

Judith Chelius Stark, Seton Hall University

Shirley Wilton, Ocean County College

1992–1993

Gerry Smith-Wright, Drew University, Chair

Donna Crawley, Ramapo College

Judith Wrase Nygard, Mercer County Community College

Nadine Shanler, Trenton State College

1991–1992

Fran Bartkowski, Rutgers University–Newark, Chair

Vivian Perry, Saint Peter's College

Kathy Vasile, Brookdale Community College

Isa Tavares Maack, Essex County College

1990–1991

Carole Krauthamer, Trenton State College, Chair

Mia Anderson, Bergen Community College

Delight Dodyk, Drew University

Barbara Seater, Raritan Valley Community College

1989–1990

Isa Tavares Maack, Essex County College, Chair

Charley Flint, William Paterson College

Adele McCollum, Montclair State University

Jacqueline Pope, Richard Stockton College

Consultants

Roberta Francis, Grants and Program Consultant, 1994–present

Wendy Kolmar, Drew University, Special Consultant and Editorial Consultant, 1986–present

Jeris Cassel, Rutgers University, Librarian Consultant, 1986–1989

Beva Eastman, William Paterson College, Technology Consultant, 1986–1989

Linda Jeffrey, Rowan College, Southern Regional Consultant, 1986–1989

Linda Langschied, Rutgers University, Librarian Consultant, 1986–1989

Naomi Miller, Sussex County Community College, Special Consultant, 1994–1995

Paula Rothenberg, William Paterson College, Consultant, 1986–1989

Advisory Board, Phase I

Leslie Agard-Jones, William Paterson College

Judith Brodsky, Rutgers University

Charlotte Bunch, Rutgers University

William Chafe , Duke University

Virginia Cyrus , Rider University

Gloria Dickinson, Trenton State College

Delight Dodyk, Drew University

Doris Friedensohn, Jersey City State College

Carol Gilligan, Harvard University

Edward Goldberg, NJ Department of Higher Education

Mary Hartman, Rutgers University

Hilda Hidalgo, Rutgers University
Helen Hoch, Jersey City State College
Karen Howe, Trenton State College
Judith Johnston, Rider University
Phillipa Kafka, Kean College
F. David Kievitt, Bergen Community
  College
Michael Kimmel, SUNY at Stony Brook
Wendy Kolmar, Drew University
Suzanne Lebsock, Rutgers University
Elinor Lerner, Stockton State
Adele McCollum, Montclair State
  University
Connie Murray, NJ Institute of Technology
Ferris Olin, Rutgers University

Paula Rothenberg, William Paterson
  College
Bernice Resnick Sandler, Association of
  American Colleges
Carol Smith, Rutgers University
Linda Stamato, Rutgers University
Peter Stein, William Paterson College
Catharine Stimpson, Rutgers University
Janis Strout, Princeton University
Adrian Tinsley, Rowan College of New
  Jersey
Rhoda Unger, Montclair State University
Joan Weimer, Drew University
Deborah White, Rutgers University
Marge Wyngaarden, Board of Trustees,
  Ramapo College of NJ

Transformations Editorial Staff

Donna Crawley, Co-editor, Ramapo
  College, 1994–1995
Frances Shapiro-Skrobe, Co-editor,
  Ramapo College, 1994–1995
Martha Ecker, Associate Editor, Ramapo
  College, 1994–1995

Kathleen Fowler, Book Review Editor,
  Ramapo College, 1994–1995
Sylvia Baer, Founding Editor, Gloucester
  County College, 1990–1994
Maryann McLoughlin O'Donnell,
  Assistant Editor, Ocean County College,
  1992–1994

Student Essay Publication Editors

Elaine Foster, Co-editor, Hudson County
  Community College, 1993–present
Jane Isenberg, Co-editor, Hudson County
  Community College, 1993–present

Sylvia Baer, Editor, Gloucester County
  Community College, 1991–1993
Martina Nowak, Editor, The New Jersey
  Project, 1990

1991–1992 Art Exhibit Jury

Janet Taylor Pickett, Essex County
  College, Curator
Judith Brodsky, Rutgers University

Nancy Einreinhofer, William Paterson
  College
Ileana Fuentes-Perez, Rutgers University
Deborah Sperry, Newark Museum

Residential Institute Coordinators

Roberta Francis, 1989
Lauren Burnbauer, 1988

Gail Kraidman, 1987

Instructional Media Services

K.C. Dietsch, Rutgers University–Camden, 1989–present

Office Staff

Judy Baker, Administrative Assistant, 1992–present; Secretary, 1991–1992; Student Assistant, 1990–1991

Helena Lota, Secretary, 1994–present

Rosanne Marrone, Secretary, 1993–1994

Martina Nowak, Secretary, 1989–1990

Arlene Nora, Office Manager, 1986–1989

Guida West, Special Projects Administrator, 1986–1989

Merle Fischer, Secretary, 1986–1989

Diana Gerace, Secretary, 1986–1989

Marie Howley, Secretary, 1986–1989

Student Assistants

Lisa Scholts, 1991–1995

Renee Channer, 1994–1995

Ruth Jean-Marie, 1995

Jennifer Nunez, 1994

Jana Gerken, 1992–1993

Barbara Victor, 1991–1993

Lynn Insley, 1991–1992

Karen Booth, 1989–1991

Belinda Curtis, 1991

Bob Mastrangelo, 1990

Rebecca Reynolds, 1986–1989

Liz Smith, 1986–1989

SUMMER INSTITUTE PARTICIPANTS

1994

Brookdale Community College: Floresta D. Jones; *Camden County College:* Lorraine Baggett-Heuser, Elisabeth Bass, Marie English, Wanda Kaluza, Robert Lorenzi, Rita Wade Perkins, Allison Sutton, Karen Thoens; *College of Saint Elizabeth:* Elena Colicelli, Kathleen Hunter; *County College of Morris:* Barbara Beauchamp, Ann Hadjiloizou, Nick Irons; *Essex County College:* Charles Bateman, Gretchen Brown, Susan Fischer, Chiu-Min Lai; *Felician College:* Teresa Bowers, Deborah Ann Jensen; *Kean College:* Sharon Boyd-Jackson, Emily Filardo; *Mercer County Community College:* Vera Goodkin, Emmaline Marks; *Ramapo College:* Susan Scher, Behzad Yaghmaian; *Rowan College:* Ronald Czochor, Beverly Horton, Wanda Larrier, Yuhui Li, Maria Rosado; *Rutgers University–New Brunswick:* Barbara Balliet, Ernest Dunn. Peter Li, Godfrey Roberts, Carmen Whalen; *Seton Hall University:* Sister Anita Talar; Sussex Coun, Cheryl Baton, Richard Linden; *University of Medicine and Dentistry of New Jersey–Robert Wood Johnson Medical School:* Patricia Carver, Michelle Harrison, Robert Like.

1993

Brookdale Community College: Renee Gaines, Newana Barnes; *College of Saint Elizabeth:* Patricia Schall; *County College of Morris:* Janice Rafalowski, Wendy Jones; *Hudson County Community College:* Issam El-Achkar, Biswa Nath Ghosh, Mohammad Nasar Imam, David Rosenthal, Jo-Ann Sainz; *Kean College:* Deborah Allen, Russ Mahan; *Mercer County Community College:* Sharmila Sen; *Montclair State University:*

Rachel Fordyce, Susana Sotillo, Valentin Soto; *Ramapo College:* James Naazir Conyers, Elaine Risch, Sara Kuplinsky; *Rider University:* Pamela Brown, Wendy Lewis Chung, Minmin Wang; *Seton Hall University:* Evelyn Plummer, Judith Chelius Stark, Rosemary Skeele; *Trenton State College:* Amelia Blyden; *Union County College:* Anthony Boyle, Sondra Fishinger, Lynn Meng, Lawrence Wollman; *William Paterson College:* Laura Tapia Aitken, Janet Pollak, Daniel Meaders.

1992

Camden County College: Barbara Brook, Lynette Cook, Lawrence Dellolio, Joseph Haro, William Marlin, John Pesda, Jill Russell; *Centenary College:* Eleanor Carducci, Barbara-Jayne Lewthwaite, Marie Peters; *County College of Morris:* Gwen Dungy, Barbara Karpinski, Stuart Siegelman, Bette Simmons; *Essex County College:* Linda Corrin; *Felician College:* Gloria Antall, Sherida Yoder; *Hudson County Community College:* Theodore Lai; *Montclair State University:* Kenneth Brook, Mildred Garcia; *Passaic County Community College:* Elaine Harrington; *Princeton University:* Janis Strout; *Ramapo College:* Louise Allerton, Joan Eurell, Christine Machorek, Kathleen, Neumann, Peter Scheckner, Alana Sherman; *Rutgers University–New Brunswick:* Shelley Myer, Diana Valle-Ferrer; *Sussex County Community College:* Patricia Bailey, Anthony Balzano, Janet Cutshall, Heather Pfleger-Dunham, Naomi Miller, William Waite; *Trenton State College:* Blythe Hinitz, Marlene Kayne, Nadine Shanler, Allan Singh, Aura Star; *William Paterson College:* Gunvor Satra.

1991

Bloomfield College: Jamileh Amirzafari; *Brookdale Community College:* Barbara Burke, Terri Hicks, Linda White; *Centenary College:* Angela Elliott, Virginia Ellsasser, John Holt, Dorothy Rhoda, Linda Schwartz Green; *College of Saint Elizabeth:* Margaret Roman, Laura Winters; *Drew University:* José Carmona, Kathryn Gray, Roxanne Friedenfels, Ann Saltzman; *Rowan College:* Lynn Nelson; *Gloucester County College:* Linda DeFelice; *Hudson County Community College:* Elaine Foster, Jane Isenberg, Theodore Kharpetian, Barry Tomkins; *Jersey City State College:* Godwin Ohiwerei; *Kean College:* Sarah Smith Ducksworth, Richard Katz; *Montclair State University:* Nancy Tumposky; *Ocean County College:* Bram Conley, Nancy Polonitza, Tamara Richardson; *Ramapo College:* Kathleen Fowler, Rosetta Geller, Frances Shapiro-Skrobe, Ramon Reyes; *Rider University:* Nancy Allen, Judith Johnston, Pearlie Peters; *Rutgers University–Newark:* Louise Taylor; *Sussex County Community College:* Penne Prigge; *Upsala College:* Gail Mansouri, Ann Oster, Bill Olson.

1990

Bergen Community College: Mia Anderson; Judi Davis; *Brookdale Community College:* Irma Lester, Cheryl Lonon, Sydelle Sipress, Kathy Vasile, Mary Lou Wagner; *College of Saint Elizabeth:* Sister Elena Francis Arminio, Harriet Sepinwall; *Essex County College:* Robert Adubato, Desiree Jett, Milena Mercado Rubinstein, Isa Tavares Maack; *Fairleigh Dickinson University–Madison:* Sharon Sweeney; *Georgian Court College:* Mary Chinery, Susan Cummings, Joyce Jacobs, Dorothy Lazarick, Suzanne Pilgram; *Rowan College:* Alice Herman, Yvonne Rodriguez; *Gloucester County College:* Crystal Bacon; *Mercer County Community College:* Judith Wrase Nygard; *Montclair State University:* Adele McCollum, Alyce Sands Miller; *New Jersey Institute of Technology:* Norbert Elliot; *Ocean County College:* Mary Ellen Carr, Kathleen McCormick, Carolyn Showalter,

Shirley Wilton; *Rutgers University–Douglass College:* Manijeh Saba; *Trenton State College:* Sally Archer, Ellen Friedman; *William Paterson College:* Sally Hand, Joan Tuohy.

1988
Bloomfield College: Linda Epps; *Fairleigh Dickinson University:* Maureen Petersen; *Rowan College:* Virginia Brown, Howard Cell, Bela Mukhoti; *Kean College:* Catherine Dorsey-Gaines, Thomas Herron, Marjorie Kelly; *Mercer County Community College:* Dori Seider; *Middlesex County College:* H. Wayne Brady, Dorothy Ivery Cole, Marge Cullen, Steven Rosengarten, Diane Wilhelm; *County College of Morris:* Patricia Bristowe, Diane Davenport, Ingeborg Haug DiGiacomo, Sandra Jackson; *Ramapo College:* Donna Crawley, Martha Ecker; *Rutgers University–Camden:* K.C. Dietsch, Marion Steininger; *Rutgers University–New Brunswick:* Mary Gibson, Jeannette Haviland, Deirdre Kramer, Kurt Spellmeyer, Monica Taylor, Linda Zerilli; *Rutgers University–Newark:* Annette Allen, Janet Larson; *Richard Stockton College:* Cheryle Eisele, Lorna Martin; *Union County College:* Jo Duvall, Eileen Kaufman; *Upsala College:* Ali Kamali, Joyce Lopez, Louise Simons.

1987
Bergen Community College: Joanne Glasgow, F. David Kievitt, Sandra Silverberg; *Bloomfield College:* Ella Handen, Douglas Poswencyk; *Rowan College:* Huguette Henderycksen, Mark Hutter, Linda Jeffrey, Corann Okorodudu; *Global Studies Consortium:* Barbara Bari Franzoi (College of Saint Elizabeth), Joanna Regulska (Rutgers University–New Brunswick), Sylvia Rudy (Upsala College); *Kean College:* Phillipa Kafka, Sylvia Strauss, Ann Walko; *Monmouth College:* Kenneth Campbell; *Raritan Valley Community College:* Olivia Bissell, Joanne Shalaby, Barbara Seater; *Richard Stockton College:* Nancy Ashton, Nancy Davis, Elizabeth Elmore; *Union County College:* Dorothea Hoffner, Judy Mayer, Theodore Vaughn.

1993 NATIONAL CONFERENCE PROGRAM COMMITTEE

Laura Aitken, William Paterson College
Fran Bartkowski, Rutgers University–Newark
Donna Crawley, Ramapo College
JoAnn Cunningham, William Paterson College
Martha Ecker, Ramapo College
Charley Flint, William Paterson College
Elaine Foster, Hudson County Community College
Kay Fowler, Ramapo College
Ellen Friedman, Trenton State College
Beth Hess, County College of Morris
Desiree Jett, Essex County College
Phillipa Kafka, Kean College
F. David Kievitt, Bergen Community College

Wendy Kolmar, Drew University
Laura Kramer, Montclair State University
Irma Lester, Brookdale Community College
Isa Tavares Maack, Essex County College
Lorraine Mayfield-Brown, Montclair State University
Adele McCollum, Montclair State University
Kathleen McCormick, Ocean County College
Naomi Miller, Sussex County Community College
Bill Olson, Upsala College
Ramon Reyes, Ramapo College
Margaret Roman, College of Saint Elizabeth

Ann Saltzman, Drew University
Fran Shapiro-Skrobe, Ramapo College
Sharon Sweeney, Fairleigh Dickinson
  University–Madison
Nancy Tumposky, Montclair State
  University

Kathy Vasile, Brookdale Community
  College
Linda White, Brookdale Community
  College
Laura Winters, College of Saint Elizabeth

PARTICIPATING INSTITUTIONS

Atlantic Community College
Bergen Community College
Bloomfield College
Brookdale Community College
Burlington County College
Caldwell College
Camden County College
Centenary College
College of Saint Elizabeth
County College of Morris
Cumberland County College
Douglass College, Rutgers University
Drew University
Essex County College
Fairleigh Dickinson University–Madison
Felician College
Georgian Court College
Gloucester County College
Jersey City State College
Kean College
Mercer County Community College
Middlesex County College
Monmouth College
Montclair State University

New Jersey Institute of Technology
Ocean County College
Passaic County Community College
Princeton University
Ramapo College
Raritan Valley Community College
Rider University
Rowan College
Rutgers University–Camden
Rutgers University–New Brunswick
Rutgers University–Newark
Salem Community College
Saint Peter's College
Seton Hall University
Stevens Institute of Technology
Richard Stockton College
Trenton State College
Union County College
University of Medicine and Dentistry of
  New Jersey–Robert Wood Johnson
  Medical School
Upsala College
William Paterson College

About the Editors and the Contributors

THE EDITORS

Charley B. Flint is an associate professor of sociology at William Paterson College, where she is also on the women's studies faculty, directs the Race and Gender Project, and is faculty coordinator of the MOST (Minority Opportunities Through School Transformation) Program of the American Sociological Association. She also coordinates special projects for the New Jersey Project, where she leads ALANA, a program of and for women of color in higher education in New Jersey. Her research concerns the social construction of social deviance as social control; gender and crime; women in prisons; the interaction of race, sex, and class and curriculum transformation; and multicultural education. She was the first black woman to receive a Ph.D. in sociology from Rutgers University in 1981, where she was an active participant in the development of the women's studies program.

Ellen G. Friedman is professor of English at Trenton State College, where she directs the women's studies program and led a curriculum transformation project. She has published numerous essays on modernism, postmodernism, and women writers in such journals as *PMLA* and *Modern Fiction Studies.* She published *Joyce Carol Oates* and edited *Joan Didion: Essays & Conversations* and coedited *Breaking the Sequence: Women's Experimental Fiction* and *Utterly Other Discourse: The Texts of Christine Brooke-Rose.* She is currently writing a book on representations of morality in contemporary U.S. culture entitled *Morality U.S.A.*

Wendy K. Kolmar is director of women's studies and an associate professor of English at Drew University. She has directed curriculum transformation projects on her own campus, served as a consultant to the New Jersey Project and as a project staff member, and worked with faculty to transform the curriculum on many other campuses inside and outside New Jersey. Among her scholarly publications is *Haunting the House of Fiction: Feminist Perspec-*

tives on Ghost Stories by American Women Writers, coedited with Lynette Carpenter.

Paula Rothenberg is director of the New Jersey Project and professor of philosophy and women's studies at William Paterson College. She is the editor of *Race, Class and Gender in the United States,* one of the first and most widely used diversity texts in higher education. She is coeditor of *Feminist Frameworks.* She has lectured at hundreds of colleges and universities around the country, and her articles and essays on race and gender scholarship and curriculum have appeared in numerous publications and have been widely reprinted.

THE CONTRIBUTORS

(affiliation at time of New Jersey Project association)

Nancy L. Ashton	Richard Stockton College of New Jersey
Crystal V. Bacon	Gloucester County College
Frances Bartkowski	Rutgers University–Newark
Susan Boughn	Trenton State College
José A. Carmona	Hudson County Community College
Susan Cavin	New Jersey Institute of Technology
Mary Cross	Fairleigh Dickinson University
JoAnn Cunningham	William Paterson College
Gloria Harper Dickinson	Trenton State College
Beva Eastman	William Paterson College
Norbert Elliot	New Jersey Institute of Technology
Lois Fichner-Rathus	Trenton State College
Kathleen Fowler	Ramapo College of New Jersey
Roxane Friedenfels	Drew University
Catherine Dorsey Gaines	Kean College
Rosetta Geller	Ramapo College of New Jersey
Joanne Glasgow	Bergen Community College
Jo-Ann Gross	Trenton State College
Jim Hala	Drew University
Ruth L. Hall	Trenton State College
Sally Hand	William Paterson College
Freda Hepner	Brookdale Community College
Blythe F. Hinitz	Trenton State College
Allen M. Howard	Rutgers University
Karen G. Howe	Trenton State College

Elaine D. Ingulli	Richard Stockton College of New Jersey
Diane Kalish	William Paterson College
John Kaltner	Upsala College
F. David Kievitt	Bergen Community College
Adam Knobler	Trenton State College
Laura Kramer	Montclair State University
Irma Lester	Brookdale Community College
Antoinette Liquori	William Paterson College
Virginia Ramey Mollenkott	William Paterson College
Lynn Hankinson Nelson	Rowan College of New Jersey
Wilfredo Nieves	Essex County College
Belkis Petrus	William Paterson College
Neil Printz	Caldwell College and Andy Warhol Foundation for the Visual Arts
Laura Hepburn Rawlins	Sussex County Community College
Ellen Romain	William Paterson College
Margaret Roman	College of Saint Elizabeth
Manijeh Saba	Rutgers University
Ann L. Saltzman	Drew University
Arlene Holpp Scala	William Paterson College
Stephen R. Shalom	William Paterson College
Frances Shapiro-Skrobē	Ramapo College of New Jersey
Toby Silverman	William Paterson College
Eleanor Smith	William Paterson College
Nancy Steffen-Fluhr	New Jersey Institute of Technology
Helen Stewart	Rider University
Andrea Tschemplik	Upsala College
Rhoda K. Unger	Montclair State University
Sara L. Webb	Drew University
Cliff Wood	County College of Morris

Index